A GAME *of* PASSION

THE NFL LITERARY COMPANION

EDITED BY JOHN WIEBUSCH
& BRIAN SILVERMAN

Turner Publishing, Inc.
ATLANTA

Published by Turner Publishing, Inc.
A Subsidiary of Turner Broadcasting System, Inc.
1050 Techwood Drive, N.W.
Atlanta, GA 30318

First Edition 10 9 8 7 6 5 4 3 2 1

Library of Congress Cataloging-in-Publication Data
A game of passion: the NFL literary companion / edited by John Wiebusch and Brian Silverman.—1st ed.
p. cm.
Includes bibliographical references.
ISBN 1-57036-115-0 (hard.) : $21.95 — ISBN 1-57036-106-1 (trade paper) : $10.95
1. Football—Literary collections. 2. American literature—20th century. I. Wiebusch, John. II. Silverman, Brian.
PS509. F6G36 1994
810.8'0355—dc20 94-26362
CIP

Distributed by Andrews and McMeel
A Universal Press Syndicate Company
4900 Main Street
Kansas City, Missouri 64112

Contents

III: THE PRESS BOX

INTRODUCTION

Not the Only Word Game in Town

THERE IS A COMMON PERCEPTION in American culture that football gets ratings, and baseball sells books.

George Will and Roger Angell extol the measured sameness and quiet civility of the game of baseball. The bookshelf bases are loaded with their efforts.

John Madden and Terry Bradshaw gesture wildly and talk in cartoon words about contact and collision. The VCR lineups are filled with the latest from NFL Films.

All of the preceding is true. And all of it adds to the misconception that football is visual, not literary. This book aims to correct that misconception.

Football does have its literary muses.

Novelists, poets, playwrights, and biographers have joined sportswriters and columnists within these pages. Where else could you find a cast so varied it includes:

Ray Bradbury, the ultimate American hyphenate (novelist-poet-essayist-critic-social commentator), who has written poems and essays about football.

Don DeLillo, whose body of fictional work is second to none over the past quarter-century, and who wrote a novel about football called *End Zone*.

James Dickey, whose body of poetry is second to none over the past quarter-century, and who has turned his muse to football on numerous occasions.

Andy Rooney, everyone's favorite prime-time curmudgeon, a man passionate about football in general and the New York Giants in particular.

Lee Iacocca, whose photograph should be next to "entrepreneur" in the dictionary. Iacocca cites Vince Lombardi as the person who had the most to do with shaping what he became.

August Wilson, a Pulitzer Prize-winning playwright who grew up loving Sunday afternoons in the fall because they meant the pro football season was on.

All of the above and more—including Irwin Shaw, Gay Talese, and Haywood Hale Broun—make up the first section of this book, Gridiron Tales.

We get personal in Section II: Voices From the Field.

Have some fun with—and get some inspiration from—men who helped make mayhem on the field or from the sidelines: Joe Namath, Jim Brown, Gale Sayers, Vince Lombardi and John Madden. They came, they saw, they conquered, they wrote books.

So did Tim Green, who while only 30, already is threatening to challenge Ray Bradbury's hyphenate record (Green is a player-commentator-essayist-novelist . . . so far). His second novel, *Titans*, published in 1994, dispels once and for all the idea that no one that big (Green is 6-2 and weighs 245 pounds) and strong can make good things come out of a word processor.

Section III: The Press Box is for traditionalists of all shapes and sizes.

Everything in this section—as well as many of the pieces in the first two sections of *A Game of Passion*—appeared in publications produced by NFL Properties—in books, in *PRO!* and in *GameDay*, in the Super Bowl program, and in other publishing ventures.

My friends are here as well, and that smacks not of cronyism but more of a round table of sports.

The writers in this section have a lot of things in common . . . warmth, sensitivity, strength, talent. But the truly common thread is they all touched me. They all made me feel good. It is the arrogant belief of editors that if we feel something, then so will our readers.

Who could not love Shelby Strother? He accepted the world around him without condition. In the china closet of humanity, he was a serving platter, and he never stopped bringing us helpings of life. The first time I met Shelby it was love at first thoughts. We were soul brothers for five special years, before cancer overcame him in 1991. Read the story here about Gene Stallings and his son and you will know why I still miss him.

Wells Twombly also was too young and too unfinished when his kidneys stopped working in 1979. Wells spun tales that made me laugh and made me cry (often at the same time). I still miss him, too.

Among heaven's literary angels, Shelby Strother and Wells Twombly stand out. Frederick Exley also flies with that crowd.

The writers in Section III: The Press Box all are, or were, sportswriters. Truth is, there is no need for the adjective. This is the kind of writing you can show your brother-in-law who would rather play tennis on weekend afternoons in October or the person with whom you live who would rather go to a movie on the afternoon of the last Sunday in January. They will like what's here as much as you will.

One of the beauties of this book is that you can read it in one sitting, from the beginning . . . or you can pick it up a dozen times, opening it at random.

Enjoy the trip, whatever your route.

Books are a product of the collaborative process, particularly anthologies such as this. Over the years, I have had a lot of literary companions. I thank them all.

Special thanks are due three people without whom this book would not have been possible—Phil Barber of NFL Properties, Kevin Mulroy of Turner Publishing, Inc., and Brian Silverman. Barber and Mulroy helped in the selection process (the orders came from a long menu), and Silverman gathered the pieces that were not originally printed in NFL publications.

—JOHN WIEBUSCH, JUNE 1994

I

Gridiron Tales

IRWIN SHAW

The Eighty-Yard Run

Irwin Shaw wrote short stories for more than five decades, and his work has appeared in Esquire, The New Yorker, Harper's Bazaar, *and* The Saturday Evening Post. *This story is about the frustrations of a man whose greatest moment of glory, during a mundane football practice, set a standard that he never again was able to meet.*

THE PASS WAS HIGH AND WIDE and he jumped for it, feeling it slap flatly against his hands, as he shook his hips to throw off the halfback who was diving at him. The center floated by, his hands desperately brushing Darling's knee as Darling picked his feet up high and delicately ran over a blocker and an opposing linesman in a jumble on the ground near the scrimmage line. He had ten yards in the clear and picked up speed, breathing easily, feeling his thigh pads rising and falling against his legs, listening to the sound of cleats behind him, pulling away from them, watching the other backs heading him off toward the sideline, the whole picture, the men closing in on him, the blockers fighting for position, the ground he had to cross, all suddenly clear in his head, for the first time in his life not a meaningless confusion of men, sounds, speed. He smiled a little to himself as he ran, holding the ball lightly in front of him with his two hands, his knees pumping high, his hips twisting in the almost girlish run of a back in a broken field. The first halfback came at him and he fed him his leg, then swung at the last moment, took the shock of the man's shoulder without breaking stride, ran right through him, his cleats biting securely into the turf. There was only the safety man now, coming warily at him, his arms crooked, hands spread. Darling tucked the ball in, spurted at him, driving hard, hurling himself along, his legs pounding, knees high, all two hundred pounds bunched into controlled attack. He was sure he was going to get past the safety man. Without thought, his arms and legs working beautifully together, he headed right for the safety man, stiff-armed him, feeling blood spurt instantaneously from the man's nose onto his hand, seeing his face go awry, head turned, mouth pulled to one side. He pivoted away, keeping the arm locked, dropping the safety man as he ran easily toward the goal line, with the drumming of cleats diminishing behind him.

How long ago? It was autumn then, and the ground was getting hard because the nights were cold and leaves from the maples around the stadium blew across the practice fields in gusts of wind, and the girls were beginning to put polo coats over their sweaters when they came to watch practice in the afternoons . . . Fifteen years. Darling walked slowly over the same ground in the spring twilight, in his neat shoes, a man of thirty-five dressed in a double-breasted suit, ten pounds heavier in the fifteen years, but not fat, with the years between 1925 and 1940 showing in his face.

The coach was smiling quietly to himself and the assistant coaches were looking at each other with pleasure the way they always did when one of the second stringers suddenly did something fine, bringing credit to them, making their $2,000 a year a tiny bit more secure.

Darling trotted back, smiling, breathing deeply but easily, feeling wonderful, not tired, though this was the tail end of practice and he'd run eighty yards. The sweat poured off his face and soaked his jersey and he liked the feeling, the warm moistness lubricating his skin like oil. Off in a corner of the field some players were punting and the smack of leather against the ball came pleasantly through the afternoon air. The freshmen were running signals on the next field and the quarterback's sharp voice, the pound of the eleven pairs of cleats, the "Dig, now dig!" of the coaches, the laughter of the players all somehow made him feel happy as he trotted back to midfield, listening to the applause and shouts of the students along the sidelines, knowing that after that run the coach would have to start him Saturday against Illinois.

Fifteen years, Darling thought, remembering the shower after the workout, the hot water steaming off his skin and the deep soapsuds and all the young voices singing with the water streaming down and towels going and managers running in and out and the sharp sweet smell of oil of wintergreen and everybody clapping him on the back as he dressed and Packard, the captain, who took being captain very seriously, coming over to him and shaking his hand and saying, "Darling, you're going to go places in the next two years."

The assistant manager fussed over him, wiping a cut on his leg with alcohol and iodine, the little sting making him realize suddenly how fresh and whole and solid his body felt. The manager slapped a piece of adhesive tape over the cut, and Darling noticed the sharp clean white of the tape against the ruddiness of the skin, fresh from the shower.

He dressed slowly, the softness of his shirt and the soft warmth of his wool socks and his flannel trousers a reward against his skin after the harsh pressure of the shoulder harness and thigh and hip pads. He drank three glasses of cold water, the liquid reaching down coldly inside of him, soothing the harsh dry places in his throat and belly left by the sweat and running and shouting of practice

Fifteen years.

The sun had gone down and the sky was green behind the stadium and he laughed quietly to himself as he looked at the stadium, rearing above the trees, and knew that on Saturday when the 70,000 voices roared as the team came running out onto the field, part of that enormous salute would be for him. He walked slowly, listening to the gravel crunch satisfactorily under his shoes in the still twilight, feeling his clothes swing lightly against his skin, breathing the thin evening air, feeling the wind move softly in his damp hair, wonderfully cool behind his ears and at the nape of his neck.

Louise was waiting for him at the road, in her car. The top was down and he noticed all over again, as he always did when he saw her, how pretty she was, the rough blond hair and the large, inquiring eyes and the bright mouth, smiling now.

She threw the door open. "Were you good today?" she asked.

"Pretty good," he said. He climbed in, sank luxuriously into the soft leather, stretched his legs far out. He smiled, thinking of the eighty yards. "Pretty damn good."

She looked at him seriously for a moment, then scrambled around, like a little girl, kneeling on the seat next to him, grabbed him, her hands along his ears, and kissed him as he sprawled, head back, on the seat cushion. She let go of him, but kept her head close to his, over his. Darling reached up slowly and rubbed the back of his hand against her cheek, lit softly by a street lamp a hundred feet away. They looked at each other, smiling.

Louise drove down to the lake and they sat there silently, watching the moon rise behind the hills on the other side. Finally he reached over, pulled her gently to him, kissed her. Her lips grew soft, her body sank into his, tears formed slowly in her eyes. He knew, for the first time, that he could do whatever he wanted with her.

"Tonight," he said. "I'll call for you at seven-thirty. Can you get out?"

She looked at him. She was smiling, but the tears were still full in her eyes. "All right," she said. "I'll get out. How about you? Won't the coach raise hell?"

Darling grinned. "I got the coach in the palm of my hand," he said. "Can you wait till seven-thirty?"

She grinned back at him. "No," she said.

They kissed and she started the car and they went back to town for dinner. He sang on the way home.

Christian Darling, thirty-five years old, sat on the frail spring grass, greener now than it ever would be again on the practice field, looked thoughtfully up at the stadium, a deserted ruin in the twilight. He had started on the first team that Saturday and every Saturday after that for the next two years, but it had never been as satisfactory as it should have been. He never had broken away, the longest run he'd ever made was thirty-five yards, and that in a game that was already won, and then that kid had come up from the third team, Diederich, a blank-faced German kid from Wisconsin, who ran like a bull, ripping lines to pieces Saturday after Saturday, plowing through, never getting hurt, never changing his expression, scoring more points, gaining more ground than all the rest of the team put together, making everybody's All-America, carrying the ball three times out of four, keeping everybody else out of the headlines. Darling was a good blocker and he spent his Saturday afternoons working on the big Swedes and Polacks who played tackle and end for Michigan, Illinois, Purdue, hurling into huge pile-ups, bobbing his head wildly to elude the great raw hands swinging like meat-cleavers at him as he went charging in to open up holes for Diederich coming through like a locomotive behind him. Still, it wasn't so bad. Everybody liked him and he did his job and he was pointed out on the campus and boys always felt important when they introduced their girls to him at their proms, and Louise loved him and watched him faithfully in the games, even in the mud, when your own mother wouldn't know you, and drove him around in her car keeping the top down because she was proud of him and wanted to show everybody that she was Christian Darling's girl. She bought him crazy presents because her father was rich, watches, pipes, humidors, an icebox for beer for his room, curtains, wallets, a fifty-dollar dictionary.

"You'll spend every cent your old man owns," Darling protested once when she showed up at his rooms with seven different packages in her arms and tossed them onto the couch.

"Kiss me," Louise said, "and shut up."

"Do you want to break your poor old man?"

"I don't mind. I want to buy you presents."

"Why?"

"It makes me feel good. Kiss me. I don't know why. Did you know that you're an important figure?"

"Yes," Darling said gravely.

"When I was waiting for you at the library yesterday two girls saw you coming and one of them said to the other, 'That's Christian Darling. He's an important figure.'"

"You're a liar."

"I'm in love with an important figure."

"Still, why the hell did you have to give me a forty-pound dictionary?

"I wanted to make sure," Louise said, "that you had a token of my esteem. I want to smother you in tokens of my esteem."

Fifteen years ago.

They'd married when they got out of college. There'd been other women for him, but all casual and secret, more for curiosity's sake, and vanity, women who'd thrown themselves at him and flattered him, a pretty mother at a summer camp for boys, an old girl from his home town who'd suddenly blossomed into a coquette, a friend of Louise's who had dogged him grimly for six months and had taken advantage of the two weeks that Louise went home when her mother died. Perhaps Louise had known, but she'd kept quiet, loving him completely, filling his rooms with presents, religiously watching him battling with the big Swedes and Polacks on the line of scrimmage on Saturday afternoons, making plans for marrying him and living with him in New York and going with him there to the night clubs, the theaters, the good restaurants, being proud of him in advance, tall, white-teethed, smiling, large, yet moving lightly, with an athlete's grace, dressed in evening clothes, approvingly eyed by magnificently dressed and famous women in theater lobbies, with Louise adoringly at his side.

Her father, who manufactured inks, set up a New York office for Darling to manage and presented him with three hundred accounts, and they lived on Beekman Place with a view of the river with fifteen thousand dollars a year between them, because everybody was buying everything in those days, including ink. They saw all the shows and went to all the speakeasies and spent their fifteen thousand dollars a year and in the afternoons Louise went to the art galleries and the matinees of the more serious plays that Darling didn't like to sit through and Darling slept with a girl who danced in the chorus of *Rosalie* and with the wife of a man who owned three copper mines. Darling played squash three times a week and remained as solid as a stone barn and Louise never took her eyes off him when they were in the same room together, watching him with a secret, miser's smile, with a trick of coming over to him in the middle of a crowded room and saying gravely, in a low voice, "You're the handsomest man I've ever seen in my whole life. Want a drink?"

Nineteen twenty-nine came to Darling and to his wife and father-in-law, the maker of inks, just as it came to everyone else. The father-in-law waited until 1933 and then blew his brains out and when Darling went to Chicago to see what the books of the firm looked like he found out all that was left were debts and three or four gallons of unbought ink.

"Please, Christian," Louise said, sitting in their neat Beekman Place apartment, with a view of the river and prints of paintings by Dufy and Braque and Picasso on the wall. "Please, why do you want to start drinking at two o'clock in the afternoon?"

"I have nothing else to do," Darling said, putting down his glass, emptied of its fourth drink. "Please pass the whisky."

Louise filled his glass. "Come take a walk with me," she said. "We'll walk along the river."

"I don't want to walk along the river," Darling said, squinting intensely at the prints of paintings by Dufy, Braque and Picasso.

"We'll walk along Fifth Avenue."

"I don't want to walk along Fifth Avenue."

"Maybe," Louise said gently, "you'd like to come with me to some art galleries. There's an exhibition by a man named Klee . . ."

"I don't want to go to any art galleries. I want to sit here and drink Scotch whisky," Darling said. "Who the hell hung those goddam pictures up on the wall?"

"I did," Louise said.

"I hate them."

"I'll take them down," Louise said.

"Leave them there. It gives me something to do in the afternoon. I can hate them." Darling took a long swallow. "Is that the way people paint these days?"

"Yes, Christian. Please don't drink any more."

"Do you like painting like that?"

"Yes, dear."

"Really?"

"Really."

Darling looked carefully at the prints once more. "Little Louise Tucker. The middle-western beauty. I like pictures with horses in them. Why should you like pictures like that?"

"I just happen to have gone to a lot of galleries in the last few years . . ."

"Is that what you do in the afternoon?"

"That's what I do in the afternoon," Louise said.

"I drink in the afternoon."

Louise kissed him lightly on the top of his head as he sat there squinting at the pictures on the wall, the glass of whisky held firmly in his hand. She put on her coat and went out without saying another word. When she came back in the early evening, she had a job on a woman's fashion magazine.

They moved downtown and Louise went out to work every morning and Darling sat home and drank and Louise paid the bills as they came up. She made believe she was going to quit work as soon as Darling found a job, even though she was taking over more responsibility day by day at the magazine, interviewing authors, picking painters for the illustrations and covers, getting actresses to pose for pictures, going out for drinks with the right people, making a thousand new friends whom she loyally introduced to Darling.

"I don't like your hat," Darling said once, when she came in in the evening and kissed him, her breath rich with martinis.

"What's the matter with my hat, Baby?" she asked, running her fingers through his hair. "Everybody says it's very smart."

"It's too damned smart," he said. "It's not for you. It's for a rich, sophisticated woman of thirty-five with admirers."

Louise laughed. "I'm practicing to be a rich, sophisticated woman of thirty-five with admirers," she said. He stared soberly at her. "Now, don't look so grim, Baby. It's still the same simple little wife under the hat." She took the hat off, threw it into a corner, sat on his lap. "See? Homebody Number One."

"Your breath could run a train," Darling said, not wanting to be mean, but talking out of boredom, and sudden shock at seeing his wife curiously a stranger in a new hat, with a new expression in her eyes under the little brim, secret, confident, knowing.

Louise tucked her head under his chin so he couldn't smell her breath. "I had to take an author out for cocktails," she said. "He's a boy from the Ozark Mountains and he drinks like a fish. He's a Communist."

"What the hell is a Communist from the Ozarks doing writing for a woman's fashion magazine?"

Louise chuckled. "The magazine business is getting all mixed up these days. The publishers want to have a foot in every camp. And anyway, you can't find an author under seventy these days who isn't a Communist."

"I don't think I like you to associate with all those people, Louise," Darling said. "Drinking with them."

"He's a very nice, gentle boy," Louise said. "He reads Ernest Dowson."

"Who's Ernest Dowson?"

Louise patted his arm, stood up, fixed her hair. "He's an English poet."

Darling felt that somehow he had disappointed her. "Am I supposed to know who Ernest Dowson is?"

"No, dear. I'd better go in and take a bath."

After she had gone, Darling went over to the corner where the hat was lying and picked it up. It was nothing, a scrap of straw, a red flower, a veil, meaningless on his big hand, but on his wife's head a signal of something . . . big city, smart and knowing women drinking and dining with men other than their husbands, conversation about things a normal man wouldn't know much about, Frenchmen who painted as though they used their elbows instead of brushes, composers who wrote whole symphonies without a single melody in them, writers who knew all about politics and women who knew all about writers, the movement of the proletariat, Marx, somehow mixed up with five-dollar dinners and the best-looking women in America and fairies who made them laugh and half-sentences immediately understood and secretly hilarious and wives who called their husbands "Baby." He put the hat down, a scrap of straw and a red flower, and a little veil. He drank some whisky straight and went into the bathroom where his wife was lying deep in her bath, singing to herself and smiling from time to time like a little girl, paddling the water gently with her hands, sending up a slight spicy fragrance from the bath salts she used.

He stood over her, looking down at her. She smiled up at him, her eyes half closed, her body pink and shimmering in the warm, scented water. All over again, with all the old suddenness, he was hit deep inside him with the knowledge of how beautiful she was, how much he needed her.

"I came in here," he said, "to tell you I wish you wouldn't call me 'Baby.'"

She looked up at him from the bath, her eyes quickly full of sorrow, half-understanding what he meant. He knelt and put his arms around her, his sleeves plunged heedlessly in the water, his shirt and jacket soaking wet as he clutched her wordlessly, holding her crazily tight, crushing her breath from her, kissing her desperately, searchingly, regretfully.

He got jobs after that, selling real estate and automobiles, but somehow, although he had a desk with his name on a wooden wedge on it, and he went to the office religiously at nine each morning, he never managed to sell anything and he never made any money.

Louise was made assistant editor, and the house was always full of strange men and women who talked fast and got angry on abstract subjects like mural painting, novelists, labor unions. Negro short-story writers drank Louise's liquor, and a lot of Jews, and big solemn men with scarred faces and knotted hands who talked slowly but clearly about picket lines and battles with guns and leadpipe at mine-shaftheads and in front of factory gates. And Louise moved among them all confidently, knowing what they were talking about, with opinions that they listened to and argued about just as though she were a man. She knew everybody, condescended to no one, devoured books that Darling had never heard of, walked along the streets of the city, excited, at home, soaking in all the million tides of New York without fear, with constant wonder.

Her friends liked Darling and sometimes he found a man who wanted to get off in the corner and talk about the new boy who played fullback for Princeton, and the decline of the double wingback, or even the state of the stock market, but for the most part he sat on the edge of things, solid and quiet in the high storm of words. "The dialectics of the situation . . . The theater has been given over to expert jugglers . . . Picasso? What man has a right to paint old bones and collect ten thousand dollars for them? . . . I stand firmly behind Trotsky . . . Poe was the last American critic. When he died they put lilies on the grave of American criticism. I don't say this because they panned my last book, but . . . "

Once in a while he caught Louise looking soberly and consideringly at him through the cigarette smoke and the noise and he avoided her eyes and found an excuse to get up and go into the kitchen for more ice or to open another bottle.

"Come on," Cathal Flaherty was saying, standing at the door with a girl, "you've got to come down and see this. It's down on Fourteenth Street, in the old Civic Repertory, and you can only see it on Sunday nights and I guarantee you'll come out of the theater singing." Flaherty was a big young Irishman with a broken nose who was the lawyer for a longshoreman's union, and he had been hanging around the house for six months on and off, roaring and shutting everybody else up when he got in an argument. "It's a new play, *Waiting for Lefty*; it's about taxi drivers."

"Odets," the girl with Flaherty said. "It's by a guy named Odets."

"I never heard of him," Darling said.

"He's a new one," the girl said.

"It's like watching a bombardment," Flaherty said. "I saw it last Sunday night. You've got to see it."

"Come on, Baby," Louise said to Darling, excitement in her eyes already. "We've been sitting in the Sunday *Times* all day, this'll be a great change."

"I see enough taxi drivers every day," Darling said, not because he meant that, but because he didn't like to be around Flaherty, who said things that made Louise laugh a lot and whose judgment she accepted on almost every subject. "Let's go to the movies."

"You've never seen anything like this before," Flaherty said. "He wrote this play with a baseball bat."

"Come on," Louise coaxed, "I bet it's wonderful."

"He has long hair," the girl with Flaherty said. "Odets. I met him at a party. He's an actor. He didn't say a goddam thing all night."

"I don't feel like going down to Fourteenth Street," Darling said, wishing Flaherty and his girl would get out. "It's gloomy."

"Oh, hell!" Louise said loudly. She looked coolly at Darling, as though she'd just been introduced to him and was making up her mind about him, and not very favorably. He saw her looking at him, knowing there was something new and dangerous in her face and he wanted to say something, but Flaherty was there and his damned girl, and anyway, he didn't know what to say.

"I'm going," Louise said, getting her coat. "I don't think Fourteenth Street is gloomy."

"I'm telling you," Flaherty was saying, helping her on with her coat, "it's the Battle of Gettysburg, in Brooklynese."

"Nobody could get a word out of him," Flaherty's girl was saying as they went through the door. "He just sat there all night."

The door closed. Louise hadn't said good night to him. Darling walked around the room four times, then sprawled out on the sofa, on top of the Sunday *Times*. He lay there for five minutes looking at the ceiling, thinking of Flaherty walking down the street talking in that booming voice, between the girls, holding their arms.

Louise had looked wonderful. She'd washed her hair in the afternoon and it had been very soft and light and clung close to her head as she stood there angrily putting her coat on. Louise was getting prettier every year, partly because she knew by now how pretty she was, and made the most of it.

"Nuts," Darling said, standing up. "Oh, nuts."

He put on his coat and went down to the nearest bar and had five drinks off by himself in a corner before his money ran out.

The years since then had been foggy and downhill. Louise had been nice to him, and in a way, loving and kind, and they'd fought only once when he said he was going to vote for Landon. ("Oh, Christ," she'd said, "doesn't *anything* happen inside your head? Don't you read the papers? The penniless Republican!") She'd been sorry later and apologised for hurting him, but apologised as she might to a child. He'd tried hard, had gone grimly to the art galleries, the concert halls, the bookshops, trying to gain on the trail of his wife, but it was no use. He was bored, and none of what he saw or heard or dutifully read made much sense to him and finally he gave it up. He had thought, many nights as he ate dinner alone, knowing that Louise would come home late and drop silently into bed without explanation, of getting a divorce, but he knew the loneliness, the hopelessness, of not seeing her again would be too much to take. So he was good, completely devoted, ready at all times to go any place with her, do anything she wanted. He even got a small job, in a broker's office and paid his own way, bought his own liquor.

Then he'd been offered the job of going from college to college as a tailor's representative. "We want a man," Mr. Rosenberg had said, "who as soon as you look at him, you say, 'There's a university man.'" Rosenberg had looked approvingly at Darling's broad shoulders and well-kept waist, at his carefully brushed hair and his honest, wrinkleless face. "Frankly, Mr. Darling, I am willing to make you a proposition. I have inquired about you, you are favorably known on your old campus, I understand you were in the backfield with Alfred Diederich."

Darling nodded. "Whatever happened to him?"

"He is walking around in a cast for seven years now. An iron brace. He played professional football and they broke his neck for him."

Darling smiled. That, at least, had turned out well.

"Our suits are an easy product to sell, Mr. Darling," Rosenberg said. "We have a handsome, custom-made garment. What has Brooks Brothers got that we haven't got? A name. No more."

"I can make fifty, sixty dollars a week," Darling said to Louise that night. "And expenses. I can save some money and then come back to New York and really get started here."

"Yes, Baby," Louise said.

"As it is," Darling said carefully, "I can make it back here once a month, and holidays and the summer. We can see each other often."

"Yes, Baby." He looked at her face, lovelier now at thirty-five than it had ever been before, but fogged over now as it had been for five years with a kind of patient, kindly, remote boredom.

"What do you say?" he asked. "Should I take it?" Deep within him he hoped fiercely, longingly, for her to say, "No, Baby, you stay right here," but she said, as he knew she'd say, "I think you'd better take it."

He nodded. He had to get up and stand with his back to her, looking out the window, because there were things plain on his face that she had never seen in the fifteen years she'd known him. "Fifty dollars is a lot of money," he said. "I never thought I'd ever see fifty dollars again." He laughed. Louise laughed, too.

Christian Darling sat on the frail green grass of the practice field. The shadow of the stadium had reached out and covered him. In the distance the lights of the university shone a little mistily in the light haze of evening. Fifteen years. Flaherty even now was calling for his wife, buying her a drink, filling whatever bar they were in with that voice of his and that easy laugh. Darling half-closed his eyes, almost saw the boy fifteen years ago reach for the pass, slip the halfback, go skittering lightly down the field, his knees high and fast and graceful, smiling to himself because he knew he was going to get past the safety man. That was the high point, Darling thought, fifteen years ago, on an autumn afternoon, twenty years old and far from death, with the air coming easily into his lungs, and a deep feeling inside him that he could do anything, knock over anybody, outrun whatever had to be outrun. And the shower after and the three glasses of water and the cool night air on his damp head and Louise sitting hatless in the open car with a smile and the first kiss she ever really meant. The high point, an eighty-yard run in the practice, and a girl's kiss and everything after that a decline. Darling laughed. He had practiced the wrong thing, perhaps. He hadn't practiced for 1929 and New York City and a girl who would turn into a woman. Somewhere, he thought, there must have been a point where she moved up to me, was even with me for a moment, when I could have held her hand, if I'd known, held tight, gone with her. Well, he'd never known. Here he was on a playing field that was fifteen years away and his wife was in another city having dinner with another and better man, speaking with him a different, new language, a language nobody had ever taught him.

Darling stood up, smiled a little, because if he didn't smile he knew the tears would come. He looked around him. This was the spot. O'Connor's pass had come sliding out just to here . . .the high point. Darling put up his hands, felt all over again the flat slap of the ball. He shook his hips to throw off the halfback, cut back inside the center, picked his knees high as he ran gracefully over two men jumbled on the ground at the line of scrimmage, ran easily, gaining speed, for ten yards, holding the ball lightly in his two hands, swung away from the halfback diving at him, ran, swinging his hips in the almost girlish manner of a back in a broken field, tore into the safety man, his shoes drumming heavily on the turf, stiff-armed, elbow locked, pivoted, raced lightly and exultantly for the goal line.

It was only after he had sped over the goal line and slowed to a trot that he saw the boy and girl sitting together on the turf, looking at him wonderingly.

He stopped short, dropping his arms. "I . . ." he said, gasping a little, though his condition was fine and the run hadn't winded him. "I—once I played here."

The boy and the girl said nothing. Darling laughed embarrassedly, looked hard at them sitting there, close to each other, shrugged, turned and went toward his hotel, the sweat breaking out on his face and running down into his collar.

RAY BRADBURY

All Flesh Is One: What Matter Scores?

Name the medium, Ray Bradbury has conquered it. Over more than 50 years of unbridled creativity, Bradbury has written six novels, several hundred stories, scripts, essays, plays, articles, and literary reviews. He also has penned countless poems, including this masterfully evocative example, written in 1970.

The thing is this:
We love to see them on the green and growing field;
There passions yield to weather and a special time;
There all suspends itself in air,
The missile on its way forever to a goal.
There boys somehow grown up to men are boys again;
We wrestle in their tumble and their ecstasy,
And there we dare to touch and somehow hold,
Congratulate, or say: Ah, well, next time. Get on!
Our voices lift; the birds all terrified
At sudden pulse of sound, this great and unseen fount,
Scare like tossed leaves, fly in strewn papers
Up the wind to flagpole tops:
We Celebrate Ourselves!
(Sorry, old Walt.)
We play at life, we dog the vital tracks
Of those who run before and we, all laughing, make the trek
Across the field, along the lines,

Falling to fuse, rising amused by now-fair, now-foul
Temper-tantrums, sprint-leaps, handsprings, recoils,
And brief respites when bodies pile ten high.

All flesh is one, what matter scores?
Or color of the suit
Or if the helmet glints with blue or gold?
All is one bold achievement,
All is fine spring-found-again-in-autumn day
When juices run in antelopes along our blood,
And green our flag, forever green,
Deep colored of the grass, this dye proclaims
Eternities of youngness to the skies
Whose tough winds play our hair and rearrange our stars
So mysteries abound where most we seek for answers.
We do confound ourselves.
All this being so, we do make up a Game
And pitch a ball and run to grapple with our Fates

On common cattle-fields, cow-pasturings,
Where goals are seen and destinies beheld,
And scores summed up so that we truly *know* a score!
All else is nil; the universal sums
Lie far beyond our reach,
In this mild romp we teach our lambs and colts
Ascensions, swift declines, revolts, wild victories,
Sad retreats, all compassed in the round
Of one autumnal October afternoon.
Then winds, incensed and sweet with dust of leaves
Which, mummified, attest the passing of the weather,
Hour, day, and Old Year's tide,
Are fastened, gripped and held all still
For just one moment with the caught ball in our hands.
We stand so, frozen on the sill of life

And, young or old, ignore the coming on of night.

All, all is flight!
All loss and apt recovery.
We search the flawless air
And make discovery of projectile tossed—
The center of our being.
This is the only way of seeing;
To run half blind, half in the sad, mad world,
Half out of mind—
The goal line beckons,
And with each yard we pass,
We reckon that we win, by God, we win!
Surely to run, to run and measure this,
This gain of tender grass
Is not a sin to be denied?
All life we've tried and often found contempt for us!
So on we hied to lesser gods
Who treat us less as clods and more like men
Who would be kings a little while.
Thus we made up this mile to run

Beneath a late-on-in-the-afternoon-time sun.
We chalked aside the world's derisions
With our gamebook's rulings and decisions.
So divisions of our own good manufacture
Staked the green a hundred yards, no more, no less.
The Universe said "No"?
We answered, running, "Yes!"
Yes to Ourselves!
Since naught did cipher us
With scoreboards empty,
Strewn with goose-egg zeros
Self-made heroes, then, we kicked that minus,

Wrote in plus!
The gods, magnanimous,
Allowed our score
And noted, passing,
What was less is now, incredibly, more!
Man, then, is the thing
That teaches zeros how to cling together and add up!
The cup stood empty?
Well, now, look!
A brimming cup.

No scores are known?
Then look down field,
There in the twilight sky the numbers run and blink
And total up the years;
Our sons this day are grown.

What matter if the board is cleared an hour from now
And empty lies the stadium wherein died roars
Instead of men
And goalposts fell in lieu of battlements.
See where the battle turf is splayed
Where panicked herds of warrior sped by,
Half buffalo and half ballet.

Their hoof marks fill with rain
As thunders close and shut the end of day.
The papers blow.
Old men, half-young again, across the pavements go
To cars that in imagination
Might this hour leave for Mars.
But, sons beside them silent, put in gear,
And drive off toward the close of one more year,
Both thinking this:

ALL FLESH IS ONE

The game is done.
The game begins.
The game is lost.
But here come other wins.
The band tromps out to clear the field with brass,
The great heart of the drum systolic beats
In promise of yet greater feats and trumps;
Still promising, the band departs
To leave the final beating of this time
To older hearts who in the stands cold rinsed with Autumn day
Wish, want, desire for their sons
From here on down, eternal replay on replay.

This thought, them thinking it,
Man and boy, old Dad, raw Son
For one rare moment caused by cornering too fast,
Their shoulders lean and touch.
A red light stops them. Quiet and serene they sit.
But now the moment is past.
Gone is the day.
And so the old man says at last:
"The light is green, boy. Go. The light is green."
They ran together all the afternoon;
Now, very simply, they drive away.

ANDY ROONEY

Oh, What a Lovely Game

Catching Andy Rooney in a serious mood usually is tougher than catching Jerry Rice on a fly pattern. But when Rooney wrote for the Super Bowl XXVI game program in Minneapolis, he waxed both nostalgic and—dare we say it?—sentimental. The long-time "60 Minutes" essayist and author of two best-selling books has been an avid follower of the sport of football since his childhood days on the vacant lots. As he says in the column, "Any other game is tiddlywinks."

I WAS AN ALL-AMERICA GUARD at Colgate University in 1940. I went on to play in the NFL, and later was voted into the Pro Football Hall of Fame.

Well, I wasn't *actually* an All-America and I never played professional football—you know how old football players and war veterans tend to exaggerate—but I did get into a few games in college when we were ahead by four or five touchdowns and coach Andy Kerr cleared the bench to give the substitutes a break.

That was as close as I ever got to being either All-America or in the Hall of Fame, but during those years as something less than a Heisman Trophy winner, I acquired a love for football that is undiminished 50 years later. In my view, any other game is tiddlywinks.

As a freshman at Colgate, I was a 185-pound running guard. In the Single- or Double-Wing formation, devised many years before by one of the great early football coaches, Pop Warner, I pulled to run interference for a halfback or fullback on half the plays. We had Bill

Geyer, one of the all-time great players in Colgate history, who had run 100 yards in 10 seconds as a sprinter. He was one of the fastest, toughest, most elusive halfbacks in the nation. Later, he played with the Chicago Bears.

There was no intermediary, no handoff, in the Single-Wing offense, as there is in today's game in which the quarterback handles the ball on every play. Everything was Shotgun. When the play was called for Geyer to sweep wide right, the center snapped the ball directly to Bill and he took off.

Everything went well in practice those first few weeks. I got by the first couple of games okay, but then we went up to Archbold Stadium to play Syracuse. They had a big, fast, rangy end who was responsible for everything that went outside.

We ran one of those sweeps during the game. From a sprinter's stance, the Syracuse end started at the same instant Geyer began his outside charge. From my crouched position, I spun to the right and headed for the gap between the end and Geyer.

The distance between the two was shorter than the distance between me and them and with my speed, which unlike Geyer's was closer to 20 seconds for the 100, there was no way I could get between them for a block.

We beat Syracuse that day, as I recall, but Geyer never gave me a lot of credit for the victory.

My career as a football player in college was one stumbling block after another. I was determined not to let the game dominate my life and become a culturally deprived jock, so I decided to take piano lessons during the football season.

The wife of a history professor undertook, at $2 for each one-hour lesson, to teach me. During my first lesson, I recall thinking that it was quite probable that I had more potential as a football player than I had as a musician. My first day of piano lessons also turned out to be my last. I went directly from that lesson to football practice. It was a game-style scrimmage between substitutes and the first team, with officials.

During the second half of the scrimmage that day, I was playing opposite Bill Chernowkowski, one of those ape-like athletes whose weight was mostly at or above the waist. He had short, relatively small legs and a huge torso with stomach to match. At 260 pounds, "Cherno" was the heaviest man on the squad.

As things turned out, it didn't matter where he carried most of his weight or how much of it there was. When he stepped on the back of my right hand in the middle of the third quarter, that ended, for all time, any thought I might have had of being another Horowitz. My hand still is slightly deformed, and I often look at it with the same sense of pride with which I view the television Emmys in my bookcase.

One of the saddest days of my life was the day I realized I'd played my last game of football. It was as final as death. As a young boy, I'd played in vacant lots—back in the days when there were vacant lots—every Saturday during the fall. By the time I got to high school, I knew I loved the game better than any other. I played all through high school and in college and then, one day, it was over. It was like the day my dog died.

It probably wouldn't occur to anyone who never played that even second stringers love the game. You don't have to be a star to enjoy playing football. You hear parents advise their children to learn to play a safer sport, a sport like golf or tennis that they can enjoy all their lives. I understand that argument but, as bad as I felt on that last day, I wouldn't trade my football days for golf if I could have started playing when I was eight and grown up to be Arnold Palmer.

People who have played football at any level watch a game with a different eye than someone who has never played. For one thing, they tend to watch the man playing the position they played. If you played center, you watch the center a lot. If you played end, you watch the ends.

I hear people say they can see the game better at home on television than they can see it sitting in the stadium. No one who knows much football thinks it's as good to watch at home as it is at the stadium. Watching at home is better than not watching football at all, but it isn't the same as being there.

The biggest difference in being there is that, good as the pictures, commentary, and replays are on television, the person at home is watching a small part of the total game that someone else has chosen to show him. What you watch is not your choice. At the stadium, the fans can watch what they want to watch anywhere on the field. I concede that if a person is not a knowledgeable football fan, he or she might get more out of watching it on television.

I often miss completely something that has happened to the ball carrier, because I'm watching what the guard is doing to the nose tackle or vice versa.

Every team played a seven-man defensive line when I played, with only one linebacker—always the toughest kid on the block. We all played both ways, of course, offense and defense. If they hadn't changed the rules, Joe Montana might have had to play free safety on defense. I don't know how that would have worked out for Joe, but I think New Orleans fullback Ironhead Heyward could hold his own as a middle linebacker on defense.

The great Frank Gifford, the most graceful football player I ever watched, was one of the last to play both offense and defense for the Giants.

Even relatively new football fans have seen a lot of rule changes. One of my prized possessions is a *Spalding Official Football Guide* that belonged to my uncle, who played for Williams College in 1900.

In those days they had to make only five yards for a first down (in three downs), and the literary style of the old rule book should embarrass the current rules committee.

"The game progresses," the rule book reads, "in a series of downs, the only limitation being a rule designed to prevent one side from continually keeping possession of the ball without any material advance, which would be manifestly unfair to the opponents.

"In three attempts to advance the ball, a side not having made five yards toward the opponent's goal, must surrender possession of the ball.

"It is seldom that a team actually surrenders the ball in this way," the rule book continues in its elegant prose, "because, after two attempts, if the prospects of completing the five-yard gain appear small, it is so clearly politic to kick the ball as far as possible that such a method is more apt to be adopted."

Eat your heart out, John Madden!

In 1925, the NFL player limit was 16. As late as 1944, a team still was limited to a roster of 28 players. And, of course, the uniform has changed.

One of the primary rules of life is that nothing seems to help, and that certainly is true of the protective equipment used by football players. Everything a player wears to a game today is better than the equipment of 35 years ago, but I don't notice that there are any fewer injuries. Of course, modern-day collisions involve bigger, stronger people. Early helmets were felt-padded leather. Today's plastic helmets are part protector, part lethal weapon.

Players used to make some individual choices about their uniforms. What a player wore frequently was not very uniform at all. There were players who liked stockings and players who didn't. In the NFL today, stockings are mandatory. I played next to a center who had an interesting theory. He refused to wear an athletic supporter because he felt he was safer from injury in this sensitive area if his private parts weren't confined like sitting ducks.

There was no rule against grabbing the face mask until 1956, for a simple reason—there were no face masks. A lot of teeth were lost. I remember Bill Farley coming back to the huddle, leaning over, and spitting his front teeth on the ground as he listened to the signal for the next play. Broken noses were common—but not considered serious. Stanley Steinberg wore a huge rubber protector over his nose that looked like part of a clown's costume. He held it in place by clenching a mouthpiece attached to it between his teeth.

The one rule I would most like to see put into effect—and never will as long as coaches dominate the rules committee—is one that would require a man on the field to call plays. If football is a game of mind and body and there are only 11 men from each team on the field, one of those players should be responsible for making the decision about which play to run. It should be illegal for a coach or anyone on the sidelines or in a booth up in the stadium to send in or signal a play.

If that seems like a rule that would be too difficult to enforce, make it the honor system. It's an honorable game.

Position names have changed over the years. We played with a quarterback, two halfbacks, a fullback, two ends, two guards, two tackles, and a center. In today's Super Bowl, each team will have 45 players available and the position names are different. There won't be anyone called a center on defense. He's a nose tackle now, assuming the team lines up an odd number of defensive linemen. On offense, the big, slower ends are tight ends and the smaller, fast ones are wide receivers. The tight ends block a lot, and, while they also catch (or drop) passes, they aren't called tight receivers.

Originally the quarterback was so called because he didn't stand back as far as the tailback and fullback in the Single-Wing. His position name has remained the same even though he usually no longer stands even a quarter of the way back.

Even the language of the game has evolved. Most of the football words used by fans have been popularized by radio and television commentators. Some assistant coach starts using a word in practice as a code for some action. The word is picked up by players and, eventually, by commentators and newspaper reporters hungry for authentic-sounding color.

Most of the words stick for a few years and then disappear in the lexicon of long ago. A few seem to have long lives. During the 1960s, the popular word for what a linebacker did when he abandoned his responsibility for a short pass and tried to break through the offensive line to get the quarterback was "red dog." I haven't heard "red dog" in years. Now, what they do is "blitz" and the word seems to be having a longer life than "red dog."

One phrase that's just come into its own this year is "red zone."

Until a few years ago, the area inside the 20-yard line was simply that, "the area inside the twenty-yard line." Now it's regularly being referred to as "the red zone."

"Run-and-Shoot" and the "hurry-up offense" are big these days, just the way the "flea flicker" pass and "the Statue of Liberty" used to be, but you can bet those phrases will be put out of their misery just the way "red dog" was. It's the kind thing to do to an old dog.

In spite of my failure to be chosen as an All-America during my playing days, I have great memories of it. Football locker rooms are good places. The talk is good, the feeling is good. Even the smell gets to you if you love the game.

When I go to the stadium, I bring either a small black-and-white television set or a radio. I don't watch the television set but sometimes, depending on who's doing the broadcasting, I prefer it to listening to the radio. Other times I stick with radio exclusively. All of the announcers broaden my knowledge of the game I'm watching by pointing out things I didn't see. Of course, I often feel like pointing out to them things I saw that they didn't. "Hey, Pat!" I yell to Summerall in my mind. "You missed the block Elliott put on so and so."

In addition to the radio and television sets with earplugs, I bring a small pair of good binoculars, a tuna fish sandwich on rye, and a thermos of chicken soup when it's cold. I am indifferent to the weather. I come prepared, and, except for a few early games when it can be too hot, I don't care what the temperature is.

When Sunday dawns cold, gray, and rainy, I invariably am asked whether I'm going to the game anyway. For 45 years I've had the same answer to that question. "Why wouldn't I go?"

Rain or snow are of no concern to me at a game. I actually enjoy sitting there, properly dressed and shielded, in a cold rain. The only minor problem I have with rain is that water tends to run up my sleeves when I hold the binoculars to my eyes for long periods.

Having sat with 70,000-odd strangers every Sunday for all these years, I think I understand fans better than the players do. Players seem to take fans more seriously than fans take themselves.

While it has become popular to suggest that anyone who spends time watching someone else play a game is an idiot, I happily profess to being one of those idiots. The Super Bowl is one of the highlights of my year.

If anyone here at the game is one of a small but inevitable number of people who come to every Super Bowl game, not because he or she wishes to but because a husband or friend had an extra ticket, you may wonder why some of us derive so much pleasure from a mere game. I ask you to look for a minute at the headlines in your newspaper any day of the week.

"RAGING FIRE KILLS 16!"

"AIRLINER DOWN IN MOUNTAINOUS AREA. ALL 237 ABOARD BELIEVED LOST."

"BANKRUPTCIES RISE AS ECONOMY FAILS TO RESPOND."

"PARENTS ARRESTED FOR CHILD ABUSE FOR THIRD TIME."

"AIDS EPIDEMIC ON INCREASE."

Do these tragic events make your day? Does the recent local murder make you happy all over for the rest of the week? Is reading about a raging flood or of corruption in government your idea of a good time?

It's for relief from such depressing world events and from the daily pressure of living our own lives that we turn to sports for entertainment. For many of us, there is nothing in all of sports quite as diverting as football . . . and no sporting event as much fun to watch as the Super Bowl.

DON DELILLO

"The Language of Football"

from *End Zone*

Don DeLillo, one of America's foremost novelists, is the author of more than a dozen books, including LIBRA, MAO II, *and* WHITE NOISE, *which won the National Book Award in 1985. His first novel,* END ZONE, *written in 1972, covered many subjects, including football. In this excerpt, DeLillo colorfully demonstrates the special language of football.*

THE SPECIAL TEAMS COLLIDED, swarm and thud of interchangeable bodies, small wars commencing here and there, exaltation and firstblood, a helmet bouncing brightly on the splendid grass, the breathless impact of two destructive masses, quite pretty to watch.

(The spectator, at this point, is certain to wonder whether he must now endure a football game in print—the author's way of adding his own neat quarter-notch to the scarred bluesteel of combat writing. The game, after all, is known for its assault-technology motif, and numerous commentators have been willing to risk death by analogy in their public discussions of the resemblance between football and war. But this sort of thing is of little interest to the exemplary spectator. As Alan Zapalac says later on: "I reject the notion of football as warfare. Warfare is warfare. We don't need substitutes because we've got the real thing." The exemplary spectator is the person who understands that sport is a benign illusion, the illusion that order is possible. It's a form of society that is rat-free and without harm to the unborn; that is organized so that everyone follows precisely the same rules; that is electronically controlled, thus reducing human error and benefiting industry; that roots out the inefficient and penalizes the guilty; that tends always to move toward perfection. The exemplary spectator has his occasional lusts, but not for warfare, hardly at all for that. No, it's details he needs—impressions, colors, statistics, patterns, mysteries, numbers, idioms, symbols. Football, more than other sports, fulfills this need. It is the one sport guided by language, by the word signal, the snap number, the color code, the play name. The spectator's pleasure, when not derived from the action itself, evolves from a notion of the game's unique organic nature. Here is not just order but civilization. And part of the spectator's need is to sort the many levels of material: to allot, to compress, to catalogue. This need leaps from season to season, devouring much of what is passionate and serene in the spectator. He tries not to panic at the final game's final gun. He knows he must retain something, squirrel some food for summer's winter. He feels the tender need to survive the termination of the replay. So maybe what follows is a form of sustenance, a game on paper to be scanned when there are stale days between events; to be propped up and looked at—the book as television set—for whatever is in here of terminology, pattern, numbering. But maybe not. It's possible there are deeper reasons to attempt a play-by-play. The best course is for the spectator to continue forward, reading himself into the very middle of that benign illusion. The author, always somewhat corrupt in his inventions and vanities, has tried to reduce the contest to basic units of language and action. Every beginning, it is assumed, must have a neon twinkle of danger about it, and so grandmothers, sissies, lepidopterists, and others are warned that the nomenclature that follows is often indecipherable. This is not the pity it may seem. Much of the appeal of sport derives from its dependence on elegant gibberish. And of course it remains the author's permanent duty to unbox the lexicon for all eyes to see—a cryptic ticking mechanism in search of a revolution.)

Blue turk right, double-slot, zero snag delay.

I was the lone setback. Nobody took out their middle linebacker. I got hit at the line of scrimmage, the 31, a high hard shot that settled my stomach and got rid of the noise in my head. Hobbs threw to Jessup on a half-moon pattern good for twelve. Taft went outside for six yards, then three, then five. I went straight ahead for five. Taft took a trigger pitch, cut inside a good block, and went to their 22. We left the huddle with a sharp handclap and trotted up to the line, eager to move off the ball, sensing a faint anxiety on the other side of the line.

Quick picket left, hook right.
Twin option off modified crossbow.
Re-T, chuck-and-go.

"How to hit," George Dole shouted out to us. "Way to pop, way to go, way to move. How to sting them, big Jerry. Bloomers, Bloomers, Bloomers. How to play this game."

Taft, stutter-stepping, juked a man into the ground and was forced out at the 5. I went off-tackle to the 1. Our line was firing out beautifully. It was crisp basic football. We were playing better than ever, in controlled bursts, probably because we were facing real talent. Taft went into the end zone standing up. Two of the receivers ran after him to slap his helmet and escort him off. Bing Jackmin kicked the extra point. I got down on one knee on the sideline, the chin strap of my helmet undone, material for a prize-winning sports photo. Commotion everywhere. Oscar Veech was shouting into my left ear.

"Gary, on the thirty-two I want you to catapult out of there. I want you to really come. I want to see you zoom into the secondary. But be sure you protect that ball."

"Right."

"Get fetal, get fetal."

"Fetal," I shouted back.

Centrex returned the kickoff to their 27. Our defense rolled into a gut 4-3 with variable off-picks. Their quarterback, Telcon, moved them on the ground past midfield, then went to the air on two of the next three plays. They tried a long field goal, wide to the right, and we took over. Hobbs hit Spurgeon Cole for good yardage but we were caught holding. Taft picked up eight. Ron Steeples was knocked cold, and we were forced to call a time out to get him off. Chuck Deering came running in to replace him, tripping and falling as he reached the huddle. I went inside tackle for three yards. Hobbs threw to Taft on a gate-delay out of the backfield. It picked up only seven, and the punting team came on. I sat on the bench, noticing Raymond Toon down at the far end; he seemed to be talking into his fist. Byrd Whiteside punted to their 44, a fair catch. Telcon moved them on the ground, inside mostly, all the way to our 19. Dennis Smee kicked somebody. That moved the ball inside the 10. Three running plays. The extra point tied it.

When we huddled at the 24, Hobbs said: "Stem left, L and R hitch and cross, F weak switch and sideline. On hut."

"What?" Chuck Deering said.

"On hut."

"No, the other thing. F something."

"F weak switch and sideline," Hobbs said.

"What kind of pattern is that?"

"Are you kidding?"

"What a bunch of fetus-eaters," Kimbrough said.

"When did they put that pattern in, Hobbsie?"

"Tuesday or Wednesday, Where the hell were you?"

"It must have been Wednesday. I was at the dentist."

"Nobody told you?"

"I don't think so, Hobbsie."

"Look, you run out ten yards, put some moves on your man and end up near the damn sideline."

"On hut. Break."

Third and eleven. They send their linebackers. Hobbs left the pocket and I had Mallon, their psychotic middle linebacker, by the jersey. He tripped and I released, moving into a passing plane for Hobbs. He saw me but threw low. I didn't bother diving for it. Creed seemed to be looking right past us as we moved off the field. I sat next to Chester Randall, a reserve lineman. He had broken his right wrist the week before, and it was still in a cast.

"Make no mistake, I can play with this thing. Hauptfuhrer gave me the go. If they need me, I can play, arm or no arm. The only thing that worries me is the dryness. I wish I could spit. I'm too dry to spit. I've been trying to work up some saliva for the past hour. I'd feel a whole lot better if I could only spit."

"Why don't you drink some water?"

"I've been trying to avoid that. It's what killed my sister's baby. There's something in it."

Centrex, starting from midfield, picked up six, eight, five, four, nine. Lenny Wells came off in pain—his left arm. George Owen screamed at him. The quarter ended. I thought of ice melting above the banks of streams in high country. Billy Mast replaced Wells. Telcon kept the ball on a bootleg and went to the 1 (flag in the air) before Buddy Shock caught him with a shoulder. Their penalty, clipping, and that put the ball outside the 20 from point of infraction. Telcon tried to hit his flanker on a post pattern. Bobby Iselin picked it off and returned to the 19. I couldn't find my helmet for a moment.

Garland Hobbs: "Let's ching those nancies."
Monsoon sweep, string-in left, ready right.
Cradle-out, drill-9 shiver, ends chuff.

Broadside option, flow-and-go.

I got bounced out of bounds and stepped on. Veech shouted down at me. Hard-earned first down for the unspectacular Harkness. Taft ran out of room and cut back into traffic. Their territory, second and eight. Hobbs looked toward Creed for guidance. The man's arms remained folded, his right foot tamping the grass.

Quickside brake and swing.

I put a light block on their end, then turned to the right to watch the play develop. Taft caught the ball about six yards behind the line and followed the center and both guards. They looked impressive, trucking along out there in front, Onan Moley flanked by Rector and Fallon, but nobody remembered to throw a block. The left cornerback sliced in to make an ankle-high tackle just as Taft was getting set to turn it on. A Centrex lineman was hurt, knee or ankle, and they had to call time to get him off. We assembled near our own 45. John Jessup took off his helmet. There was blood all over his lips and teeth.

Their linebackers seemed about to swarm-drop. Hobbs shouted numbers and colors over the defensive signals. I noticed that the knuckles on my left hand were all torn up. Hobbs kept changing plays, reacting to the defense. The whistle blew, delay of game, and we rehuddled and came back out. Hobbs threw to Spurgeon Cole up the middle. He got hit and dropped it. Centrex claimed fumble but the official paid no attention. Byrd Whiteside punted miserably.

"I wonder what we're missing on TV," he said.

Centrex stayed on the ground, going mainly over our left side, Lloyd Philpot and Champ Conway. On first down Telcon faked a handoff, rolled right, and hit one of his backs, number 25, all alone in the end zone. The conversion was good, and our kick return team left the bench. Bobby Iselin returned to the 17 where he was hit and fumbled. Lee Roy Tyler recovered for us. I jogged onto the field.

Each play must have a name. The naming of plays is important. All teams run the same plays. But each team uses an entirely different system of naming. Coaches stay up well into the night in order to name plays. They heat and reheat coffee on an old burner. No play begins until its name is called.

Middle-sift-W, alph-set, lemmy-2.

Taft went burning up the middle for fifteen. He got six on the next play. I was up ahead, blocking, and we went down along with three or four other people. I was on my back, somebody across my legs, when I realized their tackle, 77, was talking to me, or to Taft, or perhaps to all of us spread over the turf. He was an immense and very geometric piece of work, their biggest man, about six-seven and 270, an oblong monument to the virtues of intimidation. His dully hazy eyes squinted slowly deep inside the helmet.

Hobbs faked a trigger pitch to Taft, then handed to me, a variation off the KC draw. Mike Mallon and I met head-on. I went down a bit faster than he did. Hobbs called for a measurement although we were obviously short, almost a yard. I was breathing heavily as we rehuddled. I thought one or two ribs might be broken. Taft went straight ahead, bounced off Onan Moley, and tried to take it outside. A linebacker grabbed his jersey, somebody else held him upright, and then 77 stormed into him. I knew we had lost yardage, and I took off my helmet and started off. I heard a scuffle behind me. I put my helmet back on. It was Jessup and number 62 ready to go at each other. Bloomberg moved between them, and they started to circle him, cursing each other. Then somebody pushed 62 away and Anatole took Jessup by the arm and led him off. About ten yards away Taft was just getting to his feet. Tweego had Cecil Rector by the pads as I crossed the sideline.

"I want you to fire out, boy. You're not blowing them out. You're not popping. I want you to punish that man. I want you to straighten him up and move him out. You're not doing any of those things."

Moving on the ground, Centrex picked up three, eight, nine, then lost four on a good tackle by Dennis Smee, who went spinning off a block and hit the ball carrier very hard around the midsection as he hesitated while bellying out on a sweep. Third and five. Telcon rolled out, got set to throw, saw his man covered, sidestepped Dickie Kidd, and reversed his field. Buddy Shock just missed him way behind the line. Howard Lowry grabbed an ankle, and then John Billy Small was all over Telcon. He seemed to be climbing him. They both went down on top of Lowry. Punt formation. Bobby Hopper called for a fair catch. My ribs seemed all right and I went out. Three firecrackers went off in the stands. The crowd responded with prolonged applause.

Taft took a quick toss at the point and followed me inside their left end. Then I was down, and somebody was running right over me. I heard a lot of noise, pads hitting, men grunting and panting. Then it all came down on top of me. I smelled the turf and waited for the bodies to unpile. My rib cage was beginning to ache, a sense of stickiness, of glue. I felt quite happy. Somebody's hand was at the back of my neck, and he put all his weight on it as he lifted himself up.

Counter-freeze, blue-2 wide, swing inside delay.

I flared to the left, taking Mallon with me. Taft waited for a two-count and swung over the middle. Under pressure Hobbs threw high. Third and four. I couldn't contain my man. I tried to hold him. Then he and two others were all over Hobbs. I walked off without looking back. Whiteside punted sixty yards in the air. Jeff Elliott moved along the bench toward me.

"We're not moving the ball."

"I know," I said.

"That first drive was tremendous, Gary. But since then."

"We'll probably get killed. I anticipate a final score of eighty-three to seven."

"Not this team. This is a real team. We've got the character to come back. We're only down seven. This is a team that goes out and plays."

"I was just talking, Jeff. Psyching myself."

Telcon hit his tight end near the sideline for twelve. Champ Conway came off holding his left shoulder, and John Butler replaced him. Telcon completed two, missed one, hit one. He shook off Link Brownlee and threw to one of his backs who was just lounging around in the flat. The man took it all the way to our 17 before Bobby Luke caught him from behind. They picked up two on the ground, not very stylishly, Kidd and Lowry driving the ballcarrier back about ten yards while the official chased them blowing his whistle. Telcon overthrew a man in the end zone. Then he hit number 29 coming out of the backfield. Butler and Billy Mast put him down at the 9. They called time and Telcon looked toward his bench. Their head coach, Jade Kiley, turned to one of his assistants and said something. I looked at the clock. The field goal team came on. Hauptfuhrer started shouting at the defense, howling at them.

"Look out for the fake. Look out for the faaaaake. Aaaaaake. Aaaaaake. Aaaaaake."

They made the field goal. Bobby Iselin returned the kickoff to the 24. We all hurried out.

"Bed," Jerry Fallon said. "Pillow, sheet, blanket, mattress, spring, frame, headboard." Gibberish.

Hobbs hit Chuck Deering on a pony-out for nine. He worked the other sideline, and Spurgeon Cole was forced out after picking up thirteen. The bench was shouting encouragement. Hobbs came back with an opp-flux draw to Taft that picked up only two. He called time and went over to talk to Creed. I got my cleats scraped clean and watched Hobbs come trotting back; he seemed to have the answer to everything. I swung behind Deering, who was running a Q-route to clear out the area, and then I fanned toward the sideline and turned. The ball looked beautiful. It seemed overly large and bright. I could see it with perfect clarity. I backed up half a step, leaning with the ball. Then I had it and turned upfield. Somebody grabbed my ankle, but I kicked away and picked up speed again, being sure to stay near the sideline. Two of them moved in now. They had the angle on me and I stepped out of bounds. I got hit and dropped and hit again. I came up swinging. Somebody pulled my jersey, and I was kicked two or three times in the leg. I realized this was their side of the field. Fallon and Jessup pulled me away. The roughing cost them fifteen, and that moved the ball inside their 20. Hobbs hit Cole on a spoon-out to the 10, and we called time. He went off to confer with Creed again. Ron Steeples, who'd been knocked unconscious in the first quarter, came running in now to replace Chuck Deering. He was happy to be back. The scent of grass and dirt filled my nostrils. Hobbs returned and we huddled. His primary receiver was Jessup on a shadow-count delay over the middle. I went into motion, and the ball was snapped. I watched Jessup fake a block and come off the line. Hobbs looked to his left, pump-faked, turned toward Jessup and fired. The ball went off Jessup's hand and right to their free safety, 46, who was standing on the goal line. We all stood around watching, either startled or pensive, trying to retrace events. Then 46 decided to take off, evading Kimbrough and Rector, cutting inside me. I went after him at top speed. At the 30-yard line I became aware of something behind me, slightly off to the side. White and green and coming on. Then it was past me, 22, Taft Robinson, running deftly and silently, a remarkable clockwork intactness, smoothly touring, no waste or independent movement. I didn't believe a man could run that fast or well. I slowed down and took off my helmet. Taft caught 46 just the other side of midfield, hitting him below the shoulders and then rolling off and getting to his feet in one motion. I stood there watching. The gun sounded, and we all headed for the tunnel.

I sat on the floor sucking the sweet flesh out of half an orange. Onan Moley slid down the wall and settled next to me. Somebody's blood was all over the tape on his forearm.

"We're hitting pretty good," he said.

"They're just hitting better."

"They don't do anything unexpected. But they're the kind of team that gets stronger and stronger. They'll demolish us in the second half. They'll just keep coming. They'll keep getting stronger. I figure the final score to be about sixty-six to seven."

"That bad?" Onan said.

"Worse maybe."

"We'll probably have to use cable blocking more often than not in the second half."

"Imagine what it's like," I said, "to go against a major power. These people come on and on. So imagine what it must be like to go against a really major power."

"Yeah, think what it must be like to take the field against Tennessee or Ohio State or Texas."

"Against Notre Dame or Penn State."

"The Fighting Irish," Onan said. "The Nittany Lions."

"Imagine what it must be like to play before a hundred thousand people in the L.A. Coliseum."

"And nationwide TV."

"UCLA versus LSU."

"One of the all-time intersectional dream games."

"We'll never make it," I said. "We'll never even get out of here alive. They'll just keep coming and coming."

"That fifty-five is the meanest thing I ever hope to play against."

"Mallon," I said.

"That thing is clubbing me to death. He rears back and clubs me with a forearm every play. I start wincing as soon as I snap the damn ball because I know old fifty-five is already bringing that forearm around to club my head. Gary, I only go about one ninety-eight. That thing is easy two thirty-five."

"And still growing."

"I guarantee you I'm not about to get him any madder than he was the day he was born. I can take sixty minutes of clubbing as long as I know I'll never see that guy again. He is one mean person, place, or thing."

The coaches started yelling for their people. Onan went over to Tweego's group, and I went to the blackboard where Oscar Veech and Emmett Creed were waiting. Creed spoke slowly and evenly, looking from Hobbs to Taft to me, ignoring the other quarterbacks and running backs gathered behind us. Bobby Hopper asked a question about the blocking assignments just put in for the drag slant right. Creed looked at Oscar Veech. It was rather strange. He didn't want to talk to anyone who couldn't help him win.

"Right guard blocks down," Veech said. "Harkness takes out the end."

It wasn't time to go back out yet. I went and sat against another wall. Mitchell Gorse, a reserve safetyman, walked by. In his spotless uniform he looked a bit ludicrous.

"We'll come back, Gary," he said.

"Bull."

Across the room Bloomberg was sitting on a park bench that somehow had found its way into the dressing area. From somewhere I could hear Sam Trammel's voice.

"Crackback. Crackback. Crackback."

My helmet, wobbling slightly, rocking, was on the floor between my feet. I looked into it. I felt sleepy and closed my eyes. I went away for a while, just one level down. Everything was far away. I thought (or dreamed) of a sunny green garden with a table and two chairs. There was a woman somewhere, either there or almost there, and she was wearing clothes of another era. There was music. She was standing behind a chair now, listening to a Bach cantata. It was Bach, all right. When I lost the woman, the music went away. But it was still nice. The garden was still there, and I felt I could add to it or take away from it if I really tried. Just to see if I could do it, I took away a chair. Then I tried to bring back the woman without the music. Somebody tapped my head, and I opened my eyes. I couldn't believe where I was. Suddenly my body ached all over. They were getting up and getting ready to move out. I was looking into Roy Yellin's chewed-up face.

"They're putting me in for Rector," he said.

"What's wrong with Cecil?"

"Nothing wrong with Cecil. He's just not hitting. He's getting beat. His man is overpowering him. Number seventy-seven's his man. He looks real big, Gary. Big, strong, and mobile. Those are Tweego's exact words. What do you think?"

"He'll kill you," I said.

"You think so?"

"He killed Cecil, didn't he? He'll kill you, too."

"Are you serious?"

"I'm just kidding. It helps me relax."

"That's what I mean."

"You'll do the job, Roy. I just said those things to undermine my sense of harmony. It's very complex. It has to do with the ambiguity of this whole business."

I got up and punched a locker. It was almost time.

We were all making the private sounds. We were getting ready. We were getting high. The noise increased in volume.

"Footbawl," George Owen shouted. "This is footbawl. You throw it, you ketch it, you kick it. Footbawl. Footbawl. Footbawl."

We were running through the tunnel out onto the field. Billy Mast and I met at the sideline. He raised his hands above his head and then brought them down on my pads—one, two, three times. I jumped up and down and threw a shoulder into Billy. The band marched off now. We were both jumping up and down, doing private and almost theological calisthentics, bringing God into the frenzied body, casting out fear.

"How to go, little Billy."

"Hiyoto, hiyoto."

"They're out to get us. They'll bleach our skulls with hydrosulfite."

"They'll rip off our clothes and spit on our bare feet."

"Yawaba, yawaba, yawaba."

"How to go, Gary boy. How to jump, how to jump."

"They'll twist our fingers back."

"They'll kill us and eat us."

Centrex came out. We gathered around Creed again and then broke with a shout. The kickoff team went on. Bing Jackmin kicked to the 7 or 8, and they returned to the 31, where Andy Chudko hit the ballcarrier at full force and then skidded on his knees over the fallen player's body. I watched Creed take his stance at the midfield stripe. Bing Jackmin came off the field and sat next to me.

"One two three a-nation. I received my confirmation. On the day of declaration. One two three a-nation."

"They're coming out in a double-wing," I said.

"It's all double, Gary. Double consciousness. Old form superimposed on new. It's a breaking-down of reality. Primitive mirror awareness. Divine electricity. The football feels. The football knows. This is not just one thing we're watching. This is many things."

"You know what Coach says. It's only a game, but it's the only game."

"Gary, there's a lot more out there than games and players."

Telcon faked a handoff, dropped slowly back (ball on his hip), then lofted a pass to his flanker, who had five steps on Bobby Luke. The ball went through his hands, a sure six, and he stood on our 45-yard line just a bit stunned, his hands parted, a tall kid with bony wrists, looking upfield to the spot in time and space he would have been occupying that very second if only he had caught the football. They sagged a little after that and had to punt. Bobby Hopper called for a fair catch and fumbled. About six players fought for possession, burrowing, crawling, tearing at the ground. A Centrex player leaped out of the mass, his fist in the air, and their offense came back on.

Lee Roy Tyler limped to the sideline. Vern Feck stomped his clipboard, then turned his back to the field and looked beyond our bench, way out over the top of the stadium. From our 32 they picked up two, one, and five on the ground. Telcon looked across at his head coach. We rose from the bench and crowded near the sideline. Centrex broke and set.

Hauptfuhrer chanted to his linemen: "Contain. Contain. Contain those people. Infringe. Infringe on them. Rape that man, Link. Rape him. Ray-yape that man."

Dennis Smee, at middle linebacker, shouted down at the front four: "Tango-two. Reset red. Hoke that bickie. Mutt, mutt, mutt."

John Butler fought off a block and held the ballcarrier upright at the 23. We made noises at the defense as they came off. Hobbs opened with a burn-7 hitch to Ron Steeples off the fake picket. Second and one. Hobbs used play-action and threw to Spurgeon Cole, seam-X-in, leading him too much. Their tight safety came over to pick it off and ran right into Spurgeon. Their ball.

Telcon threw twice for first downs. Two holding penalties moved them back. They tried two draws. Then Buddy Shock turned a reverse inside. They punted dead on our 23. I went out, feeling the glue spreading over my ribs. Hobbs called a power 26 off the crossbow with Taft Robinson carrying. I went in low at their left end. He drove me to my knees, and I grabbed an ankle and pulled. On his way down he put a knee into my head.

Out-23, near-in belly toss.

Taft barely made it to the line of scrimmage. On a spring-action trap I went straight ahead, careened off 77, and got leveled by Mike Mallon. He came down on top of me, breathing into my face, chugging like a train. I closed my eyes. The noise of the crowd seemed miles away. Through my jersey the turf felt chilly and hard. I heard somebody sigh. A deep and true joy penetrated my being. I opened my eyes. All around me there were people getting off the ground. Directly above were the stars, elucidations in time, old clocks sounding their chimes down the bending universe. I regretted knowing nothing about astronomy; it would have been pleasant to calculate the heavens. Bloomberg was leaning over to help me to my feet. We joined the huddle. Garland Hobbs, on one knee, spoke into the crotches of those who faced him.

"Brown feather right, thirty-one spring-T. On two. Break."

I couldn't believe it. The same play. The same play, I thought. He's called the same play. A fairly common maneuver, it somehow seemed rhapsodic now. How beautiful, I thought. What beauty. What a beautiful thing to do. Hobbs received the snapback, Roy Yellin pulled, and there I was with the football, the pigskin, and it was planted once more in my belly, and I was running to daylight, to starlight, and getting hit again by Mallon, by number 55, by their middle linebacker, by five-five, snorting as he hit me, an idiotically lyrical moment. Down I went, the same play, the grass and stars. It's all taking so long, I thought. The galaxy knows itelf. The quasars repeat their telling of time. Nine-tenths of the universe is missing. I was covered with large people. In a short while they raised themselves, and I drifted back to the huddle. The chains came out. First down. Hobbs overthrew Jessup, then Steeples. Taft went wide for two. Centrex returned the punt to their 33.

Ted Joost squatted next to me on the sideline.

"This whole game could be played via satellite. They could shoot signals right down here. We'd be equipped with electronic listening devices. Transistor things sealed into our headgear. We'd receive data from the satellites and run our plays accordingly. The quarterback gets one set of data. The linemen get blocking patterns. The receivers get pass routes. Et cetera. Same for the defense. Et cetera."

"Who sends the data?" I said.

"The satellites."

"Who feeds the satellites?"

"A computer provides the necessary input. There'd be a computerized data bank of offensive plays, of defensive formations, of frequencies. What works best against a six-one on second down and four inside your own thirty? The computer tells; the satellite broadcasts to the helmet. There'd be an offensive satellite and a defensive satellite."

Centrex stayed on the ground. Their guards and tackles came off the ball. Dickie Kidd was helped off, and George Dole replaced him. They picked up nine, four, eight, three, three, six. They moved quickly in and out of the huddle. They kept grinding it out. They kept hitting; they kept moving. Billy Mast's jersey was torn off his back, and he had to come off for a new one. He removed his helmet. Both his eyes were puffed up, and there was a patch of dry blood at the corner of his mouth. Telcon skirted John Butler and picked up two key blocks. Bobby Iselin bumped him out at the 16.

Our defense called time to get organized. Larry Nix went in for Lloyd Philpot. I watched Lloyd come toward the bench. His jersey wasn't tucked into his pants. Tape was hanging from his left wrist and hand. He squatted down between Ted Joost and me.

"I didn't infringe. The coaches wanted optimum infringement. But I didn't do the job. I didn't infringe."

Two running plays gained little or nothing. Then Telcon got pressure from Howard Lowry and had to throw the ball away. Their field goal kicker came on. The ball hit the crossbar and bounded back.

Delta-3 series, saddleback-in, shallow hinge reverse.
Span-out option, jumbo trap.

I followed a good block by Jerry Fallon, tripping over somebody's leg and gaining only three. Then, on a column sweep, Taft turned the corner and picked up speed just as a lane opened. Suddenly he was gone, out into open territory, and I watched from my knees as he dipped and swerved and cut past a cornerback, one motion, accelerating off the cut and heading straight for the last man, the free safety, and then veering off just slightly, almost contemptuously, not bothering to waste a good hip-fake, still operating on that first immaculate thrust, cruising downhill from there. I was on my feet and following him. We were all running after him, running past our bench, everybody standing and yelling, jumping, looking at the back of his jersey, at 22 in white and green, the crowd up and screaming—a massive, sustained, and somehow lonely roar. I slowed to a walk and watched Taft glide into the end zone. He executed a dainty little curl to the left and casually dropped the football. Moody Kimbrough stumbled over the goal line and picked him up. Then Fallon and Jessup were there, and they were all carrying Taft back across the goal line, holding him at the waist and under the arms, and Roy Yellin was jumping up and down and smacking Taft on the helmet. Spurgeon Cole stood beneath the goal posts, repeating them, arms raised in the shape of a crossbar and uprights, his fists clenched. The crowd was still up, leaning, in full voice, addressing its own noise. Taft came off. Bing Jackmin kicked the extra point. I hit Taft on the helmet and sat next to Tim Flanders.

"We got a game going now," he said. "We got a game going. We got a game going now."

"I think my ribs are busted," I said.

"You're okay. You're okay. You're okay."

Bing kicked out of bounds and had to do it over. They returned to the 38. The quarter ended. I went over to hit Taft on the helmet again. Hauptfuhrer and Vern Feck were explaining something about gap-angle blocking to Dennis Smee. Emmett Creed moved his right foot over the grass, a few inches either way. This was his power, to deny us the words we needed. He was the maker of plays, the name-giver. We were his chalk-scrawls. Something like that.

Centrex stayed inside the tackles, making two first downs. Then Telcon handed to his big back, 35, and I watched him come right toward us, toward the bench, rumbling over the turf, really pounding along. He got ready to lower a shoulder as he sensed Buddy Shock coming straight across from his linebacker's spot. They met before the runner could turn upfield. Buddy left his feet as he made contact, coming in hard, swinging a forearm under the lowered shoulder. They went down a few yards away from us. We heard the hard blunt heavy sound of impact and then the wild boar grunt as they hit the ground and bounced slightly, grasping now, breathing desperately, looking into the earth for knowledge and power. Standing above them we watched solemnly, six or seven of us, as Buddy put his hand on the ballcarrier's head and pushed himself upright. Then 35 got to his feet, slowly, still panting. John Jessup spoke to him, conversationally, in a near whisper.

They stayed on the ground, moving it to our 16. Telcon rolled out right, threw left. Their tight end, all alone on the 5, walked in with it. I felt tired suddenly. A wave of sorrow passed over our bench. After the extra point, they kicked away from Taft, a low floater that Ted Joost fell on at the 29. Taft picked up three on a rip-slant. Roy Yellin came up limping.

"Walk it off," Kimbrough told him.

"Oh mother," Yellin said. "Oh Grace Porterfield Yellin. Oh it hurts, it hurts."

"Walk it off, shovel-head."

Zone set, triple tex, off-hit recon dive.

I was pass-blocking for Hobbs. The big thing, 77, shed Yellin and came dog-paddling in. I jammed my helmet into his chest and brought it up fast, striking his chin. He made a noise and kept coming, kept mauling me. He backed me up right into Hobbs, and we all went down. I heard the coaches screaming, their voices warming our huddle. Hobbs left the pocket and threw to Taft in a crowd. A linebacker tipped it, gained control, and brought it in. Taft got a piece of him, and Ron Steeples put him down. As we went off, Oscar Veech screamed into our chests.

"What in the hell is going on here? What are you feebs doing out there? What in the hell is the name of the game you people are playing?"

The ball was spotted at our 33. Dennis Smee moved along the line, slapping helmets and pads. Jessup sat next to me on the bench. Blades of grass were stuck to the dry blood on his face. Centrex shifted into a tight-T. Halfback picked up four. Telcon kept for six. Halfback went straight ahead for nine. Halfback went straight ahead for eight. Fullback went off-tackle for four. Fullback went straight ahead, taking George Dole into the end zone with him. The extra point was good.

"Jee-zus," Jessup said.

"It's all over."

Taft took the kickoff six yards deep and brought it out to the 44. Len Skink reported in for Yellin. Randy King replaced Onan Moley. Terry Madden came in at quarterback. He hit Taft on a snowbird flare for no gain. He threw deep to Steeples incomplete. He fumbled the snap and fell on it. Bing Jackmin met me at the sideline.

"Our uniforms are green and white," he said. "The field itself is green and white—grass and chalk markings. We melt into our environment. We are doubled in the primitive mirror."

I walked down to the very end of the bench. Raymond Toon was all alone, talking into his right fist.

"There it goes, end over end, a high spiral. The deep man avoids or evades would be better. Down he goes, woof. First and ten at the twenty-six or thirty-one. Now they come out in a flood left to work against a rotating zone."

"Toony, that's not a flood."

"Hey, Gary. Been practicing."

"So have we."

"There they go. Andy Chudko, in now for Butler, goes in high, number sixty-one, Andy Chudko, fumble, fumble, six feet even, about two twenty-five, doubles at center on offense, Chudko, Chudko, majoring in airport commissary management, plays a guitar to relax, no other hobbies, fumble after the whistle. College football—a pleasant and colorful way to spend an autumn afternoon. There goes five, six, seven, eight, nine, ten, eleven yards, big thirty-five, twelve yards from our vantage point here at the Orange Bowl in sun-drenched Miami, Florida. John Billy Small combined to bring him down. John Billy, as they break the huddle, what a story behind this boy, a message of hope and inspiration for all those similarly afflicted, and now look at him literally slicing through those big ball carriers. Capacity crowd. Emmett Big Bend Creed. Mike Mallon, they call him Mad Dog. Telcon. Multi-talented. A magician with that ball. All the color and excitement. He's got it with a yard to spare off a good block by fifty-three or seventy-three. Woof. Three Rivers Stadium in Pittsburgh or Cincinnati. Perfect weather for football. Time out on the field. And now back to our studios for this message. They're a powerhouse, Gary. They play power football. I'd like to get in there and see what I could do. It looks like some of the guys got banged up pretty bad."

"Nobody's died yet. But then the game isn't over."

"Telcon looks out over the defense. He's a good one. Hut, hut, offside. He's one of the good ones. Plenty of hitting out on that field. I'm sure glad I'm up here. D.C. Stadium in the heart of the nation's capital. Crisp blue skies. Emmett Big Bend Creed. And there's more on tap next week when the Chicago Bears, the Monsters of the Midway, take on the always rough and tough Green Bay Packers of coach something something. Gary, what's going to happen up there on the banks of the Fox River in little Green Bay when the big bad Bears come blowing in from the windy city?"

"You'd better take it easy," I said. "Try to get a grip on things. I'm serious, Toony. You'd better slow down. I really think you'd better watch yourself."

I went over and sat with Garland Hobbs. Centrex was running sweeps. They picked up a first down at our 38. People began to go home. Somebody in the stands behind us, way up high, was blowing into some kind of air horn. It sent a prehistoric cry across the night, a message of grief from the hills down to the suffering plain. Objects were thrown out of the stands.

"Fug," Hobbs said. "That's all I can say. That's the only word in my head right now. Fug, fug, fug."

Somebody fumbled, and Link Brownlee fell on it. I hit Hobbs on the pads and went out. Terry Madden left the pocket, what there was of it, and headed toward the sideline looking downfield for someone to throw to. Their left end pushed him out of bounds, and a linebacker knocked him over the Centrex bench. I strolled over there. Players were milling about, shoving each other just a bit.

Jessup to number 62: "Peach pit. Scumbag."

They got fifteen yards for roughing. We went to the near hashmark and huddled. Madden's nose was bleeding. At the snap I moved into my frozen insect pose, ready to pass block. Jessup ignored his pass route and went right at the linebacker playing over him, 62, leading with a forearm smash to the head and following with a kick in the leg. I watched 62 actually bare his teeth. Soon everybody was in it, swinging fists and headgear, kicking, spitting, holding on to pads, clutching jerseys, both benches emptying now, more objects sailing out of the stands. I was in the very middle of the rocking mass. It was relatively safe there. We were packed too tightly for any serious punching or kicking to be done. The real danger was at the periphery where charges could be made, individual attacks mounted, and I felt quite relaxed where I was, being rocked back and forth. A lot of crazed eyes peered out of the helmets nearby. In the distance I could see some spectators climbing over the guard rails and running onto the field. Then there was a sudden shift in equilibrium and I caught an elbow in the stomach. I turned, noted color of uniform, and started swinging. I moved in for more, very conscious of the man's number, 45, backfield, my size or smaller. Somebody ran into me from behind, and I went down. It was impossible to get up. I crawled over bodies and around churning legs. I reached an open area and got to my knees. There was someone standing above me, a spectator, a man in a white linen suit, his hand over his mouth, apparently concealing something, and he seemed to be trying to speak to me, but under the circumstances it was not possible to tell what he was saying or even in what language he was saying it. A player tripped over me; another player, backpedaling, ended in my lap. Then I was completely buried. By the time I got out, it was just about over. Jessup and 62 were down on the ground, motionless in each other's arms, neither one willing to relinquish his hold. But nobody was fighting now, and the offficials moved in. It took them about half a minute to persuade Jessup to let go of the other player. I felt all right. My ribs didn't ache for the moment. Both men were thrown out for fighting. The field was cleared. Randy King sat on the grass, trying to get his right shoes back on.

Twin deck left, ride series, white divide.
Gap-angle down, 17, dummy stitch.
Bone country special, double-D to right.

Papers blew across the field. I put a gentle block on their left end, helping out Kimbrough. Madden threw to nobody in particular. The stands were almost empty now. I ran a desultory curl pattern over the middle, putting moves on everybody I passed, including teammates. Madden threw behind me. I reached back with my left hand and pulled it in, a fairly miraculous catch. There was open field for a second. Then I was hit from the side and went down. One of their cornerbacks helped me up. I returned to the huddle. We went to the line and set. The left side of our line was offside. We went back again. Taft ran a new off-bike delay that picked up four. The gun sounded. I walked off the field with newspapers whipping across my legs. We went quietly through the tunnel and into the locker room. We began taking off our uniforms. In front of me, Garland Hobbs took a long red box from the button of his dressing area. The label on it read: ALL-AMERICAN QUARTERBACK, A MENDELSOHN-TOPPING SPORTS MOTIVATION CONCEPT. Carefully he opened the box. He arranged twenty-two figurines on a tiny gridiron and then spun a dial. His team moved smartly downfield. Sam Trammel went along the rows of cubicles, asking for complete silence. I assumed a team prayer was forthcoming. Next to me, Billy Mast recited a few German words to himself in the total stillness. When I asked for a translation he said it was just a simple listing of things—house, bridge, fountain, gate, jug, olive tree, window. He said the German words gave him comfort.

Hauptfuhrer was standing over us. "Shut up and pray," he said.

JAMES DICKEY

Breaking the Field

James Dickey, who played a bit of football at Clemson, has an ability to break it down into elemental emotions of fear, pride, and exultation. Dickey, Poet-in-Residence at the University of South Carolina, has been honored for his compilations of poetry, PUELLA *and* BUCKDANCER'S CHOICE. *He wrote this poem—an ode to punt returners—for the Super Bowl XXVIII game program.*

for the punt returners
A high one coming,   Nosing down it is turning
Over to make itself come down harder
And faster to me
near me.
Shift   stutter-step   back   right
Right.   Got it
now
Look everywhere at once.   left right and up the middle:
One good block out of nowhere.   Chaos   field breaking –
Closing jerseys, all wrong.   Not many friends
But the right ones.   The chaos must be better:
Let's break it more, friends.
Look everywhere
One last time. Closing colors, but in amongst
Green shows like a grasshopper: through everything, green
Of the broken field.   Men down all over.   Space closing, but
Beyond friends and enemies, green.   Green daylight:
Left.   Left.   Green still showing
A little.   Go there

GARY CARTWRIGHT

Tom Landry: God, Family, and Football

At the time of this story's publication in SPORT *magazine in 1969, the Dallas Cowboys were changing pro football with revolutionary offensive and defensive techniques. They were winning football games, but never championships. Tom Landry, the only coach the Cowboys had from the franchise's inception in 1960 until 1989, was the man most credited for the team's success. He also was blamed for its failures in big games. Written by Texas-based journalist Gary Cartwright, this is a revealing profile of a misperceived technocrat and one of the NFL's most influential coaches.*

IT IS SATURDAY AFTERNOON, early November. A chilled old-time wind chases the fire and baked bronze of dying leaves, and Tom Landry sits in his office on the eleventh floor of a suburban tower in North Dallas, looking down with the sort of detachment that Baron Frankenstein must have experienced as he watched the villagers fight fear with sticks and hayforks.

The Monster is loose again!

The extent of his capering again will be apparent in the agate type of the Sunday sports pages. Ohio U. defeats Cincinnati 60 to 48. Virginia holds off Tulane 63 to 47. Yale tears up Princeton 42 to 17. *Yale*! The blunderbuss of the dime novel, the twenty-three-pound turtleneck sweater in grandpa's attic, scoring with basketball propensity. Even Landry's old school, the University of Texas, is lacing TCU (47 to 21) with unparalleled freedom of expression.

Records fall like leaves, then blow away under the gusts of new records. Someone named Mike Richardson (forget that name) wipes Kyle Rote and Doak Walker from the SMU record book. Michigan's Ron Johnson is a jet-age ghost, cremating the memory of Grange and Harmon in his fantail. In a radio interview former Los Angeles Rams center Art Hunter refers to O.J. Simpson as "the best of Jimmy Brown and Gale Sayers rolled into one." And Texas's Chris Gilbert, the little tailback who has broken all the Southwest Conference rushing records and threatens more of the same to every career rushing record in the history of college football, will have difficulty making it as a first team All-America.

What was once a game of patience, prudence, and pogroms enacted more or less in the geographical center of a seven-diamond defense now looks as though it were invented by the French. Even the college teams which are not, strictly speaking, relying on the "pro-type" offense, are gaining three or four hundred yards a game. "Ten yards and a cloud of dust;" that's how Texas Tech coach J.T. King describes the University of Texas attack.

The Monster is everywhere, legends tumbling on his vibrations.

"I still feel that the defense will stand up to the test," Tom Landry is saying on this particular Saturday afternoon. Landry is seemingly oblivious to the riots that are at this moment taking place on the campuses across the land; Landry is talking of the National Football League, specifically of the game in the Cotton Bowl Sunday between his Cowboys and the New York Giants, a game that will go a long way in settling the winner of the Capitol Division. There are those in football, Giants' president Wellington Mara among them, who feel that Tom Landry has perfected, maybe even invented, football's modern defense. Landry credits the invention to Steve Owen the genius of the Giants from 1931–1953, though it was Landry who defined the relationship of the linebacker to the width of the playing field, thus establishing what Mara calls "the inside-out theory of defensive football"—protecting the middle while trusting the flanks to hot pursuit.

Landry was one of the first to recognize tendencies and traits in his opposition, and one of the first to devise "keys" which would unlock the secrets of the mysterious huddle. Many coaches eventually reached that conclusion, but *Landry did it as a player.* And when it was perfected—and when the Giants were the most feared defense in football—Landry started experimenting with offensive weapons which could conceivably destroy his life's work. It was a restless imitation of art and life: from the missile came the antimissile came the anti-antimissile. . . .

But listen to Landry on this Saturday afternoon:

"The defense will stand up. But sometimes you wonder (he says this with some irony in his normal monotone; his oyster eyes twinkle; his Ice Age smile, collected through centuries of slow but constant seepage, is alert to history's carnage). . . .

"You see what's happening to college football. The two-platoon rule opened it up to the multiple offense, and the multiple offense created an impossible situation in terms of how a college team can *defense* it. The key to defense is execution; in order to execute well enough to contain a multiple offense a team must play together four or five years . . . at least that long . . . which is impossible for the colleges. As long as colleges play a multiple offense . . . a T-formation offense, with quarterbacks in the pass pocket . . . as long as that happens, the colleges will never be able to defense it; they will never have enough experience to cope with the many problems. The colleges must either return to one platoon football or resign themselves to big scores."

Somewhere in the corners of your mind you hear Baron Frankenstein speak, identifying his work, preaching caution, almost amused at the misunderstanding. Lay aside your hayforks, melt down your silver bullets: your icons are powerless, your dogs less than useless. The Monster is not the creation but the creator. It is the *Landry Monster*, that gangling apparition of spreads and slots and double-or-triple wings and men-in-motion and abrupt shifts, coordinated to wreck anticipation, delight the fans, and make supermen from human tissue.

They used to laugh at it. Such great-but-stylized coaches as Buddy Parker used to warn Landry that the multiple offense would never work, that it would strangle on its own complications; and for a time in the early 1960s it seemed as though they were right. But Landry *had it in his mind* when he resigned as defensive coach of the Giants to take the head job with the newly formed Dallas Cowboys in 1960.

His conviction never wavered. "It was, and still is, the only way to attack the basic 4-3 defense," Landry says. On the other hand: "If you have the time and patience to coordinate your defense . . . the experience to handle all the complicated sets . . . defense will prevail."

Like brilliant men in every field, Tom Landry is self-made. Or, as Landry chooses to put it, he is the product of destiny, and divine counterplay.

"It is hard to put your finger on why you make the decisions that you make," says Landry. "I'm a great believer in my own convictions, but I pray a great deal that I'll make the right decision. I have no doubt that there is something other than man himself that leads man."

That something, of course, is the Christian God. There was a time eight or nine years ago, in the scruffy, early years of the Cowboys, when some of the older players referred to their coach as *Pope Landry I*. Less pious in recent years, Landry expresses his deepest beliefs in the stereotype of selected banquet speeches, and in answers to direct questions. "If Landry has ever saved any souls," says one current player, "he did it without anyone knowing."

In the early years many players found Landry confusing and noncommunicative. "He would never pat you on the behind and tell you 'good job,'" complained one former defensive back. "If you intercepted a pass, Landry looked at you like *that's what you're supposed to do!*" But that is Landry's style—taciturn without being shy, confident without being boastful; he exudes rather than expounds his philosophy. Except for the practice field or meeting room, Landry permits himself almost no personal contact. There is one minor exception: he sometimes lifts weights with the players in the offseason. Landry is as trim and maybe as strong as any man on his team. With Tom Landry, the priority is God, family, and football.

"I grew up in a Christian home," says Landry, "but I wasn't truly converted to Christ until 1958. I lived a moral life, but I wasn't a true Christian. Most people go through life always looking . . .always seeking. I found out that a Christian commitment is the only real purpose in life."

Landry says that he did not have "a religious experience" in 1958 so much as he "matured into it."

"You could never get Tom to talk about his background," recalls Father Benedict Dudley, the Giants' chaplain.

Says Cowboys president Tex Schramm, "Tom isn't the easiest man in the world to communicate with. You have to hit him with a two-by-four to get his attention: but once you get it, you get his whole attention. Tom has a rare perspective. For instance, he is known as a progressive coach, but in a lot of ways he's very conservative. He holds strong with tradition, yet he is an innovator. If you remember, he used to alternate quarterbacks (before Don Meredith reached maturity). He recognized this wasn't the ultimate answer, yet there we were in 1962 leading the league in offense. And with *nothing!*"

Sportswriters who have known Landry for a few years find him strikingly honest, easy to interview. I remember a party in 1963 after team owner Clint Murchison, Jr., destroyed Landry's original five-year contract and signed him to a new eleven-year contract, an unprecedented vote of confidence.

Everyone was whooping it up but Landry, who was sitting alone in one corner, serene as a Ming vase. "Why aren't you living it up?" someone asked him. "This is your party."

"No," said Landry. "This isn't my party. This is the team's party."

Later that night his wife, Alicia, told me: "No one will ever have to fire Tommy. He would quit if he didn't win. The new contract is a vote of confidence in the football team, not in Tommy!"

Tom Landry takes his aspirations seriously—and one at a time. Aside from beating the Green Bay Packers in a championship game,

Landry's idea of personal fulfillment is to have a positive influence on as many young men as possible. This is his passion and it traces back to his own boyhood which was, in a contemporary sense, unique.

Landry was born in 1924, a half block from the First Methodist Church of Mission, Texas. Mission is a small town with a large Mexican-American population in the lush citrus valley between the Gulf of Mexico and the Rio Grande. Tom's father ran a garage; he served as Fire Chief and superintendent of Sunday school at the church down the street. Tom played every sport in season, made mostly A's in his school subjects, and had an exemplary Sunday school attendance record.

"Mission was a great place for a boy to grow up," he recalls. "I learned something playing in the sandlots . . . something that today's youngsters aren't able to experience. Here is where you learn to cry and to fight . . . to overcome all situations according to your own abilities and initiative . . . without some (adult) supervisor always looking over your shoulder."

With characteristic clarity Landry remembers that his final high school team (1) played the Notre Dame box formation; (2) went undefeated in twelve games; (3) allowed only one touchdown—on a pass interference penalty. Landry was a good college player at the University of Texas, a standout passer until he broke the thumb on his passing hand, at which time he was forced to surrender his starting position to another passer of some ability, Bobby Layne. Converted to fullback in the week between the thumb injury and the game against North Carolina (the Choo-Choo Justice team), Landry ran for more than one hundred yards that Saturday afternoon. Though he had less speed than your average pulling guard, Landry played six seasons at cornerback with the Giants (1950–55), the last four as a player-coach. By the late 1950s he was such a valued assistant coach with the Giants that head coach Jim Lee Howell referred to him publicly as "the best coach in football."

The Giants in those glory days were pretty much the product of two assistant coaches—Landry on defense, Vince Lombardi on offense. "Jim Lee Howell gave them a lot of leeway," admits Wellington Mara. "He kept the power of veto, but he recognized their abilities. I recall back about 1956, everyone was defending the end sweep by dropping off the ends (who became linebackers) and forcing the play inside. Landry wanted to defense it inside-out, stop them up the middle with the idea that the pursuit would take care of the outside. Quite simply, Tom was talking about today's 4-3 defense—where the four (defensive) men (up front) are charged with the responsibility of keeping the five (offensive) linemen from getting a clean shot at the middle linebacker. Jim Lee accepted Tom's idea; the rest is history."

In 1959 Lombardi heard the call, moving to Green Bay. His success is football cliché. Not long after, Landry tentatively accepted a position as head coach of the new Houston Oilers of the AFL, but destiny was squeezing curious patterns. In the middle of the 1959 season, while the Giants were posting a 10-2 record and winning another Eastern Conference championship, Mara called Landry advising him that the new NFL franchise in Dallas had expressed interest in him. If Mara knew at the time that Jim Lee Howell would announce his retirement at the end of that season ("Those ten victories," said Howell "don't make up for the two defeats"), Mara did not mention it to Landry; but the opportunity to remain in the NFL (not to mention the opportunity of challenging Lombardi) prevailed. So Landry took the Dallas job.

Much of the fascination in Landry's rise is that he came up through the ranks: from player, to player-coach to coach. Only Don Shula of the Colts has approached Landry's success both as a player and a coach, making the transition while still retaining respect and command.

The message is one of pace and temperament. "The day Landry became a non-playing coach," recalls Giants' publicity man Don Smith, "it was as though he had been coach for twenty years. You pull a shade, you go to sleep, the next morning you wake up with a lifetime of wisdom under your pillow. There is no sense of time passing. Even today when I run into Tom I get the feeling—there has been *no passage of time*."

"Landry is a born student of the game," says Emlen (Em) Tunnell, the great defensive back who played with (and later for) Landry. Tunnell had been with the Giants two seasons when Landry came as part of the peace package negotiated when the old All-America Conference folded before the 1950 season. The Giants and the New York Bulldogs each picked five players from the newly defunct New York Yankees. On the recommendation of Gus Mauch, the Yankees' trainer, the Giants selected three of the four members of the Yankees' secondary—Otto Schnellbacher, Harmon Rowe, and Landry. By 1951, the Giants had the best defensive backfield in football.

"Landry was sort of weird," Tunnell recalls, "but we were a unit back there (in the secondary), getting closer and closer. I remember when we shut out the great Browns' team in 1950, didn't even let 'em get close enough to try a field goal. After the game me and Schnellbacher and Rowe would go out for beer, but Tom would disappear. He was always off with his family. You never knew what was going through his mind. He never said nothing. He just always knew what was going on. We didn't have words like 'keying' in those days, but Tom made up his own keys and taught 'em to the rest of us."

Landry remembers it well: "By training I was an industrial engineer." (He was on his way to a career in engineering when the Yankees signed him as a punter and defensive back in 1949; he also played running back with the Yankees.) "I had to know what was going on. It was my nature. I couldn't be satisfied trusting my instincts the way Em did. I didn't have the speed or quickness. I had to train myself, and everyone around me, to key various opponents and recognize tendencies."

Where Vince Lombardi was a gurgling volcano, blistering everyone in his path, Landry was placid as a mountain lake. These contrasting personalities had no small effect on the Giants.

"Lombardi was a much warmer person," says Mara. "He went from warm to red hot. You could hear him laughing or shouting for five blocks. You couldn't hear Tom from the next chair. Lombardi was more of a teacher. It was as though Landry lectured to the upper 40 percent of the class and Lombardi lectured to the lower 10 percent."

Again, that was Landry's style. Intellectual but non-aggressive. At the same time Landry's physical presence went unquestioned; it was a lineal strength that ran through the team, a central nervous system. He had been one of them through all kinds of hell.

When the Giants lost both of their quarterbacks in a game with Pittsburgh in 1953, Landry came over from defense and ran the team for most of the last half. Though Landry had never worked at quarterback, he was obviously the only man on the team who might be expected to play the position cold.

"I was lucky," Landry recalls. "Pittsburgh was the only field in the league where you could draw plays in the dirt."

The Giants lost 24 to 14. The following week against Washington, New York again lost 24 to 21. Landry played fifty-nine minutes of this game, directing both the offense and defense.

That mystical and saintly presence which sustained the Giants (in ways that it took them years to realize) has never abandoned Tom Landry.

"He tells you what's going to happen," says Cowboys halfback Dan Reeves, "and on Sunday it happens."

Says Don Meredith: "Landry used to be ultra-frustrating. I thought I knew a little about football. But Landry would be up at the blackboard saying, 'Okay, we'll do this . . . then they'll do that . . . then we'll . . . ' You'd interrupt him and say, 'Coach, what if they don't do that?' . . . Landry would just look at you and say, '*They will.*'"

But this is a Saturday afternoon early November 1968, Landry is absorbed by new peril, not old glory. Until two weeks ago his team was undefeated, rolling Packers-like to another conference championship, true to the vow he made in training camp: this time,

Landry vowed, the Cowboys would be more than a match for the Packers in the championship game. But it is beginning to look as though Landry is wrong. For one thing, the Packers show scant inclination to win their own division; coach Lombardi is now Mr. Lombardi, elder statesman to pro football. Then two weeks ago in the Cotton Bowl the erstwhile headless horsemen of Green Bay rode through Dallas as though it were Sleepy Hollow. It was no contest.

"They were the Packers of old," Landry is lamenting. "They tested us in areas (of defense) that we thought we had under control. You never know how good you are . . . or how far you've come . . . until Green Bay tests you. It's always been a measure of my defensive team how well we've been able to do against Green Bay, and up until now we have never matched them with experience and execution. When we do, we will have arrived."

Anticipating that the Packers are somehow still the team his Cowboys must beat, Landry made one key change—he moved Mel Renfro, his talented free safety, to leftside cornerback. Meanwhile, the Cowboys must win their own division. If they beat their only challenger, the Giants, on Sunday they will have a three-game lead with five games to play. Since New York in its last two games lost to lowly Atlanta and was shut out by Baltimore, victory seems simple, if not assured.

But now it is Sunday: a dark, cold, windy afternoon. Meredith's first pass is crippled by a 30-miles-per-hour headwind and falls into New York hands. Dallas gets it back on a fumble recovery, but Meredith can't get it going and after an exchange of punts Fran Tarkenton takes New York in for a 7-0 lead. Bruce Maher intercepts a second Meredith pass and runs it eighty-nine yards to the Dallas six. Tarkenton throws and New York has a 14-0 lead.

On the sideline Landry watches his pass rushers play Chinese chess with Tarkenton: "Tarkenton's uniform won't be sent to the cleaners this week," moans a Dallas sportswriter. Landry's face is tight as a coffin when he tells Meredith: "They're outhitting us. They're outplaying us every way. We've got to get tough."

Now Meredith is brilliant. He first hits Bobby Hayes, then Lance Rentzel. With touchdown passes the Cowboys struggle to a 14-14 tie by halftime. The second half opens with Tarkenton throwing a 60-yard touchdown pass to Homer Jones.

"Get tough!" one of Landry's assistants yells from the sideline. The Cowboys are on the march. Meredith scrambles for six yards and a first down, then he comes limping to the sidelines: Meredith is back in the game after three plays, but his knee cartilage is torn and won't be sound for the remainder of the 1968 season. It's more pain for Meredith, Landry knows. Fullback Don Perkins bolts for seven yards. The Vikings have just defeated the Packers, announces the public address system. Dallas halfback Les Shy drops a touchdown pass at the goal line. The Cowboys continue to march. On a great second effort, halfback Craig Baynham, who has replaced Shy, pounds over from the New York one; the game is again tied 21 to 21.

In the final quarter Dallas goes against the wind, New York with it. Tarkenton throws thirty-five yards to Homer Jones, then Pete Gogolak kicks a field goal, pushing New York in front 24 to 21.

"All the way, Lance-*baby*!" an assistant coach shouts from the sideline, but Lance Rentzel signals for a fair catch and fumbles in a gust of wind. Gogolak kicks another field goal. New York has a six-point lead. Landry has never seemed more composed. He glances at the clock. A little more than two minutes remain.

First and ten. Dallas has the ball on its forty-five. Things look normal, which is to say they look good. The toughness to pull a game out, the sacrifice of a self-extracted wisdom tooth, that has been Landry's lesson to his team. Now Meredith rolls right, now Lance Rentzel is open near the Giants' twenty, now the pass hangs on the wind, and now Spider Lockhart is making the sweet interception.

Landry is four feet out on the playing field, shouting, "Dammit, why did you . . . " but he never says who, he never says what. It is dark now in Dallas. The lights are on; dew collects on the pale green grass. It seems much later than it is, and Meredith jogs back to the sideline, his face broad with wonder, twisted with regret. The whole thing must seem too stupid for words: while the Cowboys were losing two of their last three games, Meredith went from third to first on the league passing chart. Too stupid for words . . . too painful. Landry wears that same expression you have seen so often on the lead film preceding all NFL telecasts, that classic eyes-closed-to-earth muffled sob, that God-imploring anxiety caught on film as Landry realized that an illegal-motion penalty had sealed Dallas's defeat in the 1966 championship game in this same stadium, in this same paralyzing dark cold, in this same and endless quest for something attainable in an unattainable sort of a stupid way.

"You don't think it didn't hurt to walk off that field?" Landry asked writers at his press conference the following Wednesday. "There's no criticism you could make that could hurt like that."

In Landry's mind it was simple. He had taught them offense, he had taught them defense. He had taught them how to come from behind; he had provided the leadership that gives a man confidence in the system, if not in himself. In some cases . . . in Meredith's case, for example . . . Landry had in fact saved a soul. For what? For what came *next*.

What comes next, Landry is quick to explain, is toughness. He will have to remind them of toughness. Chances are good that they have already reminded themselves, but he will call it to their attention with some very hard work.

"You don't build character without somebody slapping you around," Landry tells his press conference. "We got to the point where we thought we could take it easy and win. Why even my wife was talking of an undefeated season. That's a sure sign of death. . . . I'll tell you this, we'll be a different team next week."

FREDERICK EXLEY

"One for Steve"
from *A Fan's Notes*

In 1968, Frederick Exley won the PEN/Faulkner Award for "the year's most notable first novel." That novel, A FAN'S NOTES, *takes its title partly from the life-long fascination the author has had for the sport of football. This excerpt, a brush with the greatness of Frank Gifford picks up shortly after Exley's abortive attempt at applying for a job with an advertising agency, after which he retreats to the sanctuary of his aunt's couch.*

FOR MONTHS I HADN'T BEEN ABLE to rcad anything except advertisements. Sustaining my literary fantasy had required such fierce concentration that my energies were not in long enough supply for even cursory reading, but now, in boredom, I forced myself to read. Even then I did not at first understand what was happening to New York Giants coach Steve Owen. The newspapers kept using the euphemisms "retiring" and "resigning," and it was only after I had gone to the columnists that I began to piece together the truth. When I did so, I was outraged. Owen always had maintained that defenses win football games. Professional football was increasingly deferring to the forward pass as the ultimate and only weapon, and apparently Owen was being asked to step aside by men whose vision of the game proclaimed it unalterably given over to offensive techniques. These "men" were, of course, shadowy, never identified; but one had only to understand the childishly petulant character of the New York sportswriter (he takes every New York defeat as if he had been out there having his own face rubbed in the dirt) to know who the men were. Owen had been losing for a number of years now, and the writers had been on him. Victorious, there was something nauseatingly reprehensible in their doleful, sentimental invitations to the public to come to the Polo Grounds on Sunday to witness Owen's swan song as head coach.

I never would have left the davenport that murderously damp Sunday in 1953 had I not read that Frank Gifford was starting for the Giants at halfback. When I read that, my mind—as isolated minds are wont to do, offered the least stimulation—began to fabricate for itself a rather provocative little drama. I began to imagine how wonderful it would be if Gifford single-handedly devastated the Detroit Lions as a farewell present for Owen. I had had encounters with both of these men at different times in my life. In a way both had given me something, Gifford a lesson in how to live with one's scars, and Owen no less than perhaps my first identity as a human being. And so that bleak, cold Sunday, I rose—to the astonishment of my aunt, I might add—from the davenport, bundled up as warmly as I could, took the commuting train to Grand Central, sought directions to the Polo Grounds, and got on the subway to the Bronx.

I met Steve Owen in the late thirties or early forties, when I was somewhere between the ages of 8 and 11. I suspect it was closer to the time I was 8, for I remember very little of what was said, remembering more the character of the meeting—that it was not an easy one. My father introduced me to him, or rather my father, when the atmosphere was most strained and the conversation had lagged, shoved me in front of Owen and said, "This is my son, Fred."

"Are you tough?" Owen said.

"Pardon, sir?"

"Are you tough?"

"I don't know, sir."

Owen looked at my father. "Is he tough, Mr. Exley?"

Though more than anything I wanted my father to say that I was, I was not surprised at this answer.

"It's too soon to tell."

Owen was surprised, though. He had great blondish-red eyebrows, which above his large rimless glasses gave him an astonished expression. Now he looked baffled. As the meeting had not been a comfortable one to begin with, he said in a tone that signaled the end of the conversation, "I'm sure he's tough, Mr. Exley." Turning abruptly on his heels, he walked across the lobby to the elevator of his hotel, where this meeting took place.

This was a few years after my father had quit playing football, when he was managing the Watertown [New York] semiprofessional team, the Red and Black. A team that took on all challengers and invariably defeated them, they were so good that—stupefying as it seems—the ostensible reason for our journey to New York had been to discuss with Owen the possibility of the Red and Black's playing in exhibition against the Giants. I say "stupefying" now; but that is retrospectively fake sophistication: I thought we could beat the Giants then, and I use the "we" with the glibness of one who was committed unalterably to the team's fortunes—the water boy. On the wall in the bar of the Watertown Elks' Club hangs a picture of that team; seated on the ground before the smiling, casual, and disinterested players is an anguishingly solemn boy—the solemnity attesting to the esteem in which I held my station. I still can remember with what pride I trotted, heavy water bucket and dry towels in hand, onto the field to minister to the combatants' needs. Conversely, I recall the shame I experienced one day when, the team's having fallen behind, the captain decided to adopt a spartan posture and deprive his charges of water, and he had ordered me back from the field, waving me off when I was almost upon the huddle. My ministrations denied in full view of the crowd, I had had to turn and trot, redfaced, back to the bench. Yes, I believed we could beat the Giants then. Long before Owen so adroitly put my father down, though, I had come to see that the idea of such a contest was not a good one.

The trip began on a depressing note. The night before we were to leave, my father got loaded and ran into a parked car, smashing in the front fenders of our Model A Ford roadster. It was one time—in retrospect—that my father's drinking seemed excusable. Such a journey in those days was one of near-epic proportions, made only at intervals of many years and at alarming sacrifices to the family budget; I have no doubt that that night my father was tremulous with apprehension, caught up in the spirit of bon voyage, and that he drank accordingly. Be that as it may, because he was drunk he left the scene of the accident; and the next day, fearing that the police might be searching for a damaged car, my mother wouldn't let him take the Ford from the garage. For many hours it was uncertain whether we should make the trip at all; but at the last moment, more, I think, because I had been promised the trip than for any other reason, it was decided we should go on the train.

We rode the whole night sitting up in the day coach, without speaking. My father was hung over, deeply ashamed, and there was a horrifying air of furtiveness hanging over us, as if we were fleeing some unspeakable crime. As a result, the trip—which might have been a fantastic adventure—never rose above this unhappy note. In New York we shared a room at the YMCA (I can remember believing that only the impossibly rich ever stayed in hotels), and the visit was a series of small, debilitating defeats: bland, soggy food eaten silently in barnlike automats; a room that varied arbitrarily between extreme heat and cold; a hundred and one missed subway connections; the Fordham-Pittsburgh game's having been sold out; the astonishment I underwent at no one's knowing my father; and finally, the fact that our meeting with Owen, which I had been led to believe was prearranged, was nothing more than wishful thinking on my father's part.

I don't know how many times we went to Owen's hotel, but each time we were told that he was "out." Each time we returned to the YMCA a little more tired, a little more defeated, and with each trip the Giants' players whose names I knew, Ken Strong and Ward Cuff and Tuffy Leemans and Mel Hein, began to loom as large and forbidding as the skyscrapers. At one point I knew, though I daren't say so to my father, that the idea of such a game was preposterous. Moreover, for the first time in my life I began to understand the awesome vanity and gnawing need required to take on New York City with a view to imposing one's personality on the place. This was a knowledge that came to haunt me in later years.

It was not until my father, his voice weary, suggested that we make one final trip to the hotel that I saw that he, too, was disheartened. All the way there I prayed that Owen still would be "out." I had come to see that the meeting was undesired by him, and I feared the consequences of our imposition. The moment we walked into the lobby, however, the desk clerk (who had, I'm sure, come to feel sorry for us) began furiously stabbing the air in the direction of a gruff-looking, bespectacled, and stout man rolling, seamanlike, in the direction of the elevator—a fury that only could have signaled that it was Owen. My father moved quickly across the lobby, stopped him, and began the conversation that ended with Owen's *I'm sure he's tough, Mr. Exley.* As I say, I don't remember a good deal of the conversation prior to my being introduced; I do remember that Owen, too, thought the idea of such a contest ridiculous. Worse than that, my father already had been told as much by mail, and I think that his having made the trip in the face of such a refusal struck Owen as rather nervy, accounting for the uneasiness of the meeting. On Owen's leaving, I did not dare look at my father. It wasn't so much that I had ever lived in fear of him as that I had never before seen any man put him down, and I was not prepared to test his reaction to a humiliation that I unwittingly had caused. Moreover, my father's shadow was so imposing that I scarcely had ever, until that moment, had any identity of my own. At the same time I had yearned to emulate and become my father, I also had longed for his destruction. Steve Owen not only gave me identity; he proved to me my father was vulnerable.

On the subway going up to the Polo Grounds, I was remembering that meeting and contemplating the heavy uneasiness of it all anew when suddenly, feeling myself inordinately cramped, I looked up out of my reverie to discover that the car was jammed and that I somehow had got smack among the members of a single family—an astonishing family, a family so incredible that for the first time in my life I considered the possibility of Norman Rockwell's not being lunatic. They were a father, a mother, a girl about fifteen, and a boy one or two years younger than she. All were dressed in expensive-looking camel's-hair coats; each carried an item that designated him as a fan—the father two soft and brilliantly plaid wool blankets, the mother a picnic basket, the girl a half-gallon thermos, and the boy a pair of field glasses, strung casually about his neck—each apparently doing his bit to make the day a grand success. What astonished me, though, was the almost hilarious similarity of their physical appearance: each had brilliant auburn hair; each had even, startlingly white teeth, smilingly exposed beneath attractive snub noses; and each of their faces was liberally sprinkled with great, outsized freckles. The total face they presented was one of overwhelming and wholesome handsomeness. My first impulse was to laugh. Had I not felt an extreme discomfort caused by the relish they took in each other's being—their looks seemed to smother each other in love—and the crowdedness that had caused me to find myself wedged among them, separating them, I might have laughed. I felt not unlike a man who eats too fast, drinks too much, occasionally neglects his teeth and fingernails, is given to a pensive scratching of his vital parts, lets rip with a not infrequent fart, and wakes up one morning to find himself smack in the middle of a Saturday Evening Post cover, carving the goddam Thanksgiving turkey for a family he never has seen before. What was worse, they were aware of my discomfort; between basking in each other's loveliness they would smile apologetically at me, as though in crowding about me they were aware of having aroused me from my reverie and were sorry for it. Distressed, I felt I ought to say something—"I'm sorry I'm alive" or something—so I said the first thing that came to my mind. It was a lie occasioned by my reverie, one that must have sounded very stupid indeed.

"I know Steve Owen," I said.

"Really!" they all chimed in high and good-natured unison. For some reason I got the impression that they had not the foggiest notion of what I had said. We all fell immediately to beaming at each other and nodding deferentially—a posture that exasperated me to the point where I thought I must absolutely say something else. Hoping that I could strike some chord in them that would relieve the self-consciousness we all were so evidently feeling, I spoke again.

"I know Frank Gifford, too."

"Really!" came their unabashed reply. Their tone seemed so calculated to humor me that I was almost certain they were larking with me. Staring at them, I couldn't be sure; and we all fell back to smiling idiotically and nodding at each other. We did this all the way to the Bronx where, disembarking, I lost contact with them—for the moment at least—and felt much relieved.

It seems amazing to me now that while at USC, where Gifford and I were contemporaries, I never saw him play football; that I had to come 3,000 miles from the low, white, smog-enshrouded sun that hung perpetually over the Los Angeles Coliseum to the cold, damp, and dismal Polo Grounds to see him perform for the first time; and that I might never have had the urge that long-ago Sunday had I not once on campus had a strange, unnerving confrontation with him. The confrontation was caused by a girl, though at the time of the encounter I did not understand what girl. I had transferred from Hobart College, a small, undistinguished liberal arts college in Geneva, New York, where I was a predental student, to USC, a large, undistinguished university in Los Angeles, where I became an English major. The transition was not unnatural. I went out there because I had been rejected by a girl, my first love, whom I loved beyond the redeeming force of anything save time. Accepting the theory of distance as time, I put as much of it between the girl and myself as I could. Once there, though, the prospect of spending my days gouging at people's teeth and whiffing the intense, acidic odor of decay—a profession I had chosen with no stronger motive than keeping that very girl in swimming suits and tennis shorts; she had (and this, sadly, is the precise extent of my memory of her) the most breathtaking legs I ever had seen—seemed hideous, and I quite naturally became an English major with a view to reading The Books, The Novels, and The Poems, those pat reassurances that other men had experienced rejection and pain and loss. Moreover, I accepted the myth of California the Benevolent and believed that beneath her warm skies I would find surcease from my pain in the person of some lithe, fresh-skinned, and incredible lovely blonde coed. Bearing my rejection like a disease, and like a man with frightfully repugnant and contagious leprosy, I was unable to attract anything as healthy as the girl I had in mind.

Whenever I think of the man I was in those days, cutting across the neat-cropped grass of the campus, burdened down by the weight of the books in which I sought the consolation of other men's grief, and burdened further by the large weight of my own bitterness, the whole vision seems a nightmare. There were girls all about me, so near and yet so out of reach, a pastel nightmare of honey-blond, pink-lipped, golden-legged, lemon-sweatered girls. And always in this horror, this gaggle of femininity, there comes the vision of another girl, now only a little less featureless than all the rest. I saw her first on one stunning spring day when the smog had momentarily lifted, and all the world seemed hard bright blue and green. She came across the campus straight at me, and though I had her in the range of my vision for perhaps a hundred feet, I only was able, for the fury of my heart, to give her five or six frantic glances. She had the kind of comeliness—soft, shoulder-length chestnut hair; a sharp beauty mark right at her sensual mouth; and a figure that was like a swift, unexpected blow to the diaphragm—that to linger on makes the beholder feel obscene. I wanted to look. I couldn't look. I had to look. I could give her only the most gaspingly quick glances. Then she was by me. Waiting as long as I dared, I turned, and she was gone.

From that day forward I moved about the campus in a kind of vertigo, with my right eye watching the sidewalk come up to meet my anxious feet, and my left eye clacking in a wild orbit, all over and around its socket, trying to take in the entire campus in frantic split seconds, terrified that I might miss her. On the same day that I found out who she was I saw her again. I was standing in front of Founders' Hall talking with T., a gleaming-toothed, hand-pumping fraternity man with whom I had, my first semester out there, shared a room. We had since gone our separate ways; but whenever we met we always passed the time, being bound together by the contempt with which we viewed each other's world and by the sorrow we felt at really rather liking each other, a condition T. found more difficult to forgive in himself than I did.

"*That?*" he asked in profound astonishment to my query about the girl. "*That?*" he repeated dumbly as if this time—for I was much given to teasing T.—I had really gone too far. "*That,*" he proclaimed with menacing impatience, "*just happens to be Frank Gifford's girl!*"

I never will forget the contempt he showered on me for asking what to him, and I suppose to the rest of fraternity row, was not only a rhetorical but a dazzlingly asinine question. Nor will I forget that he never did give me the girl's name. The information that she was Gifford's girl was, he assumed, quite enough to prevent the likes of me from pursuing the matter further. My first impulse was to laugh and twit his chin with my finger. But the truth was I was getting a little weary of T. His monumental sense of the rightness of things was beginning to grate on me; shrugging, I decided to end it forever. It required the best piece of acting I've ever been called upon to do; but I carried it off, I think, perfectly.

Letting my mouth droop open and fixing on my face a look of serene vacuousness, I said, "Who's Frank Gifford?"

My first thought was that T. was going to strike me. His hands tensed into fists, his face went the color of fire, and he thrust his head defiantly toward me. He didn't strike, though. Either his sense of the propriety of things overcame him, or he guessed, quite accurately, that I would have knocked him on his ass. All he said, between furiously clenched teeth, was: "*Oh, really, Exley, this has gone too far.*" Turning hysterically away from me he thundered off. It had indeed gone too far and I laughed all the way to the saloon I frequented on Jefferson Boulevard, sadly glad to have seen the last of T.

Frank Gifford was an All-America at USC, and I know of no way of describing this phenomenon short of equating it with being the Pope in the Vatican. Our local *L'Osservatore Romano*, *The Daily Trojan*, was a moderately well-written college newspaper except on the subject of football, when the tone of the writing rose to an hysterical screech. It reported daily on Gifford's health, one time even imposing upon us the news that he was suffering an upset stomach, leading an irreverent acquaintance of mine to wonder aloud whether the athletic department had heard about "milk of magnesia, for Christ's sake." We were, it seems to me in retrospect, treated daily to breathless items such as the variations in his weight, his method of conditioning, the knowledge that he neither smoked nor drank, the humbleness of his beginnings, and once we were even told the number of fan letters he received daily from pimply high school girls in the Los Angeles area. The USC publicity man, perhaps influenced by the proximity of Hollywood press agents, seemed overly fond of releasing a head-and-shoulder print showing him the apparently proud possessor of long, black, perfectly ambrosial locks that came down to caress an alabaster, colossally beauteous face, one that would have aroused envy in Tony Curtis. Gifford was, in effect, overwhelmingly present in the consciousness of the campus, even though my crowd—the literati—never once to my knowledge mentioned him. We never mentioned him because his being permitted to exist at the very university where we were apprenticing ourselves for Nobel Prizes would have detracted from our environment and been an admission that we might be better off at an academe more sympathetic with our hopes. Still, the act of not mentioning him made him somehow more present than if, like the pathetic nincompoops on fraternity row, we spent all our idle hours singing his praises. Our silence made him, in our family, a kind of retarded child about whom we had tacitly and selfishly agreed not to speak. It seems the only thing of Gifford's we were spared—and it is at this point we leave his equation with the Bishop of Rome—was his opinion of the spiritual state of the USC campus. But I am being unkind now; something occurred between Gifford and me which led me to conclude that he was not an immodest man.

Unlike most athletes who could be seen swaggering about the campus with *Property of USC* (did they never see the ironic, touching servility of this?) stamped indelibly every place but on their foreheads, Gifford made himself extremely scarce, so scarce that I only saw him once for but a few brief moments, so scarce that prior to this encounter I had begun to wonder if he wasn't some myth created by the administration to appease the highly vocal and moronic alumni who were clamoring incessantly for USC's Return to Greatness in, as the sportswriters say, "the football wars." Sitting at the counter of one of the campus hamburger joints, I was having a cup of chicken noodle soup and a cheeseburger when it occurred to me that he was one of a party of three men seated a few stools away from me. I knew without looking because the other two men were directing all their remarks to him: "Hey, Frank, how about that?" "Hey, Frank, cha' ever hear the one about . . ." It was the kind of given-name familiarity one likes to have with the biggest man on the block. My eyes on my soup, I listened to this sycophancy, smiling rather bitterly for what seemed an eternity; when I finally did look up, it was he—ambrosial locks and all. He was dressed in blue denims and a terry-cloth sweater, and though I saw no evidence of *USC* stamped anyplace, still I had an overwhelming desire to insult him in some way. How this would be accomplished with any subtlety I had no idea; I certainly didn't want to fight with him. I did, however, want to shout, "Listen, you son of a bitch, life isn't all a goddam football game! You won't always get the girl! Life is rejection and pain and loss"—all those things I so cherishingly cuddled in my self-pitying bosom. I didn't, of course, say any such thing; almost immediately he was up and standing right next to me, waiting to pay the cashier. Unable to let the moment go by, I snapped my head up to face him. When he looked at me, I smiled—a hard, mocking, so-you're-the-big-shit? smile. What I expected him to do, I can't imagine—say, "What's your trouble, buddy?" or what—but what he did do was the least of my expectations. He only looked quizzically at me for a moment, as though he were having difficulty placing me; then he smiled a most ingratiating smile, gave me a most amiable hello, and walked out the door, followed by his buddies who were saying in unison, "Hey, Frank, what'll we do now?"

My first feeling was one of utter rage. I wanted to jump up and throw my water glass through the plate-glass window. Then almost immediately a kind of sullenness set in, then shame. Unless I had read that smile and that salutation incorrectly, there was a note of genuine apology and modesty in them. Even in the close world of the university, Gifford must have come to realize that he was having a fantastic success, and that success somewhat embarrassed him. Perhaps he took me for some student acquaintance he had had long before that success, and took my hateful smile as a reproach for his having failed to speak to me on other occasions, his smile being the apology for that neglect. Perhaps he only was saying he was sorry I was a miserable son of a bitch, but that he hardly was going to fight me for it. These speculations, as I found out drinking beer late into that evening, could have gone on forever. I drank eight, nine, ten, drifting between speculations on the nature of that smile and bitter, sexually colored memories of the girl with the breath-taking legs back East, when it suddenly occurred to me that she and not the girl with the chestnut hair was the cause of all my anger, and that I was for perhaps a very long time going to have to live with that anger. Gifford gave me that. With that smile, whatever he meant by it, a smile that he doubtless wouldn't remember, he impressed upon me, in the rigidity of my embarrassment, that it is unmanly to burden others with one's grief. Even though it is man's particularly unhappy aptitude to see to it that his fate is shared.

Leaving the subway and walking toward the Polo Grounds, I was remembering that smile and thinking again how nice it would be if Gifford had a fine day for Owen, when I began to notice that the redheaded family, who were moving with the crowd some paces ahead of me, were laughing and giggling self-consciously, a laughter that evidently was connected with me in some way. Every few paces, having momentarily regained their composure, they would drop their heads together in a covert way, whisper as they walked, then turn again in unison, stare back at me, and begin giggling anew. It was a laughter that soon had me self-consciously fingering my necktie and looking furtively down at my fly, as though I expected to discover that the overcoat that covered it somehow had disappeared miraculously. We almost were at the entrance to the field when, to my surprise, the father stopped suddenly, turned, walked back to me, and said that he was holding an extra ticket to the game. It was, he said, the result of his maid's having been taken ill, and that he—no, not precisely he, but the children—would deem it an honor if I—"knowing Owen and all"—sat with them. Not in the least interested in doing so, I was so relieved to discover that their laughter had been inspired by something apart from myself—the self-consciousness they felt at inviting me—that I instantaneously and gratefully accepted, thanked him profusely, and was almost immediately sorry. It occurred to me that the children might query me on my relationship with Owen—perhaps even Gifford—and what the hell could I say? My "relationship" with both of these men was so fleeting, so insubstantial, that I unquestionably would have had to invent and thereby not only undergo the strain of having to talk off the top of my head but, by talking, risk exposure as a fraud.

My fears, however, proved groundless. These people, it soon became evident, had no interest in me whatever, they were so bound up in their pride of each other. My discomfort was caused not by any interest they took in me but by their total indifference to me. Directing me by the arm, father seated me not with the children who, he had claimed, desired my presence but on the aisle—obviously, I thought, the maid's seat (accessible to the hot dogs)—

and sat himself next to me, separating me from his wife and children who had so harmoniously moved to their respective seats that I was sure that the family held season tickets. Everyone in place, all heads cranked round to me and displayed a perfect miracle of gleaming incisors.

It only had begun. The game no sooner was under way when father, in an egregiously cultivated, theatrically virile voice, began—to my profound horror—commenting on each and every play. "That is a delayed buck, a play that requires superb blocking and marvelous timing," or, "That, children, is a screen pass, a fantastically perilous play to attempt, and one, I might add, that you won't see *Mr.* Conerly attempt but once or twice a season"—to all of which the mother, the daughter, and the son invariably and in perfect unison exclaimed, "Really!" A tribute to father's brilliance that, to my further and almost numbing horror, I, too, soon discovered I was expected to pay—pay, I would expect, for the unutterable enchantment of sitting with them. Each time that I heard the *Really!* I would become aware of a great shock of auburn hair leaning past father's shoulder, and I would look up to be confronted by a brilliant conglomeration of snub noses, orange freckles, and sparkling teeth, all formed into a face of beseechment, an invitation to join in this tribute to Genius. I delayed accepting the invitation as long as I could; when the looks went from beseechment to mild reproachment, I surrendered and began chiming in with *Really!* At first I came in too quickly or too late, and we seemed to be echoing each other: *Really! Really!* Though this rhythmical ineptness chafed me greatly it brought from the family only the most understanding and kindly looks. By the end of the first quarter I had my timing down perfectly and settled down to what was the most uncomfortable afternoon of my life.

This was a superb Detroit team. It was the Detroit of a young Bobby Layne and an incomparable Doak Walker, of a monstrously bull-like Leon Hart and a 300-pound Les Bingaman, a team that was expected to move past the Giants with ease and into the championship of the Western Division. Had they done so—which at first they appeared to be doing, picking up two touchdowns before the crowd scarcely was settled—I might have been rather amused at the constraints placed on me by the character of my hosts. But at one thrilling moment, a moment almost palpable in its intensity and unquestionably motivated by the knowledge of Owen's parting, the Giants recovered, engaged this magnificent football team, and began to play as if they meant to win. Other than the terrible fury of it, I don't remember the details of the game, save that Gifford played superbly; and that at one precise moment, watching him execute one of his plays, I was suddenly and overwhelmingly struck with the urge to cheer, to jump up and down and pummel people on the back.

But then, there was father. What can I say of him? To anything resembling a good play he would single out the player responsible and say, "Fine show, Gifford!" or "Wonderful stuff there, Price!" and we would chime in with "Good show!" and "Fine stuff!" Then, in a preposterous parody of cultured equanimity we would be permitted to clap our gloved right hands against our left wrists, like opera-goers, making about as much noise as an argument between mutes. It was very depressing. I hadn't cheered for anything or anybody in three years—since my rejection by the leggy girl—and even had mistakenly come to believe that my newfound restraint was a kind of maturity. Oh, I had had my enthusiasms, but they were dark, the adoration of the griefs and morbidities men commit to paper in the name of literature, the homage I had paid the whole sickly aristocracy of letters. But a man can dwell too long with grief, and now, quite suddenly, quite wonderfully, I wanted to cheer again, to break forth from darkness into light, to stand up in that sparsely filled (it was a typically ungrateful New York that had come to bid Owen farewell), murderously damp, bitingly cold stadium, and scream my head off.

But then, here again was father—not only father but the terrible diffidence I felt in the presence of that family, in the overwhelming and shameless pride they took in each other's being and good form. The game moved for me at a snail's pace. Frequently I rose on tiptoe, ready to burst forth, at the last moment restraining myself. As the fury of the game reached an almost audible character the crowd about me reacted proportionately by going stark raving mad while I stood still, saying *Really!* and filling up two handkerchiefs with a phlegm induced by the afternoon's increasing dampness. What upset me more than anything about father was that he had no loyalty other than to The Game itself, praising players, whether Giants or Lions, indiscriminately. On the more famous players he bestowed a *Mister*, saying, "Oh, fine stuff, *Mr.* Layne!" or, "Wonderful show, Mr. Walker!"—coming down hard on the *Mister* the way those creeps affected by The Theater say *Sir* Laurence Olivier or *Miss* Helen Hayes. We continued our *fine show's* and *good stuff's* till I thought my heart would break.

Finally I did, of course, snap. Late in the final period, with the Giants losing by less than a touchdown, Conerly connected with a short pass to Gifford, and I thought the latter was going into the end zone. Unable to help myself, the long afternoon's repressed and joyous tears welling up in my eyes, I went berserk.

Jumping up and down and pummeling father furiously on the back, I screamed, "Oh, Jesus, Frank! Oh, Frank, *baby! Go! For Steve! For Steve For Steve!*"

Gifford did not go all the way. He went to the one-foot line. Because it was not enough yardage for a first down, it became fourth and inches to go for a touchdown and a victory, the next few seconds proving the most agonizingly apprehensive of my life. It was an agony not allayed by my hosts. When I looked up through tear-bedewed eyes, father was straightening his camel's-hair topcoat, and the face of his loved ones had been transfigured. I had violated their high canons of good taste, their faces had moved from a vision of charming wholesomeness to one of intransigent hostility; it was now eminently clear to them that their invitation to me had been a dreadful mistake.

In an attempt to apologize, I smiled weakly and said, "I'm sorry—I thought *Mr.* Gifford was going all the way," coming down particularly hard on the *Mister*. But this was even more disastrous: Gifford was new to the Giants then, and father had not as yet bestowed that title on him. The total face they presented to me made me want to cut my jugular. Then, I thought, *What the hell*; and because I absolutely refused to let them spoil the moment for me, I said something that had the exact effect I intended: putting them in a state of numbing senselessness.

I said, my voice distinctly irritable, "Aw, c'mon, you *goofies. Cheer. This is for Steve Owen! For Steve Owen!*

The Giants did not score, and as a result did not win the game. Gifford carried on the last play, as I never doubted that he would. Wasn't this game being played out just as, in my loneliness, I had imagined it would be? Les Bingaman put his 300 pounds in Gifford's way, stopping him so close to the goal that the officials were for many moments undetermined; and the Lions, having finally taken over the ball, were a good way up the field, playing ball control and running out the clock, before my mind accepted the evidence of my eyes. When it did so, I began to cough, coughing great globs into my hands. I was coughing only a very few moments before it occurred to me that I also was weeping. It was a fact that occurred to father simultaneously. For the first time since I had spoken so harshly to him, he rallied, my tears being in unsurpassably bad taste, and said, "Look here, it's *only* a game."

Trying to speak softly so the children wouldn't hear, I said, "F—— you!

But they heard. By now I had turned and started up the steep concrete steps; all the way up them I could hear mother and the children, still in perfect unison, screeching *Father!* and father, in the most preposterously modulated hysteria, screeching *Officer!* I had to laugh then, laugh so hard that I almost doubled up on the concrete steps. My irritation had nothing to do with these dead people, and not really—I know now—with anything to do with the outcome of the game. I had begun to be haunted again by that which had haunted me on my first trip to the city—the inability of a man to impose his dreams, his ego, upon the city, and for many long months had been experiencing a rage induced by New York's stony refusal to esteem me. It was foolish and childish of me to impose that rage on these people, though not as foolish, I expect, as father's thinking he could protect his children from life's bitterness by calling for a policeman.

Frank Gifford went on to realize a fame in New York that only a visionary would have dared hope for: he became unavoidable, part of the city's hard mentality. I never would envy or begrudge him that fame. I did, in fact, become perhaps his most enthusiastic fan. No doubt he came to represent to me the realization of life's large promises. But that is another part of this story. It was Owen who over the years kept bringing me back to life's hard fact of famelessness. After that day at the Polo Grounds I heard of Owen from time to time, that he was a line coach for one NFL team or another, that he was coaching somewhere in Canada—perhaps at Winnipeg or Saskatchewan. Wherever, it must have seemed to him the sunless, the glacial side of the moon. Owen unquestionably came to see the irony of his fate. His offensively obsessed detractors had been rendered petulant by his attitude that "football is a game played down in the dirt, and always will be," and within three years after his leaving, his successors, having inherited his ideas (the Umbrella pass defense for one), took the Giants to a world championship with little other than a defense. It was one of the greatest defenses (Robustelli, Patton, Huff, Svare, Livingston, et al.) that the game has ever seen, but, for all of that, a championship won by men who played the game where Owen had tenaciously and fatally maintained it was played—*in the dirt.*

HAYWOOD HALE BROUN

Farewell the Gods of Instant Legend

Was Davey O'Brien really 3 feet tall, and could he truly throw a football 100 yards? Or do the images of the sporting field become hazy and distorted through the years and through the games? Those are the rhetorical questions asked by Haywood Hale Broun for a LIFE *magazine insert in 1969, prepared in conjunction with the NFL's 50th anniversary. Broun, a veteran CBS-TV commentator, also wrote pieces for* SPORTS ILLUSTRATED.

IN THE DIM YESTERDAY when athletes traveled on trains, the back platform of the observation car was the framework in which many Americans saw their sports heroes for the only time in their lives.

When the train stopped at a crossroads town to drop mail or pick up water, the whole population would be waiting for the magic moment when the great man, up to then a smudgy newspaper picture, appeared in the round, in the flesh, in that nearness which was just short of the bliss suggested by the old line "Shake the hand that shook the hand of John L. Sullivan."

When my father was a baseball writer traveling through spring training with the New York Giants it used to amuse Ring Lardner to take him onto the back platform and introduce him to the circle of sport worshipers as Jess Willard, a man my father resembled only in weight. The fake Willard would say a few modest words, clasp his hands in the traditional fighter's gesture and withdraw, leaving a knot of excited Floridians discussing their unexpected celebrity bonus.

There are probably still old folks down there who remember

seeing Willard when they were kids, a Willard whom even today they remember as appearing shockingly out of shape for a fighter, but a jolly good fellow for all of that.

This is, in a sense, a perfect example of an old-time sports memory. It is vivid, exciting, highly personal, and wildly inaccurate. Of course, lots of other people saw the actual Jess Willard but if you were to ask for a description they would strain the reality through so many layers of subsequent experience that they might well come up with a picture of my father.

So great was the hunger in those old days for a look, a touch, a close view of the gods of games that when it happened, excitement and near hysteria vibrated the eye and the ear and turned the memory into the broad and golden outline of instant legend.

When George Halas announced that he had signed Red Grange to play with the Chicago Bears, the lines began to form next morning outside the Spalding store where tickets were announced as available, and stretched four abreast, around and around the block. Later that year people paid twelve and a half Coolidge dollars per ticket to see him play a Florida exhibition.

If now, fifty-odd years later you asked those ticket buyers to tell you about the Grange they saw, they would take out a memory as loved and polished as old ivory and give you a description of something no human being could ever have accomplished. They would describe to you the flight of a bird in a football suit and they would tell you that nobody they see nowadays on the television has over come close.

Television has, of course, given us a closer and more accurate view of what goes on. By the use of instant replays, it permits us to see exactly what happened in the detached atmosphere of hindsight so that we are infinitely more knowledgeable, and our memories are a great deal more accurate. What it has taken from us in exchange for this is the moment of mad immediacy when adrenalin has blinded us to the true picture and given us a myth disguised as an observation.

My own first memories of professional football go back to a man I remember as being approximately three feet high, Davey O'Brien, quarterback of the Philadelphia Eagles. In my mind's eye—and the mind is that of a frenzied college freshman now somewhat tattered through being stored in the head of a middle-aged man—O'Brien is a tiny creature who has to reach up to take the ball from the center and who then fades desperately back like someone from one of Charles Schulz's Peanuts teams lost in a nightmare of ill intentioned monsters. Somehow the little O'Brien escapes the huge linemen and passes the ball 100 yards through the air and we are all cheering and crying and dealing to each other almost as much punishment as the players are managing on the field.

Some factual researches have revealed to me that O'Brien, though small for a football player, actually weighed 160 pounds at the time, and is a person whom I, at 163 pounds, am not entitled to regard as spectacularly undersized. My factual researches have no impact on the vivid picture I project on my personal screen when I summon up that impossible sunny Sunday in the Middle Jurassic Age, however.

Neither is it true or rather can it be true that the head of Bill Hewitt, who never wore a helmet, actually changed shape like a squeezed melon as he dove in for a tackle? It seems medically unlikely, but that is the way I remember it.

"There were giants walking the earth in those days" cry all we middle-aged and more than middle-aged rememberers of the sports figures of our childhoods and youths and there are no tapes or films or objective views of a small glass square to say us nay.

It is, of course, the refuge of all of us to feel, when youth is far enough behind us, that it was the world's last age of innocence. The medieval adventurers who went on the First Crusade used to shake their heads over the sad lot who marched off to the Second, as my father thought my 1930s idols, Carl Hubbell, Tuffy Leemans, and Davey O'Brien to be pale shadows of such demigods as Christy Mathewson or Charley Brinkley, who drop-kicked five field goals against Yale—a feat mysterious to me because I never saw anybody drop kick anything against anybody.

The young of my son's generation and those who came after, are, and will be, so impressively informed that one wonders if they will have the chance to make or hold those larger-than-life images which are such stuff as dreams are made on.

Split screens, isolated cameras, and slow-motion replays will give a heretofore impossible dimension to watching. As the astronauts know far more about the moon than is contained in all the poets' speculations, so tomorrow's fans will see more than did the wisest of coaches and scouts twenty years ago. Also, in the new trend to absorb sports heroes into the worlds of commerce and entertainment, there is inherent a more extensive acquaintance with Olympus than was possible to those who waited in the depot for the glimpse of Jess Willard waving from the observation car.

Of course, the facts and photos brought back from the moon have the immediacy and excitement that goes with authenticity, but the poetry and fantasy tend to fade and the pale-faced moon from which we hoped to plunk bright honor is no longer a ghostly galleon tossed upon cloudy seas.

There will still, naturally, be the special excitement of being actually on the scene, but even then the following day's delayed tape will show what really happened, thus fixing and clarifying the memory. It is a remarkable prospect and as the techniques are refined, it may be possible to check through, at will, an electronic box of great moments which can be mixed according to the whim of the viewer.

It is going to be remarkable and I am sorry that I am not going to be around for much of it. I have a consolation, however. I have a recollection, uncontradicted by any earthbound film, of Davey O'Brien, no taller than my knee, throwing a football the length of the field on the fly.

LEE IACOCCA

AS TOLD TO MURRAY OLDERMAN

The Lesson I Learned from Vince Lombardi

In 1972, a year after Vince Lombardi died of cancer, Lee Iacocca, then the president of Ford, wrote a tribute for SPORT *magazine. In the piece, Iacocca tells of his few encounters with Lombardi and how, despite their limited time together, he was influenced by the great Green Bay Packers coach.*

THE LAST TIME I SAW Vince Lombardi—it was in a private club in New York over plates of pasta at a feast fit for a Roman emperor—I asked him a very specific question which had long been on my mind: "Just how tough are you?"

And he replied in that sharp, quick way he had of talking: "Well, I'm tough with guys who have talent and goof off."

Then I said, "Coach, tell me who was the best football player you ever had, and why."

I thought he'd say, "Gee . . . well, I've coached a lot of guys." Instead, he answered, "Paul Hornung."

I wasn't ready for the quick reply. So I went on: "I don't know Hornung personally. I know him only as a man who played great ball for you. You made something out of the guy—I know that. What made *him* so great?"

Lombardi thought this over a second and said, "It's tough for me to answer because it's not a matter of a team but of the individuals who make up that team—and this man, Paul Hornung, had one priceless ingredient as an individual. The guy had to win; he just wanted to win. If he got into a tight game and we needed five yards or a vital touchdown, you just knew this man would break it open. It wasn't luck, or that he trained harder than the other guys, or didn't smoke."

Now *that* interested me because Vince Lombardi had at least 25 players on the Green Bay Packers he could have named, and he picked this man without saying he was good at blocking or good at running or any other special skills. Only that he simply wanted to win.

"That's what my life has always been about," continued Vince. "I've always wanted to win. I had this desire. When I play and when I coach, I just got to win."

It has stuck with me, this singular devotion of a man to his goal. The truth is, I had met Vince Lombardi only twice, and already he was a legendary figure to me. The first time was, I believe, at one of the All-America Golf dinners in New York. Then in May of 1971 I was coming into New York from Detroit on business. Edward Bennett Williams (whom I'd known for some time) was there with Coach Lombardi for the National Football League meetings. Ed is a famous lawycr, a fanatic football devotee (as I am), and also the president of the Washington Redskins. I med Ed for a drink one evening. He had the coach with him, so he said, "Let's have dinner."

We went to the Columbus Club, which has a number of prominent Italian men in New York, and the next three hours were among the most enjoyable and rewarding I've ever experienced. It was one of those regular impromptu banquet-type evenings. I sat next to Lombardi, and we spent the three hours eating everything in sight. We kidded each other that with all the problems and pressures we had running a ballclub or a company, we could pride ourselves on still having pretty good stomachs. We had pasta and put a lot of pepper on the pasta—that's what started us talking about our stomachs—and we had veal and chicken. We must have had 10 courses. I remember we ended up with something called sambucco, an anisette with a little coffee bean on top, which is supposed to be just the thing to perk you up after you've had a 10- or 12-course dinner. Anyhow, I really had a chance to meet the man and sit with him over a period of hours, talking about everything.

The image I retain is that of a warmhearted man, with no nonsense in his talk. What sticks in my mind are the questions I asked him about all the things I'd read about him and what it took to put together a winner. I remember him saying, "Yeah, you got to teach fundamentals in anything."

But then he'd blurt, almost self-consciously: "Lee, what the hell am I telling you for? You run a company. It's the same way, whether you're running a ballclub or a company." And he'd keep repeating, "What the hell am I telling you for?"

He provided me, however, with three salient points in his formula for leadership. "You teach them the fundamentals," he said, "that's one thing. The guy's got to know the basics of the game. He's got to know what he's talking about. Then you keep the boys in line. That's what you call discipline. They play as a team, not as one individual guy. No prima donnas on the team. They may not like it, but that's the way it is.

"But there've been a lot of people who put good clubs together in many sports who missed the third ingredient: That if you're going to play together as a team, you've got to care for one another. You've got to love each other. You can't just go out and say, 'I'm going to do it alone.'"

You only had to see the Packers play to understand what he meant. Every visit they made was a special occasion to me, an exhilarating display of football as it should be played. The last time Lombardi brought a Green Bay team to Detroit was in October 1967, his last season as the leader of the Packers. The Lions had surprised the Packers in the season opener by tying them in Green Bay and actually felt they should have won the game. Remember, Green Bay was the defending NFL champion and was going for a modern record of three straight titles. The Lions, in their first season under Joe Schmidt, were on the way back. A victory over the Packers in their second meeting would hoist the Lions into a first-place tie.

The Packers, moreover, were hurting. This wasn't the same team that had dominated football with its beautifully meshed "49sweep"—Hornung following Jimmy Taylor through the off-tackle hole, preceded by the blocking tandem of Jerry Kramer and Fuzzy Thurston, the pulling guards—literally blasting through the NFL. Both Hornung and Taylor, the one-two punch of the running game, were gone. Thurston, bruised and aging, was on the bench. Bart Starr, the peerless quarterback, the extension of Lombardi on the field, was hurt and would miss the Detroit rematch. Zeke Bratkowski, his stand-in, was 36. The Packers generally were beginning to show signs of age. Willie Davis, Henry Jordan, Willie Wood, Bobby Jeter, and Ray Nitschke were prime defenders, all over 30. Many of the key offensive people, such as Starr and Kramer, Forrest Gregg and Boyd Dowler, were also over 30.

The Lions, starting fast, zipped into a 10-0 lead by the middle of the second quarter. Just before halftime, Donny Anderson got the Packers back into the game by grabbing a touchdown pass from Bratkowski. A field goal by Don Chandler in the third quarter tied it, and then in the last 15 minutes the Packers broke the game open by ripping loose for 17 points. They were on their way to Lombardi's third straight NFL title.

The numbers on some of the uniforms were different—Elijah Pitts and Jim Grabowski carried the ball that day—but the precision and synchronization were there, plus the willingness to knock people down. "Pro football is a violent game," Lombardi once said. "There is nothing wrong with violence, if it is controlled."

The Packers also showed a team cohesion that went beyond the mere execution of play-book assignments. There was a responsiveness of one player to the other, all stimulated by the coach.

"The difference between mediocrity and perfection," the coach told me that night at dinner, "is the the feeling these guys have. They call it team spirit. When the guys are imbued with that, then you know you've got a team."

He made no bones about it. He said, "That's all there is to a team."

The funny thing is, I've often used the same analogy at Ford. I said to Lombardi that night: "I've used your name many times, Coach." And I have. Often. I told my people: "You know Lombardi—they say that for him there's nothing in life but winning." That's true. He's in a competitive venture. What did he say about ties? It's like kissing your sister. But—and I told this to a group of auto dealers in Palm Springs—"you win first by caring."

When I asked Vince a special question about motivating people he'd say to me: "What do you do at Ford? Sure, it's a business, but it's also a team of people. Does one guy bring out a car?"

He kept repeating it, and I said no. The man doing the engineering has to work with the man doing the manufacturing. If they don't really care about each other's role in putting a car together as a team, what do you get? You get lousy cars. And in Lombardi's world, you get losers.

Because he was so forceful in relating these thoughts, and because I knew he lived by this creed, he made a believer out of me. When I was made president of Ford last December, I received a letter of congratulations from a friend, Jerry Jacob, reminding me of that night with Lombardi. It said: "You may recall the quote Ed Williams attributed to Vince Lombardi that night you had dinner in New York. 'Success is a great deal like narcotics. You rapidly become addicted to it. It tends to deepen the depression of defeat and dulls the elation of victory. There are a very select few who make winning a way of life. And after a while some of the day-to-day victories can become dull, routine. But when you lose one, it sure hurts.'

"But winning the Super Bowl, that's something else. Even Vince got excited about that one. My sincere congratulations to you."

Lombardi, you may remember, was almost like a missionary in his attitude toward the Super Bowl when the Packers first approached it after the 1966 season. Despite statements that came out later, he didn't really take the Kansas City Chiefs lightly. "I go into every game scared," he said. "I'm scared for this one."

Because the Packers in that era were so omnipotent, memories get distorted. They thoroughly beat the Chiefs in that first Super Bowl—on the final scoreboard. But at halftime it was still a toss-up ball game. Green Bay led, 14-10, yet Kansas City had been raising hell with the Packers defense, which found Lenny Dawson's moving pocket a puzzle.

During the intermission, Lombardi reminded his veteran team this was more than a simple game and another payday. "You," he said to them, "are representing the whole National Football League."

When the second half started, the Chiefs were on the move again, crossing midfield. The situation was third down and five yards to go. The Packers, under Lombardi, were fairly conservative in their tactics. They seldom blitzed on defense. But this time, when Dawson slid out to his right behind a covey of blockers, the linebackers came shooting through and penetrated the moving pocket. Dawson had to unload, and his hurried pass was short. Safety Willie Wood intercepted the ball, scooted down the middle of the field, and then cut to the sidelines for 50 yards before he was tackled on the Chiefs' 4-yard line. On the next play, Elijah Pitts scored, and the Kansas City effort crumbled into a rout.

After the game, Lombardi was pressed for his opinion of the Chiefs. He really didn't want to say anything, but in the emotion of the moment he let himself go. With characteristic honesty, he said that he felt they were below the top rung of NFL teams and that their defensive secondary didn't measure up to NFL standards. He didn't claim later he was misquoted either.

This brings to mind another stage of my conversation with Lombardi, a very important one. I asked him how long it would take him to win the Super Bowl again in his rebuilding job with Washington. You know, he'd just had the one season with the Redskins under his belt, in 1969, and had produced their first winning record in 14 years. Again you can call it a dogmatic way of thinking, but he didn't say, "Oh, that depends."

He said, "Oh, Lee, I'd say two years."

With positiveness. Like: "Yes, I have the material now, a lot of young guys, but give me two years, I'll be a real contender. We'll have everything put together at Washington to win the Super Bowl."

The point about this is that you hear about a Vince Lombardi, but here you see the private person, positive in his emotions that what he was doing would produce results. And results meant winning.

Also when you asked him, "Have you thought about winning?" it was like asking, "Have you thought about breathing?"

Washington, you know, had some pretty ratty seasons before Lombardi came in, and he talked about the defense being a little weak. Yet he didn't hedge about needing three or four years, or a five-year plan, or the right kind of schedule. Two years was *it*, just like that.

My impressions of Lombardi during our dinner were of the tough disciplinarian, even in his clipped conversational tones. But there was a warmth there, too, and you felt a kinship. Anybody who knew him could relate to him.

Take that business of "love" which was part of the Green Bay championship syndrome. It's difficult when you put quotes around "love." And yet, as I mentioned earlier, I quoted Lombardi at great length on this subject in my speeches to big dealer-groups. I tried to convey that even though it's more impersonal in your relationships with people in a big company, there's a line-staff relationship as in football. You don't go around saying, "Be my buddy, and I'll love you." But there is a feeling of rapport in any big team.

On an emotional level, I couldn't zero in specifically on one guy, as Lombardi is supposed to have done when he grabbed a big lineman by the neck and chewed him out, but they hear about it at Ford when things go wrong. "You guys blew it," I've said often. "Somebody missed his g—— d—— block. We got clobbered and we shouldn't have."

I suppose the football analogy comes naturally to me. As a kid in Allentown, Pennsylvania, I used to watch the Eagles play when they still had the wooden stands. I'd go to every game. This was before Steve Van Buren. Then came that backfield with Tommy Thompson,

Bosh Pritchard, and Joe Muha. My interest in the pros continued over the years. In our kind of business, you need a hobby. I like to watch good competition. I like a good scrap. We've had fairly good teams in the 20 years I've been in Detroit, and I've never missed a Green Bay game with the Lions. And I became interested in Vince Lombardi as soon as he joined the Packers.

Suprisingly enough, when I saw Lombardi that night for dinner, I sensed that he was as interested in me as I was in him, which is why we had a nice evening together and a lot of laughs. He said, "I've always known a lot of things about Ford. The car business has fascinated me. I want to come out some time and have lunch with you and, believe it or not, be a tourist and see how they make cars." I said, "Okay, you don't have to call me. I'll write you."

But I never got to write him. Less than a week later, I found out that he was in the hospital with what was diagnosed as his fatal illness.

I remember I was really shocked, particularly because we had been reveling just a few days earlier in our Italian-style feast, boasting about our cast-iron stomachs. I felt a profound sense of loss, not only for myself personally, but for all Americans.

Vince Lombardi had something to offer that was unique and went beyond sports. An introspective man, he was aware of social change in this country and once expressed a sense of personal failing. He felt he let himself get so wrapped up in the Green Bay Packers, in how they walked and talked and dressed, that he was oblivious to the revolt of the young which was taking place around him. He admitted he should have been more aware. At the same time, he also defended football as an endeavor translatable to the life experience.

"Football," he said, "requires spartan qualities to be a part of it. Sacrifice, self-denial—they're cliché words—but I believe in them with every fiber of my body. I'm not saying everybody who plays football is a spartan or denies himself. But it's a symbol of courage: it's a symbol of teamwork, which I think is a great American attribute."

And he came back to football, ironically, with the Washington Redskins because he couldn't stomach the idea of Vincent Thomas Lombardi being a living legend, the Super-coach.

"There's no way I could live with that kind of thing," he said. "A lot of people are anxious to see me fall flat on my face. I don't say it with malice. I think that's just a human reaction. Someone said the reason I came back to coaching was to destroy a legend. I'm sure I'm going to destroy it. But this is where I want to be."

He didn't destroy the legend, he embellished it.

By today's standards, some people would call Vince Lombardi square. He talked about imbuing kids with the qualities that really make good citizens. Cycles come and go, but honesty is honesty and working hard is working hard. We've always been told in our educational system that one way to make better people is through competitive sports.

Lombardi the competitor certainly personifies to me, a legend.

AUGUST WILSON

Hero Worship on Sunday Afternoon

How important can one football game or one hero be? Ask four 14-year-olds from a working-class Pittsburgh neighborhood as they make a pilgrimage to Forbes Field to watch the great Jim Brown. The game didn't turn out exactly as they guessed, but then, August Wilson points out, a lot of things don't. Wilson is a Pulitzer Prize-winning playwright whose works include TWO TRAINS RUNNING, MA RAINEY'S BLACK BOTTOM, *and* FENCES. *The Minnesota native wrote this piece for the Super Bowl XXVI game program in Minneapolis.*

THE SUPER BOWL has become so much a part of American popular culture that it is difficult to imagine or remember a time before there was a Super Bowl, when the price of a Broadway theater ticket was anywhere from $2 to $10 and you could see your local professional football team for $3.90. A time before cable TV and VCRs and microwave ovens. A time before "Monday Night Football," when all the games were played on Sunday afternoons, and Sunday evenings were dedicated to Ed Sullivan, watched on 19-inch black-and-white televisions. This was before the Beatles, Bob Dylan, or the Supremes. This was years before you could transport an entire football team, its staff, and 200 fans on the same airplane, and long before anyone ever had heard of Bill Gates or Microsoft, back when the letters DOS might have stood for Defensive and Offensive Strategy. It was a time when professional football was played on grassy fields, though with the same skill and intensity with which it is played today.

In 1959, I was 14 years old and lived in Hazelwood, a working-class area of Pittsburgh made up mostly of steel workers who worked at the Jones and Laughlin steel mill. On Saturdays, they drank beer and cut their lawns, and on Sundays, they took their wives and daughters to church. Their sons, it seemed for the most part, were left to their own devices. The numerous events and sports teams sponsored by the local Knights of Columbus and the Moose and Kiwanis Clubs served better than the church for the molding of their character.

Sports in Hazelwood was a pretty serious proposition, and almost every kid had the opportunity to play for one team or another. These teams were started and sponsored and supported by stout men with large hands and broad backs who sought ways to teach their sons rules of conduct and ideas of fair play, and to instill in them a competitive spirit that would serve them well when they grew up and became lawyers or shoe salesmen or advertising executives. Sports might even lead to college and a job other than the arduous and all-consuming work of making steel.

Sunday afternoon, weather permitting, was given to listening to the Steelers football game on the front porch. In 1959, Steelers football fans were hardy; they had well-developed loyalties despite the fact the team consistently was at the bottom of the standings. There were few victories to celebrate, as guys named Terry Bradshaw, Mean Joe Greene, Jack Lambert, Franco Harris, and Lynn Swann still were in junior high school, and it would be many years before Pittsburgh sportswriters ran out of metaphors to describe the "Steel Curtain" Steelers teams of the seventies.

To a 14-year-old in a world of rapidly shifting values and expectations, sports is a way of discovering and defining yourself, of testing and exploring the limits of potential. A way of being and becoming. It is a world unto itself, and nothing is as important within that world as its Heroes. Every home run by Hank Aaron and every knockout by Sonny Liston became a victory for you, an announcement of your presence in the world, flush with an exciting armada of possibilities. You lived through your heroes' flesh and sought to reenact their accomplishments, whether in a pick-up touch game or on the playing field of the local high school or in the world of your imagination.

In the minds of the boys I grew up with, no one loomed larger as a Hero than Jim Brown, who had blazed his way into our consciousness in 1957. Jim Brown was everything we wanted to be. Big, quick, and powerful, he ran right over the linebackers, leaving would-be tacklers scattered like bowling pins. He stood head and shoulders above any other running back playing the game. And he did it all with grace and style. He was, in a word, magnificent. As we were. Or wanted to be. And could be through him. Every 100-yard game, every touchdown was a salute to our possibilities. We named ourselves after him and argued our right to do so.

This year, 1959, also was the year when we, as incoming freshmen, began our sports careers at Gladstone High School. The baton was passed to us to avenge the litany of crushing defeats suffered at the hands of Westinghouse High School, the powerhouse perennial city football champions. We doubted we could beat them, but we took a solemn vow that we would not be beaten 66-0, we being Earl, Jesse, myself, and Ba Bra (pronounced Bay Bra, short for Baby Brother), whose real name was Arthur.

On a crisp, autumn morning (what other kinds of autumn mornings are there?), the four of us rendezvoused at Earl's house to begin an adventure that has stayed with me for 32 years. We were determined to see Jim Brown and the Cleveland Browns play the Pittsburgh Steelers, despite the fact we had all of $2 among the four of us. Familiar with the security at Forbes field, which we had tested (sometimes successfully) during innumerable Pittsburgh Pirates baseball games, our plan called for an early arrival, long before the ticket-takers and the small army of security, vendors, ushers, and other official personnel took their places. A short walk from Hazelwood, along Second Avenue up the winding road into Oakland, would put us at the foot of the 15-foot wall that surrounded the stadium. Though we never had done it before, we did not for a moment doubt our ability to scale even a 30-foot wall to see the great Jim Brown.

The four of us were friends, comrades, neighbors who lived on the same street, fell in love with the same girls, and learned, each in his own way, the same things. We also were each others' nemeses and delighted in our small victories. Earl was the tallest, Jesse the strongest, Ba Bra the fastest, and I was the best all-around athlete. Nobody could hit a baseball farther than me, nobody could throw a football like Ba Bra (a beautiful spiral that was deadly accurate, he was the presage, both in size and temperament, to the gifted Joe Gilliam), nobody could block shots or hook a basketball better than Earl, and nobody could catch a baseball or a football more skillfully than Jesse. We were good kids with a strong sense of community. We cut lawns, washed the neighbors' cars, and made yearly expeditions to a hidden and abandoned apple orchard, learning the location of which was in itself a rite of passage. There we picked bushels of apples that we sold for $3 to get enough money to buy a pair of $7.98 Converse tennis shoes.

Our conversation up the winding road probably was about football, Jim Brown, and the dreaded confrontation with Westinghouse High School, which followed us everywhere like a gathering storm.

At 10 A.M. the security guards were nowhere to be found, and the wall proved difficult, but somehow surmountable. Finding ourselves alone among 35,000 empty seats, we took the best seats in the house and waited for the game to begin. The best seats in the house proved to be too visible and when the security guards went on duty, we eventually were spotted. But Forbes Field was a large place, and we ran and took seats in the third deck until the gates opened and the crowd began to arrive.

It never occurred to us that the game would be sold out, and every time we settled into a seat someone would come to claim it, until ultimately we were forced to watch the game standing up in the aisles, ducking ushers. And watch it we did.

What a magnificent spectacle! It was big and it was beautiful and it was alive. It was number 32, the Great One himself, now carrying for a 6-yard gain, a 12-yard gain, a 3-yard gain, an 8-yard gain. And then, somewhere in the middle of the game, it happened. To the best of my recollection, what happened was this: Jim Brown broke a 73-yard run. On a quick burst up the middle, he ran over a linebacker and shook off two or three would-be tacklers on his way down the sideline, where some brave defensive back risked life and limb to save the touchdown by lunging and grabbing him by his ankles two yards short of the goal line. Now maybe I have embellished this over the years. Often in the retelling of an event, we exaggerate it until we ourselves come to believe it, to the point where we no longer can separate fact from fiction. So I concede beforehand that some football historian, some NFL statistician, some discriminating fan or sportswriter may prove that it was a 43-yard run, or maybe a 37-yard run, but what happened next is indisputable and irrefutable.

Overjoyed, we held our breath and secretly prayed in the name of poetic justice that Jim Brown be given the ball so he could score the touchdown he had so narrowly missed. The dictates of poetic justice prevailed and the handoff went to Brown who, while negotiating the 2 yards into the end zone, did the unspeakable. He fumbled.

We were, to a man, crushed. It is not an easy thing at 14 years old to see your hero falter. Not that we were unaware that fumbles and missteps were part of the game. We had seen Roberto Clemente drop a fly ball, and we had seen Hank Aaron strike out. But somehow this was different. This was bigger. Maybe because no matter how brilliant the run, it was incomplete and needed the two yards to legitimize it. Maybe, and I think this is more accurate, we simply had invested too much of ourselves in Jim Brown's heroics. Whatever it was, our spirits were bruised, and as we began the walk back down the winding road, the fumble stayed with us. It hung in the air, unspoken. We walked in silence and gradually it came to us: The possibility of failure carried with it the possibility of success. If the great Jim Brown could fumble the ball, then maybe just maybe, the great Westinghouse High School football team could stumble on its way to the championship. It was a thought where there had been none before.

"Hey, man, you think Westinghouse take City again this year?"

"I don't know. They ain't so tough. They only beat Carrick by twenty-six points."

"If you don't be scared . . . Half the time that's how they win, 'cause the other team be scared."

"We got a good defense. All you got to do is stop Henderson. He the one be scoring all their points."

The road opened and our pace quickened. It was, after all, only a game.

"Hey, Earl."

"What?"

"Why you got such a big head, man?"

"Yeah. And look at them feet."

"I don't know how you walk with them size twelves."

We turned onto Second Avenue, the wind at our backs and the road home welcoming us as heaven welcoming a saint.

RAY BRADBURY

A Game of Passion

When the NFL's publishers assembled a collection of works in 1975, they asked Ray Bradbury to write the Prologue. The revered writer struggled to find the right angle—until it found him at a classic USC-Notre Dame game. Bradbury, author of noted works such as THE MARTIAN CHRONICLES, FAHRENHEIT 451, SOMETHING WICKED THIS WAY COMES, *and* THE OCTOBER COUNTRY, *recently produced an award-winning cable television series, "The Ray Bradbury Theater."*

THE EDITORS OF THIS BOOK wanted me to say something fresh, something incredibly new, something amazingly forceful and surprising about football.

How do you do that?

How do you find a way to say new things about such a familiar subject?

I looked at a few hundred exceptional photographs.

Nothing happened.

I went to a few football games.

Nothing happened.

Nothing except the old miracles, the old and dearly similar rushes and cries and amiable brutalities.

But even those, I saw, were not as brutal, close up, as I had imagined they might be. I had somewhat dimly hoped for bonecrushing, rib-destroying, skull-crunching truths delivered in avalanches around, about, over, and on me.

The harder I looked the less I knew. The more I searched the less I found. Gazing around at the running teams, the crowd, the blue sky, I thought, come on, God, give me a day like the day when I was ten years old and discovered I was alive for the first time.

Don't give me facts; give me Revelations. Hit me with a bolt.

Nothing happened.

Except, suddenly, something did happen.

On a particular Saturday in November 1974, I stumbled into the Los Angeles Coliseum to see some college teams play football.

All the lightning and fever and pandemonium in history flattened me.

Because what I saw was the Notre Dame-USC game.

Remember that one?

During the first half I drank beer to console myself, since USC was losing its soul, heart, guts, and shoes out there in a dreadful weather of loss.

During the second half I drank beer to celebrate.

It was all magical, of course. I made it happen. At the kickoff for the second half I prayed:

Run it all the way for a touchdown.

Which is exactly what happened.

The people, on their feet, raved and screamed and yelled for the next hour.

Because USC just kept running that ball and totaling out the Irish. The people never once stopped shouting and shrieking. When all the yells stopped and we dragged ourselves out laughing and staggering, my daughter, whose first game this was, turned and said:

"Is it always like this?"

"If you're lucky, once every ten years!" I replied, laughing wildly. And we blundered happily off among all the delirious, feverish, similarly blundering people who had been sitting in electric chairs for the last 90 minutes with a billion volts full on, charging and recharging their dynamos. Everywhere you looked were sunburst faces, eyes exploding with fire, mouths wreathed in Greek comedy smiles. With, of course, a few Notre Dame losers lurking here or there, dodging the crowds, shadowing themselves away to their cars to unearth triple martinis or quadruple scotches.

I warmed my hands at the passing throng. I warmed my face at their faces. I warmed my soul at the sunfires that absolutely blazed in their flesh as they went away in the autumn afternoon.

We are sun worshippers, I thought, and this has been a day of fire and light and joy and such dazzling energy as shucks the years and puts on youth like a bright suit.

I was reminded of this again a few nights later. Still not knowing what I would write in this Prologue, I was in a book store when a friend nudged me and we stood talking weathers and sports and elations.

"My God," he said at last, "wouldn't it be wonderful if medics could plug in on the energy that jumps out of a crowd at the Coliseum?"

"Hey, yeah!" I said, waiting.

"Compact all that energy in a machine and shoot that juice into all the cancer victims in the world and—"

"Cure them?" I supplied.

"Cure them clean through and through!"

"What an idea!" said I. "That's it, by God, that's it! The thing I've been searching for. Eureka! It's found!"

And I wandered off imagining a machine that made a conduit to channel the lava fires, the crowd-electricities, the mob-energies to be delivered into hospital rooms to raise Lazarus, and into old folks' hordes to tap-dance the palsied feet and rear up the fragile white-moth people into incredible dances.

What a world that would be!

Will we ever do it, treat the football stadium and its running buffalo tribes on the field and its surging pulses of men and women in the stands as Numero Uno energy-producing field hospitals for the dead to be raised and the sick to be cured?

We've only begun to think of it.

Sport might one day soon teach us so much about energy and spirit as will revitalize the whole area of medicine, psychic medicine, geriatrics, and microbiology. One really grand game of football might be enough to kick over 10 trillion bubonic germs, send the rats and their fleas back to the seaports, and evict the graveyard tenants forever.

One could easily imagine teams in 2001 playing under such names as the Lazarus 11, the Resurrection Reds, the Easter Morning Whites, or the Ascensionists.

The American Medical Association would tabulate the teams, and the Bureau of Power and Light would lay the cables and transmit the impulses. Football fields would become vast hearthing places where the burning of happy souls would be broadcast by new equipment to the nearest emergency hospital or children's ward. Cables might be run out along the Pacific deeps to the nearest lepers' colony and for the first time in 10,000 years the people with the look of the lion, the lost souls on abandoned isles, might be shaken to health, flaked of their illness, washed in the blood of the lambs and colts, which of course are names for other teams in any years, and caused to swim home singing the praise of pigskins to form new churches. Said churches having coaches for ministers, priests, and—pigskin aside—rabbis, where confession might be admitting you don't like hockey, so Lord forgive me, and baseball? That's not so hot, either. A church, affiliated with a hospital where Mary is on one side in a chapel, Knute Rockne on the other, and Christ in between, wears a helmet and does not despair.

All pretty wild? Yes, no, maybe.

I remember the fire, I remember the warmth. I remember the joy. I remember the hearthing place of that game with 100,000 Jehovah's Witnesses whether they knew they wore the label or not.

You've all been to similar games and come out dressed in coats of many colors, made up of a thousand invisible lights and shared moments.

Which is the long way around to finally telling you what in hell I'm doing up front here in this book. I was concerned about taking the assignment because I was afraid of repeating threadbare clichés.

But in accepting this task, I remembered going to Houston eight years ago to meet all the astronauts and move around in the training areas where the Apollo missions prepared for their moon flights. I saw everything. I saw too much. I telephoned *LIFE* and asked them to fire me. No, sir, they said. We believe in you.

How much time do I have? I asked.

Twenty-four hours, they said.

I woke the next morning with the handle I needed to fit the astronauts and their jobs: I was looking at a theatre of history where men rehearsed history in the same minute detail as actors, directors, script-writers, on simulation-stages, in order to run out to the moon and make time and history real.

I finished my article for *LIFE* in five hours.

The metaphor, the lightning, had struck me.

And now here, on the green field, asking, the lightning has struck again and the answer, the concept, the idea is: ENERGY.

What you have in this book is a collection of photographs of energy frozen for a moment so you can look at it, enjoy it, warm your hands in recollection, warm your hearts with remembrance. The fire is here. The wild blood is here. The joy is here. The freedom is here for you to touch, turn, and rekindle.

Will the Lazarus teams one day a century from now play at eternal scrimmages and total up grand points not only on the lit board but in the tubercular sanitariums and cancer encampments of the world? Who can say? Who would dare predict? Who knows? We know so little of the miracle of stuffs that we humans are. The mystery of our blood and fire and energy is just that: still a mystery after 10,000 years of religion, and a few hundred of truly operative medicine. We have sunlight, and atomic energy, and the tumults and shoutings of fire in football crowds to examine and put on like gear, to run in like founts.

Maybe somewhere along the yardages from one goal to another, we may just catch immortality, turn into a mob of sunflowers looking up at that passing symbol of freedom and elation, that football that drifts forever and may never come down.

Worth thinking about, anyway. Worth trying to figure an AC-DC plug that might fit and run the wires from stadium to sickroom and tune the Life Force in after the evening news on Channel 5.

If the fire fits, put it on. If the energy suits, wear it like a glove. If the joy is just the right size, tilt it on your head. If the sun at noon and a football at four on a late autumn day look much the same, reach up, grab, carry. Run for your life, laughing. Pursued not by fates and furies but by outrageous laughters and incredible delights.

Here's the book. Here are the photographs of men on their way to becoming fire, burning their images in chemistries on papers in darkrooms to be leafed in later years.

Aren't you glad I waited in the middle of the field for something to touch me?

Aren't you glad that I was lucky and something did at last touch and burn and change?

What a relief to know what I now know about football.

The shadow races on the grass. The ball drifts like an eternal balloon in a sky that is always sunrise.

If you don't mind, I'll just run out after the long toss. Years from now, I may even catch it.

GAY TALESE

Alias Little Mo

Before turning his journalistic eye toward subjects such as the Mafia, sex, the NEW YORK TIMES, *and his own family, Gay Talese wrote several memorable sports features, including "The Loser," about boxer Floyd Patterson, and "The Silent Season of the Hero," about Joe DiMaggio. In this piece, written for the* TIMES *in 1957, Talese studies the relationship between the two football-playing Modzelewski brothers, Dick—"Little Mo," who played with the New York Giants—and Ed—"Big Mo," who played with the Cleveland Browns.*

DICK MODZELEWSKI, ALIAS LITTLE MO, is 260 pounds of tough tenderloin with shoulders so broad that he often has to pass through doors sideways.

When he is not playing tackle for the New York Giants, Modzelewski is a warmhearted, gentle soul who loves to baby-sit for his 108-pound wife, Dorothy. But when he is playing football, he is thoroughly bellicose. He wants to win more than any man since Machiavelli, Dillinger, or Leo Durocher.

Leo Durocher once said that if he were playing shortstop and his mother were rounding second, he'd trip her—accidentally.

"I'd help her up, brush her off, and tell her I'm sorry," the ex-baseball manager said, "but she wouldn't get to third."

Modzelewski feels likewise and, whenever he can, he tries to knock his brother down and steal the football.

His brother is Ed (Big Mo) Modzelewski, a fullback on the Cleveland Browns.

"Ed is my brother and I love him," said Dick yesterday at Yankee

Stadium, where the Giants will meet the Washington Redskins on Sunday. "But on the field he wears a white shirt and I wear a blue shirt and we don't know each other."

Dick is paid considerable money by the Giants for pushing people around. His contributions have had much to do in giving the Giants a defensive line that is virtually unbeatable, unstoppable, and unpronounceable. On the line with Modzelewski are John Martinkovic, Andy Robustelli, Jim Katcavage, and Walt Yowarsky.

Dick Modzelewski was born in West Natrona, Pa., a small coal-mining town near Pittsburgh where boys begin to play tackle in the streets at eight and where a majority of the male population have had their noses broken at least once.

He is one of six children in a family that weighs collectively about 1,540 pounds. His father, a muscular miner, weighs 220 pounds; his mother, 235 pounds. His two sisters steadfastly refuse to testify.

Big Mo, who is 28, weighs 215; he is called Big Mo because in high school he was larger than Dick, who is 26. The newest Mo in the family is Eugene, who, at 13, weighs 192 pounds and is called Dyna-Mo.

There is also Joe, a 30-year-old brother who weighs 205 and used to be one of Ezzard Charles's sparring partners. Joe won seventeen out of twenty-one fights, but quit when his jaw was broken. He now works in a glass company in Pittsburgh.

Little Mo and Big Mo played high school and college football together and both were All-Americans at Maryland in 1952. They wish they were professional teammates but since they are not, they are enemies whenever the Giants and Browns play. Last year Little Mo stopped Big Mo with a throttling tackle on the l-yard line in a successful goal-line stand.

Dick estimates that he gets hit between sixty and seventy times a game. Sometimes he gets hit three times on one play.

When he lines up, his nose is usually a foot from that of the opposing tackle's. But professional linemen, he says, don't talk to each other during the afternoon of crouching.

"Oh, once in a while I talk to my brother," Dick said. "When I tackle him, I say, 'You didn't get too many yards, did you?' Or he'll say, 'Is that the hardest you can hit?'"

Dick has never been knocked out in five years of pro football, though he says the person making the tackle generally suffers more than the person being tackled. He was "fogged up" once when a knee owned by a Cleveland Browns player clobbered Dick. The knee, Dick said, did not belong to Ed Modzelewski.

"If you get the wind knocked out of you," Dick said, "the trainer comes out and says to you, 'What time is it?' 'Where are you?' 'Who are we playing?' If you say, 'We're playing Hawaii,' the trainer leads you off the field."

No matter how excellent the players' conditioning might be, a pro lineman is fatigued before the game is over, Modzelewski said.

"You start feeling the bumps and bruises in the final quarter, but if your team is winning you don't mind. But if you're losing, those bumps and bruises hurt like hell."

Modzelewski stands 5 feet 11 1/2 inches and claims to be the shortest Giant on defense. He has an 18 1/2-inch neck and his shirts, all tailor-made, cost $14 each. His sports jackets are size 48.

He has blue eyes, over which he wears contact lenses. Lenses were recommended when he was in high school on an afternoon when the foe's halfback ran right past him with the football and Little Mo didn't see him.

With his wife and two-year-old son, Mark, Dick lives in a hotel near the Stadium. He would like to sleep late on Mondays because he is usually sore and scratched, but Mark usually falls out at 8 a.m. And Monday is the day that his wife and Mrs. Ken MacAfee often spend eight hours shopping and spend lots of money downtown, and Ken and Dick baby-sit.

"Me and Ken take the kids out for a walk, then give them lunch, then put them to bed," Dick said. "Then Ken and me go back to sleep."

On Dec. 15, when the Browns come to town, Dick will probably entertain Big Mo with dinner and drinks.

"We'll go to the movies the night before the game," Dick said, "and Ed will try to pump me for information and I'll try to pump him for information. After that we'll come home to my place and talk and have a few drinks."

And then, with a smile totally lacking in fraternalism, "Maybe I can slip Ed a couple of quick ones."

JAMES DICKEY

In the Pocket

With very few words, James Dickey has a way of dropping the reader, unprepared, into the swirling heart of tumultuous action. In this poem, which appeared in the book MORE THAN A GAME *in 1974, he chooses the quarterback as embattled protagonist. Though he is known primarily for his poetry, Dickey also is the author of two celebrated novels,* DELIVERANCE *and* TO THE WHITE SEA.

Going backward
All of me and some
Of my friends are forming a shell   my arm is looking
Everywhere and some are breaking
In   breaking down
And out   breaking
Across, and one is going deep   deeper
Than my arm.   Where is Number One hooking
Into the violent green alive
With linebackers?   I cannot find him he cannot beat
His man   I fall back more
Into the pocket   it is raging and breaking
Number Two has disappeared into the chalk
Of the sideline   Number Three is cutting with half
A step of grace   my friends are crumbling
Around me the wrong color
Is looming   hands are coming
Up and over between
My arm and Number Three: throw it hit him in the middle

Of his enemies   hit move scramble
Before death and the ground
Come up   LEAP STAND KILL DIE STRIKE
Now.

SANDY GRADY

Cruncher

This story, written by syndicated columnist Sandy Grady for SAGA *magazine in 1960, is about the last of the great two-way players, Chuck Bednarik. Bednarik, who played both linebacker and center for the Philadelphia Eagles and helped lead them to an NFL championship in 1960, is best known as the man who put the ferocious hit on Frank Gifford that nearly ended the halfback's career. Bednarik's persona remained true to his hardscrabble Pennsylvania roots.*

HE DIDN'T NEED AN ALARM CLOCK. The big man had his own private clock wound tight. At 8:30, it clanged deep in his mind. The big man shuffled his 230 pounds and stared blinking at the ceiling. He had taken two sleeping pills to sink him into this dreamless coma. Now he fought his way back to life, like a fighter getting off the deck. The big man could hear his four daughters squealing over their toys downstairs—it was the day after Christmas. He could hear the subdued murmur of Philadelphia suburban traffic from outside on Pennsylvania Route 611.

This was going to be the biggest damn day of Chuck Bednarik's life, and suddenly he knew it, and he catapulted out of the bed as if burned. In five hours he would be on the winter-gray turf of Franklin Field. He would have to play almost 60 minutes against Green Bay. If they were 60 good minutes, Philadelphia might win the pro football championship. Bednarik was 35 years old. He had endured jolts and bruises through a dozen games for this moment. Now he had to wad up the whole ball of his middle-aged comeback and gamble it on one hour of action.

"Hey, Chuck," Emma Bednarik called, "I've got coffee and scrambled eggs and toast and jelly and . . ."

She was kidding. It was a ritual. Bednarik scowled at the unshaven, heavy jaw in the mirror. The thought of food almost made him sick. He knew the tension was starting early.

By 9:30 Bednarik was dressed. He went outside to taste the weather, the way a fisherman will sniff the wind before shoving off. Bednarik walked on the lawn, still patched with old snow. The quiet Abington street of $40,000 homes was a long way from the old Bednarik household, hidden in the steel-slag haze of Bethlehem.

He checked the watch: 9:45. The tigers inside him were doing cartwheels now. Even at Bethlehem High he'd felt them some. At Penn during those All-American years, he'd felt the tigers churning a little before the big games. Before each of the 30 missions as a B-24 gunner over Europe, the tigers had somersaulted in Bednarik's stomach. That was different. The 11 pro seasons had quieted the old tigers. Until this year, that is. It had been one helluva season, every game for the money, ten wins, with Bednarik under pressure as a center and linebacker. The tigers flipped inside before every game, but he knew this was going to be the worst.

"Emma, I think I'll drive down and start dressing," said Bednarik.

It was casual as a broker, a salesman, a 9-to-5 clerk telling his wife he was heading for the office. "It's gonna be a cinch, baby," said Bednarik, going out the door. "It's gonna be nice and cold. I could play all day in this weather."

He knew he was lying, backing the maroon Pontiac station wagon out of the garage. He had been tired, racked up and the air coming in hot gasps, a couple of times this year. The first time he'd tried this 60-minute trick, the sultry day in Cleveland, had been no picnic. He'd been mad as hell at Paul Brown or he would never have gone the route. He was 35 and he couldn't lie to his legs. He had retired twice before, but this time he had meant it. He had the good job with the concrete outfit. He was still amazed when he thought about the whole weird deal. Here he was, a beat-up old linebacker, driving to a stadium to play for the National Football League championship, when he should be out hustling concrete.

Bednarik began wheeling faster, beating the cars away from the lights, the tension gnawing. He had to stop Hornung on that option pass play. Hell, Gifford was the best at that play and the Eagles had handled him, hadn't they? He had to watch Starr on those swing passes. There were going to be a lot of trap plays. If somebody sucked in, he'd have to handle Jim Taylor alone. The movies don't lie about Taylor. He runs like hell.

The tigers were doing their acrobatic williwaws inside Bednarik now. Before he reached Franklin Field he'd pick up two candy bars. He needed the energy. He hoped he could get one of them down.

Chuck Bednarik didn't know where the big season began. How do you reach back and put a finger on the flow of time and say, This is where it started? Maybe it began the year he was 16, a skinny kid who wanted to be a fullback, and Jack Butler at Bethlehem High said, "C'mere, Bednarik, you got three days to learn to be a center." Did it start that far back—or the day he came out of the Army Air Corps and decided to go to Penn? Or the day on the train he popped off to Greasy Neale. Bednarik was a rookie then on the 1949 championship Eagles, and Neale was a tough guy, but Bednarik cornered him on the train: "I'm tired of sitting on my butt—play me or trade me to somebody who will." Greasy stuck him in against the Chicago Cardinals, and somehow he avoided getting killed. There were 145 pro games after that one, and Bednarik missed only one. Bednarik liked to remember that. When he could walk, he would play.

But this season had been wildly absurd. It was something Bednarik hardly dared dream after a half-dozen gin-and-tonics. Bednarik knew this shouldn't be a championship team. Too many rookies, too many old guys. Bednarik knew at 35 he shouldn't be playing 60 minutes. Sam Huff, Les Richter, Joe Schmidt—those guys wouldn't do it. Yet here he was.

Maybe it began last spring on the day he went to the Eagles' office. Just a nice, spring day in Philadelphia, the girls swishing along Locust St. in their summer dresses.

"I hear you and Emma have a new baby on the way, Chuck," said Vince McNally. "Congratulations."

"Thanks," said Bednarik. He watched McNally light another cigarette across the desk. McNally is an ex-Knute Rockne quarterback, a trim, white-haired man who is general manager of the Eagles.

"Chuck, you might regret quitting football. All right, so you'll be 35. You're still in great shape."

"I don't want anybody pitying me," said Bednarik. "I couldn't stand to slow up and look like a bum out there."

"Believe me, Chuck," said McNally, his eyes narrowing behind the horn rims, "the Eagles need you this year. I wouldn't make this offer if I thought you'd slowed up. I think you need us, too, with your new responsibilities."

"I've got a job. It's time I started to earn a living."

McNally lit another cigarette. He picked up an envelope on the desk. He penciled down a figure: $2000. It wouldn't look a decent raise to a baseball player. A pitcher would laugh. A quarterback would laugh. Bednarik is an old lineman. Old linemen don't laugh at two grand.

"You know we haven't made any money," said McNally. "We've had losing teams. Buck Shaw wants you badly. Talk to Emma about it. Think it over."

"I've thought it over," said Bednarik. "Hell, maybe I knew I'd do this all along. Gimme the contract."

McNally stubbed out the cigarette and grinned.

An old lineman's version of hell starts in July. The pro training camps are stuck in alien hamlets of Wisconsin and Minnesota and the Pennsylvania hills. It is supposed to be cool. It never is. The old lineman's enemy is the sun that sweats out the beer and the sirloin steaks and the mashed potatoes. The wind sprints are brutal, and the scrimmages are no rest. There is always a rookie who wants to make a quick reputation. There is always a rookie who wants to knock an old lineman on his sweaty, disgusted, bored, tired rear end.

The Eagles train in Hershey, Pennsylvania. There is the aroma of chocolate on the wind. The hills are green. The heat beats on them in brassy waves. The rookies dress quickly in the gray sweat suits, eager for the calisthenics the old pros hate.

"You're going for a nice vacation," Emma Bednarik said, needling her husband. "You're getting away from the girls and all the racket here. You'll loaf up in those cool hills."

Bednarik groaned. Cool hills. Nuts. He had tried to stay in shape always. A little gin in the summer didn't hurt. He cut down the cigarettes. No bread-and-butter. Plenty of golf. Still it hurt to run the first few days in that damnable sun.

"He's a three-beer man, Chuck Bednarik," said the bartender proudly in one of Hershey's few spas. "Chuck's in here 15 minutes after practice. Whoo-eee, he's hot. Fast as I can draw 'em, he knocks off three draft beers. That's all I see of Chuck Bednarik. He's in bed by 10. Thirsty, but a good boy."

Bednarik was toughening the 240 pounds now. His snapbacks to Norm Van Brocklin were sharp. Bednarik watched the kids passing through camp rapidly as street cars. The Eagles had won seven, lost five, the year before. Buck Shaw needed blocking. He needed a lot of things. The club was too patchy for a title, even with Van Brocklin's arm. Maxie Baughan, a red-haired kid from Georgia Tech, looked tough working at linebacker with Chuck Weber and Bob Pellegrini. Huh, linebacking wasn't Bednarik's worry now, though. He was a center.

"Why don't you come over to the defensive meetings, Chuck," said Jerry Williams, who drew the defense's diagrams. "You can't tell. You may need this stuff someday."

"Okay, I'll drop in," said Bednarik. He did sit through a half-lecture, but he sneaked out the door, restless with the Xs on the blackboard. What did they expect him to do, play 60 minutes?

Chuck Bednarik's season began in Cleveland. The Eagles had

played a lot of football before that. They had mildly surprised themselves by winning all five exhibitions. In Philadelphia people snickered that McNally was staging another ticket-selling drive. It looked true when the Browns waffled the Eagles, 41-24, in the home opener. The Eagles went to Dallas and stole one, 27-25. They came home and beat the Cards, then stopped the Lions solidly. The plane ride to Cleveland was quiet. Beating the Browns in their own park was like trying to steal a hunk of beef from a lion.

"Hey, Chuck, get in! Get in! Pelly's hurt!"

Guys were banging Bednarik on his back, shoving him toward the field. It had been the third play of the game. Bednarik had been resting on the bench. A Cleveland run swept out of his line of vision. He didn't see Bob Pellegrini flattened in the violent mob, painfully hurt. When he leaped up, Bednarik knew Pelly was down, though. The fire bell in his mind clanged. Hell, this might be a ball. He hadn't gone both ways since he was at Penn.

"Wait a minute, Chuck." Shaw grabbed his arm. "Don't be a hero. If you get tired, let me know."

Bednarik jammed on the helmet. He took the wide, crouching stance at the left linebacker slot. Tom Brookshier yelled something about a pass pattern. Bednarik didn't hear. He was suddenly embroiled in a gulf of Brown blockers.

They came at him again on the second play. There was a sharp twinge in his thigh. He felt as though he'd been stabbed with an icepick. Bednarik didn't want to limp. He wanted to stay in now.

The Cleveland slotback had lined up on his right. The end, Gern Nagler, was on his left. The slotback feinted a block. Bednarik turned to bounce him off, catching a glimpse of Bobby Mitchell hurtling around his end. What he didn't see was the end, who hit him from the blind side, because this was a play the Browns call "The Clip." Bednarik's 235 pounds somersaulted in the air so viciously he landed on his feet. Somehow he helped Jimmy Carr bring down Mitchell.

Bednarik lay in the grass in front of the Cleveland bench. He didn't really want to move. Then he glanced up and saw Paul Brown.

Under the snapbrim hat, Brown was laughing as though Bednarik was the most comic figure since Fatty Arbuckle was hit with his last lemon pie.

"Bednarik," said Brown, "you're too damn old for this game."

Bednarik was off the grass now. Fast. He unleashed a torrent of abuse. His thick neck was red with anger. When someone jostled Bednarik away, Brown wasn't laughing.

"How's the leg, Chuck?" Dr. Mike Mandarino said at the half.

"It's nothing," mumbled Bednarik. "A little muscle pull. Damn, it's hot out there."

They packed ice around the leg, but anger was Bednarik's private antidote for the pain. "Jeez, I called that Brown things I oughta apologize for," said Bednarik in the clubhouse. "Not even my own father could say that to me, though—that I'm an old bum. I'm gonna show that sonofabitch how old No. 60 is."

The chance came quickly. The Eagles had to stop the Browns on the goal stripe. Jimmy Brown came rumbling through the hole, churning high. Bednarik had the open shot, and he hit Brown with every ounce of his anger, lifting him like a sack of sugar. There were 30 seconds left when Bednarik snapped the ball to the field goal kicker, Bobby Walston. Bednarik held the block for the three-count.

"Boot like hell, Cheewah," Bednarik thought.

The wind was in his face, and the posts were 38 yards away, but the kick was good. The Eagles had won, 31-29. Bednarik had made 15 tackles, 11 of them unassisted.

"How d'ya like that Paul Brown?" Bednarik said to Walston as they sat in the clubhouse. "He had a real smirky smile on his face when he left the field."

"Helluva game, Chuck," said Pellegrini.

"Thanks, Gringo," said Bednarik.

He limped off the plane at Philadelphia and skipped the parties. Emma Bednarik had to massage the left thigh until Bednarik could sleep. The long ordeal of Charles Bednarik had begun.

Buck Shaw laughed the next day. "No, I can't expect Bednarik to play 59 minutes the next seven games. Oh, he'd try to do it if I asked.

"But that routine would be too tough for a guy 15 years younger than Chuck."

Bednarik wasn't laughing. He woke up with a numb leg. Emma fixed a dish he loves, called "pig-in-a-bag." He didn't want to eat. In the late afternoon, Bednarik and defensive end Ed Khayat hoisted a ladder and hung storm windows on the big house. Bednarik felt better.

The next two weeks were almost a holiday. The Eagles caught Bobby Layne with his dauber down, and they blew through Pittsburgh, 34-7. Bednarik intercepted a pass to set up a touchdown. He was a linebacker now, as Shaw tried to rest him by using rookie Bill Lapham at center. The next game was with the Redskins, who almost blitzed Van Brocklin loose from his handsome teeth before Dutch pulled it out, 19-13.

After the game, Bednarik threw a wingding. The pros, who won't avoid a little fluid celebrating after a victory, said it was the best party of the year. Chuck had 78 people milling through his paneled den in the basement. Bednarik likes gin-and-tonic, a drink associated with Bermuda shorts and sunny beaches. He likes 'em in the snow, if necessary. Usually the Bednarik limit is two. That night he was in a swinging mood.

"I got a lot of trophies in this room," Chuck said to a few of the bulls at the party. "I want one more."

"Which one, Chuck baby?"

"You know damn well which one," said Bednarik. "The big one. See all those team pictures? I want one of the 1960 Eagles. And under it I want it to say, 'NFL CHAMPIONS.'"

"That's a surprise," said somebody. "I thought you wanted it to say, 'To hell with Paul Brown.'"

Bednarik laughed. It was a good party. But the Giants would be ready in Yankee Stadium the next Sunday. The Giants didn't give a damn about Bednarik's dream or the Eagles' 6-1 record. The Giants would be cruel and crafty—they had not overlooked the way the Redskins had blitzed Van Brocklin flat on his satin britches.

Bednarik could have reached into the grab bag of Manhattan and picked any bauble on this crisp, lively Saturday night. Mary Martin was packing them in with *The Sound of Music*. Tammy Crimes had opened a new musical and Ethel Merman was still blaring through *Gypsy*. The taxis hooted through the canyons to the good East Side restaurants, and the night clubs were jumping. But Bednarik is not a bright lights guy. He was in New York to play the Giants and, as usual, the tigers of tension had their claws in him.

So he stood on a corner of Times Square with his roommate, John Nocera, for two hours, watching the swirl of the mob past the hot dog joints on 42nd Street.

"It's a big town, Nose," said Bednarik, unrecognized by the shoals of milling sightseers.

"Yeah? Well, we'll shake it up tomorrow," said Nocera.

Bednarik grunted. "Huh. Know how long since we've beaten these guys over here, Nose? Not since Jim Trimble's first year, 1952, when we caught 'em 14-10. That's seven in a row here. I think about those things, Nose." Bednarik flipped a cigarette, Bogart-style, and headed for the hotel. Maybe he could sleep a little.

The Eagle blocking pattern for a pass has the center sliding back to form one rim of the passer's cup. The halfbacks swing out for a safety valve pass. The Giants had howling success with this gimmick the first half. They roared through it like pillaging Indians. Bednarik, assigned to be a linebacker only, watched in dismay as center Bill Lapham was knocked into inept confusion by the blitz. The Giants gobbled up Van Brocklin like barracuda hitting a wounded porpoise. They led 10-0 at the half. Goodbye, Dreamsville.

"Okay, Sam, the fun's over," Bednarik said to Sam Huff, the Giant linebacker. "The veterans are taking over."

Huff and Bednarik like each other, and Sam grinned at Bednarik's bravado. He knew the Giants could win if they kept the blitz moving. Bednarik had the plan from line coach Nick Skorich to stop it. No more fancy blocking. The halfbacks would stay tight. Bednarik and the other linemen would form a wall. It worked, and Van Brocklin tied it 10-10.

Now Bednarik, back at his full-time job, caught the jungle flavor and smell of the game. Mel Triplett, the good Giant fullback, came through the hole on a slant. Bednarik bombed him, the ball squirted up like a hunk of wet soap, and Carr took it on the fly for a touchdown. It was 17-10, but the Giants were driving back to tie it. They flipped the ball to Gifford, the one guy who could run all the way for the money.

Gifford, a runner who never made a mistake, made a near-fatal one now. He tried to feint Don Burroughs. He took his eye off Bednarik. Chuck hit him chest-high with every ounce of power, trying to shatter the ball loose. Gifford flopped on the turf, inert as stone. Most of the 63,571 fans would not soon forget the sight of Bednarik, dancing wildly over Gifford's body, shaking his fist in conquest, yelling his triumph.

"We got the ball! We got it!" Bednarik was screaming.

The Giants doctor, bent over Gifford, snapped, "Shut up, you damn gorilla. You've almost killed this man." He said worse things, too, and Bednarik suddenly realized Gifford might indeed be hurt.

"You hit him hard, Chuck," said Huff, level-eyed.

"I got excited, Sam," said Bednarik.

"Pros don't get excited, Chuck," said Huff.

In the locker room, though, Huff shrugged off the smashing tackle. Gifford was in the hospital with a severe concussion, his career ended. "It's a tough business," said Huff. "Chuck hit him clean."

Chuck Conerly, the only pro on the field who had been around as long as Bednarik, was burning, though. "Bednarik's a cheap-shot artist," snarled Conerly. "I told him so, too."

"The Giants will take care of Bednarik next week," said a New York writer walking out of Yankee Stadium. "They're mad as hell. The pros know how to handle a guy like that."

All week the telephone rang in the Abington house. Did Bednarik figure the Giants would gang him in revenge for Gifford? "If they do," Bednarik said, "you'll see the biggest coward in the world. I'll run like hell. Nobody's gonna suck me into a fight to get me out of the game. This one we've gotta win."

He sent Gifford a card of apology and a bowl of fruit. It was only a token, though. Bednarik knew the tackle had been hard—but necessary and legitimate. Bednarik vastly enjoys publicity. He loves flash-bulbs popping and the interviews and the headlines and the kids swarming for autographs. Now he was getting a bad rap coast-to-coast for hurting Gifford. He tried to ignore it, but he didn't know how the Giants would.

Bednarik remembered another old pro, his rookie year, who felled Charlie Trippi and almost crippled him. He remembered the way the Chicago Cardinals waited for this guy until the next game. Then they took turns whacking him with everything, getting 15-yard penalties in bundles. After the game in the runway the old pro was trapped by a half-dozen Cardinals, swinging helmets. Bednarik didn't want this sort of scene with the Giants.

"To hell with it," Bednarik said, "we've got a title to win now. The only Giant who blew his top is Conerly, who's a sour grapes bum with a glorified column in that New York paper."

Bednarik was right. No Giant took a shot at him. They had their opportunities, because before the game, Shaw tapped Chuck on the shoulder pad: "Sorry, Chuck, I'll need you both ways again today." He played almost 60 minutes again, and the Eagles, running as always like Silky Sullivan on his good days, bellowed back on two Van Brocklin touchdowns to win it, 31-23.

"How'd you like to play 60 minutes, Sam?" Bednarik said sweetly to Huff.

"Man," said Huff, "there ain't that much money in the world."

The cops said there were 15,000 people at the airport. The Eagles had taken the Eastern title in St. Louis, and Bednarik peered in astonishment out the DC-6 window at the mob, the TV flood lights, the bands blaring. Most of the Eagles tried a flank movement, sneaking out the front hatch and running for their cars. Not Bednarik. He had waited 11 years for this crowd.

"I promise you," said Bednarik, "no matter who we play, we'll win the world title for Philadelphia."

Immense roar. He might have offered to abolish taxes and give away free booze. Bednarik, beaming over the bow tie, shuffled through the victory pack, shaking hands, scrawling his name on kids' windbreakers.

There were two left now, the Steelers and the Redskins, meaningless games, and Shaw wanted to keep Bednarik out of them. It was like inviting Jackie Leonard to a cocktail party and forbidding him to tell jokes. Bednarik's No. 60 seemed to appear in the midst of every gang tackle.

"It's not luck, it's instinct," marveled Skorich. "You've heard of people being accident prone, Bednarik is tackle prone. If the play's on his side, he'll get a piece of it. Sure, Huff and Les Richter and Joe Schmidt get the publicity. This guy is the best."

Now it was four days before the Green Bay match. On the snow-lined practice field, the seven bulls made seven puffs of blue vapor in the frozen, bruised air. They looked like seven laundry bags in the grey sweat suits.

"Kamikaze!" yelled Bednarik as the bulls rumbled after an imaginary Green Bay punt receiver.

"Kamikaze!" the bulls bellowed in a ragged chorus.

"Kamikaze, baby, kamikaze!"

Later a guy asked Bednarik who started this curious battle yell. "I did," said Bednarik. "We're like those Japanese pilots. This is our last fight and we're not coming back."

A couple of newspaper types were having a glass of grog to fight off the cold later. One shook his head at Bednarik's theatrics.

"Can you imagine Cousy or Mantle or Spahn or Musial coming up with that kamikaze stuff," he said. "On anybody else it would sound absurd. On Bednarik it sounds normal, because he's really the gung-ho type. He plays for the money, but beneath it all, he's still a soph at Penn, getting ready for Notre Dame."

His companion quaffed the glass. "Yeah, I guess that's one reason

I hope Bednarik has one helluva game against Green Bay. He reminds me a little of Archie Moore. Not only the newspaper color. I mean the way Chuck's been beating around for years, playing his guts out, but not getting the championships or the big money or the national acclaim."

"It's like Van Brocklin said," agreed the other. "If he were in New York, they'd build a statue of Bednarik in the centerfield of Yankee Stadium."

"Well, here's to a big one Monday."

"To Monday. . . ."

Now Monday's clock ticked loud as a hammer on a tin roof inside Bednarik. It was 10:30. He walked into the Eagles' clubhouse. The stadium above was warming with pale sunlight and early clots of people. Bednarik had a cup of hot chocolate. Other Eagles drifted in. It was explosively quiet. You could hear shoes plop on the concrete.

"We gotta win this one, you jokers," yelled Bednarik. "My wife's already spent the money."

The tension rippled but it did not break. The Eagles dressed in taut silence. No one laughed when Van Brocklin tried to put his left shoe on his right foot a half-dozen times. Bednarik, who sometimes makes fight talks before Eagle games, was wise enough to stay mute. Shaw walked into the cluttered, narrow room and said that no matter what happened against Green Bay, this has been the proudest year of his life. Shaw, too, knew the money and the pride was out in the field now, and no speeches were needed.

"Let's go kick a few tails," said Bednarik. The Eagles clumped out into the pasty sunshine, following the "60" on the green back. The Star-Spangled Banner floated over the jammed arena, and Bednarik felt the tigers inside, snarling and leaping. They did not subside until he hit the first Packer. He hit him hard.

Bednarik had to work like hell the first 15 minutes. The Packers twice got the ball inside the 25. Jim Taylor, their fine fullback, and Paul Hornung, the gifted halfback, had to be stopped. The Eagles scrambled ahead, 10-6, but Hornung threatened to run them out of the park in the second half. It was fourth down. Tough yardage. Hornung stormed right and cut for a hole. Bednarik crunched a shoulder into him with the mindless violence of a freight train hitting a sports car. Hornung dropped and twisted in terrible pain. Trainers came running.

"Oh, my God," thought Bednarik. "First Gifford, now this."

In the time out, Bednarik turned to one of the Eagles. "I hit him a good shot. There wasn't nothing wrong with that tackle." They had carried Hornung away, finished with a pinched nerve in the shoulder that hurt like a hundred toothaches.

"You hit him damn good, Chuck," said the Eagle.

The Eagles had a 17-13 lead, but the last nine minutes would be frenzied. The Packers looked for the knockout punch, like a tough fighter losing a decision. Bednarik gobbled up a Max McGee fumble, which helped. Then the clock was spinning in chill blue dusk.

Last play. A pass to Taylor. He came rumbling, knocking down Eagles, 17 yards away from the championship.

"I saw guys bounce off him," Bednarik would say later, bringing back the vivid moment. "I saw Baughan hit and bounce, Burroughs hit and bounce. I said, by God, I'm not gonna bounce, I'm gonna catch him in a bearhug and hold him. I wrestled him down and I held him tight, watching the clock run. Then I said, 'Okay, Taylor, get up. This is one game that's over.'"

Bednarik had made 11 tackles and played 58 minutes and been incredibly good for a shaky antique. He wanted one more gift now: the white Corvette a sports magazine bequeaths to the game's outstanding player. The writers voted for Van Brocklin, though. Somebody told Bednarik.

"Quarterbacks," he said with a shrug. There was no malice. Quarterbacks are part of the lineman's world, like flying elbows and cracked teeth.

He had the picture he wanted for the den now: the three tiers of hard-jawed faces, 37 guys in the green blazers, Bednarik looming over them all in a candy-striped tie, with the legend: "1960

Eagles—World Champions." He had the fame that only a championship can harvest in American sports. He could laugh at Paul Brown for sneering at his age, and he could forget the years he played savage football while other linebackers on winning teams got the acclaim.

One ingredient was left for Bednarik's apple-pie world: the money.

"I've never given you a hard time about the salary," Chuck said, sitting again in Vince McNally's office at Locust and 12th Streets. "You've always had the contract ready and boom-boom I signed."

"True, Chuck," said McNally, beginning to chain smoke, knowing what was coming. "We wanted to pay you more but—"

"I know. You weren't drawing people and couldn't pay big salaries. Only now it's different. You drew 350,000 people. You made money. I played my heart out for you. Nobody else in the league went 60 minutes."

"You did a wonderful job," said McNally. "What's on your mind?"

"This," said Bednarik. It was his time to scribble on the envelope. The figure was close to a $6,000 raise. McNally began to blow smoke in furious clouds. It was a modest request compared to paychecks of Mantle, Mays, or Spahn, but pro football doesn't make millionaires of its linemen.

"That's a quarterback's salary," said McNally.

"I'm your quarterback on defense," said Bednarik, stung in his lineman's pride. "Look, Vince, I think I can play another year, either as center or linebacker, not both. But maybe I'm wrong. Maybe I'm too old. Maybe I ought to hang them up."

"Mary," yelled McNally to his secretary, "type me up a contract for Charles Bednarik."

Now he had the respect and the glory and the money, but one moment from the big season stuck in his craw: the tackle that finished Frank Gifford. No one had ever called Bednarik an easy-going football player, but no one had called him a dirty one either. He had seen other bulls get the tag "hatchet man" for banging a star such as Gifford. Bednarik is a rough, swaggering guy, full of noisy gusto about his trade, but he did not like the idea of playing his last years with a gunman's reputation.

On a summer day, Gifford called. He wanted to do an interview for his New York radio show. He congratulated Bednarik on his signing. It was the first time Bednarik had heard from the Giant back since he smashed him to earth in November.

"Before we go on the air, Chuck," Gifford said, "I want to tell you something. I've never resented the way you hit me. It was a good, clean tackle. The whole thing was my fault for not seeing you coming. I'll tell the world that. You've always been tough but you're clean, buddy."

Bednarik hung up the phone, immensely happy. He sat down in the backyard, the newest and fifth Bednarik daughter gurgling in his tattooed arms. The other girls, Charlene, Donna, Pam, and Carol, skittered and tumbled on the shady lawn.

"It took a real pro to say what Giff did," Bednarik said. "Did you ever hit a golf ball just right, so it just clicked and shot 250 yards? That's the way the Gifford tackle was. It felt like a feather, I hit him with such lucky timing. Not lucky for Giff, though."

"Did you ever have a guy you really wanted to hurt, Chuck? A guy you really hated?"

Bednarik bounced Jacqueline Bednarik softly, thinking. You could almost see his mind shifting from this tranquil yard, the cries of the girls like bright pennants on the muted air, to the cursing, thudding wars of the bulls on a hundred other afternoons.

"Yeah, you get in those situations," he said slowly. "Guys pop you, and you say, 'Damn you, I'll get you for that.' But you don't get the chance for a game or two, and then you've got a feud. Lou Creekmur with the Lions, he was a bad guy, but I never got a shot at him. Don Colo was another I missed. Oh, I skip those team riots if I can. We had two big, bloody things against the 49ers in San Francisco, but I just watched. What's the percentage? I've had to fight some guys, though—and one I remember good was Chuck Noll."

He swung the baby gently against his chest, remembering. Noll was a 220-pound guard for the Browns. On a kickoff he had met Bednarik with an uppercut that had Chuck seeing galaxies of shooting stars. "You'll get yours, buddy!" said Bednarik. He nursed his anger a year, waiting for the moment. It came at Philadelphia in a game the Eagles were losing badly to Cleveland.

"Hey, Frank," Bednarik said to his roommate, Frank Wydo, "let's get that No. 65."

On the kickoff, Wydo hit Noll high and Bednarik creamed him low. Noll came up frothing. "I'll come to the locker room after the game and kill you, Bednarik," he screamed.

"Don't bother," said Chuck. "I'll meet you right here."

Bednarik forgot the incident. The game ended on that precise spot of turf, though. Noll came running, eyes full of fire, yanking off his helmet as he got in firing range.

"That was a mistake, taking off the helmet," said Bednarik. "I dropped him with one shot to the jaw."

The fight had more spectators in Cleveland than some championship matches, because the TV cameras had closed in on the scene. The cameras also caught the Browns helping Noll stagger away—and Bednarik, enraged now, chasing him to the dugout. Bednarik dropped him again with a hook. The Lake Erie TV watchers were so irate that Bednarik had to stay in his hotel room on the Eagles' next visit. Commissioner Bert Bell fined him $50 and demanded he apologize.

"Hey, this thing between me and you has been going on two years," Bednarik said to Noll during a pre-game warmup. "Let's forget it."

Noll put his chin a half-inch from Bednarik's chin.

"—— you," he said.

Bednarik shrugged and walked away. Noll grabbed his shoulder and spun him. He stuck out a hand. "Okay," he said, "let's start from scratch, No. 60."

"Wydo hit me like that once," Chuck laughed. "He was later my best buddy and roomie on the Eagles. But this was when he was a Steeler rookie. He clipped me a good shot on the jaw. I asked him what the hell that was for. 'For hitting me in the Penn-Cornell game,' he said. I told him I didn't even know he was on the Cornell squad. We still laugh about it.

"The rookies are the worst, though," said Chuck. "You get to recognize the old cheap-shot artists. You watch 'em close. But the exhibitions are murder, because every green kid from Slippery Rock Tech wants to get a quick reputation belting you on your pants."

In the dying light, we worked on a pitcher of ice tea. Bednarik talked of each Eagle team, even the bad ones, with tremendous pride. "He may not remember his own phone number," said Emma, "but I don't think he's ever forgotten an Eagle score, or a touchdown, or a play. That goes for Penn, too."

Over the dozen years, the small failures nag at his mind as well as the larger triumphs. He was fined $50 once for dogging it on a touchdown play and it still rankles.

"We're playing the Steelers and Lynn Chadnois comes around end and Fran Rogell brushes me out. Trimble yells, 'You quit, Bednarik—that'll cost you $50.' I yelled back, 'What about those ten other guys?' I liked Jim but he was going through a rough season. He fined some other guys that day and the ball club turned against him. I never quit."

Bednarik does not hide his job and his booming pride in the career he has carved out of muscle and pain. We walked slowly around the walls of the basement den, swarming with trophies and photos. Bednarik belting a Navy halfback for Penn. Bednarik at an All-America party. Bednarik at a Penn banquet. (The ends gave him a trophy that year for making all of their tackles.)

Bednarik and the crew of the Liberator bomber in which he flew over Europe. ("Sometimes one engine would be shot out, once the tires were blown off, always there seemed to be 100 or 200 flak holes—Lord, we were lucky.") Bednarik wearing a huge cigar and a huge grin after beating the Giants.

"Where do you think you'd be now if it wasn't for football, Chuck?" I asked him.

"I dunno. Working in the steel mill like my dad did, I guess. If the war hadn't come along, I wouldn't have gone to college. I always hung around with older guys in Bethlehem and I was in a hurry to get a job and make some pocket money. John Butler suggested I try to get in Penn. I remember the day I walked into the dining room and George Munger saw me—I was 210 pounds, 6-3, mature compared to those college kids—and Munger's eyes popped. I had to carry mail on the campus, a dollar an hour, though, until I became eligible."

We walked up the stairs and into the quiet dusk.

"If it hadn't been football, though, I think I would have had a good crack at baseball," said Bednarik. "That's what I really regret. In 1952 I worked out before every game with the A's. I'd hit those good pitchers—Shantz and Kellner and Coleman. I got to be a close pal of Gus Zernial and we'd hit homers in batting practice for dimes. I didn't lose money.

"Jimmy Dykes and Art Ehlers—he was the general manager—liked me, I knew. One Sunday night Ehlers called me. They needed a catcher at Ottawa. Hell, yes, I'd go. That was triple-A, and just a step to the majors. But I called McNally and he said no. 'You're the heart of our defense,' he said, 'and I'm not going to let you break a leg in a baseball game.' I'm sorry I never had the chance to prove I could catch in the majors."

Bednarik stood on the front lawn and looked up at the house towering in the circle of trees. Dogwood and holly and ferns lined the walk.

It was a long way from the steel mill, a long way from the profane, sweaty crash of a hundred battles with the bulls in the big arenas.

"Football gave me all this," said Bednarik, standing in the velvet dusk. "I gave everything I had to football, though, and I'm not so old that I haven't got some more to give."

At the moment on the cool suburban street, the tigers inside Chuck Bednarik were still, resting, waiting. The tigers would get their chance.

II

Voices From the Field

JOHN MADDEN
WITH DAVE ANDERSON

"Those Raider 'Renegades'"

from *Hey, Wait a Minute (I Wrote a Book!)*

It's easy to forget that John Madden, bombastic color commentator and devoted bus rider, was, first, one of the NFL's most respected coaches. In 1976, he steered the Oakland Raiders to victory in Super Bowl XI. Madden also is a successful author who teamed with NEW YORK TIMES *sports columnist Dave Anderson to write three popular books. The following excerpt is from Madden's first,* HEY, WAIT A MINUTE (I WROTE A BOOK!). *It profiles the group of rowdies and oddballs who gave the Raiders their storied reputation.*

BEFORE ANY NFL COACH makes a trade, he usually checks around with other coaches who know the player involved, especially if he's a player with a past. One day late in our 1976 training camp, George Allen, then coaching the Washington Redskins, phoned me about John Matuszak, a big defensive end then with the Kansas City Chiefs.

"You played against him twice last year," George said. "Is he worth getting?"

"I wouldn't take him, George," I said. "I just don't think he'll help your team."

I'm sure George thought later that I was setting him up—hoping he would ignore "Tooz" so that the Raiders could get him. Or maybe he thought then that I was trying to con him. Whatever, the Redskins traded a 1977 eighth-round choice and a 1978 seventh-round choice to the Chiefs for Tooz, whose value had deteriorated after he had been the very first choice in the 1973 draft. But only a couple of weeks into the 1976 season, George released him.

By then, my thinking on Tooz had changed. We had planned to continue using our 4-3 defense that year—four defensive linemen and three linebackers. But injuries had decimated us. Two of our defensive ends, Tony Cline and Horace Jones, and a defensive tackle, Art Thoms, suddenly were out for the season.

Out of necessity, we had to switch to a 3-4 defense. Willie Hall now was our fourth linebacker. But we still needed help at defensive end.

In a 3-4 defense, I've always believed that you need three defensive-tackle types, big guys who can hold their ground, who won't allow themselves to be moved by the offensive push. And that season there weren't many defensive linemen bigger than big Tooz, at 6'7" and 270 pounds the prototype of the bigger, heavier defensive ends you see now.

"What about Matuszak?" Al Davis asked.

"Yeah," I said, "he's worth a shot."

When he arrived, I wasn't about to talk to Tooz about his past. In his travels, every coach and every amateur psychologist had lectured him. He was more experienced at hearing that speech than I was at giving it. He had a reputation as a disruptive influence, but I hadn't phoned George Allen or the coaches in Kansas City and Houston for his report card. Whatever he did that they got rid of him for, if he did it with us, he was gone, too. If you know too much about a guy, you tend to pre-judge him, to hold his past against him. I wasn't a psychiatrist or a psychologist. I was a football coach. If you play football for me, good. If you screw up, goodbye.

"I've got three rules," I told him. "Be on time, pay attention, and play like hell when it's time to."

Those rules were for all my players—not just the "renegades," as people liked to call some of them. Yes, the Raiders took a few players that other teams had given up on—not that Al and I thought we had a magic formula to reform them. Our reasoning was, when a player's back is against the wall, when he realizes that no other team wants him, when he knows that the Raiders will be his last stop, that's when he should realize that if he doesn't shape up, his career will be over. We also never gave up much, if anything, to get that type of player. Other teams in every sport make the mistake of trading good players or high draft choices for somebody who has been a problem. But for us, it was always a no-lose situation. If the guy didn't work out, we hadn't lost any important players or draft choices. But some of our renegades really worked out, like Matuszak, who became the left defensive end on our Super Bowl XI team.

I think the only harsh words I ever had with Tooz developed the week after he joined us. We were practicing in the Houston Astrodome on Saturday for our game there the next day.

I was a little edgy. Kenny Stabler was hurt and we had cut George Blanda in training camp. My quarterback suddenly was Mike Rae, who had played in Canada for three years but was a rookie with us. The day before the game I always believed in a long practice. Not hard, but long. I wanted to go through every situation. I wanted my players to be thinking football as long as possible. And having to start Mike Rae meant that we really had to go over everything in the game plan. Finally, we were running short-yardage plays down near the other team's goal line, which we usually did at the end of Saturday's practice. After a play down there, Tooz looked around at everybody.

"All right," he said, "let's make this last one a good one."

This *last* one. I thought I was the coach. I thought I decided which play would be the last one. I ran over and started screaming at him.

"I'll tell you when the *last* one is," I yelled. "*I'll* tell you, *you* don't tell me."

In the short time Tooz had been with us, he had never seen me explode. As big as he is, he jumped back like he thought I was crazy—which I was, especially with Stabler out. I don't remember how many more plays we ran after that, but it was more than I had originally planned. Quite a few more. The next day, Mike Rae threw two touchdown passes, just enough for us to win, 14-13.

Tooz fit in quickly at left end, next to Dave Rowe at nose tackle and Otis Sistrunk at right end. Like with any new player, I just wanted Tooz to get in the circle with the other players, not try to be a leader. He got in the circle. He was on time, he paid attention, he played like hell when it was time to. And he never again tried to decide which would be the last play in practice.

Otis Sistrunk had arrived in 1972 from the Rams, but beyond that we never had much of a line on him. You know how all NFL players are listed with their names, their position, and their college. Trunk's college was the same as the hair on his head—none. With his shaved head, I had no idea how old he was. For all I knew, he could have been anywhere from twenty-five to forty when we got him. He was a good guy, happy-go-lucky, a fun guy. He always had an answer whenever anybody tried to figure out his age.

"When did you play high school ball?" I once asked him.

"I worked in a factory in high school, coach," he said.

Try to figure that out. But he could play. When we needed a defensive tackle in 1972, I phoned Tommy Prothro, then the Rams' coach. He had just signed Phil Olsen, the younger brother of Merlin Olsen, so we thought the Rams would have to cut one of their defensive tackles.

"That's right, I'll have an extra one," Tommy told me. "Send somebody down to look at them, and tell me who you want."

Ron Wolf went down to watch the Rams practice in training camp. That night, he phoned and told me that one of the best defensive tackles there was Otis Sistrunk, but he doubted the Rams would trade him. I figured, hey, take a shot. I phoned Tommy.

"How about that, what's his name, Treetrunk?" I said.

"Sistrunk," he said. "Yeah, we'll let you have him."

We got "Trunk" and a fifth-round draft choice in a trade for our fourth-round choice. He played through the 1979 season, but by then he had an unofficial college. In his first Monday night game as a TV analyst, Alex Karras looked at his monitor showing Trunk on the sideline, the steam rising from his shaved head.

"He's from the University of Mars," Alex said.

Bob Brown, another ex-Rams player and known as The Boomer, joined us in a 1971 trade for Kent McCloughan and Harry Schuh after he told the Rams he deserved as much money as Roman Gabriel, their quarterback. Earlier he had been traded by the Eagles when he objected to the firing of Joe Kuharich as general manager.

In his three seasons with us, I never had any trouble with The Boomer—but one of our goal posts did.

When he and the Raiders' veterans reported to training camp that year, we had two days of meetings before any formal practice. But when the afternoon meeting ended that first day, the veterans and the rookies worked out on their own, running around and throwing the ball. His first day, The Boomer, 6'4" and 280, emerged from the locker room in his black jersey and marched across the field toward the wooden goal posts at the other end. He stopped at one of the goal posts, got down in his three-point stance, put his right foot back for leverage, then put a forearm smash on the goalpost. The goalpost swayed, then toppled backward, the crossbar tipping down. The Boomer had knocked down a goal post.

Without a word, he got up and strode back toward his awed teammates. The Boomer had arrived. With a boom.

To strangers, he would introduce himself as Robert Stanford Brown, professional right tackle. But around the team, he just wanted to be called The Boomer. He even called himself that.

"Coach," he told me the day he reported, "The Boomer is here."

Over his career, The Boomer was All-Pro eight times—six times with the Eagles and the Rams, twice with us. Psychologists say that, by nature, offensive linemen are passive people whereas defensive linemen are aggressive. But in personality, The Boomer was more like a defensive tackle. After he arrived, he imposed his personality on some of our best offensive linemen—Art Shell, Gene Upshaw, George Buehler.

"Attack your man, don't let him attack you," he told them. "Always attack."

The Boomer attacked pass rushers the same way he attacked that wooden goal post. He had the biggest, strongest arms I've ever seen. He didn't just try to block a pass rusher, he tried to punch a pass rusher, preferably in the solar plexus where there's no protective equipment. After one of those punches, the guy he was blocking puked right there on the field. Even in practice, The Boomer didn't want to be beaten. When he was with the Rams, he had some tremendous battles with Deacon Jones, their Hall of Fame defensive end, on the practice field. In those years, the rules permitted a pass rusher to head slap a pass blocker, whack him across the helmet. I don't know if Deacon invented the head slap, but he popularized it. Except that The Boomer didn't like it.

"Don't do it anymore," The Boomer told him time after time. "I'm warning you, don't do it anymore."

Deacon just laughed. Until the day he swatted The Boomer and realized his left hand was impaled on The Boomer's helmet. On each side of a helmet, a small padded screw holds the inner cushion. The Boomer had replaced one of these screws with a longer screw that had been sharpened like an ice pick. As soon as Deacon slapped The Boomer's helmet, his hand was stuck on that sharpened screw. Howling, he stared at his bloody hand.

"What the hell's that on your helmet?" Deacon screamed.

"I warned you not to do it anymore," The Boomer said.

Deacon never did it anymore, at least not to The Boomer in practice. To this day, Deacon has a big scar in the middle of his left hand. I know nobody slapped The Boomer around in our practices. He was not only one of the toughest players I've ever known, but also one of the smartest. Not just football-smart either. As an All-America guard at Nebraska, he earned a bachelor of science degree in biology. Even before he joined the Eagles as their first-round draft choice, he enrolled at the University of Pennsylvania and later got a master's degree in education administration.

Bob Brown was nobody's fool, and nobody to fool with. He has settled in Oakland, so I see him every so often. He still works out and lifts weights every day. He's still The Boomer.

The season we won Super Bowl XI, we picked up Carl Garrett from the Jets for a tenth-round draft choice. Not much of a price for a running back who rushed for 220 yards on only 48 carries, an excellent 4.6 average. Playing behind Clarence Davis in the Super Bowl, he had a 13-yard run to the Vikings' 13 that led to our first touchdown. When we got him, I remembered I had tried to scout him on a spring trip in 1968 when he was at New Mexico Highlands. The day I got there, I went to practice to see him.

"Which one is Garrett?" I asked.

"He's not here," somebody said.

"What's wrong? Is he injured?"

"No, he doesn't like spring practice. He only shows up if he feels like it."

"Oh," I said. "One of those."

But in the fall he obviously felt like playing. He rushed for 3,862 yards in three seasons there. As the Patriots' third-round choice in 1969, he was voted the AFL's rookie of the year over O.J. Simpson, the very first choice that year as the Heisman Trophy winner. Four years later Carl was traded to the Bears for a first-round choice, then he drifted to the Jets in 1975 for Mike Adamle and a fourth-round choice.

But when we got him, we didn't care why he had been traded so often. In those years some teams might trade a player if he didn't wear a necktie on a trip. No matter what it was, Carl started fresh with us. And he gave us a big year.

As good as he was, though, Carl Garrett was never really a Raider to the other veterans. That's true of anybody who joins your team after he's been with a few other teams.

The season we won Super Bowl XI, we also had Ted Kwalick,

once an All-Pro tight end with the 49ers, who had jumped to the World Football League before we signed him as Dave Casper's backup. He hung out with our players. That wasn't the problem. But he had been such a good player with the 49ers and now he wasn't really that good for us. If you watched him closely, you saw he was still a 49ers' tight end. Our tight end had to be a really good blocker; he wasn't a good blocker. Our tight end had to run disciplined square-out and comeback pass-patterns; he had always been more of a freelance pass receiver.

It works the other way, too. As great a tight end as Dave Casper was with the Raiders, after he was traded to the Oilers in 1980, he has never been that good again. To me, he was a Raiders' tight end playing for Houston, just as Ted Kwalick had been a 49ers' tight end playing for Oakland.

Young players from other teams sometimes fit in quickly. Daryle Lamonica hadn't played much in Buffalo, he hadn't established himself as a Bills' player, so he was able to be a Raider almost immediately. For his first five seasons, Ted Hendricks had been with the Colts and the Packers, so it took him a little more time before he felt like a Raider, before the other players accepted him as a Raider.

Warren Wells, a wide receiver who had too short and too sad a career, was another young player who became a Raider quickly after having bounced around. I had several great players, but Warren may have been the most talented of them all. He could run like a deer. He could catch the ball. He could block. He could tackle on special teams. And he was my son Mike's favorite player. Mike was just a little kid when Warren used to give him gum and talk to him. I have a picture of Mike sitting on Warren's lap. And wherever Mike has played football, he has always worn Warren's number, eighty-one, if it was available. One day after Mike had gotten to know Warren, a friend of ours who didn't know Warren asked Mike about him.

"Is he white or black?" our friend said.

Mike thought and said, "I don't know."

Warren had been with the Lions in 1964 before spending two

years in Alaska in the army. After his discharge, the Lions cut him and the Chiefs were looking at him at training camp in 1967 when we spotted him while watching a film of an exhibition game. At the time Otis Taylor was the Chiefs' best wide receiver. We were watching this film when one of the Chiefs' wide receivers made a big play.

"Otis Taylor," I said, "is really tough."

"He sure is," Ron Wolf, our personnel director, said. "Hey, that's not Taylor, that's not eighty-nine."

"Who is it then?"

Checking the Chiefs' roster, we found out that Warren Wells had made that catch. Several days later Al Davis got a phone call from Lloyd Wells, a scout for the Chiefs who was not related to Warren but who had known him at Texas Southern.

"Lloyd told me the Chiefs are going to cut that kid you saw on film," Al told the coaches. "I think we'll sign him for the special teams and work with him as a receiver."

As great a wide receiver as he turned out to be, Warren was also the best special-teams player I ever had. Covering kickoffs or punts, he had a way of snaking through to make the tackle. Nobody could block him. His instincts were amazing. And he was even better as a receiver. Of the 13 passes he caught as a rookie, 6 were for touchdowns. The next year, he caught 53 passes for 1,137 yards and 11 touchdowns; in 1969, he caught 47 for 1,260 yards (an incredible 26.8-yard average) and 14 touchdowns before a shoulder injury knocked him out of the playoffs; in 1970 he caught 43 passes for 935 yards and 11 touchdowns.

One of those 1970 touchdowns came on the most amazing catch I've ever seen. We were playing the Jets at Shea Stadium, trailing 13-7, with 28 seconds left when we got the ball at our own 30-yard line. On first down, Warren drew a pass-interference penalty against Earlie Thomas, the cornerback who was covering him. Now we were on the Jets' 33 with 22 seconds.

After two incompletions, only eight seconds were on the clock. Lamonica dropped back and threw a pass into the left corner of the end zone where Warren was surrounded by Thomas and W. K. Hicks, a Jets' safety. From where I was standing along the sideline, I saw the ball pop up in the air as if Warren had bobbled it. Next thing I knew, Warren had caught it for a touchdown with :01 showing on the clock. George Blanda kicked the extra point, and we won, 14-13.

On our game film the next day, it still looked as if Warren had bobbled the ball. The next spring when we got our Raiders highlight film that NFL Films produced, we saw that one of their cameramen had a shot that showed Warren reaching between the two Jets, tipping the ball away from them, and then catching it as he fell to the ground. Damndest catch I've ever seen.

But in 1971 he didn't play. He would never play again. Back in 1969 he had pleaded guilty in Oakland to a charge of attempted rape. He was put on three years' probation, which required him to stay out of bars. Warren couldn't drink. Not that he drank a lot. But after one drink, some of my players told me, Warren was a different person. He had several other problems with the police—drunken driving, carrying a concealed weapon. Then shortly before he was to report to training camp in 1971, he was stabbed by a woman in Beaumont, Texas, his hometown. In a bar. That revoked his probation. He did 10 months in confinement, some of it in state prisons, before a judge ordered him to a Synanon commune at Santa Monica in what had once been an expensive hotel. Some of the inmates were living there with their wives and kids, but Warren was alone. Warren was always alone. His marriage had broken up. He had nobody.

"I'm making the best of it," he told me when I visited him. "I'll be ready for training camp."

But when he arrived at training camp in 1972, he was a totally different athlete. He was running in slow motion. At first I thought he was just taking it easy to avoid pulling a muscle. But as the exhibition games approached, I decided that he had to speed up. I wanted him to start showing me the Warren Wells that I had to see, the Warren Wells who always had thrived on great one-on-one duels with Willie Brown in practice.

"It's time," I told him, "to kick it into high gear. Let's see you really run."

Warren nodded and lined up for a deep post pattern. But when he took off, he was still running in slow motion. On his way back, I walked over to him again.

"That's not your high gear," I said.

"Yeah," he said. "I was really moving."

Whatever had happened to him in that year off, Warren was running as fast as he could, but it was nowhere near fast enough. I had to cut him, and it was as tough a cut as I've ever made. I think I worried about it more than he did. The day I told him, he didn't seem to mind.

"That's all right, coach," he said. "You gave me my shot."

I don't know why or how, but Warren had changed in that year off. Physically, his whole system had slowed down. Mentally, he was placid, passive. He had lost his drive, lost his desire. And his problems had just begun. In 1976, in Beaumont, he was arrested for attempted robbery of a woman outside a Houston supermarket. He later was sentenced to three years at Huntsville, a maximum-security prison. He was still there when Al Davis organized a Raiders' alumni reunion. As the Raiders' director of special projects, I was in charge of contacting all our former players.

"I know Warren's in jail," Al said, "but I want him here. Tell those prison people the Raiders will pay all the expenses for Warren and as many guards as they want to send with him."

But the Huntsville warden wouldn't let Warren leave. The last I heard, he was in Houston, trying to make a go of his life. I've always thought that his problem in Oakland was being single. After practice, a single player is on his own. He has no wife and kids to go home to, only an empty apartment or hotel room. So a single player tends to go to bars, stay out late, not eat right, not get enough sleep.

"If you've got a nice girl, get married," I used to tell my single players. "Buy a house, get a station wagon, a dog, and a lawn mower."

When they see me, confirmed bachelors like Clarence Davis,

George Atkinson, and Tom Keating still laugh about that little speech. But they were able to handle being single. Warren wasn't. Even when Warren tried to do the right thing, it backfired.

"You can't play this game forever," I once told him. "If you build a good reputation, you'll have an opportunity to do something solid with your life. Get involved with the community."

Not long after that Warren visited some kids at a local hospital. When he told me one little kid in particular had really enjoyed seeing him, I thought of how Warren was my son Mike's favorite player. I thought Warren had really found something to do with his spare time, especially when he showed me a big get-well card he had bought for the kid at the hospital.

"I'm going to get all the players to autograph it," he said. "He'll love it."

In the locker room that day, Warren handed the card to some of the players and asked them to write something nice on it for the little kid who was in the hospital. Our players were always autographing cards like that. But some of them couldn't believe Warren had gone to see a little kid in a hospital.

"This isn't for some kid," I heard one of the players say. "This must be for some chick Warren is trying to impress."

I didn't think anything of it at the time but a few minutes later I happened to be standing near Warren when the card made its way back to him. Instead of wishing the kid a quick recovery, some of the players had written obscene phrases on the card. As soon as Warren read what was on the card, he tore it up. I can still see the pieces of that card falling to the floor.

As far as I know, Warren never went back to see that little kid in the hospital.

JOE NAMATH
WITH DICK SCHAAP

"Who Did They Think They Were Messing With—the Rams?"

from *I Can't Wait Until Tomorrow 'Cause I Get Better Looking Every Day*

One of the most memorable upsets in NFL history, Super Bowl III, in which the New York Jets defeated the Baltimore Colts 16-7, was, in Joe Namath's estimation, no upset at all. In this chapter from Namath's brash 1969 autobiography, I CAN'T WAIT UNTIL TOMORROW 'CAUSE I GET BETTER LOOKING EVERY DAY, *written with Dick Schaap, Namath recalls his good-natured confidence as the big game approached. Schaap has collaborated on a number of well-known sports books, including* BO KNOWS *and* INSTANT REPLAY.

THE DAY AFTER WE BEAT the Oakland Raiders for the 1968 American Football League championship, one of my friends came running up to me. "Hey, Joe," he said. "You hear the spread for the Super Bowl game?"

"No," I said. "What's the spread?"

"Seventeen points," he said. "Seventeen mother points."

"Hell," I said. "That's crazy. We should only be favored by nine or ten."

I wasn't serious, of course. I knew that Baltimore was going to be favored over us. But when I heard that they were favored by seventeen points, I couldn't believe it. I couldn't believe anybody would be dumb enough to give us seventeen points.

Sure, I knew the Baltimore Colts had a great team. I knew some people were saying they had the greatest team in the history of professional football. They'd only lost two games in two years, so they had to be pretty damn good. But I knew we had a great team, too. We were the New York Jets, man, and you just couldn't give the New York Jets seventeen points. Who'd they think the Colts were going to be playing—the Los Angeles Rams or the Cleveland Browns or one of those teams?

Back in the middle of the season, when it began to look as though we had a good shot at the American Football League title, I started thinking a little about playing against Baltimore. I was really looking forward to it; it was like a dream game to me. The Colts had always been my favorite team before I began playing pro ball myself, and Johnny Unitas had been my favorite player. I used to think Johnny was the best quarterback of all time. I still rate him one of the top two.

I didn't get much time to think about the Colts during the year because I had to be thinking more about the Oakland Raiders and the Kansas City Chiefs. We were pretty sure we'd end up playing either the Raiders or the Chiefs in the American Football League championship game, and I wasn't looking beyond that game. I didn't have any strong opinion about exactly how good the Colts were. I don't judge a team until I've watched their game movies, until I've studied what they can do and what they can't do. I don't just believe what somebody writes in the newspapers. I've met a few sportwriters who can't read without moving their lips.

For a few days after the Oakland game, while sportswriters all over the country were telling everybody how bad Baltimore was going to beat us, I just relaxed and enjoyed the feeling of being a part of the champions of the American Football League. The day after New Year's, we flew to Fort Lauderdale to start getting ready for the

Super Bowl. When I was a teenager, I thought about joining the Air Force—it looked like one good way for me to stay out of the Pennsylvania steel mills—and becoming a pilot. I still think I'd like to learn how to fly, but I don't enjoy commercial planes. I don't enjoy them at all. On the way down to Florida, I managed to calm my nerves with a few Johnnie Walker tranquilizers.

From the airport, we drove over to the Galt Ocean Mile, the same hotel the Green Bay Packers had stayed in the year before, and Jim Hudson and I checked into our room, the Governor's Suite, the same room Vince Lombardi, the Green Bay coach, had lived in the year before. I think Lombardi's a helluva coach, and he's always said nice things about me, but I'm not sure he would have approved of everything I did in his old room the week before the Super Bowl.

All year, wherever the Jets went, Hudson and I took a suite. Just so the club wouldn't go broke, we shared the difference in price between a regular double room and a suite. I actually need a suite, because I get a lot of visitors, people who want to come up and talk about football and things like that—you'd be surprised how many girls there are who like to talk football in my hotel room—and I don't like to disturb Hudson. It's good having Jim around, though, because he's a married man, and a lot of girls wouldn't feel safe in a hotel room with just a bachelor. As long as I've got Jim around as a chaperone, all the girls feel safe.

The very first morning in Fort Lauderdale, I had a couple of visitors, but they didn't want to come up to my room, and they didn't want to talk football. They said they were law enforcement officials. On our last trip to Miami, to play the Dolphins, some distinguished citizen had threatened to kill me. (Later, when all those stories were going around that I was the new headman of the Cosa Nostra—hell, I'm not even eligible; I just look Italian—this gentleman was rumored to be one of my closest friends. I don't think that's a very nice way to show friendship.) I lived through that previous trip, and the two visitors said they hoped I'd do just as well on this one. "A routine checkup," one of the guys told me. He was very happy about the particular room I'd picked. He said that, because of the position of my balcony, anybody who wanted to shoot me would have to fire from a wide-open spot on the beach behind the hotel. "There's nothing to worry about," said the investigator. "If he shoots you, he can't possibly get away." That really made me feel a lot better.

I've got to admit that I'm not one of the biggest fans of the law enforcement agencies these days. I mean, I don't mind them tapping my phones. I don't even mind them playing the tapes for every tourist who walks into their offices. I just wish to hell that they'd pay their share of the phone bill. That's only fair.

It wasn't nice of the law enforcement people to send complete strangers to talk to me in Fort Lauderdale. The least they could've done was send the guys who'd been tailing me during the season. I'm pretty sure they started keeping me company right after we lost a couple of games to Buffalo and Denver. It was nothing personal, but, as I mentioned earlier, I had five passes intercepted in each of those games, and the D.A. or the C.I.A. or somebody like that got a little curious. Nothing serious. They just checked all my bank deposits. I don't blame them, I guess. I know that some people actually do bet on professional football games. Guys kid me now and then: "C'mon, Joe, you want to make fifty thousand dollars this weekend?" and I kid them right back, "Who do I have to kill?" and they just laugh. They're only fooling around, but some people just don't have any sense of humor.

Not too long after the Denver game, Ray Abruzzese, my roommate, and I began to get the feeling that we were being trailed and that our phone in our apartment was being tapped. Ray, who used to play for the Jets, thought maybe the phone was being tapped by an irate husband, but I told him it probably wasn't that serious, probably just the C.I.A. We were both pretty amused, but we stopped cracking funny jokes on the phone about point spreads.

Then I had to go out of town for a road game. We were taking a ridiculously early chartered flight, about ten o'clock in the morning, and Ray and I slept through the alarm. We didn't wake up till about nine thirty. We got dressed quick and I just grabbed a toothbrush, figuring I'd pick up some clothes out of town, and Ray started driving me to the airport. I kept hoping that the plane had taken off. I knew I'd get fined for missing the flight, but I was more worried about keeping everybody waiting. I knew I could catch a later plane.

We were about twenty minutes from the airport when, suddenly, Ray started cursing like crazy. "Why didn't that mother wake us up?" Ray said.

"Who you talking about?" I said.

"That mother that's following us," Ray said, nodding at the rear-view mirror. "Shit, he knew what time we had to be at the airport, the bastard. Why didn't he call us up? Why didn't he wake us?" Ray was really mad at the guy. He went down at least a notch or two in Ray's estimation that day.

When I wasn't busy talking to the law that first morning in Fort Lauderdale, I was down in the Imperial Room of the Galt Ocean Mile attending a team meeting and getting my first look at the Baltimore movies. Like always, I only watched their defensive team, the guys I'd be facing, and, I'll tell you, I enjoyed that show as much as a good Lee Marvin movie. I saw what the Colts could do and what they couldn't do, and I liked what I saw. Some people were saying that the Jets'd be scared of the Colt defense. Scared, hell—the only thing that scared me was that they might change their defense.

What I liked best was the Baltimore safety blitz. Lots of times, just before the snap or on the snap, they moved their two safeties, Rick Volk and Jerry Logan, up to fill in the gaps between the linebackers. Sometimes, one safety would blitz—shoot through and try to get the quarterback—and, sometimes, the other one would blitz. No matter who blitzed, they had to leave part of the middle open. I knew I could hit my wide receivers slanting in. (Of course, I knew I was going to get hit, too. You get hit almost every time on those blitzes—and I don't enjoy getting hit—but it's worth it to have those receivers open.)

The more I saw of the Baltimore movies, the better I felt. Cleveland and Minnesota and Los Angeles were just plain dumb against the blitz. The Browns kept trying to run through the packed Baltimore line. The Rams used some quick sideline patterns that didn't disrupt the blitz at all. The Vikings didn't do a damn thing to throw the Baltimore defense off balance; as far as I could tell, they never varied their count, never took a real long count or a real quick count to break the rhythm of the Colts. I'd been telling people all year that the American Football League had caught up to the National Football League and people kept telling me I was wrong. Well, I was wrong. We'd already passed them in a lot of things.

I just prayed that the Colts would blitz us. If they did, I figured, they were dead. Our backs are just the best there are at picking up a blitz. Matt Snell and Bill Mathis are fantastic, and Emerson Boozer keeps getting better and better, both blocking and reading defenses. And our ends, Don Maynard and George Sauer and Pete Lammons, can smell a blitz a mile away. They've got a whole bunch of little signals to change their patterns; like, if Maynard winks at me, he means he's going to run an I pattern. In the 1968 season, we handled the blitz like crazy. Against Miami, we completed five touchdown passes, and all five came against the blitz. Anybody that's ever played in the American Football League will tell you not to blitz against New York. Of course, the Colts didn't know that; they didn't have any regulars—just one substitute—who'd played in the American Football League. We had three or four guys on our club who'd spent some time with the Colts before they moved up in class.

After our first look at the movies, we went to the practice field for a light workout. Somebody told me that I'd been assigned the same locker Mickey Mantle used in spring training with the Yankees. Mickey and I are pretty good friends; between us, we've got almost one good pair of legs.

Our uniforms were hanging in the locker room. Because we'd been designated the visiting team in the Super Bowl, we had our white uniforms. It was only right that the good guys should be wearing white; besides, I always wear white football shoes, and I like my outfits to be coordinated. All the omens looked good—white uniforms plus we were playing the Super Bowl game on the twelfth, my uniform number.

The days leading up to the Super Bowl game passed quickly. I was busy, debating Lou Michaels, sleeping through our picture session, keeping Jimmy Fazio out of bankruptcy. I practiced, too. I practiced damn hard, and I watched Baltimore movies in my room, as well as at our team meetings. I loved what the projector showed me; the one-eyed monster tells no lies. I guess my teammates felt the same way. "Damn, Joe, we better stop watching those movies," Pete Lammons said to me, after one meeting, "or we're gonna get overconfident." I cracked up laughing. Then I realized Pete was right; I wondered which one of us was going to call up the Colts and tell them they didn't have a chance.

Three days before the game I went down to the Miami Springs Villas to receive an award from the Touchdown Club as the outstanding player in pro football. I knew the place pretty well. Eastern Airlines stewardesses train there; I've done some training there myself during the off-season.

"We're going to win Sunday," I told the people at the Touchdown Club dinner. "I'll guarantee you."

I was just telling those people the truth. I know I'm not allowed to bet on football games, but, what the hell, all those people were nice enough to give me an award, I figured I'd be nice enough to give them a good tip. They should have mortgaged their houses and put everything on the Jets. Hell, they could have bought their own llama rugs and their own fur coats. Instead, some of them thought Namath's a real joker. I don't joke about football. I don't joke about the game.

I honestly felt that we had a better team. Judging from the movies, as I said before, I wasn't too impressed by the Baltimore defense. Come to think of it, judging from a couple of their games I saw on television, I wasn't too impressed by their offense, either. And I felt that we had a stronger team physically. Almost all of us were under thirty, and a lot of us were twenty-four and twenty-five and twenty-six. Yet, because we'd started with the Jets when the Jets were down, we had just as much playing experience as the older Colts. I bet I'd thrown almost as many passes in four seasons as Earl Morrall had thrown in thirteen. I felt Maynard, Sauer, and Lammons, as a group, were better receivers than Baltimore's Jimmy Orr, Willie Richardson, and John Mackey; I felt Snell and Boozer were better runners than Baltimore's Tom Matte and Jerry Hill. I didn't see any way they were better than us.

I study football, and I understand it—well, I understand some of it—and when I say we're a better football team, you can go to sleep on that. I know the better team doesn't always win, but when you've got the better team plus eighteen points—the price had gone up a point by then; there must've been a lot of stupid people running to the bookmakers—it's like stealing.

Still, some people said I was just shooting my mouth off, I was just whistling in the dark, I was just trying to act confident so that my teammates wouldn't be afraid of the Colts. Now, that's absurd. I know my teammates, and they're not afraid of anything. What's going to frighten Gerry Philbin? He'd tackle a tank. And Winston Hill and Dave Herman and Johnny Sample and Verlon Biggs and Jim Hudson, shoot, those guys don't scare. I'm the only guy on the whole team who doesn't go around looking for physical contact. And, once in a while, Emerson Boozer'll stay back just to keep me company.

The Colts didn't act any smarter than the people who bet on them. "When he gets a little older," Baltimore's Billy Ray Smith said about me, "he'll get humility." He was just mouthing words. He never met me. He didn't know me. He didn't know what the hell he was talking about. Who says when I get older I'll get humility?

Two days before the game, my father and my brother Bob came down to Florida from Beaver Falls. My father took time off from his job in the steel mill; my brother took time off from his bar and grill in Monaca, just outside Beaver Falls. Neither of them took time off to watch me lose. My mother was supposed to make the trip, too, but she gets very nervous about flying and she wasn't feeling too well, so I told her to stay home and watch us win on television. I didn't want to take any chance on her getting hijacked to Havana and missing the game.

The night before the game, after our ten o'clock team buffet, a ritual before road games, I went up to my suite. I didn't go up alone. I took some Baltimore films with me. About eleven o'clock, Clive Rush, our offensive coach, stopped by my room, the regular pregame bed-check. He saw I had the projector set up. "See anything new?" he asked me. "Same stuff," I said. Clive didn't have to worry about me missing curfew. Weeb Ewbank had put in a curfew starting Tuesday night, and just like everybody else on the team, I made curfew every night. It wasn't that I felt I had to get to bed so early—I can't fall asleep before two or three o'clock, no matter what—but I knew that if I were missing, Weeb wouldn't be able to sleep, and I wanted him fresh and rested for the game.

I had only one real problem the night before the game. Jim Hudson had deserted me. His wife had come down for the game, and he'd moved into another room with her, leaving me all alone. I hate to watch movies by myself. Maybe I'm afraid of the dark. . . .

It was a nice peaceful way to spend the eve of a game. It really calmed me down. I'm supposed to be a big swinger, but I can enjoy a Saturday-night movie just as much as anything else. I got plenty of sleep. I was wide awake for breakfast at eleven o'clock. I didn't feel like eating. I was looking forward to the game too much. I was looking forward to a lot of fun.

On the bus going to the Orange Bowl in Miami, I thought about the game, thought about specific situations. I didn't exactly daydream, but I could almost visualize certain things happening. I could see Maynard flying down the sidelines, for instance, sprinting beyond the man covering him, breaking into the clear, and I could see me lofting the ball, over the defender, into Maynard's arms, and I could see Maynard scoring. I could see the safety blitz, too. It looked beautiful to me.

In the dressing room, Jeff Snedeker, our trainer, wrapped tape all around my right knee. Then, just as he had for every game for four years, he taped a steel-and-rubber brace to the knee. Personally, I don't think the brace does anything except make it a little more difficult for me to move around, but Weeb thinks it does some good and Jeff goes along with him. I don't want to hurt their feelings.

After Jeff helped me off the table, I walked back into the locker room and listened to Weeb's pregame speech. I don't need a speech to get me up for a big game. I just half-listened. Weeb reminded a few of the guys that the Colts had gotten rid of them and that they now had a chance to get even.

I went out on the field, loose and relaxed. I just had the normal butterflies, just enough inner tension to get the adrenaline flowing good. The way I figured, I didn't have anything to worry about. It was just going to be another triumph for clean living.

The Colts kicked off to us, and on our first play from scrimmage, I called our shift, our left guard moving over between our center and our right guard. I just wanted to let the Colts know right away that we had the shift, that they were going to have to adjust their defenses to us, that we were going to act and they'd have to react. I just wanted them to realize they weren't playing with children.

I wasn't too surprised by the way the game went. I was a little surprised how well the Colts moved the ball against our defense the first couple of times they got the ball. I watched from the sidelines and I thought, "Well, hell, maybe they're gonna score a touchdown or two." It didn't worry me. It just meant we'd have to score a few more.

I don't think we played a particularly great game, not by our standards. We played pretty much the way we'd played in our better games all year. Of course, any game's a great game when you win, but I know my own performance wasn't anything special. The second time we had the ball, I sent Don Maynard out on a fly pattern, and it worked almost the way I'd been seeing it in my head. Don streaked down the sidelines and he got past Jerry Logan and I lofted the ball downfield and Don stretched for it, and the goldang ball sailed about two inches beyond his reach. When the game ended, Don came up to me, shaking his head. "Durn, I'm sorry, Joe," he said.

"What for?" I said.

"Well, shucks," he said, "if my leg hadn't been hurt, I would have got to that."

"Your leg still bothering you?" I said. Maynard's leg had really been killing him the last four, five weeks of the season.

"Yeah," he said.

Hell, if I'd known that, I would have thrown the ball two inches shorter.

The next play right after that, George Sauer was wide open on the left, and I threw the ball five yards over his head. Just a miserable pass. I had trouble throwing to my left on and off all day; sometimes, I'd throw perfect to my left and, other times, I'd just get my thumb and my grip all messed up and throw terrible. In the third quarter, my thumb got hit, and it hurt like hell, but I came out of the game for just one series of downs.

Our plays against the Baltimore blitz worked beautifully. Every time I came up to the line of scrimmage, I thought to myself, Please let them blitz, please. And they did. I didn't complete every pass play against the blitz. I missed two or three times, but we hurt them a lot more than they hurt us. On one of those misses, George Sauer broke clean, and he was just wide open, but I couldn't find him. He was in a dead spot in my vision. We had a communication problem on the play. I thought George was going to go to the inside, and George thought I was expecting him to go to the outside. I had to run with the ball that time, and I got tackled, and we had to settle for a field goal. We should've had a touchdown; Sauer could've picked up thirty yards on that play if I'd spotted him.

I must have called more than a third of our plays—at least half of our running plays—at the line of scrimmage, looking over the Baltimore defense, anticipating their moves, deciding what to do. It got to the point where I was just telling the guys in the huddle, "Check with me," meaning I'd call the play at the line. There was no sense wasting time calling a play in the huddle, because I knew I'd change it to a better play with an automatic, an audible, at the line. During the weeks after the Super Bowl, I started learning how to play chess, with pawns and rooks and bishops, but I was really learning during the game. You don't have much time to stop and appreciate what you're doing while you're playing a football game, but it's the same sort of strategy as a chess match.

I can't say enough about how good our guys were in picking up the plays at the line of scrimmage. I mean, it's really a hard thing for them. When I change a play at the line, they've got to drive the play they've been thinking about from their minds and they've got to replace it with a new one and, in a few seconds, they've got to be ready for a different assignment, maybe on a different snap count, maybe in a whole different direction. Our guys didn't bust one play all day, didn't miss a single assignment as far as I could tell, never jumped offsides or anything. Two or three years earlier, if I'd tried calling all those audibles, before we really knew each other, our guys would have been flopping all over the field, getting in each other's way, missing blocks, fouling up everything. But, against Baltimore, their coordination, their discipline, was just fantastic. It was a bitch of a test, and every guy on our club passed it.

I varied our snap count all through the game. Sometimes we went on the first sound; the ball was snapped to me the first sound I made. Sometimes we went on the color I called, sometimes on the first number and sometimes on the third and sometimes on the sixth. I had a rhythm of my own going, an erratic rhythm inside my head, and it was upsetting the Baltimore rhythm, just like I knew it would.

Take our first touchdown—hell, our *only* touchdown; it just seems like we had more. We were down near the Baltimore goal line, and when I saw Lou Michaels come on the field, I knew positively that the Colts were going into a tight five-one defense. From watching the movies, I knew that with Michaels in there on a short-yardage situation the Colts wouldn't use any other defense. Up until then, as far as I can remember, I hadn't called any plays on the first sound because, when the play's on the first sound—when I say, "Now!"—there's no way I can check off the play at the line of scrimmage. Against the Colts, obviously, I liked to be able to check off. But the first play with Michaels on the field, I said, "We'll go on the first sound." I called a 19-straight, a handoff to Snell, and Matt bounced around the left side and scored. We had the Colts off balance then, and they never really got their balance back.

Weeb and some other people said afterward that I called a perfect game, but that's not true. I made a couple of mistakes. I threw one pass that I shouldn't have thrown. In the third quarter, on a third-down-and-long situation, I threw to Pete Lammons on a hook pattern, and Jerry Logan almost intercepted. I should never have released the ball. I was really forcing the pass. But even though I did a bad thing, I did one thing right on the play. I kept the ball outside Lammons. I saw Logan lying in the grass, wanting to go for the ball, so I threw on the far side of Lammons, away from Logan. Well, Logan lunged for the ball and touched it, but he couldn't hold it. If I'd thrown right at Lammons, Logan would have intercepted. He might even have run the ball back for a touchdown. I still don't know why I threw the ball; I should have eaten it.

I threw two other passes during the game that looked like they might've been intercepted, but I don't consider them mistakes. One Lenny Lyles reached for and missed and Sauer caught, and the other was a miserable end-over-end job that Don Shinnick of the Colts knocked down. I watched the films afterward, and they were good smart passes; they weren't going to be intercepted. If I'd thrown that damn pass right, the one Shinnick knocked down, we'd have gained twenty yards; Sauer and I had both read the Baltimore defense just right, and then I flopped the ball through the air like a girl.

My only other mistake came in the fourth quarter. When we were leading, 16-0, I ran a play on the first sound. At that stage, when we were trying to use up the clock, I shouldn't have done that. It was just plain stupid on my part. But, outside of that and the pass to Lammons, I guess I've got to admit that Weeb was right.

Hell, our whole club came pretty close to being perfect, which didn't surprise me at all. That's the way we play. We don't expect to make any mistakes. Jim Hudson was practically sick after the game because he'd missed a tackle on Tom Matte when Matte got off a long run right after our touchdown. "I had him, I had him at the line of scrimmage," Hudson said. "I was gonna kill him and I closed my eyes and I missed him. Damn." We'd just won the championship of the whole world, and Hudson was almost sick because he'd missed one tackle.

I don't want to take anything away from the Colts. Taking the world championship is enough. They're a helluva football team. Matte's a great runner, and they hit hard, and they play clean, tough football. But, just like I'd been saying all along and everybody'd been laughing, the Jets are a great football team, too. People say Sauer and Maynard and Lammons are good, and that's not half enough to describe them. And our defense was just beyond belief. The people who came to the Super Bowl saw a great defensive team, but it wasn't the Colts.

All of our guys really hit. On our first series of plays, Rick Volk tackled Matt Snell, and Matt hit him so hard Volk was shook up the rest of the game. He wound up in the hospital with a concussion. When I heard about that, I was really sorry he'd been hurt. I mean it. Sure, Volk was trying to get to me and kill me on the blitzes, but that's football, that's his job. The name of the game is kill the quarterback, and Volk was just playing the game. On the field and off the field are two different things. I hate to see anybody get hurt. Especially me, of course.

The only thing that really upset me all day was that, after the game was over and we'd won, 16-7, we didn't have any champagne in our locker room. That was just plain ridiculous. Weeb and Milt Woodard, the president of the American Football League, said that it wouldn't look right on television for us to be drinking, that it'd be bad for our image, bad for the sport, a bad influence on children. They were acting childish themselves. It was pure hypocrisy, and hypocrisy hurts our image a lot more than a couple of glasses of champagne. We were the champions, man, the best in the world, and we had Cokes and Gatorade to drink. The whole thing left a bad taste in my mouth. I washed it out later with Johnnie Walker.

I had some night. I stayed up till the sun rose the next day. Hell, I'd been getting too much sleep all week, anyway. We were on top of the world. Number one. We were Number one. Sometimes, for no reason at all, I just broke out laughing, I felt so good.

On television that night, I watched the replay of the game. Some people were already saying that if we played the Colts again on another day, the result would be different. I watched the game on TV and I saw how conservatively I'd played, how I went for field goals instead of touchdowns, and I guess I had to agree with those people.

On another day, we would have beat Baltimore worse.

GALE SAYERS
WITH AL SILVERMAN

"Pick"
from *I Am Third*

The friendship of two running backs for the Chicago Bears, Gale Sayers and Brian Piccolo, was a special one. Piccolo was there for Sayers when the star made his comeback from a serious knee injury, and Sayers was there for Piccolo during the backup's ordeal with lung cancer. This chapter from I AM THIRD, *Sayers's autobiography, written with Al Silverman, covers the relationship between the two players and was the basis for the popular television movie,* BRIAN'S SONG. *Silverman was the editor of* SPORT *magazine from 1960 through 1972 and, more recently, coeditor of the anthology,* THE TWENTIETH CENTURY TREASURY OF SPORTS.

BRIAN PICCOLO AND I began rooming together in 1967, and we became close friends. It's easy to make a big deal out of the fact that he was white and I'm black and to wonder how we got along. But there was nothing to it, although I admit at first we did feel each other out. I had never had a close relationship with a white person before, except maybe George Halas, and Pick had never really known a black person. I remember him telling me that he wondered at first, "Are they really different? Do they sleep in chandeliers, or what?"

The best thing about our relationship as it developed was that we could kid each other all the time about race, do our thing in perfect ease. It was a way, I guess, of easing into each man's world. It helped take the strangeness out of it.

Like, before that 1969 exhibition game in Washington, a writer came into our room to interview me, and Pick really laid it on.

"How do you get along?" the writer asked.

Pick said, "We're O.K. as long as he doesn't use the bathroom."

"What do you fellows talk about?"

"Mostly race relations," I said.

"Nothing but the normal racist stuff," he said.

"If you had your choice," the writer went on, ignoring all the digs, "who would you want as your roommate?"

I was very tactful. "If you're asking me what white Italian fullback from Wake Forest, I'd say Pick."

Piccolo was born in Massachusetts and raised in Fort Lauderdale, Florida. At Wake Forest, he was the campus honcho. He made All-America running back. He led the country in rushing and scoring in his senior year, but he wasn't drafted. They claimed he didn't have too much size or too much speed, but the Bears took him as a free agent. Like all free agents, he was a long shot to make it in the pros. But he hung in there with determination and guts, and he turned out to be a helluva football player.

How good was he? Well, he was always proudest of the fact that one year he graded higher than I did. At the end of the season the coaches review all the game films and grade each player. And in 1968 Pick graded about 98 and I graded like 74. "If I do something," Pick said, "I do it. If I'm told to block the linebacker, I do it. I'm a ballplayer's ballplayer. They got to go with me."

I first met Pick at the All-America game in Buffalo, New York, after my senior year. There were four of us in that game who were going on to the Bears' camp—Dick Butkus, Jimmy Jones, Pick, and myself. And Butkus and I never said a thing to any of the others, or to each other. "You were so bad then," Pick once said to me. "You were a real hotshot."

The thing is I was very shy then. I'm not outgoing anyway. I don't try to push myself on people. And I was really quiet. I was always listening—I still am a very good listener, which I think is a good trait—but I was no talker. While the other Bear rookies socialized among themselves, said, "Hey, how you doing? We'll see you in training camp," Butkus and I didn't have one word to say to anyone, including ourselves. Piccolo claimed we both changed amazingly over the years, and I guess that's true.

Anyway, I did give Pick a glancing hello that first time in Buffalo and that was it. We were on different teams in the All-America game, and he didn't play because he had a pulled hamstring. Every year we have a 10-day rookie camp at Soldier's Field, and he wasn't in there because of the pull. The hamstring really ruined his rookie season.

The next year, 1966, we got a little closer. We lockered next to each other, his number being 41 and mine 40 ("I had Dick Gordon on my left," he once said, "Sayers on my right. I felt like an Oreo cookie.") And we got to know each other a little better. We became friendlier and friendlier.

I had to get friendly with him because he was my backup man, and I needed him. When I was tired, I depended on him for a blow. He always said, "I have the distinction of never being put into a game by a coach." We always worked it between ourselves. Mr. Halas was head coach then, and he never liked to take me out of a game. But there were times when I just ran and ran and ran and I was completely whipped. And Piccolo knew it, but he would have to engage in a lengthy charade before they'd take me out.

First Pick would ask me, "Gale, are you tired, do you want a blow?" If I said yes, he'd go to Ed Cody, our backfield coach, and say, "Gale's tired, he wants to take a blow." And then Ed would come back to me and say, "Gale, are you tired?" Just to make sure, you know. Then, if I said yes, Ed would go to Mr. Halas and the old man would turn to Piccolo and say, "Pick, come here, Gale's tired. I think maybe you ought to go in for him." That was always kind of interesting, except it was a little tough for Piccolo to get into the games. By the time that ritual was finished, the game would be over.

But after a while, the coaches just let us do it by ourselves. And Pick got on to my ways and could tell when I wanted to take a blow.

All I had to do was look over to the bench and he would see. He would know by the way I was standing in the huddle, by the way I hung my head. If I made a long run, starting at one side of the field and ending on the other, he'd know to come in for a play. And he was always around the side lines ready to come in.

There were times, of course, when this didn't work to Pick's advantage. Once, against Minnesota, I had just finished running what we call a "sucker play." On a sucker play, the guard doesn't block the defensive tackle. He tries to pull the tackle the opposite way, making the tackle think he's leading a sweep or something. He takes the tackle with him and the runner shoots through the hole. And I shot through for forty yards. Naturally, I was tired and Pick went in.

In the huddle, our quarterback, Jack Concannon, called, "Same play," and Pick's jaw hit the ground. After a tackle has been had on a sucker play—which you never call more than once a game—you know the tackle wants to kill somebody. He just wants to sucker somebody himself. And Piccolo got hit good. He came out of the game and his nose was bleeding and his eyes were watery and he was muttering something about being the biggest sucker of all.

But the worst moment for Pick came in a game against Detroit in 1967. We had played the first game with the Lions at Wrigley Field and beat them 14-3. Afterward, their linebacker, Wayne Walker, came out with this comment: "Every time the Bears play us they nickel-and-dime us to death. This time we're gonna get 'em."

So we went to Detroit about three weeks later and they tried very hard to get us. It was a pretty physical game—a tough game. It was one of the most physical, most vicious games I've been in since I've played pro ball. They were punching and gouging and twisting legs in there and getting away with a lot of stuff the referee couldn't see.

In the fourth quarter, we had a 14-point lead, and I decided to get out. I really wasn't that tired, but I said to myself, "We're ahead, our defense is playing good ball, enough to hold them, I'll take a blow." With eight minutes to play, we punted and I came off and said to Pick, "Finish it up."

That puzzled him because it was not like me to leave a game with eight minutes still left. The puzzle was solved right away the first time he carried the ball. He hit into the line and someone started twisting his ankle and another guy started punching him in the guts and Alex Karras was hollering at our center, Mike Pyle, "When the season's over I'm coming to Chicago and I'm gonna kill you." And Pick came back and said, "This is one of the great favors you have done for me over the years, Gale."

And, in the summer of 1967, we began rooming together. In Birmingham, Alabama.

I was in the room when Pick came in. "What are you doing here?" he said.

I said, "We're in together."

He was a little surprised, but I had known about it. They had asked me if I had any objections to rooming with Brian. I said no, none at all. I had been rooming with a fellow who got cut, and I think Pick was rooming with a quarterback, Larry Rakestraw, and they decided maybe they ought to room guys together by position. But I think Bennie McRae, one of our cocaptains, also suggested that they start some integrated rooming, to get a little better understanding with the guys. And Pick and I were the first on the Bears.

But it really didn't make any difference. I think they tend to make too much out of it. Friends like to room with friends, and it has nothing to do with segregation or anything like that.

You can bet we didn't have dinner together in Birmingham that weekend. We joked a lot about it, but we went our separate ways. I don't know if we ate dinner with one another but a couple of times that first year. It was always that when we got into a place, I'd call the guys that I normally went out with and he'd call the guys that he normally went out with, and we'd split. It was just that he had his friends and I had mine. I think we were both a little unsure about the whole thing at first. And I guess I was a little distant that first year. I think once people get to know me, I'm easy to get along with. Pick always knew that on the day of a game I liked to be left alone—just let me be—and this is what he did. But by the end of that first year, we had both loosened up quite a bit.

I think he actually helped open me up because he was such a happy-go-lucky guy. He always had a joke or two in him. One day, he read me this letter he had just received from a guy in Chicago who actually signed his name. It went: "I read where you stay together with Sayers. I am a white man! Most of the people I know don't want anything to do with them. I just don't understand you. Most Italians I have met say that they stink—and they really do!" And Pick couldn't resist his own P.S.: "Well," he said, "that's true, of course, you can't get away from that."

He was always getting in a dig about something. Like we'd be having breakfast in the coffee shop and a waitress would say to me, "Can I ask you your name?" And before I could answer, Pick would mumble, "They all look alike."

When Pick heard that Vince Lombardi had taken over in Washington, he said he thought he would like to play a little bit for Lombardi before his career was over.

"I can arrange that," I said.

"Would you?" he said. "I'm tired of playing in your shadow. I want to be a legend in my own time."

But he never was that much in my shadow. He meant a lot to the Chicago Bears. One game in 1967 he got the game ball for his performance against Minnesota. He had a way of playing a good game when I was having a good game. When I was going well, I'd be making a lot of long runs and so I'd be taking a blow more often and maybe my playing time would be a little less. And Pick would come in and play a helluva game. You'd have to say he was an opportunist. The day I tore up my knee against San Francisco, Pick came in and ran for eighty-seven yards on eighteen carries and caught four passes for fifty-four yards.

And he did a beautiful job the rest of the year. Against New Orleans, he rushed twenty-one times for 112 yards. He ended up rushing for 450 yards, a 3.8 average. He had a favorite line then: "I won't get you sixty [meaning sixty yards in one run] but I'll get you ten sixes." Every time I saw him that year and into 1969, he'd look at me and say, "I won't get you sixty, but I'll get you ten sixes." And he'd burst out laughing.

He was really a comfort to me during the 1969 exhibition season and into the regular season, especially those early games when the writers had written me off. He was one of the few guys who seemed to have confidence in me, who built up my morale. He would read what they were saying about me and he'd say, "Don't worry about them. You're running fine. The holes aren't there, you know, just keep your chin up." Which I was trying to do, but it wasn't always easy.

And he knew I was tight in those early days, wondering if I had lost something, and he did his damndest to loosen me up. One time in camp, a writer asked about my knee. "There's one big difference in Gale now," Pick said, standing right beside me. "He runs all right until the knee starts to wobble."

The trouble was that a lot of writers began to believe that. We have one local writer who is always sneaking around, trying to pick up conversation among the players. He wants to know everything and he always edges in trying to hear what doesn't concern him. So one day after practice, we saw him coming. I put my back to him and Pick made believe he didn't know he was there, and he started in.

"It really feels that bad, huh, kid?" he said.

I said, "Yeah. I don't know if I can make it."

"Well, don't worry about it. Hell, I filled in for you last year. I'll do the job. The team will get along okay, Gale. We can do it."

"Well, I hope so, but I'm just not so sure. Damn knee. I may have to hang it up after the season."

"Well, what the hell," Pick said. "It's your fifth year. You've got your pension in."

That writer stole away, not sure that he had heard right and wondering, probably, "Was it a put-on, or should I write it?"

It's ironic the way things happen. Because of my injury and my mental state afterward, I got to know Pick even better and became closer to him than almost anybody else on the team. And then when he became ill, it seemed that our friendship deepened and we got to understand each other even better. And that's when I found out what a beautiful person he really was.

In July, when we report to camp, we all have to take complete physicals. And of course Brian had one and he had a chest X ray and nothing showed. Brian didn't smoke, didn't drink much, and he always took good care of himself. And when Ronnie Bull tore up his knee in the Detroit game, Piccolo was switched to fullback and played alongside me and was doing a helluva job.

But just about this time he began to develop a cough. It wasn't much at first. He wouldn't cough much at night, but he'd get up in the morning and start to cough, maybe four or five times, then stop for a while, then start again. Later, he was coughing at night. He would excuse himself every few minutes—because, I guess, he thought he was disturbing me.

We went up to Minnesota on November 2, and the cough got a little worse. It was kind of cool and damp, and he figured maybe he was catching cold, so he got a prescription from one of the team doctors and started taking cough medicine. Then we played in Pittsburgh, and he still had the cough. And in the Atlanta game, it really got bad.

It was warm down there, and he coughed so bad that he almost lost his breath a few times. Dick Gordon was sitting on the bench next to him. Brian was hacking something awful, and Gordon just couldn't believe it. He looked at Pick and said, "How the hell are you playing?" But he played the whole game and played well, and he scored a touchdown.

And at this time, he could still joke about it. He would get this coughing jag and then say to Ralph Kurek, another of our running backs and a good friend of Pick's, "I think I'm having a coronary."

Kurek, who's nuts, said, "Try this heart massage. I use it all the time when my heart stops."

Pick got back at Kurek by spraying his roll-on deodorant with a sticky substance, "Firm Grip." Every day he'd load it up with "Firm Grip" and Ralph never caught on to it. Pick swore that Kurek never raised his arms once he put that stuff on.

The Tuesday after the Atlanta game Pick decided he better see Doctor L. Braun, our medical doctor. Maybe he just needed a stronger cough syrup or something. So he went to the doctor's office at Illinois Masonic hospital and Doctor Braun wasn't in. Louis Kolb took Pick upstairs for a chest X ray.

He threw the X ray up on the light, and Piccolo, no medical man, nevertheless knew when an X ray wasn't right. He saw a big spot on his left lung, a clear area where all the rest was dark. He said, "Hey, doctor, what's this?"

Dr. Kolb said, "I don't mean to be an alarmist, but it's something that shouldn't be there. But we'll have Dr. Braun come down and look at it and we'll see what we can figure out. Don't worry about it, it could be a swollen gland or something."

Piccolo told me he waited an hour or so, because Dr. Braun was busy, and while he waited, he said, he sat there looking at that X ray and just wondering about a lot of things.

Finally, Dr. Braun came around, took a look, and told Pick he wouldn't be playing the game Sunday against the Baltimore Colts. He thought Brian had better stay in the hospital for some tests.

And he did. The chest specialist came in and looked down Pick's throat with a tube and he couldn't see anything. So they made an incision in his chest. And that's when they discovered it was a tumor. And it was malignant.

The doctor told Pick that he apparently had had a tumor there all his life, lying there benign, and for some reason it just decided to take off.

The first time I heard about the seriousness of Brian's illness was Friday night, when coach Halas called me at home. He said, "Brian's very sick. He's got a malignant tumor in his chest that's got to come out. We're sending him to New York to the best hospital in the country for this type of tumor."

I was stunned. I was absolutely stunned, and shocked. I just didn't know what to say; or think. After practice Saturday, I went over to the hospital to see him. He was in a fantastic mood. "I'm ready to play, man," he said. "It's just a little cough, you know." He was disappointed that he couldn't play. His wife Joy was with him, and she was in good spirits, too. I really didn't know what to say to him. We kidded around a bit, and then I left.

That night, the night before the Baltimore game, Mr. Halas called me again. He said, "Gale, I think maybe you ought to say something to the team before we go out tomorrow, try to dedicate the game to Brian. You're Pick's roommate. I think it would he appropriate."

And I said I would. The more I thought about it, the more I liked the idea. Because I think a lot of the fellows didn't realize just how sick Brian was. There had been no announcements in the papers, and the Bears wanted to make no announcements until Brian got to New York and was operated on.

I had never in my life talked to a team. I don't consider myself a leader. All the leading I do is by example, by the way I go out and play the game. And I didn't know how it would go. I was a little nervous, but that didn't matter. I wanted to get something across to the guys, that was all.

Sunday morning, I went to church, which I seldom do during the football season. I went mainly to pray for Brian.

Before we went out for our pregame warmup, I told Jim Dooley I wanted to say something to the team about Brian. He said it was okay. So after the warmup and just as we were getting ready to go back on the field, Dooley told the team, "Gale has something to say to you."

I just told them that we have a tradition after a winning game to give a game ball to the outstanding player of that game. I said. "As you all know, Brian Piccolo is very, very sick. If you don't know it, you should know it. He's very, very sick, and he might not ever play football again. And I think each of us should dedicate ourselves to try to give our maximum efforts to win this ball game and give the game ball to Pick. We can all sign it and take it up to him. . . ."

About this time I was getting pretty choked up, and they probably didn't even understand the last part of what I was saying, because I had started to cry.

As we went on the field, they started playing "The Star-Spangled Banner," and I couldn't help crying then. We were going to kickoff, so I went to the bench and just leaned over with my head down, sobbing. Jim Ringo came over to me and said, "Gale, I've been in football for twenty years and never heard anything like that before." And Abe Gibron came over and said it was a great thing to do.

And then I went over to Ross Montgomery, who was my backup man now, and I told Ross that although he was a fine football player he might as well not suit up because I wasn't coming out of this game. I was going to play this game for Brian.

And we went out and we played ball and we should have won the damn game. We had them by a touchdown with six minutes to go, and Johnny Unitas came in and drove them eighty yards. Then, as we were getting into field-goal range, they intercepted a pass and they got the field goal and we lost the game. But most of the players had given their all, I knew that.

After the game, Linda and I went to the hospital to see Brian. He was leaving the next morning for New York, and a bunch of the players came by. Mike Pyle was there with his wife, Ronnie Bull and his wife, Jack Concannon and his wife, Ed McCaskey was there, Jim Ringo, and Ralph Kurek and his wife. McCaskey ordered a bunch of pizzas and a few beers and stuff and everybody sat around.

Linda and I stayed for two hours. At one point, Pick, Concannon, Kurek, and myself went upstairs to see this little girl who had dived into a shallow swimming pool and broken her neck. She was about thirteen and was paralyzed from the neck down. She had kind of become the darling of the Bears, because every time a player came to see Dr. Fox he would send him up to see this girl. Mainly because of the girl, Brian said, he wasn't as concerned about his own troubles. The next morning, the day he left for New York, he went into the girl's room to give her a signed photograph of himself. She was asleep and he left it. Some weeks later we heard that the girl had passed away.

We talked a lot that Sunday. We clowned a little bit, but it was sort of a serious mood, considering Pick's normal disposition. But he was in fine spirits. Listening to him, I found it hard to believe that here he had played football so long without getting knocked out by an injury and, all of a sudden, this terrible thing had struck him down. It was a tough thing to believe that this kind of thing could happen to him. But he was such a strong person. He just said, "It's a tumor and it's got to come out, and it's got to come out now." And he was loose about it because that was his way. He's always been loose about things. His attitude was, What's the use of getting solemn and serious? It doesn't change things. He said he felt he was fortunate in that respect because he knew a lot of people who just couldn't look at things that way. He said he was resigned to anything that happened to him. He felt, he said, that all our lives are plotted out in advance and nothing we do can change things. His only concern, he said, was for his wife and his three small daughters.

What he was really doing, I think, was carrying through the I Am Third philosophy of life. Really carrying it through. And yet it was a very positive attitude. And I think you have to be that way. I wasn't really impressed by Brian's courage because I knew Brian. I knew he was a very courageous person, and I expected that of him.

Pick flew into New York Monday and they operated on him on Friday. Dr. Edward Beattie, who is a famous specialist on such tumors, performed the operation. He told Brian beforehand that he might have to quit playing football for a couple of years. Pick knew that would be the end for him. Because if he laid out two years, he would be trying to make a comeback at twenty-eight. So he told the doctor, "Well, listen, don't worry about it. We won't talk about it now. We'll wait and see."

Dr. Beattie also told Pick the tumor figured to be the size of a baseball. When they got it out—after a four-and-a-half-hour operation—it was closer to a grapefruit.

We had a Saturday game in San Francisco, and right after the game, I flew back to Chicago, then into New York for an appearance. Sunday morning, I went in to see Pick.

Same old Piccolo. He had watched the San Francisco game—it was on national television—and he gave me hell for not fielding a punt that went on to roll seventy yards. He said, "I kept yelling, 'Gale, pick it up, pick it up.'" Well, I caught hell from Abe Gibron for not picking it up, too.

Considering everything he had gone through, he looked well, and he was in his usual good spirits. The room was full of flowers. "I don't have any oxygen for myself," he said to me. And he had gotten thousands of cards and letters. Then he showed off a personally autographed picture and album he had received from Frank Sinatra. He flipped over Sinatra.

And, naturally, he showed me his scar. It made my knee look like nothing. It was a wicked one, coming almost from his throat down to two inches above his navel, with another scar from the middle of his sternum to just under his armpit.

Brian's attitude after the operation was so phenomenal it made me feel all the worse about how I had acted just after my knee surgery. The day after I was operated on, Pick and Bobby Joe Green came to see me. Bobby Joe was still on crutches from his knee surgery and he had a struggle to get to my room. And I just lay there and said nothing. Pick tried to make small talk, but it was like talking to a wall. Pick was so mad. He told me later, "Gale, I really felt like saying to you, 'You're a miserable S.O.B. and I won't come and see you again. Just lay in there and be miserable and feel sorry for yourself.'"

It was true. The first day or two I was terrible. Pick would say something that would normally get a chuckle, and it was like I was deaf. I lay there like stone.

And here was Brian Piccolo, after probably the most critical moment in his whole life, in fine spirits, cool and hopeful and so positive about things. He really helped lift your spirits.

He spent fifteen days in the hospital in New York. Pete Rozelle visited him on Thanksgiving Day and brought an autographed book about professional football, *The First Fifty Years*. And he watched part of the Vikings-Rams game with Pick. I expected that from a man like Rozelle. He's a straight, down-to-earth guy. A helluva man.

When Pick got back home, he naturally took it easy for a while. The doctor said he could go outdoors and do anything he wanted as soon as he felt up to it. And he did make one of our last practice sessions, before the Detroit game, our next-to-the-last of the season. And the guys were all glad to see him.

We talked on the phone a lot and Linda and I visited him a few times, and he seemed to be making terrific progress. He had gotten his weight back up to 188 and was getting ready to play a little golf and start working out a little in the gym.

When I got back from the Pro Bowl game in Los Angeles, I called him. I had been named MVP on offense in that game, and Piccolo said, "I missed the first half. I was at a meeting at the country club. But somebody there had been watching it and was saying what a great game Sayers was having. So when I got home I turned on the TV. As soon as it goes on, the nigger fumbles. That's when I turned you off. I didn't watch another play. Typical nigger play."

I couldn't stop laughing on the phone. "You're terrible," I said, "you're so bad. You haven't changed at all. You're as big a racist as you've ever been."

Shortly after, he went out to play in the Astrojet golf tournament in Phoenix, in which they pair a pro-baseball player and a pro-football player from the same city. Pick was paired with Ernie Banks of the Chicago Cubs. "Wouldn't you know?" he said. "You can't get away from them."

When he came back from the golf tournament, he called me to tell me about it. He also said that he had to go back to New York for more tests. He had discovered a lump on his chest.

That night, we played basketball together. The Bears had a team, if that's what you want to call it, and Pick was player-coach. He played pretty well, too, and he was a very tough coach. He pulled me out of the game for taking those eighty-foot shots. Well, I'm a guard. When you're a guard, you can't get under the basket and you have to take the long shot. I was pretty bad, though, I admit it.

He was in good spirits, as usual, he was the same old Pick, playing down his little lump, which turned out to be a big swelling under his chest.

He went to New York, and they put him on medicine for a while. I came in and spent some time with him. His wife Joy was staying with him, and we took in movies, went to a couple of New York Knicks basketball games, and ate pizza, which was Pick's favorite food.

They hoped that the medicine would reduce the tumor, but finally they decided he had to be operated on. He was operated on once, and a few weeks later he underwent his third operation.

Ed McCaskey and I flew into New York to see him before his second operation. He was coughing quite a bit and all the medication and stuff had weakened him physically. But mentally, he was as strong as ever. I thought to myself, "If anybody can lick it, it's got to be Pick. He can do it.

It happened that I have the same blood as Pick—B positive—so I gave a pint. A couple of days later, just before he was to undergo his second operation, he was telling friends about how Gale Sayers had given him blood.

"I don't know what it is," he said, "but lately I've gotten an awful craving for chitlins."

As much as they cut into this man, as much as he was inflicted with terrible pain and discomfort, as much as he suffered because of this wicked disease that struck him like a thunderbolt flashing out of a clear sky . . . as much as he was faced with all these tortures, his spirit would not be destroyed. That was the beautiful nature of Brian Piccolo.

There was the time, just before he went into the hospital again, that he sat down at home and wrote a letter to Freddy Steinmark of the University of Texas. Steinmark had played on Texas's 1969 national-championship football team. Just after the season, they discovered that Steinmark had bone cancer. They amputated his leg. And Pick sat down and wrote him a letter. I asked him what he said to the boy.

"I told him that I, more than any other football player, understood a few things that must have gone through his mind. Because I had gone through the same thing. I told him never to lose courage and to remember that there was always hope."

At the end of May, I came into New York to attend the Professional Football Writers annual dinner and receive the George S. Halas award as the most courageous player in pro football. I had wanted Brian to attend with me if he was strong enough, but the day I arrived in New York was the day Brian and Joy left the hospital to go back home. He had finished a series of cobalt treatments, and the doctors said he could spend a few weeks at home, then return to the hospital for more treatment.

One reason I wanted Brian with me at the banquet was that I intended to give him the trophy right there. But at least I was able to tell the audience something about Brian Piccolo.

"He has the heart of a giant," I said, "and that rare form of courage that allows him to kid himself and his opponent, cancer. He has the mental attitude that makes me proud to have a friend who spells out the word courage twenty-four hours a day of his life."

I concluded by saying, "You flatter me by giving me this award but I tell you here and now that I accept it for Brian Piccolo. Brian Piccolo is the man of courage who should receive the George S. Halas award. It is mine tonight, it is Brian Piccolo's tomorrow. . . . I love Brian Piccolo and I'd like all of you to love him, too. Tonight, when you hit your knees, please ask God to love him. . . ."

The next day I flew back to Chicago and called Pick on the phone. He had read about the speech in the paper and the first thing he said to me was, "Magic, you're too much. If you were here now I'd kiss you."

I said, "Yeah, well I'm glad I'm not there."

The next day, Linda and I did go to see him. He was wearing

shorts and sitting on the couch and he looked very small. But his spirits were as high as ever. Virgil Carter and his wife dropped by and we talked football and I cracked a couple of jokes, which was a big upset. "Gale, what is this?" Pick said. "I'm supposed to be the joker around here."

We left feeling better about him because he kept us in a lighthearted mood. He cheered us up. I'm glad of that last memory of Pick, since I was not to see him again.

He and Joy went to Atlanta to see their little girls, who had been staying with Joy's mother. He got very sick down there, and they immediately flew back to New York.

Joy told us later that he had suffered a great deal the last week of his life. She said that up to then, they both still had hope, but that last week, coming back to New York, they knew the end was near. And Brian faced up to it and started talking about it. "You know I love you, Joy," he said to his wife, "and I hope I have been a good father to the girls." And he told Joy things he would like for his girls. And when Joy would start to cry Pick would cheer her up the only way he knew how—by ridiculing his own condition. "Joy, can you believe this?" he'd say. "Can you believe this, Joy? Nobody would ever believe this."

I wanted to come in to New York to see him but at that time, my parents were involved in an automobile accident. My mother got off light with some broken ribs, but my father suffered a fractured skull and was in a coma, and I flew to Omaha to see them. And when I got back to Chicago, I had a temperature of 104, and they put me in the hospital with a strep throat.

Tuesday morning, June 16, at six-thirty, Linda called me at the hospital to tell me that Brian had passed away a few hours earlier. A few minutes later, I got another call from Ed McCaskey, who had been in New York with Joy and Brian until the end. I couldn't talk. I wasn't able to say a word to anyone the rest of that day.

I was discharged from the hospital that afternoon. When I came home, I found that my trophy had arrived from New York. I sat down and wrote Brian's name on a piece of paper and pasted it over mine on the trophy. The next morning I went to the wake with the trophy and gave it to Joy and told her I wanted it buried with Pick. Joy said no, she wanted to keep it because it meant so much to her.

The funeral was held that Friday, a clean lovely morning in Chicago, and I went through it like a sleepwalker. I was one of the pallbearers along with Dick Butkus, Ralph Kurek, Ed O'Bradovich, Mike Pyle, and Randy Jackson. I think the only thing I remember about that funeral service was one line recited from the scripture: "The virtuous man, though he dies before his time, will find rest."

It was at the cemetery, as the priest was delivering his final words, that I broke down. He referred to the trophy and to our friendship, and it was too much for me. I couldn't control myself. I just started to cry.

As soon as the service was ended, Joy came over to me and put her arms around me and we embraced, and I told her how sorry I was. "Don't be sorry, Gale," she said. "I'm happy now because I know Brian is happy, and I don't have to watch him suffer any more. He's through suffering now."

She comforted me. I thought to myself, "If she can really be that composed, Brian must have really given her something." And I thought, "Well, he gave us all something, all of us who were privileged to know him." And that helped compose me.

TIM GREEN

The Dream Is Alive

When it comes to authenticity of subject matter, few football writers can top Tim Green. That's because Green spent the last seven years as a linebacker and defensive end for the Atlanta Falcons. Between sacks and stunts, he found time to write two novels, weekly commentary for National Public Radio, and a column for the SYRACUSE HERALD-JOURNAL. *It all started with a dream, as he described in a first-person essay for* GAMEDAY *magazine in 1993.*

A FRIEND TOLD ME that Dick Butkus used to have a football dream where he'd tackle a guy in a movie theater and watch the guy's head roll down the aisle. I don't know if I really believe that Butkus had this dream, at least not all the time. Of course, dreams have more to do with NFL football than you might think.

Everyone who plays in this league has some kind of football dream. We have to. Football is a part of our souls. My football dreams are much less violent than Dick Butkus's. For the sake of intrigue, I wish I could tell you my dream was about Joe Montana's head flying from his body as I dealt him a devastating blow, but I can't. I have two kinds of dreams; one is clear-cut, the other is Freudian in nature.

I always have the clear-cut dream the night before a big game. It's a simple dream in which we are beating our opponent soundly. Despite the fact that my team is clearly winning, the fumbled ball I scoop up or the interception I grab and run back into the end zone ends up being the score that wins the game.

This dream more or less came true when I was at Syracuse

University. We were playing Navy at Annapolis, and I scored the winning touchdown by returning a blocked punt. I wish I could say that I had the dream the night before, but it's not true. Instead, it seems the only times I have that dream are the times I end up losing. In college, I had it every night before we played Penn State.

My Freudian dream is enigmatic as well as slightly embarrassing. This dream plagues me for at least five weeks before every football season. I always find myself on the sidelines watching the game. The stands are at full capacity, and although the sun is shining, an eerie mist pervades the stadium. Things aren't going well on the field for my team, and my position coach turns to me and tells me to get in there.

I start out onto the field, only to be jerked to a halt. My coach is gripping my arm and scowling angrily at me. I don't have my helmet, so I can't go into the game. "Hurry and find it," he tells me. I turn and make my way through my teammates toward the locker room, but I can't find the tunnel that will lead there. I search and search as the game goes on. People in the stands point and stare. Now, not only is my helmet missing, but my pads, my uniform, everything except my undershorts. I wake up in a cold sweat. A friend once told me that it represented my anxiety at being unprepared for the season. I don't know.

I do know my first football dreams were my most important, even though they were just daydreams. In my youth, I'd come home on a cool autumn Sunday afternoon and find my dad planted in front of the TV watching NFL football. How could I fail to envision myself then, heavily laden with pads, sweating and steaming and bleeding from my nose, dressed in an NFL uniform? Maybe I'd wear the green and white of the Jets, or the silver and blue of America's Team, the Cowboys. It didn't matter which one. The important fact was that I dreamed of playing in the NFL.

Once, when I was 10 years old, I sat attentively listening to a speaker at our annual little league football banquet. I can't remember who he was, just that he was a college coach from somewhere. I was proud then, as proud as a 10-year-old can be. I had been a starting guard for the league champion Cowboys, as our team was called. At the time, my future was bright and my dreams were alive and well. Then he spoke:

"I know many of you hope someday to play high school and then college football. Maybe some of you have even dreamed of playing pro ball."

I nodded quietly to myself. "But you boys should know this," he continued. "There are about two-hundred of you here tonight, and probably only fifty of you will ever play varsity ball in high school. Of those, only one, or maybe two, will ever play big-time college football."

I knew that big-time college ball was a prerequisite for the NFL. I looked around, critically examining my competition, searching for the two who might supplant me. There were several older boys who were much faster and stronger than I—maybe they would be the ones. But our guest speaker wasn't through . . .

"The two who ever get to college ball," he said, "they will go into another group just as big as this: two hundred college players. Then, statistics tell us that only two more from those two hundred will ever play pro ball."

On the way home that night, I was quiet. I clutched my championship trophy, relishing the cool, smooth form of the golden figure. It disturbed me to think of the overwhelming odds stacked against my dream. Looking back now, I have to wonder why? Why would anyone say something like that to us kids, even if it were true? I don't know how my fragile child's dream survived that night. Maybe it was the glint of the golden figure that sat atop my dresser, given life by the street lamp outside my window.

Whatever it was, I know the spark of that dream stayed alive, and later it roared into a flame and burned out of control. Without that spark, I would not be doing what I do today. I would not be who I am. So it's easy for me, very easy to keep the promise I made to that 10-year-old boy on a winter night 19 years ago.

"If I ever do make it," I said to myself, pulling the covers tight, "I'll be famous, like O.J. Simpson. When I go to kids' football banquets I'll tell them they can play in the NFL, they can do anything they want to do, so long as they aren't afraid to dream."

JIM BROWN
WITH MYRON COPE

"Big Daddy"
from *Off My Chest*

In Jim Brown's 1964 autobiography, OFF MY CHEST, *one of the NFL's greatest running backs sounded off on a variety of issues that were controversial at the time. In this chapter, Brown reminisces about playing against the legendary, almost mythical Gene (Big Daddy) Lipscomb, a huge defensive lineman for the Baltimore Colts. Lipscomb, noted for his on-field ferocity and off-field sweetness, died tragically, in the prime of his career, of an overdose of heroin.* OFF MY CHEST *was written with Myron Cope, the esteemed author of numerous books about football, including* THE GAME THAT WAS.

IN PRO FOOTBALL a good many players indulge in a practice known in the trade as "psyching." Psyching an opponent usually takes the form of trying to con him with conversation. Maybe you try to taunt him into committing a foul, or maybe you try to intimidate him with tough talk and threats. Personally, I don't go in for verbal nickel psychology; I don't converse with opponents during a game. But there was one man in the National Football League I always tried to psyche. He was the late Gene (Big Daddy) Lipscomb.

Naturally, I did not taunt or try to intimidate Big Daddy. Only a fool or a man bent on suicide would have tried that. What I did was try to psyche him into a frame of mind that would not allow him to get mad at me. I won't say I was afraid of Big Daddy, but on the other hand, I was conscious of the damage Daddy was capable of performing on us mortal men.

Six-feet-six and 290 pounds, Daddy rose up in the middle of the enemy line like the Empire State Building with a mustache. He had the strength of an elephant and was so fast he frequently ran down backfield men from behind. He was the one man in the league who by himself could practically control a play. What gave me pause was the known fact that Daddy could stop a ball carrier in his tracks with a great bear-hug, then straighten him up like a board, and then bend him every way imaginable. There was nothing illegal or dirty about this sort of thing. But just thinking about it, you could feel your spine splintering. You knew it wouldn't take much to give Daddy an excuse for twisting you into a piece of abstract sculpture. For one thing, he was the supreme showman: His shirttail always hung loose so it could flap in the wind when he ran. Crowds tittered when Daddy considerately leaned over and helped us little 230-pounders to our feet after smashing us to the ground. But above all, Daddy had the sensitive soul of an artist.

He was great when he wanted to be great, and the one thing that inspired him most was the chance to make mincemeat out of a star. That's where I first came in—in 1959, my third year of pro ball. Daddy played for Baltimore then, and this was our first meeting with the Colts since I had come into the league. He announced to the press that he was going to get "that Cleveland cat."

As it happened, I had a five-touchdown day—one of the best days that I have ever had. This was largely due to the fact that a guard named Jim Ray Smith was putting blocks on Daddy. Jim Ray was, and still is, the best blocking guard in the league. He and I were giving it to Daddy good in the first half. Just as Jim Ray would hit him, I would run straight at him. The next time Jim Ray hit him, I would slide off a couple yards to the side of Daddy. And the next time I would hit right behind Jim Ray again. Daddy was having a bad time. I could tell by the look on his face that he wasn't enjoying it.

At halftime, as I was walking off the field, Daddy trundled up alongside me.

"Look, Jimmy," he said, frowning. "You were laughing at me out there. I don't like that."

Laughing at Daddy? Man, I'd been running for my life.

"Daddy, I didn't say a thing. What are you talking about?"

"You were making fun of me, boy," Daddy insisted. "I'm gonna get you in the second half. You look out, I'm gonna get you. I thought you were my friend."

With that, Daddy disappeared, stomping into the Colts dressing room.

Fortunately, Daddy was not quite able to get me in the second half. Bobby Mitchell kept him too busy. Mitchell, then our halfback, kept sweeping the ends, and with all his ducking and dodging he was making Daddy look bad. Daddy didn't like that at all. Whenever he managed to get to Mitchell he tried to run him up on the bench. He looked like he wanted to kill Mitchell. He sort of forgot about me.

After the game Daddy came up alongside me again and looked down at me and said, "You had a pretty good one today. After you're dressed, come into my dressing room and talk to me."

Obediently I paid my respects to Big Daddy before leaving the park that day, and even though I'd run well against him I made up my mind that I would never again let him get mad at me. So in future games I psyched him.

"Daddy, you're really looking good out here today," I'd say after he'd knocked me down.

"You think so?" said Daddy, craving reassurance. "Thank you, Jimmy."

"Keep up the good work," I'd say as he helped me to my feet.

Sometimes I'd say, "Gosh, Daddy, I really hope you make all-pro this year."

"I'm tryin', Jimmy. I'm tryin'."

I was careful not to overdo the conversation, but I always made a point of inquiring about Daddy's health, usually after the first time he had bashed me to the ground, and wishing him a successful campaign.

In the off-season of 1963, when Big Daddy Lipscomb suddenly died in Baltimore and the police theorized that he'd had an overdose of dope, all of us who knew him well were stunned. He and I had become good friends. If Daddy was using dope, he certainly was fooling every friend he had. If he did pick up the habit later, it had to be only shortly before his death. I am still puzzled by the mysterious circumstances surrounding his death.

One thing I am sure of is that Daddy's obituaries did not always give a true picture of him. For example, it was written that he wore red neckties so bright that they would fairly burn your eyes at ten feet, and that he wore alligator shoes that looked like the alligator was still living. Actually, Daddy was one of the neatest, most conservative dressers you would want to see, and at one time was even considered a square. Lenny Moore, his Baltimore teammate, used to josh him because he bought old men's shoes—the kind with high tops. They were of soft leather, because Daddy apparently had corns. When he emerged from his square phase, he dressed mostly in tasteful blue business suits. Though a huge man, he never looked sloppy.

Many people considered Daddy uncouth. I suspect this stemmed from the fact that if he didn't like you he would tell you in a loud voice to get out of his way and actually wipe you aside. He was afraid of nobody, but I never saw him in a fist fight. He had good common sense and knew instantly when someone was trying to be smart with him in a subtle way. And he had a great sense of indignation. When a Baltimore teammate once threw a party for the team and excluded the Negro players, Daddy expressed himself the best way he knew how—by marching into the party and turning the place inside-out.

I liked him because he was, while many other things, basically a gentle man, and I liked him because he was outspoken. He would tell his coach or anybody else where to go when convinced he was being wronged. But if he liked you, there was nothing he wouldn't do for you.

Shortly before his death I played with Big Daddy in the Pro Bowl at Los Angeles. He was a Pittsburgh Steeler then, so we were both on the East squad. Both of us had goals that day. I wanted to win the Most Valuable Player trophy, which is voted by the press to the best back on the field, and Daddy wanted to win the Lineman of the Day trophy. Each of us had special reasons for wanting the trophies.

In the previous year's Pro Bowl game I'd won the MVP trophy but circumstances had rubbed some of the shine off it. The press box had been polled minutes before the game ended. No sooner had the reporters voted me the award when I committed a fumble. The West recovered and scored a touchdown to win by one point. With trophy in hand, I was the Most Valuable Goat. Now I wanted to win the award legitimately, and for another reason. I had just come off my poorest season, gaining less than a thousand yards for the first time since I was a rookie. A sprained wrist that had bothered me throughout the season was completely healed now, and I felt I could reestablish myself with a good game. Daddy wanted a trophy because he had been neglected somewhat by the press the past year, even though an all-pro. He wanted to prove he was still huge, fierce, foreboding Big Daddy.

From the opening whistle he played a tremendous game. He swarmed over the passer. Two or three times he actually ran down speedy Dick Bass on end sweeps. "Boy, Daddy, you're really looking good," I told him. "Keep it up and you gotta get the trophy." "You think so?" Big Daddy would say, and then he would go out and smear the passer again. "How you think I'm looking?" he'd keep asking me anxiously. He would march up and down the sidelines, clearing his head with smelling salts—in other words, putting on a show for the press box. He let them know he was there in a way nobody else in football could. He was still Big Daddy.

We both won our trophies. Daddy held his to his chest like a kid with a new Christmas toy. "We showed 'em, huh, Jimmy?" he said.

Daddy left this world with a victory. If there is a heaven above, I think bighearted Big Daddy had to make it. And if he did, those angels up there better be playing it smart and psyching him like I did.

VINCE LOMBARDI

WITH W.C. HEINZ

"The Morning After"

from *Run to Daylight*

In 1963, during the heat of the NFL season, legendary Green Bay Packers coach Vince Lombardi teamed with journalist W.C. Heinz to write a diary of a week in the life of a pro football coach. The result, RUN TO DAYLIGHT, *was a revealing look at Lombardi, in his own words, as he pondered both football and life. This selection begins early on Monday morning, the day after his Packers had demolished the Chicago Bears, and the beginning of a week of preparation for the following Sunday's game against the Detroit Lions.*

MONDAY

3:15 A.M.

I have been asleep for three hours and, suddenly, I am awake. I am wide awake, and that's the trouble with this game. Just twelve hours ago I walked off that field, and we had beaten the Bears 49 to 0. Now I should be sleeping the satisfied sleep of the contented but I am lying here awake, wide awake, seeing myself walking across that field, seeing myself searching in the crowd for George Halas but really hoping that I would not find him.

All week long there builds up inside of you a competitive animosity toward that other man, that counterpart across the field. All week long he is the symbol, the epitome, of what you must defeat and then, when it is over, when you have looked up to that man for as long as I have looked up to George Halas, you cannot help but be disturbed by a score like this. You know he brought a team in here hurt by key injuries and that this was just one of those days, but you can't apologize. You can't apologize for a score. It is up there on that board and nothing can change it now. I can just hope, lying here awake in the middle of the night, that after all those years he has had in this league—and he has had forty-two of them—these things no longer affect him as they still affect me. I can just hope that I am making more of this than he is, and now I see myself, unable to find him in the crowd and walking up that ramp and into our dressing room, now searching instead for something that will bring my own team back to earth.

"All right!" I said. "Let me have your attention. That was a good effort, a fine effort. That's the way to play this game, but remember this. You beat the Bears, but you know as well as I do that they weren't ready. They had key personnel hurt and they weren't up for this game. Those people who are coming in here next week will be up. They won again today, so they're just as undefeated as we are. They'll be coming in here to knock your teeth down your throats, so remember that. Have your fun tonight and tomorrow, but remember that."

"Right, coach!" someone behind me, maybe Fuzzy Thurston or Jerry Kramer or Ray Nitschke, shouted. "Way to talk, coach!"

Am I right and is that the way to talk, or has this become a game for madmen and am I one of them? Any day that you score seven touchdowns in this league and turn in a shutout should be a day of celebration. Even when the Bears are without Bill George, who is the key to their defense, and Willie Galimore, who is their speed, this is a major accomplishment. But where is the elation?

Once there was elation. In 1959, in the first game I ever coached here, that I ever head-coached anywhere in pro ball, we beat these Bears 9 to 6 and I can remember it clearly. I can remember them leading us into the last period and then Jimmy Taylor going in from the 5 on our 28-Weak, and Paul Hornung kicking the point, and then Dave Hanner breaking through on the blitz and nailing Ed Brown in the end zone for the safety. The year before, this team had won only one game and tied one out of twelve, so now they were carrying me off the field because a single league victory was once cause enough for celebration.

What success does to you. It is like a habit-forming drug that, in victory, saps your elation and, in defeat, deepens your despair. Once you have sampled it you are hooked, and now I lie in bed, not sleeping the sleep of the victor but wide awake, seeing the other people who are coming in next Sunday with the best defensive line in the league, with that great middle linebacker, that left defensive halfback who is as quick and agile as a cat and a quarterback who, although he is not as daring as Johnny Unitas or Y. A. Tittle or Bobby Layne, can kill you with his consistency.

I don't see them as I do from the sideline, but as I have seen them over and over in the films. I see them beating us 17-13 in our opener in Milwaukee in 1961. I see them beating us 23-10 in their own park the year before, and that's what I mean about success. My mind does not dwell on the two games we beat them in 1959 or the single games we took from them in 1960 and again in 1961. For the most part you remember only your losses, and it reminds me again of Earl Blaik and West Point after Navy beat our undefeated Army team 14-2 in 1950.

"All right," the Colonel would say whenever there was a lull. "Let's get out that Navy film."

You could see the other coaches sneak looks at one another, and although you couldn't hear the groans you could feel them in the room. Then we'd all file out and into the projection room once more.

"Look at that," the Colonel would say. "The fullback missed the block on that end."

How many times we had seen that fullback miss that block on that end I do not know. I do know that every time we saw that film, Navy beat Army again, 14-2, and that was one of the ways Earl Blaik, the greatest coach I have ever known, paid for what he was.

So what I see now is that opener in '61, the last time they beat us. I see them stopping us twice inside their 5-yard line. I see us running their quarterback out of his pocket, the rhythm of that pass play broken, and both their split end and Jesse Whittenton relax. I see that end start up and Whittenton slip and that end catch it and run it to the 1, and on the next play their fullback takes it in. Then I see them on our 13-yard line and their fullback misses his block and falls. As he gets up, their quarterback, in desperation, flips the ball to him and he walks the 13 yards for the score.

Lying there like this, in the stillness of my house and conscious of any sound and every sensation, I am aware now of the soreness of my gums. It is this way every Monday, because for those two hours on the sideline every Sunday I have been grinding my teeth, and when I get up at eight o'clock and put in my bridge I'll be aware of it again. That, come to think of it, is only fitting and proper, because that bridge had its beginnings in the St. Mary's game my junior year at Fordham. Early in that game I must have caught an elbow or forearm or fist, because I remember sitting in that Polo Grounds dressing room during halftime and it felt like every tooth in my head was loose.

8:40 A.M.

"So I judge you won't be home for dinner," Marie says, while I am having my second cup of coffee.

"No," I say, and that is another part of the price that you and your family must pay. Maybe I'm wrong, but the only way I know how to coach this game is all the way, and what it costs, Marie once explained.

"From Monday until Wednesday night," she said, "we don't talk to him. On Wednesday he has to go out there and convince himself and five other coaches and thirty-six football players."

8:50 A.M.

I drive down our street to the corner, and I have to wait there because at this hour the traffic is heavy going into town. It is heavy with men who must convince other men that they need more insurance or new storm windows or a new car or who must solve a heat-conduction problem or an efficiency lag, and there is not much difference between us. Some of us will do our jobs well and some will not, but we will all be judged by only one thing—the result.

"That's where I can't see that it means much," Vincent, Jr., said one evening last summer just before we went into training camp. Marie and our Susan were at the Fond Du Lac horse show, where Susan was showing her mahogany mare, and Vincent and I were eating out.

"I don't know what you're talking about," I said.

"You're always saying," Vincent said, "that the only way to play the game or do the job is the way you're convinced is right for you."

"That's correct," I said. "The rest will follow, or it won't."

"Then I can't see where there's much difference between winning or losing," Vincent said, "as long as you've done your job."

"There isn't much difference," I said, "except economic. You know that scoreboard doesn't begin to tell the story, but what goes up there controls your economic future and your prestige."

"They can keep the prestige," Vincent said.

He was twenty years old last summer, and I know what he meant. He was seventeen when we moved here from the East, and he had no vote in our move, nor had Susan. He was 5 feet 10 and weighed 180 and had been an all-conference fullback in New Jersey, but one of the Wisconsin papers listed him as 6 feet 2, 210 and all-state, and another carried that ridiculous story that he was being offered cars to pick between the four high schools.

"I'll never forget that first day out here," he has said since. "There are a thousand kids in that school, and the first time I walked into that cafeteria a thousand heads turned and a thousand kids looked at me."

One afternoon Marie drove out to watch Vincent practice. While she was sitting in her car another car drove up and one of the kids in it shouted to someone on the sidelines.

"Which one is Lombardi?" he shouted, and Marie said she

thought: Oh, please. Please leave him alone! He's just a seventeen-year-old boy. Please get off his back.

It must have been just about then that Marie came off the phone one evening. Someone had wanted her to do something and she had turned it down.

"Sometimes they claw at you," she said. "Just because your husband knows how to coach football they claw at you."

And Vincent looked up from that book he was reading and said, "Join the crowd, Mom."

8:52 A.M.

I'm in the line of traffic now, and I guess what it comes down to is that success demands singleness of purpose. In this game we're always looking for catch-phrases, especially with a connotation of masculinity, so I call it mental toughness. They have written about the mental toughness with which I supposedly have instilled this team and, when they ask me what it is, I have difficulty explaining it. I think it is singleness of purpose and, once you have agreed upon the price that you and your family must pay for success, it enables you to forget that price. It enables you to ignore the minor hurts, the opponent's pressure, and the temporary failures, and I remember my first year here. I remember that first day of full practice in training camp, and when I walked back to the dressing room I wanted to cry. The lackadaisical ineptitude, almost passive resistance, was like an insidious disease that had infected almost a whole squad. The next morning, when I walked into the trainer's room, there must have been fifteen or twenty of them waiting for the whirlpool bath or the diathermy or for rubdowns.

"What is this?" I said. "An emergency casualty ward? Now get this straight. When you're hurt you have every right to be in here. When you're hurt you'll get the best medical attention we can provide. We've got too much money invested in you to think otherwise, but this has got to stop. This is disgraceful. I have no patience with the small hurts that are bothering most of you. You're going to have to learn to live with small hurts and play with small hurts if you're going to play for me. Now I don't want to see anything like this again."

Then I walked out. The next day when I walked into that room there weren't fifteen or twenty in there. There were two, so maybe that's how you do it.

III

The Press Box

JOHN WIEBUSCH

Barnstorming

It is a story unlike any of the modern age. In 1925, the Chicago Bears took the road for two whirlwind barnstorming tours to promote their prize acquisition: famed halfback Red Grange. The 17-game spree made fistfuls of money for Grange and his flamboyant manager, C.C. Pyle, and included stops in outposts such as New Orleans, Los Angeles, and Portland. John Wiebusch, the guiding editorial force behind NFL publications, chronicled the tours for PRO! *magazine in 1977.*

RED GRANGE WAS SITTING in the back row of the Virginia Theater when an usher tapped him on the shoulder.

"Mr. Pyle wants you to have this," said the usher, handing Grange a piece of paper.

Grange turned the paper over and read the handwritten note. It said that Red Grange and a friend were entitled to see movies, free of charge, at either the Virginia Theater or the Park Theater in Champaign, Illinois. The note was signed by C.C. Pyle.

"Look," said Grange to Earl Britton, who sat next to him. "It's the first free thing I've gotten since I came to school here."

Britton laughed. "Maybe this Pyle just wants some football tickets," he said.

In October, 1925, Harold (Red) Grange was the biggest name in college football. He had been an All-America tailback in 1923 and 1924 and no one doubted he would be honored again after his senior season.

Two weeks later Grange used his movie pass for the first time. The Pathé newsreel, which included an item about Illinois's recent loss to the University of Michigan, had just ended and *The Freshman*, starring Harold Lloyd, was about to begin when the usher leaned in to Grange and whispered, "Mr. Pyle wants to see you in his office upstairs."

C.C. (Charley) Pyle's office was one door past the men's room. He was on the phone when Grange entered but he motioned the young man to sit down.

Pyle was talking about buying a movie theater somewhere in Indiana. "You tell me if that's a good buy or not," he said into the phone as he cradled the receiver on his shoulder and rubbed his thin mustache. Pyle was immaculately dressed in a blue pin-stripe suit. In his early 40s, he looked more like a dandy out of a *Liberty* magazine clothing ad than someone you'd expect to see in a windowless theater office.

"Got to run," said Pyle. "An important visitor just walked in."

Pyle hung up the phone and rose to shake Grange's hand. "If you only knew how much I admire your style of play on a football field," he said.

Pyle sat down and clipped the end off a Cuban cigar. "Red, how'd you like to make a hundred thousand dollars . . .maybe even a million?

"Well yes, of course," stammered Grange. "On the up and up?" For a moment he thought maybe Pyle was with the Capone mob.

"Playing football, my boy," said Pyle. "I believe I can work out a deal with the Bears for you to go on tour with them after your last game here. It'll be the biggest thing this country's ever seen."

"I'm flattered," said Grange. "But how?"

"You leave that to me, Red." Pyle leaned back in his swivel chair. "Only thing is, you keep our conversation here under wraps, see? When your pals ask you what I wanted, you tell them something else."

The two men rose and shook hands and Grange returned to his seat. The Harold Lloyd movie had begun.

"What'd he want?" said a voice in the dark.

"Tickets," said Grange. "Earl was right."

Pyle called Grange the following week. "Charley Pyle has just made you a very wealthy man," he said. He told Grange about his meeting with the Bears' co-owners, George Halas and Ed (Dutch) Sternaman. He said that he had worked out a fifty-fifty financial agreement. Grange would be guaranteed $3,000 minimum per game for a tour of major American cities.

"But that's just chicken feed," said Pyle. "You'll make a lot more than that. People want to see you."

Grange and Pyle agreed on the division of Grange's share of the money. Grange would get 60 percent, Pyle 40. The same arrangement would hold true for money from endorsements. Grange's contract would be with Pyle, not with the Bears.

"Now sit tight and wait," said Pyle. "We're all right as long as no money changes hands. Believe me, a lot of money will change hands later, though."

Pyle shook his head. "Never seen anything like it. What you did against Penn last Saturday! I'm looking at the *New York World* right now and Ford Frick says here, 'In the annals of play on the American gridiron no man has equalled what Red did here Saturday against the University of Pennsylvania.' It's the same in Granny Rice and Damon Runyon . . . all of 'em. They write about you like you were some kind of messiah. What a natural!"

"Mr. Pyle, those words are nice. But I don't believe . . ."

"Believe, believe! We could put you in vaudeville right now. George White would die! Money can't buy things like that ride they gave you from the station here Monday! What a thing!"

When the Illinois team arrived from Philadelphia by train, over 20,000 people were in and around the Champaign-Urbana station to meet it. Playing in the East for the first time and against a team that had been favored, Grange scored three touchdowns and rushed for 363 yards in a 24-2 Illinois victory. The man they were waiting for tried to avoid the bedlam by sneaking out the back of the train, but he was spotted by a group of students and carried more than two miles on their shoulders to the Zeta Psi fraternity house. Grange had tears in his eyes most of the way.

Pyle said he was leaving the next day for Miami, Tampa, Jacksonville, and New Orleans to begin making tour arrangements. "Plan on spending Christmas under the sun," he said. "A few lovelies, a little football. The time of your life."

At a party on Saturday night after a victory over the University of Chicago, Grange was dancing a new dance called the Charleston with a girl named Louise.

"Is it true what I hear?" she asked.

"What do you hear?" said Grange.

"That J.P. Morgan soon won't be able to hold a candle to the great Red Grange."

"Hell," said Grange, "don't believe everything you hear." It was a time of intensely competitive journalism—radio was the electronic rage, newspapers sought the real story, and newsreels reported the wonders of the world to theater audiences—and there were Red Grange rumors everywhere. He had signed a contract with two baseball owners, Charles Stoneham of the New York Giants and Jake Ruppert of the New York Yankees, to head a team in a new pro football league. He had signed a contract with Tim Mara of the New York Giants of the National Football League. He would tour with the Four Horsemen of Notre Dame, who had finished their college careers in the January 1925 Rose Bowl. He had signed with the Chicago Bears. He had signed with a millionaire theater magnate named C.C. Pyle.

Warren Brown, the *Chicago Tribune* sports editor who had first named Grange the Galloping Ghost, had the Pyle story. "People who know C.C. Pyle," he wrote, "claim the initials stand for Cash and Carry. Mr. Grange is hereby forewarned."

The *Champaign News-Gazette* summoned Grange to its office and claimed it had learned that he had signed a contract to play pro ball. "We know you've gotten money," said the managing editor.

"A damned lie," said Grange. He grabbed his hat and stormed out of the office.

More than the money or even the violation of ethics, it was the sport—the pro sport—that rankled most people. College football was one of America's favorite sports toys; professional football was a rag doll.

"He is a living legend now," wrote Irving Vaughan in the *Chicago News*. "Why go and sully it?"

"I'd be glad to see Grange do anything else except play professional football," said Fielding Yost, the athletic director at Michigan.

The should-he-or-shouldn't-he furor was a national sensation and most so-called "good and decent" men opposed the money.

Only the usually unkind Westbrook Pegler of the *Chicago Tribune* was sympathetic. Writing in response to a suggestion that Grange should try his skills at writing and movie acting, Pegler replied, "To be an imitation writer or a fake movie actor would surely be less virtuous than becoming a real football player."

In the next-to-last game of the season, Illinois defeated Wabash. Bob Zuppke, the Illinois coach, stopped by Grange's locker after the press had gone.

"You tell me you have not signed a contract to play professional football," said Zuppke, "and I believe you."

Grange nodded.

"But I want to tell you to keep away from professionalism and you will be another Walter Camp." The man who did more to shape football than any other had died in the previous spring. "Football just isn't a game to be played for money."

"You get paid for coaching, Zup," said Grange. "Why should it be wrong for me to get paid for playing?"

"I want you to visit your father next week."

"Fine, but it won't change my mind."

On Tuesday, Grange rook the train to Wheaton, a small town near Chicago. His father, Lyle, the chief of police, met him at the station.

They drove in silence for most of the way to the family home. Then Lyle Grange spoke. "You know how I feel about all this," he said. "But whatever decision you make, I'll stand by you."

"I've got a chance to turn pro, dad," said Red. "It'll give me a chance to pay you back for all the things you did for me and Garland since mom died." Sadie Grange had died when Red was five and Lyle then moved the family from Forksville, Pennsylvania, to Wheaton.

They drove into the driveway and Lyle Grange turned off the ignition. "Is this fellow Pyle on the up and up?" he asked. "I don't like this Cash and Carry thing."

"I got a call from him yesterday," said the son. "He's in Tampa and the reports he's getting all over are the crowds for our games will really be big ones . . . record ones. He's talking about all sorts of things—movies, the stage, endorsements. Charley's a showman—and he's not timid, boy, I'll say!—but I feel in my bones that he's honest as the day's long."

Lyle Grange squeezed his son's shoulder.

Illinois's final game—the last in the remarkable collegiate career of Red Grange—would be in Columbus, Ohio. "GRANGE TO BE INELIGIBLE" screamed one headline but L.W. St. Johns, the Ohio State athletic director, said, "If Red Grange denies the rumor that he's signed a contract with the pros, then that's good enough for me."

In a parade in Columbus the night before the game, Zuppke had an Illinois reserve impersonate his storied running back. "You get some rest," he told Grange. Red spent the night in his room. Later, he told his roommate, Earl Britton, the Illinois fullback, "I'm all mixed up. I'm all worried. I hope what I'm doing is right. I think it is . . . but they make me feel guilty already."

"Hell," said Britton, "you'd be a damn fool to turn it down."

Grange accounted for 192 yards against Ohio State, passing for one touchdown and intercepting a pass to end an Ohio State threat. Illinois won 14-9 and reporters poured onto the field and surrounded him.

"I intend to sign an agreement to play with the Chicago Bears," said Grange. "I have nothing to say right now."

Grange took the train from Columbus to Chicago, where he

registered under an assumed name at the Belmont Hotel. The reporters who filled the lobby of the Morrison Hotel, where Charley Pyle had opened an office, never found Grange that night.

Late the following morning, Grange and Pyle met with Bears owners Halas, who also was the team's coach as well as its right end, and Sternaman. It was the first time Grange had met either man. The agreement was confirmed and there were handshakes all around.

The contract would be signed the following morning. On this day Grange would watch from the bench in street clothes while the Bears played the Green Bay Packers.

The game was secondary to the presence of the superstar. At halftime nearly 3,000 people attempted to storm the field to get to Grange and the police had to be called in.

They went to a speakeasy that night, Grange and Pyle, and Charley Pyle lifted a glass of scotch and said, "I don't give a tinker's damn what they call me. Cash and Carry. Cold Cash. We'll have the last laugh, you and me."

"It's a lot of games to play in not much time," said Grange, "but we can do it."

"Your check, Mr. Pyle," said the waiter.

"Thank you, Eddie," said Pyle. The check was for $18. Pyle left two twenty-dollar bills.

The signing took place in the Bears' office on Monday morning.

"You look tired, Red," said a reporter.

"He's exhausted trying to figure out ways to spend the money," said Pyle.

The next morning in the *Chicago Examiner* Harry MacNamara wrote, "Mr. Charles Pyle has done the very best he could do to keep Harold 'Red' Grange busy during the interval between Thursday [November 26] and December 13. 'Red' and his supporting cast, the Chicago Bears, will be asked to do something that probably has never been attempted by an individual player or team previously.

"Pyle has succeeded in scheduling a total of 10 games in 18 days, which is a pretty fair achievement for a young manager. While going about the country playing the schedule Pyle has mapped out and 'getting the money while the getting is good,' Grange and his team will travel approximately 3,000 miles around the East . . .

"There are rumors that another, longer tour will follow."

The 10-game schedule began at Wrigley Field against the Chicago Cardinals on Thanksgiving Day, November 26, and the Columbus Tigers on Sunday, November 29. Following that were eight games in 12 days, a journey by train that had Grange and the Bears in St. Louis against the Donnelly All-Stars on Wednesday, December 2; in Philadelphia against the Frankford Yellowjackets on Saturday, December 5; in New York against the Giants on Sunday, December 6; in Washington against the Washington All-Stars on Tuesday, December 8; in Boston against the Providence Steam Roller on Wednesday, December 9; in Pittsburgh against the Pittsburgh Semipros on Thursday, December 10; in Detroit against the Detroit All-Stars on Saturday, December 12, and, finally, back in Chicago against the Giants on Sunday, December 13.

On Tuesday night Grange was having dinner at a Chicago supper club with Britton and two coeds who had driven up from Champaign.

"Don't kill yourself," said Britton.

Grange shrugged and offered his glass. "To good times," he said. "To prosperity."

"Oh, Red!" said one of the girls.

"Earl," said Grange, "maybe you should come along and get rich, too!"

"Tell 'em I'm in the book," said Britton.

The band was playing "Show Me the Way to Go Home," but there was no chance of that. It was only 11 o'clock.

When tickets went on sale at Spalding's store on State Street the next day, the line extended outside the door, up the block, around a corner, and down the next street. No one had anticipated a demand like this, particularly not the ticket printer. Only 20,000 tickets were ready and all of them were sold in three hours.

Wrigley Field overflowed with people on Thanksgiving Day. The largest crowd ever to see a pro football game—over 36,000—ignored a snowstorm that came howling out of the western prairies into Chicago.

There had been rumors that Grange would be given "free rein to run up and down the field" but the man who wore number 77 managed only 36 yards and was outplayed by the Cardinals' Paddy Driscoll.

Grange was despondent with his performance afterward but Pyle entered the locker room beaming. "Holy cow," he announced, "that was the damnedest crowd I've ever seen. I saw one guy coming over the fence with the gate around his neck. Did you hear those cries for you, Red?"

Grange was peeling off his muddy uniform. "How could I not hear them?" he said.

It snowed on each of the next two days in Chicago and it was snowing again on Sunday, when the Columbus team was the opponent. A crowd of over 28,000 watched Grange rush for 140 yards and pass for a touchdown in Chicago's 14-13 victory.

On December 1, Britton signed a contract with the Bears.

"Whoever said they don't hit hard up here is full of it," Grange told the fullback. "Two games and I've got bruises like I've never had."

It was 12 degrees in St. Louis on December 2 when Grange and the Bears came to town to play a game against a team assembled by a local mortician, Francis Donnelly. Only 8,000 people braved the fierce weather to see Grange score four times and lead the Bears to a 39-6 triumph.

On the train bound for Philadelphia, Pyle stood up in the dining car and made an announcement. "Just wanted you boys to know that I talked on the phone with Mr. Tim Mara in New York this morning and he tells me that over 40,000 tickets have already been sold for our game there Sunday. We've set a record and we aren't even there yet."

Grange fell asleep at 9:30 that night. He slept all the way to Philadelphia.

On Saturday, December 5, a driving rainstorm hit the Philadelphia area and the game that day was played in a sea of mud. Remarkably, 35,000 people sat through the downpour in Shibe Park as Grange scored both Chicago touchdowns in a 14-0 victory.

The Bears dressed on the train to New York, where they would play the Giants the following day. They were faced with the uncomfortable predicament of having to wear the same jerseys, wet, muddy, unlaundered.

“This tour will make you so wealthy, Halas,” said Pyle to the Bears’ co-owner. “that next year you’ll be able to afford two sets of uniforms.”

Tim Mara, the New York Giants’ owner, was in the lobby of the Astor Hotel when the Bears arrived. “It’s been raining here for four days,” he said to Halas and Pyle. “But we’ve got over a hundred thousand dollars in the bank already. Wait’ll you see the Polo Grounds tomorrow.”

The Polo Grounds were filled to official capacity—over 65,000—but gate crashers probably swelled the figure by another 8,000 people.

“I looked out the window of my office at 12:30,” Mara said to a group of reporters in the press box, “and I saw ladders being put up against the lower section of the bleachers on Eighth Avenue. Kids began pouring over the wall like ants. For every one the ushers caught, a dozen made it into the crowd. Looks like a few got into this press box.” Over 125 reporters were covering the game, another record.

Grange scored a touchdown after intercepting a pass and the Bears won 14-7. The star running back took a savage physical beating, however. He nursed his wounds with Pyle that night at an East Side speakeasy.

“A lot of players might be taking after you because of the money you’re making,” said Pyle. “The hundred, two hundred bucks a game they’re getting isn’t bad but it isn’t what Red Grange is getting, either.”

Grange felt a cut on his chin. "Make me feel good. Tell me how much I'm up to now."

"Your share," said Pyle, "is close to fifty thousand already."

Monday was a day away from football but it was not a day away from business. Pyle had scheduled a series of business appointments with various interests that sought Grange's endorsement and, most important, with Joseph P. Kennedy of Boston, who was producing films in Hollywood.

They came, one after another, and Grange signed contracts that would permit the use of his name in cigarette advertising (Grange to Pyle: "But I don't even smoke." Pyle to Grange: "But in the ads you'll only be saying you like the *aroma* of their cigarette smoke.") and in various clothing ads. There also would be a Red Grange doll, a Red Grange candy bar, a Red Grange meat loaf, a Red Grange sweater, Red Grange socks, Red Grange shoes, and a Red Grange fountain pen.

In the early afternoon, a surprise visitor dropped by Grange's suite. "Kid, I want to give you a bit of advice," said Babe Ruth of the New York Yankees. "Don't pay any attention to what they say or write about you. And don't pick up too many checks."

Kennedy and the movie people came by later and when they left, Charley Pyle flashed a check for $300,000 in front of a large press conference.

"Gentlemen," he said, "this young fellow here made more money today by just signing his name to various documents than anyone in the history of sport. I'm not at liberty to tell you how much the endorsements brought—although I can tell you that it amounts to a tidy sum."

On the train to Washington Monday night Grange questioned Pyle's judgment.

"We got less than a quarter of the $300,000 you said we got," said Grange. "Why'd we have to go and show a phony check."

"Publicity, my boy," said Pyle. "Every newspaper in the country will have that $300,000 in its headlines tomorrow."

Pyle lit a cigar. "And you took care of the matter with the actress?"

"I told her I'd try to call her when we got to Hollywood." A noted movie actress had called Grange at the Astor on Monday morning and suggested her name as a possible Mrs. Harold Grange.

In Washington, Grange had a message to call Illinois Senator William Brown McKinley.

"I'd like to take you and Mr. Halas by the White House before the game," said McKinley, "and have you say hello to President Coolidge."

Senator McKinley sent his car down in the morning to pick up Grange and Halas, and he met the two men at the White House. The senator proudly introduced his noted guests to Coolidge.

"Mr. President, this is Mr. Red Grange and Mr. George Halas with the Chicago Bears."

Coolidge nodded. "Glad to meet you young gentlemen," he said. "I always did like animal acts." The President did not follow sports. He had no idea who Grange and Halas were.

Grange was a tired, unimpressive figure in the football game that afternoon, contributing little to the Bears' 19-0 victory. Despite the first moderate weather of the trip, the crowd was only 8,000.

On the train from Washington to Boston, Grange held a portable phonograph in his lap. Alone with his aches and pains in a corner of the Pullman car, he was playing jazz records.

Ford Frick stopped by to see how Grange was feeling. "Gosh, I'm tired," he said. "I wish I could get away somewhere." It had been only 13 days since his first pro game.

Later, Frick would write, "The strain of this tour is starting to show on Grange. He is tremendously human, in his quiet, shy way, and just a little bit nervous and bored by the laudations which suddenly have come his way. And the pace has begun to tell. Deep lines showed about Red's face today . . ."

Most of the Bears were ailing when the team took the field against the Steam Roller in Boston December 9 for their fifth game in eight days. Grange's play was poor and the crowd of 25,000 began to boo him early in the game. The Providence team, with three of the Four

Horsemen in the backfield, outmanned the Bears 9-6. Grange managed just 18 yards.

The Bears had begun the trip with only 18 players and injuries were taking a heavy toll. On the following day in Pittsburgh, Chicago had only 10 reasonably healthy players, among them Grange.

"Lotshaw," said George Halas in the lobby of the hotel that morning, "you're playing tackle today."

Andy Lotshaw was the Bears' trainer. He had not played football for years and he was out of shape.

"I've got to warn you," said Lotshaw. "I've signed a personal service contract with Charley Pyle."

It was the Bears' only laugh of the day. They lost to a pickup Pittsburgh team 24-0 before 18,000 fans and Grange lasted only one play. A muscle was torn in his left arm and a blood clot began to form as he sat on the sidelines.

Grange was unable to play a day later in Detroit and over 20,000 people requested refunds. A gathering of 6,000 viewed the Bears' 21-0 loss to another recently assembled team.

The Bears returned to Chicago that night to face the Giants on the following day. The weather was stern again and if Grange did not play, advance sales would almost certainly melt into refunds. Two days before, a doctor in Pittsburgh had said, "Grange should not attempt to play football for two weeks. To do so might bring lasting injury." But on the morning of December 13, the Chicago newspapers announced that Grange's injury was "not near as bad as had been thought and he will play today against New York."

Grange saw only minimal action in the game but the crowd of over 18,000 was unfazed. They cheered every move he made on the bench and it took police escorts to get him to the dressing room at halftime and off the field when it was over. The Bears lost their fourth consecutive game, 9-0.

Halas met with his walking wounded in the dressing room. On the last three games of the trip, the trainer had played tackle, a fullback had played end, a guard had played quarterback. Not a man on the team did not have at least one major or minor injury, including Halas.

"You have eight days to lick your wounds," he said. "Be back here on the twenty-first and we'll go and see what sunshine looks like. See you at the station!"

Grange and Pyle celebrated that night with two showgirls.

"No dancing," said Grange. "I'm too stiff to even think about any of that hot stuff."

Pyle was euphoric. He and Grange had netted nearly $150,000 from their share of the tour. Then there were the endorsements and the movie deal. And there still were nine games left to play—in Miami, December 25; in Tampa, January 1; in Jacksonville, January 2; in New Orleans, January 10; in Los Angeles, January 16; in San Diego, January 17; in San Francisco, January 24; in Portland, January 30; and in Seattle, January 31. The reports of advance ticket sales were good. They might draw 70,000 alone in Los Angeles.

"This country is mad for sports events," said Pyle. "For any diversion. See what you kids think about this one. A cross-country marathon race . . . get a lot of people to enter, create a lot of excitement, then sell programs in each city for a quarter apiece and make out like a bandit."

"I don't know," said Grange. "Think people would care about running?"

"They care about dance marathons, don't they?" snapped Pyle. "No, this would work, I'm sure of it." He took a sip from his glass. "Talked with Hollywood today. They wanted to call our movie *The Halfback*. I talked them into something a bit more jazzy. *One Minute to Play*. Here, I says, you've got the most exciting athlete in history and you got to take advantage of what he does. They're writing a real potboiler for you. We start shooting in June. Pardon me, girls, but if you think the ladies are lovely here, Redhead, wait till you get a gander of Hollywood!"

Grange laughed and got up with his date to go to the dance floor. He had decided to try a Charleston after all.

He went home to Wheaton the next day driving a new Auburn

roadster that was a present for his brother. He was wearing his personal extravagance, a $500 raccoon coat, and in his pocket was a $5,000 check made out to Lyle Grange.

"Get everything you need," he said to his father. "Do it up brown!"

"How did it go?" asked Lyle Grange. "Or is that a silly question?"

"It went great," Red said. "I was right about Charley Pyle."

The team that left for Florida on December 21 was augmented by some players who had played for other NFL teams during the regular season. The league president, Joe Carr, had given the Bears permission to increase their roster to 22 men for this special tour.

The first game would be played in Coral Gables, a Miami suburb in the midst of a building boom. When the Bears arrived, however, they found that work had nor yet begun on the stadium that was to hold the game. But nearly 10,000 tickets had been sold at prices ranging from $5.50 to $18.

The promoter raised his hands at Pyle's outrage. "A miracle will happen before your eyes," he said. An army of carpenters invaded a large open field and, working round the clock, built a 25,000-seat stadium in less than 48 hours. It was ready on Christmas day.

Grange gained 98 yards and scored the game's only touchdown as Chicago beat a local all-star team 7-3. As the team was leaving the field, workmen were already beginning to dismantle the stadium. "In two weeks there'll be forty houses on this site," said the promoter.

After a week in the sunshine of Miami Beach, the Bears moved on to Tampa on New Year's Day to play a local team that included 37-year-old Jim Thorpe. Over 12,000 people saw Grange run 73 yards for a touchdown, gain 135 yards, and lead Chicago to a 17-3 victory.

Grange's fast money had encouraged other speculators to go after big-name college stars and a Jacksonville promoter had secured the services of another All-America back, Ernie Nevers of Stanford. Nevers would get $25,000 for two games, one against the Bears and another later exhibition against the New York Giants.

Grange vs. Nevers was billed as "The Football Match of the

Century" and tickets were priced at $8.50 and $5.50. Temporary seats were hastily built to increase the Jacksonville stadium's capacity to 35,000. Raymond Hitchcock, still famous for his Broadway success in *Kitchy-Koo* two years earlier, came from New York to see the game. The noted gatecrasher, One-Eyed Connelley ("there's not an event I can't get into") was in the park, too.

Nevers won the epic confrontation if rushing yards are the measuring stick (101-55), but Grange threw a touchdown pass and made some spectacular plays on defense as Chicago won 19-6.

The coast-to-coast tour that eventually would cover over 7,000 miles was off to New Orleans. Pyle had made accommodations for the Bears to have their own private Pullman car and dining car.

"Nothing but first class," Pyle said to Grange. "By the end of this trip you'll be purring like a kitten."

There were poker games on the train and one afternoon while they passed through Alabama, Grange won over $500.

"Lucky son of a gun," said an angry loser. "He don't need it, he wins it."

Words were exchanged and Halas had to intercede. "No more five dollar limit," he said. "From now on it's ten cents."

The team arrived in New Orleans the day before the game and Grange was invited out to the Fairgrounds racetrack for the running of the Red Grange Handicap. A horse named Prickly Heat ridden by a jockey with red hair was the winner and Grange made the winner's circle presentation of an enormous pink floral football.

The next day he ran for 136 yards and one touchdown in Chicago's 14-0 victory before nearly 10,000 people. The gross gate was over $21,000 and Pyle had guaranteed the visiting all-star team $6,000. At halftime, Lester Lautenschlaeger, the New Orleans quarterback, cornered Pyle under the stands. "Pay us half the money now and the other half later," said Lautenschlaeger, "or we don't go back on the field." Pyle counted $3,000 in small bills from a satchel he was carrying. He paid the balance later.

Southern California was the end of the rainbow in the 1920s.

Movie money was everywhere and the living was easy. Stars were the idols of the masses and Red Grange was a star.

His picture was on the cover of *Variety* and he told an interviewer, "My favorite actor on the screen is Douglas Fairbanks. I like him because he's got a lot of pep and is athletic. When I go to a movie I prefer to see some redblooded man playing the lead in preference to a woman."

And was he looking forward to his own movie career?

"I can't promise any great shakes. I'll just do the best I can and hope the people like it. Mr. Pyle and I also are talking about a vaudeville tour. But I'm not much of a comic and I'm not sure just what I'll do."

The interviewer responded parenthetically, "Does it matter? He's just our Red and that's enough. Or should be."

The Bears were staying at the Biltmore Hotel and Pyle, looking down out of his window at Pershing Square, had an inspiration. He called the papers and the next morning there were 5,000 people in the square attempting to catch footballs thrown off the Biltmore roof by Bears players. The first man to catch a ball was given $100.

"They know we're here," Grange said to Pyle that night. "You're amazing!"

Over 75,000 people were in the Coliseum on January 16. It was the third time on the trip that the pro football attendance record had been broken. George (Wildcat) Wilson, an All-America back for the University of Washington, made his pro debut that day. He would remain a member of the opposing team for the balance of the tour.

Grange did not disappoint the boisterous crowd. He tackled Wilson from behind on the first play from scrimmage to save a touchdown, then later scored twice himself in Chicago's 17-7 victory.

Grange played poker that night in a group that included Adolphe Menjou, Andy Devine, and Pyle.

"A crowd like that for an exhibition game in January is beyond belief," said Menjou. "My hat's off to you boys."

"Red Grange is magic," said Pyle and then he proposed a toast to his client's Hollywood successes. "Can't miss."

"Agreed," said Menjou.

Grange and the Bears drew nearly 65,000 people on the remaining four dates of the tour—San Diego, San Francisco, Portland, and Seattle—and the running back scored five more touchdowns. The Bears won three of the four games, losing only in San Francisco when Wilson scored both touchdowns in a 12-7 triumph.

The 10,000-mile journey that had begun on Thanksgiving day, 1925 in Chicago ended in Seattle January 31, 1926. The Bears had played 18 games before nearly 400,000 people.

Grange and Pyle took the train back to Chicago. They would return to Los Angeles four months later to begin *One Minute to Play.*

"No one will ever attempt anything like this again," said Grange.

Pyle finished signing a check for $75,000 and passed it across the table. He winked. "Don't be so sure, my boy. Don't be so sure."

The train moved across Montana and they drank Dom Perignon champagne, 1921.

Red Grange went on to make two movies, One Minute to Play *(1926) and* Racing Romeo *(1927), and a serial,* The Galloping Ghost *(1929). The movies were successful, especially* One Minute to Play, *but his acting was wooden. He also toured the vaudeville circuit with a routine entitled, "Hi, I'm Red."*

Grange and Pyle each demanded one-third ownership in the Bears in 1926 as compensation for the successes of the tour, but Halas and Sternaman refused. Grange and Pyle then sought a second franchise for New York, but Tim Mara turned that request down. The two entrepreneurs then began their own league, the American Football League, and were co-owners of two teams, the New York Yankees, for whom Grange played, and the Los Angeles Wildcats, a road team that was led by Wildcat Wilson.

The AFL lasted one year and Grange and Pyle both lost money. When the league folded, the Yankees were added to the National Football League. Early in the 1927 season, Grange suffered a disabling knee injury, ironically against the Chicago Bears. He was on crutches for eight months and missed the entire 1928 season which was the Yankees' last.

Grange's contract with Pyle expired at the end of 1927 but the two men remained friends and Grange joined Pyle in a deluxe motor home that accompanied a successful cross-country marathon promotion in the summer of 1928.

Finally rehabilitated under the care of a Los Angeles doctor in 1929, Grange accepted Halas's invitation to rejoin the Bears. He played six years with the Bears, distinguishing himself on defense. "I was a straight-ahead runner those years," he says. "The Galloping Ghost went down that day in 1927." He was a participant in three of the most memorable games in NFL history—the indoor playoff game against Portsmouth in 1932, the first championship game in NFL history in 1933 (a 23-21 Chicago victory), and the "Sneakers Game" loss to the Giants in the 1934 championship game (a 30-14 loss ruined Chicago's bid for a perfect 14-0 season).

Grange was an assistant coach under Halas for three seasons after he retired as a player, then participated in various business and sales ventures. He met Margaret (Mugs) Hazelberg in the fall of 1940 and the two were married October 13, 1941. In ensuing years, Grange became a radio and television sports commentator. He was a charter member of the Pro Football Hall of Fame in 1963. Now retired, he lives with Mugs in Indian Lakes Estates, Florida. He is 74 years old.

C.C. (Charley) Pyle died in Los Angeles on February 4, 1939. He was 56. "Charley was as honest as the day is long," says Grange. "I got every cent I ever had coming to me . . .and I got most of them because of him. If he were active today there'd be no end to the money he'd make. He was a great promoter . . .the greatest."

George Halas is still the owner of the Chicago Bears. He is 82 years old.

MICKEY HERSKOWITZ

Once Upon a Time in Dallas

Before the Dallas Cowboys, before Lamar Hunt's Dallas Texans of the American Football League, there was another Dallas Texans. They played in the NFL for one season, 1952, and if you don't remember them you are not alone. HOUSTON POST *columnist Mickey Herskowitz dredged up some Lone Star ghosts for* PRO! *magazine in 1972. Herskowitz familiarized himself with the Texans while writing* THE GOLDEN AGE OF PRO FOOTBALL, *a warm and hilarious remembrance of the NFL of the fifties, in 1974.*

IT CONVULSED THEM IN DALLAS, in 1960 when Lamar Hunt decided to call his pro football team the Texans. He could have called them the Aardvarks, or the Zombies, or any of 10,000 splendid names in between. But he chose the Texans. Possibly he was trying to cash in on the success of the last team to own that name.

The original Dallas Texans were so successful they did not even finish the season. They lost 11 out of 12 games and established what was, to that time, a world record for returning kickoffs, 67. The Texans—we think of them as the first, or vintage Texans—folded up like an old road map at midyear and were left in the lap of the National Football League. It was a team without a flag, living on the league's purse, playing its last five games on the road.

This was 1952. And you know that we are in a cycle, that we are indeed belly surfing across a wave of nostalgia, when people resurrect the memory of the '52 Dallas Texans. They were the product of a curiously mixed decade, one that gave us Elvis Presley, hula hoops, the bop, duck-tail haircuts, and the soda fountain as a center for the American youth culture.

Has it been more than 20 years? It has. And today, in the city where the Texans failed so utterly, the Dallas Cowboys now hang their headgear. The Texans are to the Cowboys what Wallis Warfield Simpson is to the British monarchy. Related if not by blood, at least by legend.

It is surprising how few people are aware that there existed in 1952 a team called the Texans. On the other hand, maybe it isn't.

The Texans did not leave much of a footprint on the sands of professional football. Yet it was not a team bereft of talent. It had Buddy Young, an exciting little runner who could move like a wisp of smoke at his peak. There were soon-to-be stars in Gino Marchetti at end and Art Donovan at tackle. And a few tough, willing pros such as Dick Hoerner and Tom Keane, part of a carload of 11 players obtained from the Rams in a sensational trade for Les Richter. But the Texans were a team in between.

When they lost, which was nearly always, they did so with regret. Once Frankie Albert offended them by faking a punt and passing deep, looking for a quick one with the 49ers ahead by 30 points. "When the ref wasn't watching," recalls Art Donovan, "one of our guys coldcocked him. He tells Albert, 'If you get up, I'll kill ya.' He didn't get up!"

The owners, the city, and the team suffered separately but equally. "It was," decided Tex Maule of *Sports Illustrated*, "a screwed up operation from the beginning."

It isn't widely known, and he does not go out of his way to enlighten people, but Maule served as publicity man for the old Texans. To get a break like that he had to walk away from the same job with the Rams, world champions the year before.

"I was convinced the Texans couldn't miss," reflects Maule, today pro football's best-known historian. "I was hired by Frank Fitzgerald, Ted Collins's son-in-law. When I got to Dallas I asked for Fitzgerald. He had been fired the day before. I was off to a great start."

The new owners of the team were the Miller brothers, Giles and Connell, heirs to a textile fortune. They were men of the cloth, so to speak, but they were quite unprepared to lose their shirts in a game that was not yet our national mania.

Formerly the New York Yanks, the team had made a large dent in the bankroll of Ted Collins, who made his pile managing Kate Smith. In 1952, larger crowds were turning out to hear Kate Smith sing "God Bless America" than to see the Texans play.

By the end of the season, pro football was a dead issue in Dallas. As a prospect for any kind of future revival, it looked about as appealing as the Los Alamos Testing Grounds. In January 1953, Al Ennis, who had been dispatched from the home office of commissioner Bert Bell to help organize the franchise, wrote a sad, bitter letter to the club's executive secretary, Marilyn Cunningham:

"It is almost certain that Baltimore will receive the franchise so nonchalantly thrown overboard by the Texas millionaires. They have already sold over fifteen thousand season tickets and are still going strong—a most amazing performance, and one that indicates tremendous civic pride. This is the sort of civic interest which all of us in the league confidently expected Dallas to exhibit—but we were wrong . . .it will be a long time, if ever, before anyone outside of Texas will believe that any group of Texans would not quit *cold* if the going got rough."

Still, the team might have been saved for Dallas. The wealthy Clint Murchison, Jr., had indicated an interest in bailing out the Millers. But when the crunch came, Murchison was in South America, and Bert Bell declined to give the team's management time to contact him.

The ominous signs were present in training camp—an uncertain coaching staff, a team composed of strangers. And a city that hadn't really asked for this blessing wasn't tuned up for it.

The team trained in Kerrville, where after practice one day Maule discovered a solitary Buddy Young still on the field doing sit-ups. Taking in the deserted landscape, Maule grinned and said, "What's the matter with you, Buddy?"

Between grunts Young replied, "Tex, a man is going to have to be in peak physical condition this year just to survive."

Young was, and he did. A black man playing in a city then still largely segregated, Buddy became the team's most popular player. Whatever else, the Texans quietly struck a blow for social justice. "There was talk of segregated seating at the Cotton Bowl," says Young. "But the Texans knocked out Jim Crow. I think that was a breakthrough."

As the season wore on, few of the players shared Buddy Young's intensity. During their final days on the road the Texans bivouacked in Hershey, Pennsylvania, the league taking the position that everyone has to be some place.

The five-week sentence in Hershey was an exercise in playing out the clock. Most of their practice time was spent playing volleyball over the goal posts. They were as restless as sailors waiting to be discharged.

The Texans were a mixed collection of styles and temper. "We had some characters," recalls Young. "Chubby Grigg, we got him in the Weldon Humble trade. Chub was mean as a snake, fat as a hog, on the downside of his pro career. His whole disposition was mean."

Once, when Buddy tried to break up a fight, Grigg picked him up and threw him into the phonograph, around which the team would gather and listen to Kay Starr sing "Wheel of Fortune" night after night. "We sure hated to lose that record player," said Donovan.

Young remembers the starting quarterback, Bob Celeri, as "almost uncoachable. It wasn't the Age of Aquarius, but he was the first guy I knew to do his own thing, and he was doing it in 1952. He liked to throw in situations like fourth and twenty."

The purest character of all, the one around whom the deeds of the season unwound like a fire hose, was the head coach, Jimmy Phelan, a handsome, whimsical Irishman.

"We had a good time in spite of everything," insists Donovan, "mostly because of Phelan. He had a great line of bull. It was a picnic just being around him. One day we were working out at a field near the Rose Bowl, getting ready for the Rams, and we ran off a couple of plays without fouling up. Phelan stopped practice, loaded everybody on a bus and took us to the racetrack. Jimmy loved the races."

Donovan was out of Holy Cross, in his third year as a pro, and on his way to greatness with Baltimore teams still to come.

He was Phelan's favorite, and in the sight of his coach, in the midst of a season where little went right, he could do no wrong. "Phelan went to Mass every morning. I'd be dragging in around six o'clock and he'd be waiting there for me with a cab, and he'd take me to church with him.

"He cared about the game. If he thought you were laying down, he wouldn't stand for it. But football had passed him by. He was one of the only coaches I ever knew who hated practices more than the players did."

It was a season of continuing bumps and bruises, a season without pity. "I hurt my leg against the Rams in the Coliseum," Donovan went on. "A guy fell into the back of it. It was killing me, but I stayed on the sideline and watched the rest of the game. When it was over everybody runs off and leaves me on the bench. I can't walk! I have to crawl all the way off the field, up the ramp and into the dressing room. The team doctor checks me over and starts looking for some crutches.

"*Phelan* stops him. He screams, 'That son of a bitch is an *Irishman*. He don't need no crutches!' Jimmy, he loved me. It turns out I got a broken knee. I was back playing three weeks later."

As an organizer, Phelan's idea of planning was the kind that made Pearl Harbor famous. His assistants, Cecil Isbell, Will Walls, and Alex Agase, did most of the coaching, and he sent them to Kerrville for a week of early practice with the quarterbacks. At the time, the Texans had neither an offense nor a defense.

"What the hell will we work on for a full week?" asked Isbell.

"Work on the cadence," said Phelan. "One-and-two-and-three."

When Phelan arrived in camp a week later, the first thing he did was change the cadence.

Later in the training period the Texans acquired Don Klosterman from the Browns. Klosterman had led the nation's passers at Loyola in 1950.

He joined the team in San Antonio, where the Texans were to play the Redskins that night in a preseason game. "I went to the Saint Anthony Hotel to meet Phelan and go over the plays and terminology. When I got there he told me we'd do it before the game. All I had to do was punt and kick.

"Now, I had come from Cleveland, where Paul Brown ran a super organized camp. With Brown, you go into a game knowing the first three plays—what to look for, where the kickoff will go, who will run it out.

"In the Texans' locker room, the first thing they did was give me the shoulder pads that belonged to Mike McCormack, a big tackle. Finally, Phelan quiets the team and says, 'Okay, hit somebody and we'll win the game.' That was it. The players went by me so fast I thought a deluge of dysentery had hit the team."

The Texans made their Dallas debut on September 28, 1959, against the New York Giants in the Cotton Bowl. A crowd of 17,000—it was to be their largest home audience—turned out to see the return of SMU heroes Kyle Rote and Fred Benners.

The Giants won 24-6, and the only Texans' touchdown was set up on a punt fumbled by a New York halfback named Tom Landry.

Klosterman missed a 33-yard field-goal attempt and was released by Phelan the next day. Klosterman was dumbfounded, a condition he had been in steadily since his first day on the job.

"Hell, I was a quarterback, not a kicking specialist," he fumed. "The ball hit the uprights and bounced back. And the next day I got cut. I was mad as hell. I couldn't believe it." Hurt, angry, disappointed, Klosterman left after exchanging a few X-rated words with Phelan.

Weeks later, preparing for their second date against the Giants, the Texans were viewing the film of their first encounter when Phelan stood up and cried, "Stop the camera. Run that back." The film spun backwards until there, again, was Klosterman's kick hitting the uprights and bouncing away.

Phelan sat down, folded his arms and looked smugly around the room. "Now," he demanded, "who says I didn't give him a chance?"

Anyone connected with the Texans can recite verbatim two stories that have become classics of the pro football genre. It is a ritual so automatic as to leave no variation in the retelling. It is like asking Francis Scott Key to sing a medley of his hit songs.

A conversation with Tex Maule begins with a half-sentence: "Tex, every ex-Texan tells the same two . . ."

And Maule interrupts: " . . . stories. The one about Phelan calling off practice so the players could cash their checks, and the one at Akron, where the crowd was so small Phelan told them they should shake hands with each fan."

"Yeah, that's it."

"Well, after a while, the whole thing got to be a comedy."

It wasn't easy to keep up with either the team or the front office. The owners decked them out in cowboy hats and colorful shirts, which the players refused to wear. Donovan gave his to a truck driver. At one point, Bob Celeri was released and hired back at a lower salary. One lineman was suspected of being paranoid. When Phelan tried to send him into a game he refused. "Why me?" he said. "I went in last time." He thought people were out to get him.

The team's only win, over the Bears 27-23, came after the club had tapped out in Dallas. That was the game played at Akron before a crowd of around 3,000, where in his pregame pep talk Phelan suggested that "we dispense with the customary introductions, and the players go into the stands and shake hands with each fan." It loosened them up, or something, and they played the hell out of the Bears ("George Halas," says Donovan, "nearly croaked").

In no other game that season did the Texans come within 17 points of a tie.

The week of what turned out to be their last game in Dallas, the Texans picked up Frank Tripucka, the former Notre Dame quarterback, from the Cardinals. When it was announced that Tripucka would start that Sunday against the Rams, Maxwell Stiles, a Los Angeles columnist, asked Maule how he could be ready on such scant practice time.

Maule, who was not your typical press agent, sighed heavily. "Well, hell," he said, "it only took Phelan thirty minutes to give him the offense, and it wouldn't have taken that long except Jimmy went over it twice."

The game was played in a blinding rainstorm. From the press box it was impossible to see any fans at all. Those who did attend had taken shelter under the stadium overhang. The Texans tried, and did not play badly, but the Rams outgunned them 27-6.

So the adventure in Dallas ended, almost unobserved, on a day without sunshine.

The Texans had moved to Dallas to drum rolls of optimism. They were pioneers, bringing the blossoming sport of pro football into the lusty southwest. The city meant jobs, futures, riches. The players had also heard that the American Airlines stewardess school was based there, and they were excited.

The day the franchise folded, Phelan announced it to the squad by canceling that afternoon's practice. "Boys," he said, "the league has decided to make us orphans. We're through in Dallas. Here are your checks. It is my opinion that you should get to the banks with all due haste."

Some had money coming they would never collect. One of them was Alex Agase, the assistant coach, who was in charge of the film projector during their last five weeks on the road. Alex had designs on that piece of equipment. It was worth $250, and he planned to hock it. "I had just been married," he recalled, "hadn't been paid in months, and really needed the money. I was sure Phelan had forgotten about the projector. The day before the season ended Jimmy walked into my hotel room, opened the closet door, and walked out with it."

Cecil Isbell, who had been on the wagon for years, tumbled off it the team's last night in Dallas. He placed one phone call, to a depressed Giles Miller, and what he told him will never be printed on a Hallmark card.

A building team, a town with a college tradition, weak management . . . those were not the ingredients to inspire the faint-hearted. But when the team took its leave of Dallas, the Miller brothers showed up at the airport to see them off. Giles was crying.

There were several neat, human twists and turns to the legend of pro football's Lost Battalion:

Murchison, who was out of town when the Texans lost their lease, became the owner of the Dallas Cowboys, who kept theirs.

Don Klosterman, who as a young quarterback lasted one week under Phelan, is today the general manager at Los Angeles.

The second Texans, owned by Lamar Hunt and raised in the new American Football League, also fled Dallas and now reside happily and successfully in Kansas City.

Buddy Young retired in 1955 and is a member of the commissioner's staff, working in player relations.

Maule, who quit a job with the Rams to return to Texas, was succeeded in Los Angeles by a fellow named Pete Rozelle.

There is, of course, a remaining touch of irony that demands expression. I asked Tex Maule what would have happened if . . . the Millers had shown the staying power to see it through, or if . . . Clint Murchison had been allowed to save the 1952 Texans.

"That's easy," said Maule. "Today they would be the Baltimore Colts."

RAY DIDINGER

A Remembrance of Paul Brown

Paul Brown once was asked how he would like to be remembered when he was gone. "I'd hope they remember my teams," the legendary Cleveland Browns coach said. We do, but we remember much more—from his farsighted football innovations to the humanity with which he treated his players. Ray Didinger, gifted columnist and feature writer for the PHILADELPHIA DAILY NEWS, *interviewed the people closest to Brown and compiled their thoughts for the Super Bowl XXVI game program in Minneapolis.*

PAUL BROWN SEEMED *to vanish almost immediately after his team, the Cincinnati Bengals, arrived in Michigan for Super Bowl XVI.*

Cincinnati's coaches and players were available to the media each morning that week, but Brown, the team's founder and patriarch, was nowhere to be seen.

He wasn't in the team's hotel headquarters. He wasn't in his suite. His secretary told reporters that Brown was in meetings. It was all very frustrating.

On Thursday before the game, NFL executive Don Weiss asked Brown to grant at least one press conference. Brown agreed, but he stipulated it be kept quiet and limited to a handful of reporters.

As usual, P.B. got his way.

So at noon, after the great media horde had departed, eight writers were escorted down a long, winding hallway to the South Wing of the Troy Hilton Hotel.

Waiting there in a makeshift meeting room, seated next to a film projector, was Paul Brown, vice president and general manager of the Bengals, former head coach of the Cleveland Browns. Pro Football Hall of Fame member. Legend. Brown was dressed neatly—brown suit, white shirt, and tie. He folded his hands and waited while the newsmen opened their notepads. He crossed his legs and tapped his foot in the air. Swiftly. Nervously. It was obvious he wasn't thrilled with this arrangement.

"Why were you so reluctant to meet with the press this week?" someone asked.

"I just feel all this attention should be going to our coaches and players," Brown said. "They're the ones who have done the work. They're the ones who brought us here. They should get the accolades.

"I'm not cut off from the team, you understand. I've been around all week. I've been to our practices. But the interviews, the pictures . . . I'll leave that to Forrest [Gregg, then head coach] and the players."

"But are you enjoying this week?" another reporter asked. "Oh, yes," Brown replied.

"These are exciting days for the O.C."

Heads shot up. Brown smiled.

"O.C. stands for Old Coach," he said

Anyone who ever met Paul Brown has a favorite memory of the man. That's mine: sitting in a Michigan hotel room 10 years ago, watching him slowly warm to the discussion of his life and times in pro football. Brown talked for an hour that day, tracing his coaching roots back to Massillon (Ohio) High School, winding through 17 seasons with the Browns and finally to the American Football Conference championship in Cincinnati. It was a fascinating journey, full of insight and wit.

I replayed that conversation in my mind last August when I learned that Brown had died at 82 from complications of pneumonia.

Other people who knew Brown as a coach, a friend, or a football rival had their own memories which, when pieced together, form the portrait of a unique individual, a man who put the word "modern" in the modern era of pro football. Teacher. Innovator. Taskmaster. Brown was all those things, certainly. He could be stern and stubborn in the extreme. But he also was a loyal and caring man who enjoyed a good joke, an afternoon of gin rummy, and a quiet Scotch with a former player.

What follows is a profile of this complex man as seen by those who walked the fields with him, from Massillon High School to the Super Bowl.

"I always felt that before Paul Brown came along, football coaches just rolled the ball onto the practice field and blew the whistle," says Sid Gillman, who, like Brown, made the Pro Football Hall of Fame for his many coaching innovations.

"Paul was the first one to bring a system to pro football. He brought a practice routine. He broke down practice into individual areas. He had position coaches, and they worked the year round. They weren't part-timers like they were on other teams.

"Paul was the first true organizational genius of football. His approach was that of a college professor. He didn't coach the game, he taught it in a classroom with films and blackboards and meticulous notebooks. He was a stickler for details that other coaches would shrug off.

"Paul and I attended quite a few coaching clinics in Ohio in the forties.

"Paul was a frequent lecturer, and his impact was tremendous, even in ways that were rather comical.

"For example, Paul pronounced football as 'fuhball.' He left out the 'T.' During those years, I would often hear other coaches talking about 'fuhball.' They would be imitating Paul right down to the way he spoke.

"If Paul said it was 'fuhball,' then, by golly, it was 'fuhball.'"

"I coached with Paul at Great Lakes [Naval Training Center] during the war, then he hired me as his backfield coach with the Browns," says Weeb Ewbank, who later directed the Baltimore Colts and New York Jets to a total of three league championships.

"I learned a lot working with him. What Paul proved, more than anything else, was that organization and preparation win football games. If you don't prepare, it doesn't matter how good your pregame talk is, you're still gonna lose. Paul wasn't much for pep talks, but he was hell on preparation.

"When Paul drew up each week's game plan, the first paragraph would be the breakdown on how we would attack and defeat this team. It was all there in a nutshell, and it was the first thing every player saw when he opened his folder that week. The guys read it over and over until it sank in."

"Pro football was really a ragged, thrown-together game until Paul came along," says Mike McCormack, who developed into a Hall of Fame tackle under Brown in Cleveland (1954–1962), then served as head coach in Philadelphia, Baltimore, and Seattle.

"I remember George Halas once saying that Paul's greatest contribution to football was that he made the other coaches compete with him. He made them all better.

"When I first signed with the New York Yankees [in 1951], we had little copy books with a play drawn here and a play drawn there. It was like high school football. We had two assistant coaches; one was a part-time card dealer in Reno, the other one was a salesman for a soda company.

"When I joined the Browns [1954], I couldn't believe how thorough everything was. Paul would lecture, and we would take notes on everything from how to do calisthenics to how to make the double-team block.

"There were times when I would think, 'Is all this really necessary?' But then I'd look to my right and see Lou Groza writing down every word, and Lou already had been in the system for ten years. There was a very specific way of doing things with the Browns. If you didn't grasp that, you didn't last."

"I remember the 1950 championship game very well," Paul Brown said that day 10 years ago, in a hotel room in Michigan. "It was a game much like this Super Bowl, a game with a lot of meaning for me, personally.

"We had just come into the NFL that year, of course, and we were playing the Los Angeles Rams. The Rams had just moved from Cleveland to the West Coast a few years before, so the feeling between the teams was very intense.

"It was a very evenly played game—a lot of offense on both sides. What I remember was the finish. And I remember it for a reason you'd probably never imagine.

"We were losing [28 to 27], but we had driven the ball down the field and we were lining up for a final field-goal attempt. It was a pretty short kick [16 yards], but it was by no means a sure thing in those cold and windy conditions. We had missed an extra point earlier.

"All the players on our sideline were celebrating, and we were still behind. I let them know how I felt. They settled down and watched what was happening on the field with a bit more interest.

"Lou Groza made the kick and we were the NFL champions. It was probably the most exciting game I've ever been involved in."

"I remember that game, too," says Otto Graham, who quarterbacked Cleveland for 10 seasons and is one of a dozen former Brown disciples in the Hall of Fame. "That was the game when I first saw the other side of Paul's personality, the soft side.

"Paul could be very cold and cutting if you made a mistake. He wouldn't shout, but he would cut you in half with a look or a remark. You'd want to go hide some place.

"This time, I was running with the ball late in the game, and I fumbled it away. I thought I had cost us the championship. It was the lowest moment of my life. Honestly, I was more devastated at that moment than I was a few years ago when the doctor told me I had cancer.

"I came off the field and there was Paul. I thought, 'Uh-oh, here it comes.' But he patted me on the back and said, 'Don't worry, Otts.

We'll still get 'em.' That was like a shot of adrenalin. Boy, I couldn't wait to get back out there. Sure enough, we got the ball back and drove down the field to win the game.

"People praised me for my poise and leadership in that game, but if it wasn't for Paul giving me that pat on the back, I couldn't have done it. He knew exactly what I needed in that situation, and he gave it to me. Paul knew football, but he knew people as well."

"Paul was tough, but he was fair and, as players, we respected that," says Dante Lavelli, the pass catcher who starred for Brown's 1942 national championship team at Ohio State, then joined him in Cleveland for 10 seasons.

"Two nights before we played the Yankees for the [All-America Football Conference] championship in 1946, our captain, Jim Daniell, was arrested for drunk driving. I heard the news while riding to practice the next morning with Lou Groza. We both knew that was it, Daniell was as good as gone.

"Paul walked into the meeting that day and the first thing he said was, 'Jim, is it true what I read in the paper?' Jim said yes. Paul said, 'Turn in your uniform.' Jim said, 'Do you want to hear my side of the story?' Paul said, 'No.' That was Paul's way. You played by his rules or you didn't play.

"Can you imagine a coach today cutting the team captain two days before the Super Bowl? But Paul's feeling was if a player was out until two in the morning two days before a championship game, then [the game] couldn't mean that much to him. We understood that.

"I don't think anyone on the team was surprised when Paul let Daniell go. We would have been surprised if he hadn't."

"Paul Brown and Vince Lombardi were very different personalities," says Willie Davis, the Hall of Fame defensive end who played for Brown in 1958 and 1959 before joining Lombardi in Green Bay for 10 seasons.

"Both men were tough on the practice field, but Vince was more vocal. He'd jump all over you. Paul was quieter, but when he said something [critical], it was so cold and nasty it cut your heart out.

"I remember my rookie year, Paul came up to me once and said, 'It's obvious this team has scouted you and they are picking on you. I just want you to know that.' The man cut me lower than grass, and I couldn't understand it because the plays were actually breaking inside me. I wasn't the one getting beat.

"The next day, we were looking at the films and Paul said, 'Willie, I owe you an apology.' He didn't elaborate, but I knew what he meant and I appreciated it. The man was very honest. I respected that.

"Several years after he traded me [to Green Bay], Paul looked me up after one of our games in Cleveland. He said, 'Willie, I just want you to know we made a big mistake letting you go.' Then he said, 'But I'm happy for you. Keep up the good work.' Coming from Paul, that meant a lot."

"I got to know Paul much better in later years, long after I played for him," says Miami's Don Shula, the second-winningest head coach in NFL history, who began his pro career as a defensive back with the Browns in 1951.

"When we were both in the coaching end of it and serving on various league committees, we developed a social relationship that was a lot of fun. We'd go out to dinner with our wives, we'd play golf. That's when I saw the other side of Paul. He was a witty guy who loved telling stories and laughing.

"But on the field, he was all business, and as a player, I found him to be very intimidating. He was a legend in my eyes. He kept a distance [from the players], which I understand now that I'm a coach myself. He needed to take the broadest possible view of things and he had to be objective. I'm the same way now.

"Paul had a knack of addressing the squad in generalities, yet making each player feel as if [Brown] was talking directly to him. There would be times when he was talking about missed assignments and mental lapses and I'd think 'Uh-oh, that's me.'

Then the guy next to me would duck his head and say, 'That's me, I know it.'

"Paul was like an army general, he had a presence about him that was unique. He affected you in ways that went well beyond football. He taught you valuable lessons about life and responsibility."

"I remember when I acquired the Cincinnati franchise," Paul Brown said. "I had a friend ask me, 'Paul, why are you doing this? Why are you taking over an expansion team? You'll get killed every week. You'll tarnish your reputation.' I said, 'You don't understand. It's pro football. I'm not getting into this for the glory or the money. I love the game.'

"It's a great game. I can't get it out of my system."

"If I learned anything from Paul, it was the philosophy of how to operate a winning franchise," says Bill Walsh, who was an assistant coach under Brown in Cincinnati [1968–1975] before leading the San Francisco 49ers to three Super Bowl titles in the 1980s.

"With Paul, everything besides winning was cosmetic. It didn't matter. He didn't concern himself with which person had what title and who had the nicest office. To Paul, all those trappings were beyond insignificant. They were a detriment. All that mattered was winning on Sunday.

"Speaking as an assistant coach, Paul was great to work with because once he gained confidence in you, he gave you a free hand. He was always the ultimate authority as head coach and general manager, but he would discuss what you were doing and if he liked it, he would say, 'Fine, go ahead.'

"There was little sentimentality in the way Paul dealt with players and the outside world in general. He had very little use for the press. He didn't care that it created the image of a cold, unfeeling person. He was cold when he felt he needed to be cold, and that was in operating his football team.

"With his friends, away from the office, he was a different person.

If that side didn't come out [in the press], he didn't care. He didn't want that side of his personality on public display."

"Paul was a determined and single-minded individual when it came to football," says Chuck Noll, who played guard and linebacker for the Browns (1953–59) and later coached the Pittsburgh Steelers to four Super Bowl victories.

"He didn't see it as a jolly, fun time. He took it as a job, and he was very serious. Personally, I found him easy to play for. If you were prepared and you played hard, you usually didn't have too many problems.

"The year after Otto [Graham] retired, we went from league champions to 5-7. That was the only losing season Paul ever had in Cleveland, and he was miserable. After the last game, when everyone was getting ready to leave, I remember Paul saying, 'Have a merry Christmas . . . if you can.'

"I listened to Paul's football philosophy for so long that I simply took it on as my own. Now that I'm a coach, I hear myself mouthing the same things Paul said about football being a game of mistakes and preparation being the key to success.

"I also picked up a few things from Paul that got me in trouble. When I talked about the 'criminal element' in football . . . I heard Paul say that originally. He was just smarter than me. He never said it around the press."

"I thought the funniest thing about Paul was his paranoia," says Len Dawson, who was a backup quarterback with the Browns (1960–61) before establishing himself as a Hall of Fame player in the American Football League with the Dallas Texans and Kansas City Chiefs.

"When we were on the road, Paul would insist we take our notebooks and game plans everywhere we went. He thought if we left them in our rooms, a maid or a bellhop would pick them up and sell them to the other team.

"When we practiced, Paul was always looking around for spies. One time Paul saw this guy in a parked car near the field. He was there for forty-five minutes, never moved. Paul was convinced the guy was spying, so he sent our equipment manager, Morrie Kono, over to check him out. Turns out it was some poor guy sleeping off a drunk.

"I laughed to myself. I thought, 'Who needs to spy on our practices? All we ever do is run Jim Brown right and run Jim Brown left.'

"But I'll always be grateful to Paul because he gave me a chance to play, not in Cleveland but in the AFL. I was stuck behind Milt [Plum], and I knew Paul wasn't about to change quarterbacks. I needed to find out if I could play pro football, and I saw the AFL as an opportunity.

"I went to Paul and asked him to release me so I could sign with the other league. He could have said, 'Forget it, you're under contract here,' but he didn't. He said he understood, and he let me go. When I hear people talk about how cold Paul was, I tell that story. A really cold person wouldn't have done what Paul did for me."

"When I think of Paul Brown, I think of a man who believed in doing things the right way, not cutting corners," says Stan Walters, an offensive tackle with the Cincinnati Bengals from 1972 to 1974.

"One morning in the dining hall at training camp, they're serving bacon and eggs. There's some bacon sitting there, left over from the day before. The cook starts to put it on my plate and right away, Paul is there.

"He says, 'What's that?' I say, 'That's okay, coach. I don't mind yesterday's bacon.' Paul says, 'I'm paying for fresh bacon.' He stared a hole through the poor cook. We had fresh bacon every morning after that.

"That was Paul. I found him up-front about everything. I was a ninth-round draft pick, and I didn't have an agent when I signed. First six games, I was on the cab squad making five hundred dollars a week. The last eight games I played and made ninth-round money.

"The next year, I came to camp and won a starting job, but I was still working under my old contract. I figured Paul was getting me cheap, but I didn't say anything. I didn't want to cause any trouble.

"The Friday before the opener, Paul called me into his office. He said, 'You're a starter now so we're giving you the same salary we're giving Tommy Casanova and Sherman White.' They were the [Bengals'] top two draft picks that year. My jaw dropped. Paul said, 'You've earned it.'

"You'd go through a wall for someone like that."

"I never thought much about my public image," Paul Brown said. "I know most people based their impressions on what they saw on the sidelines, so they only saw my serious side. I'm not like that all the time. My friends know that.

"Most of that [image] business is silliness anyway. One year in Cleveland, I wore the same brown suit to every game. We kept winning, and the players insisted I keep wearing it for good luck. When it got cold, I wore the same overcoat.

"When the season was over, a magazine named me one of the ten best-dressed men in America. It is all so superficial, how can anyone take that sort of thing seriously?"

"Paul wasn't the easiest man to talk to or to get to know when you were a player," says Jim Brown, the Hall of Fame fullback who led the NFL in rushing eight of the nine seasons he played for the Browns (1957–1965). Brown now heads a coalition of minority youth groups in the greater Los Angeles area.

"I was more outspoken than other players, and I fought with Paul over changes that I thought should be made in our offense. I thought we should diversify our attack, pass more on first down, that sort of thing. Teams were keying on me all the time.

"Other [players] felt the same way I did, but they wouldn't say anything to Paul. I would, but it didn't make much difference. Paul had his own way of doing things, and he was reluctant to change, because his way had always been successful.

"I'm able to understand that a lot better now that I'm older and I'm in charge of my own organization. It's lonely at the top, and you have to take a broad view of things. You can't waste time changing what already works. Really, I've used a lot of Paul's ideas in putting this movement together. Organization, maximizing the potential of each individual, focusing on essentials and not trivia.

"I always respected Paul, and I was grateful for the opportunity he gave me to showcase my talents. Even when we disagreed, we disagreed respectfully."

"Jim and Paul had a tug-of-war about the offense, we all knew that," Willie Davis says. "But they knew each other well enough not to have it out in front of the squad. Neither one would've backed down, and it would've been a mess. So they went back and forth in subtle ways.

"Paul sent in all the plays, of course, and when Jim didn't like the call, he'd start growling and muttering things under his breath. It was kind of funny, really. Jim would make suggestions and Paul would usually go along with him, but not right away because then it would look like Jim was calling the shots. He would wait one series, maybe two.

"One time I was playing [offensive] tackle and Jim said, 'Tell Paul to call Thirty-eight Flip.' That was a pitch to Jim going around end. I went to the bench and said, 'Coach, Jim wants to run Thirty-eight Flip.' Paul glared at me and said, 'I'm calling the plays here.' Then he called a dive up the middle.

"The next series, Paul sent in Thirty-eight Flip and Jim went sixty-five yards for a touchdown. Paul looked at me and said, 'You see, the play will work when we want it to work.'"

"I had problems with the whole system when I played, and Paul Brown was part of that," says Mike Reid, a Pro Bowl defensive tackle with the Bengals who quit the NFL to pursue a music career in 1975. He now is a Grammy award-winning songwriter in Nashville.

"I enjoyed playing the games, but I felt as if I was suffocating with all the rules. Curfews, dress codes, team meals. It was the seventies, and I was very much into myself and my freedom. I hadn't had my Copernican revelation yet. I still thought the world revolved around me.

"I saw Paul as very cold, treating players as if they were chess pieces. I had very little contact with him. I never got the feeling that he cared to know me as a person. I played seven years in Cincinnati until, finally, I was emotionally burned out. I knew it was time to do something else with my life.

"I went to see Paul to tell him I was retiring. He wasn't surprised. He knew I was unhappy. I thought he would try to talk me out of it, but he didn't. Instead, he put his hand on my shoulder and said, 'If things don't work out [in music], I just want you to know you'll always have a place here.'

"At that moment, I saw a side of Paul Brown that I'd never seen before, and I wished I had.

"Years later, I performed at a dinner for the College Football Hall of Fame, and Paul attended. I dedicated a song to him, and he told me later how touched he was. I could see that he had mellowed and by then, so had I."

Paul Brown asked how many people were expected to watch Super Bowl on TV. One hundred million, he was told.

"That's a lot," he said. Everyone in the room agreed.

"Television has had the greatest impact on pro football, more than anything else over the years," Brown said. "Television is what made the game. Television sold it.

"When the Browns joined the NFL in 1950, I went to Cleveland Gas and Electric Company and tried to sell them our exclusive TV rights for five thousand dollars. They said that seemed high. I had to convince them.

"They gave me the money, but it was more to humor me than anything else. Things have really changed. You can't even buy a

ten-second commercial for five thousand dollars today. It's really a different game."

"Paul Brown wanted people to think he was a big, bad dragon, but he was really a cream puff," says Jim Houston, a Cleveland linebacker from 1960–1972. Jim's older brother Lin also played for Brown at Massillon High, Ohio State, and the Browns.

"I never saw Paul as just a head coach. He always seemed greater than that to me. I grew up around his teams. My brother used to bring me to practice, and I'd be star-struck watching Otto Graham, Marion Motley, Lou Groza, people like that.

"The longer I was around Paul, the more I understood why he won. He had very solid values, and he stuck to them. He didn't cater to me because of my brother. He was straight down the middle with everyone. In meetings, in practice, it was all business.

"But I heard stories through my brother about things Paul did for his former players who needed a favor or needed some help. Paul was right there. He talked about *'my guys'* and he really meant it."

"I was still an immature youngster when I joined the Browns in 1958," says Bobby Mitchell, a Hall of Fame running back. "Paul taught me how to walk, talk, and eat before he ever taught me how to play football. He molded me like a piece of clay.

"There wasn't a day that Paul didn't talk to us about being a winner in life. He would say that football was just a stepping stone. He encouraged us to get jobs to prepare for the future. I went to work for a meat company. We all did something. Paul saw to that.

"That was a side of Paul that most people never saw. He could cut you to pieces on the practice field, then talk to you like a father an hour later.

"One time my wife visited me at training camp and brought our infant daughter. We were taking a walk when Paul came up behind us. He said, 'Bobby, is this your family?' I said yes, and this big smile came across his face. I had never seen that from him before.

"The next morning on the practice field, it was business as usual. I dropped a ball, and Paul gave me the stare."

"I thought going to a Paul Brown team, it would be football, football, and more football," says Bill Bergey, a linebacker with the Bengals from 1969–1973.

"I was really surprised at our first team meeting when Paul talked for two hours about everything *but* football. He said, 'You're in the big leagues now, and you'll have a lot of people patting you on the back and whispering in your ear. Be careful. Be responsible. Act like men.'

"He seemed more like our guardian angel than our coach, talking about the evils of drinking and smoking and chasing around. I thought, 'Where am I, Boys Town? Is this really Paul Brown talking? Where's the football?' But this was the foundation. The X's and O's came later.

"Paul was very straight-laced, the straightest man I ever met. Every Saturday night before a game, he would take the whole team to a movie. It was always a G-rated movie, too. *Bambi*, *Son of Flubber*, something like that. A lot of players hated it, but it was mandatory. You had to go.

"Other teams knew about it, and they would needle us. They'd say, 'What did you see last night? *Snow White*? *Cinderella*?' But Paul's attitude was, hey, if we put more points on the scoreboard, that's the best put-down in the world. And Paul's teams usually did that."

"Paul had tremendous charisma," says Tom Bass, who served as defensive coordinator under Brown in Cincinnati. "When he walked into a meeting room, everyone stopped talking. I saw players turn off the air conditioner at summer camp so they could hear Paul better. It has been said that players feared Paul, but I think it was more respect than fear. They respected who Paul was and what he stood for.

"We got most of our first [Bengals] team through the allocation draft, which meant we got players the other teams didn't want. We got a lot of guys who weren't, shall we say, the best citizens in the world. Yet these same characters joined our team and never missed a bed check, never caused a fuss, nothing.

"They knew they would have to answer to Paul, and no one wanted to do anything that would reflect badly on the organization.

"Paul Brown is probably the most misunderstood figure in the history of professional football. I think it's unfortunate that so few people ever got to see the man that I knew so well. He wasn't cold, he was just the opposite."

In his 1974 book of poetry, *Pro Football from the Inside*, Bass wrote a poem about Brown entitled "Old Paul."

Pro Football from the Inside read, in part:

I wish you knew him as I do, I wish you saw him with my eyes.
I wish you felt the feelings I have felt, but that will never be.
Your feeling of the man is based solely on those Sunday afternoons and the outcomes of the games.

The interview was winding down, and someone asked Brown how he would like to be remembered. He looked puzzled.

"What do you mean?" he asked.

"When you're gone," the reporter said. "What would you hope that people remember about you?" Brown thought a moment.

"I'd hope they remember my teams," he said. "My teams were what I was proudest of. Those players gave me so much happiness over the years.

"When I look back, I feel that I never worked a day in my life. What I did in football wasn't work, it was fun. It was sheer joy."

"I talked to Paul four days before he died," Otto Graham says. "I told him, 'You always told us to fight until the end. It's never over until you stop fighting.' He said, 'Otts, I'm just so tired.' That's when I knew it was almost over. It broke my heart to hear him say that.

"He was such a big part of my life, it didn't really hit me until he was gone. I went to his funeral, and when I saw him in the casket, tears came to my eyes. I leaned over and kissed him on the forehead. I said goodby. It was so hard to do.

"All I know is I'm a better person for having known Paul Brown. And football is a better game for having him be a part of it."

STEVE CASSADY

The Search

From the mid-seventies through the mid-eighties, no one wrote more for NFL publications than Steve Cassady. He wrote a series of columns with John Madden, and he wrote this story for PRO! *magazine in 1981 after tagging along with an NFL scout for part of a trip through the South. Cassady was there for the meetings with coaches, the film sessions, the practices, and the hours of dead time that define a scout's existence.*

SUNDAY

"Sixty percent of this job is going someplace and waiting," said the scout as he settled into the middle of a row of armless chrome and vinyl chairs. The scout was dressed in the wrinkle-proof ensemble of the habitual traveler: dark brown polyester sports jacket, light brown polyester slacks, white knit logo shirt, and brown oxfords. He set his attaché case on his lap like a tabletop and drummed on it with his fingertips. "After a while, you learn how to sit and let your mind go blank," he said.

The scout had just endured the slow crawl of time aboard a transcontinental jet. Now he was in a boarding lounge of the Atlanta airport awaiting his connection to a Southeastern Conference university town, the initial stopover on the first leg of a three-week swing into the Deep South. The flight would not depart for an hour. The scout slumped in his chair. Behind him, throngs of people moved in blurs, thousands of chattering travelers streaming in all directions toward myriad destinations.

A uniformed attendant finally announced the flight through a podium phone that garbled the numbers and destination. The scout rose and headed for the gate. Outside, lightning crackled and lit the horizon. "You know," said the scout, "the disasters in the West all happen on the ground, like earthquakes. Down here, they come from the sky." He walked into the fuselage of the stretch DC-8 and selected a seat next to the emergency exit, not for reasons of contingency planning, but because it afforded extra leg room.

The plane lumbered along the tarmac then lifted laboriously into the stormy night. Turbulence hit immediately, and the plane jostled through its ascent. Over the public address speaker, the captain said the seat belt sign would stay lit for the duration. The scout reclined in his seat and cinched his belt tighter. For the next hour, he drank muddy coffee that sloshed from the turbulence and watched the sky turn bright from lightning.

The aircraft lurched along, eventually beginning its descent. It broke through the clouds, sparkles of city lights rising to meet it. The big jet scorched the runway in a spine-jarring three-point landing, then taxied in. The scout broke through the people milling around the gate. He strode briskly to the baggage area, then across the aisle to the car rental desk. He had been penned inside breathing stale air for eight hours. He longed for the feel and smell of outdoors.

He secured a local map and the keys to a Japanese subcompact. He walked through a seeing-eye door that opened with a whoosh and was hit by a savage blast of Southern night air. "Jeez," he said, "I forgot how muggy it gets." He located the car, threw his bags into the back seat, jumped in, kicked over the engine, and switched on the air conditioner. Soon he was speeding along a two-lane road toward town.

Lush green foliage on the shoulders gave way to asphalt parking lots and blazing neon store-fronts. The scout drove on, gazing at the lengthy string of fast-food huts. "After a week of eating at those places," he said, "you'd kill for a good meal."

He found his way to the center of town and drove under the archway in front of a Holiday Inn. It was 9 p.m. in the South, 6 p.m. on the West Coast, and the scout had not yet eaten dinner. He checked in, stowed his bags in the room, then returned to the car. Following the desk clerk's directions, he motored several blocks to a boulevard that was lined with campus eateries.

The scout found an open pizza parlor and pulled in. He walked past waitresses gathered idly around the cashier's counter and sat down, one of two patrons in the darkened dining room. He ordered what proved to be an unpleasant hero sandwich, served abruptly and without charm. He ate hurriedly, washing down his sandwich with a beer. He shoved an insulting tip under the rim of his dirty plate, paid at the register with a traveler's check and returned to the motel.

The scout spread the contents of his attaché case over the green and blue floral bedspread. He was reviewing the list of prospects he would inquire about the next day.

His morning charted, he repacked the case, leaned it against the wall, and undressed for bed.

MONDAY

At mid-morning, the scout was driving past the unmanned security booth separating the entry and exit lanes of the main road into campus. This was a big school, rolling across 400 grassy acres that ended at the banks of a mud-brown river. Broad brick buildings rose in clusters and were set off by stately trees with weighty limbs and thick, gnarled trunks. The scout followed blue signs that pointed toward the gymnasium. He parked in front, under a "15 Minutes—Violators Will Be Towed" sign, reasoning that traffic laws were being ignored in the summer.

He walked through a double glass door, found a staircase at the back of the foyer, and descended to a basement corridor. His first stop was the sports information director's office. "He won't know much football," the scout explained, "but these guys get paid for knowing what the local newsmen know. Most of the time, they know more."

The scout was well informed, too. He carried a list of eight of the school's seniors, a distillation from three years of intelligence gathering. The scout's team subscribed to a computerized combine that operates as an informational clearing house. The combine subdivides the country and assigns permanent area scouts to every region. The area scouts track prospects from the time they first appear as freshmen to the time they finish spring drills in their junior year. The scouts annually file reports that itemize the prospects' height, weight, speed, toughness, intelligence, training habits, and composite score. These data are fed into a computer, and the printout traces a profile of the players' NFL potential.

When the players become seniors, the team's own scouts take over. Generally they view a prospect three times during his senior season: once at the beginning, once as the year progresses, and once after—at any bowl or all-star competition. The eight seniors on the scout's list would be eligible for the NFL draft eight months from now. He was rating them all personally for the first time.

The lone occupant of the sports information director's office was a student assistant who proved more cordial than helpful. The scout asked for a chart of seniors, a press book, and any other current handouts. He slipped easily into Southern dialect as he talked.

Down the corridor, he ran into a veteran assistant coach of casual acquaintance. The scout engaged him in conversation. The coach spoke highly of a kicker on the scout's list. He said he was academically superior and mentally tough. The scout asked him about a running back.

"You won't see him around," answered the coach. "We kicked him off the team for missing too many practices. Gave him every chance, but he just wouldn't respond. We took away his scholarship. He's not the kind of kid who'll stick around to attend classes. I hear he got himself an agent and is trying to hook on in Canada."

The scout noticed a group of people coming up the hall. They stopped several doors away and entered an office.

"Who's that?" the scout asked.

"Our recruiting coach, our backfield coach, and that big kid walking with a limp is our tight end."

"What happened to him?" asked the scout.

"A knee. He had an arthroscope on it just a couple of weeks ago. But he's making good progress. Practically no swelling. We hope he'll be ready by the third game."

"How's he done for y'all?"

"Great—been named to some All-America preview teams. He likes to catch more than block though."

The scout cut short his conversation and headed toward the office. The end was on his list, and he wanted a closer look. The injury was not a concern, at least not yet.

The end was bantering with the recruiting coach when the scout walked in and introduced himself.

When he left the room, he already had rated the tight end in his mind. "I'll watch film on him," he said, "mostly so I can say I did, but I'll tell you right now, he'll never play for our team."

The tight end was slim from the waist down, his legs as slender and sculpted as a race horse's. "If he plays at all in the pros, it will be for a team that uses its tight end more as a wide receiver like Cleveland uses Ozzie Newsome. Our coaches like a tight end who can drive-block a defensive man off the line one-on-one. This guy doesn't have the body for it."

The scout had arranged to meet the head coach's administrative assistant for a rundown on the college's seniors. He caught him in between appointments and settled into a straightback wooden chair across from his assistant's large oak desk. He took out a steno pad and pen from his attaché case and held them poised.

By the second name on the list, he was doodling in his pad. He already knew more than the assistant, who kept squinting over half-glasses at one piece of paper or another, trying to double-check heights, weights, medical histories, and majors. He spoke in generalities when it came time to rate athletic ability. The scout sat politely for a half hour, breaking in at the first possible interval.

"Where can I check out some film?" he asked. The assistant told him the film library was next to the equipment office and that a viewing room was adjacent to the coaches' lounge. "An idiot," mumbled the scout under his breath as he departed.

The coaches' lounge smelled of recent renovation. The walls were glossy white, the woodwork trimmed in the school's dominant color. Thick carpeting in the same shade as the trim ran wall-to-wall underfoot. The room was furnished in overstuffed chairs and a couch was covered in new saddle-tan leather. The alumni had not stinted.

The door opened, and the head coach strutted in. He was a regal, erect man, polite, but in a way that discouraged further conversation. "Nice talking to y'all," he said after a few amenable exchanges. "You know, our practices are closed, but you're sure welcome to watch all the film you need in the other room."

The projector whirred all that afternoon. The scout had borrowed a stack of 15 reels, all the footage from three of the previous year's games. He handled the remote switch, backing up the film and rerunning it often, slowing it down just as often. He wrinkled his forehead, concentrating on murky images. He entertained new insights, confirmed others, all the while reassuring himself he was being thorough. "After an hour-and-a-half of this, you're probably in diminishing returns," he said, "but you go on anyway."

In the second offensive reel, he found what he needed to evaluate the tight end. The end had performed superbly as a receiver in the first reel, working free with fluid cuts, catching the ball aggressively, even in a crowd. Now the scout was backing up the frames of a strongside sweep. He pushed the forward button and set the projector in slow motion. The tight end stepped toward the outside linebacker at the snap, but instead of driving into the backer's midsection, he flopped into his path, apparently hoping to trip him.

"It isn't the coaching," the scout observed, "because the technique looks good everywhere else. The kid just doesn't like to block." The scout backed up the play and reran it once more. "Look at the tackle next to him. Now that's a blocker." The scout was referring to another prospect, a 6-foot 7-inch, 271-pounder with 5.2 speed. "A guy that tall, you worry about his footwork, whether he can be knocked off balance." But in the sequence now flickering across the screen, the big tackle beat the defensive end to the point of attack. He curled his body low and, while stuttering his feet in rapid rhythm, rose to deliver an explosive uppercut of a block.

"That's what you like to see," said the scout, his voice heating. "He's got fast feet, good balance, and excellent delivery. He's big and strong, but he's agile enough to get low so the defender can't drive underneath him."

Subsequent footage disqualified a short (6-1) guard with somewhat sluggish reactions. "He always seems to be accepting the defensive charge instead of exploding to meet it." It showed the truant halfback, a 215-pounder, making good, long runs against Notre Dame and Mississippi. The runner exhibited deliberate instincts for the hole, though he was not blindingly fast. The combine scout had timed him at 4.72 seconds for the 40, and that was a consideration. "We'll look at head cases if they run a 4.6 or better," he said with a laugh. "But who wants an attitude problem with only average speed?" Still, the scout jotted a reminder in his steno pad. Later that year, he would ask the Canadian bird dog for a follow-up report.

Evidence on the kicker proved scant. From the number of times he backed up the opposing return men, it was obvious he owned a strong leg. But that was all the films revealed. "We'll find another way to check him out," said the scout.

In the defensive reels, the scout was viewing a marginal end prospect. "At 5.4 in the forty, he isn't fast enough to switch to linebacker, and at 243 pounds, he'd better be quick." He also was watching two linebackers with impressive speed, size, and intelligence. "But you have to be careful with linebackers. You can be fooled by speed and physique. What you're really looking for is instinct and first-step quickness. Do they have a nose for the ball, and can they get to it in time?"

The scout had been justifiably skeptical. Over the course of three games, the linebackers had made a substantial number of tackles, but most of them took place in the secondary, after a gain had been recorded. "See that left-side backer," said the scout while a play was rolling in slow motion. "He's in the pros now, a fourth-round pick. I didn't like him when I saw him last year, and that's why. He reacts fast enough once he figures where the play is going, but he never anticipates. He hits, but he doesn't react. Those other two guys are just like him—stiffs."

The end fared no better in the scout's estimation. His feet seemed to tangle when fighting off angle blocking. He always seemed to be slowing offensive momentum, but never stopping it or thrusting it back. Like his linebacking teammates, he was lacking first-step quickness.

"None of these guys would make the cut on our team," said the scout.

The sun was low on the horizon when the scout emerged from the gym. It had been a grueling day, hard on the eyes, and he still was feeling weighted by travel and humidity. "That's it for today," he said.

He ate dinner in the motel dining room, drank a couple of beers in the adjacent bar, then went to his room to read and watch television. By 9 o'clock he was face down on the pillow, asleep.

TUESDAY

After breakfast, the scout drove the opposite direction from the university: underneath the freeway, along a two-lane street rutted with chuckhole puddles. He passed rows of dilapidated wood-frame houses sitting on two-by-four stilts in grassless yards. "The poor section," he said dryly.

At an intersection marked by an open lot piled helter-skelter with junk, he turned and drove up a gradual hill. He drove past clusters of project housing where overweight women in floral dresses hung laundry from front-yard clotheslines, and old men in hats, slacks, and undershirts sat on porches in kitchen chairs and talked without animation.

The road climbed to a knoll that was guarded by two weathered stone sentry posts. Beyond them, the road branched both ways around a grassy rise. The scout took the right fork, and it led to a cul-de-sac parking lot above a one-story square brick building.

This was one of a legion of struggling black colleges, financed mostly by contributions, existing year to year on the guile of its grant writers and the sacrifices of its students and faculty. The scout was not here checking on a listed prospect. He was answering a fear endemic to his trade: that another team would sign a free agent of whom he never had heard. A scout is credible only to the extent he is familiar with every prospect in his region.

Around the side of the gym, a gangly youth in a practice suit strolled out. His attire bespoke the poverty of the program. His pants were torn around the knees and caked all over with brick-colored stains. His socks sagged around his ankles, and the horizontal piping around one—red and blue—did not match the orange and aqua of the other. His once-navy practice jersey was faded and fraying.

"Y'all headed for practice?" the scout asked.

"Yeah, you, too?"

"How do you get there?"

"You'll have to follow me. It's hard to find."

The scout and player walked along an asphalt path, then skittered down an embankment to a field area featuring a backstop screen in one corner and old wooden goal posts on the sides. "This is where we have night practice," the player said.

"Y'all still in two-a-days?" the scout asked.

"I wish. We're in three-a-days," the player said. "I'm a transfer student. I played at Morehouse in '75. I quit a good job in Atlanta to come here and play ball. I was a roofer. Every night when I'm dressing for that last practice, I wish I was still a roofer."

They were walking parallel to a gully grown thick with leafy dogwoods. At a small break in the foliage, the player ducked under a bushy limb and slid into the gully. He climbed up the other side to a flat expanse. The scout followed.

The field was bald, scraped red from pounding cleats. What few clumps of grass had survived were baked brown by the sun. The sounds of grunts and clouds of red dust indicated a scrimmage at the far end of the field. The scout headed toward it. A large young man dressed in red coaching shorts, a blue T-shirt, and a mesh cap ambled over. The scout identified himself. The young man said he was the head coach.

"Y'all running three-a-days, I hear," the scout said noncommittally.

"Got to," said the coach. "We got no scholarship players. Most of these guys are walk-ons without much experience. We need the repetition. We open in a week."

"Got anybody I should know about?"

The coach pointed to an oversized defensive lineman crouching in a four-point stance so a fleshy midsection bubbled below his flapping jersey. "He's about our best, our nose tackle. He's got pretty good size and he's aggressive."

The coach paused. " . . . I got to tell it like it is. We got no prospects." He thought for a minute, then seemed to brighten. "You see that kid over there in the T-shirt?" He pointed to the opposite end of the field, where a figure in cut-off jeans was conducting linebacking drills. "His name is Price. Now, if a pro team were to give Price a shot, I think they'd find they have a diamond in the rough."

"How come he's not playing now?"

"He graduated year before last. Then he got himself an agent. I think that was the problem. The teams didn't want to deal with no agent, so they didn't invite him for a tryout. I tried to tell him, 'Prove yourself first, then get an agent.' Should I tell him to come over?"

"Sure," said the scout.

Jesse Price was built like a man who pumped iron with ferocity. His biceps and thigh muscles bulged powerfully from his shirt sleeves and pants legs. He was built so well, in fact, he probably could accommodate no more functional weight.

"How tall are y'all?" the scout asked, after jotting down Price's name and address.

"Six-one," replied Price, who looked down shyly when he spoke. The scout jotted that figure, too, but he knew Price was exaggerating. The scout was 6-2 himself, and Price's hairline came even with his chin.

"I need your weight and birth date."

"About 215, 220, and I was born in January of 1956." He hesitated, then smiled nervously, flashing a gold-edged front tooth. "I just want the folks in pro ball to know Jesse Price is ready to play some football."

The scout thanked him and the coach and returned through the underbrush toward the parking lot. "I'll write a report on him," he said, ducking under a dogwood branch, "but it's hopeless. He's too short, too light, probably no more than 205 pounds, and too old. He probably was a good player at this level, but right now he's dreaming."

That afternoon, the scout drove back across town to the university. He spent an hour or so huddled with the team trainer, primarily for an exact medical history on each of his eight prospects. He also was looking for hints of malingering or poor responses to pain. When the players filtered in to dress for afternoon practice, the scout departed.

He waited in the car for a while, then he drove along a road leading to the stadium. Before long, he spotted a slender young man in a football suit jogging in the same direction. "That's our boy." He pulled alongside, slowed the car, and rolled down the window.

"Y'all practicing in the stadium today?" the scout called out.

"Yeah," said the kicker, gasping from his jog. "At 3:15."

The scout drove on. "That's what I thought," he said. "At these big schools, the kickers usually practice off by themselves where they have to perform. The head coach will be with the rest of the team over at the practice field. Let's hope the kicking coach doesn't know that practice is closed."

At the gate, the scout walked sternly by a student assistant, who looked ready to voice an objection if only he could think what to say.

He went down the tunnel, out onto the spongy blue-green artificial surface. The 85,000-seat stadium rose in a high oval around him. The scout strolled behind the goal post and merged with a swarm of white-shirted students who had been hired to retrieve kicks. He took off his watch and held it in his right hand.

For the next hour, he timed the loft of the kicks and scrutinized the young man's motion. Few of the kickoffs reached the end zone, but all rose in dizzying arcs, creating enough hang time to insure adequate coverage inside the 20. The placekicks were even more impressive. From whatever distance, they seldom strayed from the center of the crossbar. Even from 55 yards, none of his shots drifted, hooked, or sliced.

"The best test of a kicking leg," said the scout. "That means the force of the kick is stronger than normal wind currents. Kicking is like playing golf. The distances don't mean as much as the mechanics of the swing, and this kid has a great motion."

The scout left the stadium for the motel. It was relatively early but his work for the day was done. He decided to clean up, search around for a higher class of coffee shop, and find a pleasant way to kill the evening.

At 8 o'clock, he was chewing the remnant flakes from a piece of strawberry pie and asking the waitress about the social life in her town. "I was in New Orleans once," she began. "Now, that's a town. But there ain't nothing doing here, especially before school starts."

The scout found a shopping mall down the road. He drove in and noticed a large barnwood structure in the middle of the parking lot. In green neon, it advertised itself as a western bar. The scout wandered in and saw a headless naugahyde bull in the middle of a rink that was arrayed with squares of mattress foam. At the bar, women in jeans and cowboy hats were chatting, ignoring the beers in front of them. Nearby, men stood around spitting tobacco juice into styrofoam cups. "Not my kind of place," the scout said on his way out.

He walked along the mall, stopping to browse in a book-and-card shop, later in a menswear emporium. At another storefront, he looked through the plate glass window at a formal party kicking up. He backed up off the curb so he could read the overhead marquee. It said, "Arthur Murray Dance." He entered. A pink-faced middle-age man wearing horn-rimmed glasses and dressed in a tuxedo, ruffled white shirt, and patent leather pumps approached. He looked at the scout's khaki pants, tennis shoes, and knit shirt and asked if he could help.

The scout said he was just passing by, a visitor from the West Coast, and he had seen the party. The man was faced with an awkward decision. He stared for a moment, then broke into a smile and held out his hand. "My name is Ross," he said. "I'm the host for the evening. Come on in and enjoy yourself. If anybody asks, say you're my guest."

The party was a graduation dance for the latest class of beginning ballroom students. They each were requested to bring a guest, thus advertising the appeal of the studio. The room was filling rapidly with men in tuxedos and women in formal gowns. The scout entertained anachronistic thoughts about high school proms. He searched out a table and stayed there, drinking rose wine poured from a half-gallon jug by Ross's wife Freddie. He nibbled on jack cheese and crackers and carried on witless conversations with some of the curious among the dancers.

"You from around here?"

"No, the West Coast."

"Whose guest are you?"

"Ross and Freddie's."

"Oh, how long have you known Ross and Freddie?"

"About an hour."

Nervous laughter followed, and the exchanges trailed into "see-y'all-laters" and "Y'all have a nice time." The scout danced occasionally when pert female instructors sashayed by and beckoned him to the parquet floor. He was buzzing pleasantly from Freddie's frequent refills when he left the studio two hours later.

"They'll never believe it at home," he said as he drove back to the motel.

WEDNESDAY/THURSDAY

The scout had written reports in his room until checkout time Wednesday. The rest of the day he spent on the highway. About dinner time, he pulled in front of another Holiday Inn in another small town, this one in the northeast quadrant of the state. He ate a hamburger and French fries in his room, then watched television and read 100 pages in the ponderous novel *Shogun*.

By 10 o'clock Thursday morning, he was parked behind the gymnasium of a small Baptist college. Here, he was checking out only one name on his current list, a good-sized (6-1, 195) defensive back with good intelligence and acceptable speed. The scout located the sports information director in his quarters on the first floor. He was a gaunt, bespectacled man of about 35 who walked with a limp.

"He's a former quarterback," said the sports information director of the defensive back once the conversation was underway. "He changed positions because he just loves to hit. He's also a person of high moral character. He's a good mixer and a leader in the FCA [Fellowship of Christian Athletes]."

The scout hunted down an assistant coach who escorted him to an unused room down the corridor. Minutes later, the coach returned with a projector and five or six canisters of film.

"You'll like this kid," the coach said. "He's a real hitter, the leader of our secondary."

The scout was plugging in the projector when he noticed the films had not been broken into separate offensive and defensive reels. That meant watching three entire games to assess the performance of one player. The sun was beating through the window panes; the room was cramped and stifling, equipped neither with air conditioning nor fan. "Dammit," he muttered.

The first reel was rolling when the door opened and scouts from the Falcons and Broncos ducked in. The scout switched off the film, and the three exchanged pleasantries while the other two shuffled folding chairs in front of the screen. The scout pushed the forward button. For the next two hours, he and the others sat stiffly in their metal chairs, sweat beading on their foreheads as they tried to glean a rating from footage that resisted it.

The opposition teams threw infrequently so the defensive back's pass defending skills remained under cover. His play against the run also was inconclusive. At free safety—the deepest man in the secondary—he seldom was in position for a solo tackle. He had chances on a couple of sweeps, but he pursued badly on both, slicing in at angles the ball carriers could elude. On two other occasions, he was flagged for late hits.

"Wait till I talk to the area scout," one of the others complained. "He said this guy really could play. He shows me nothing."

The scout did not reply. In fact, he said little in the two-hour viewing session. He studied the film intently, backing it up at his own discretion or upon request of one of the others. He saw nothing to deny the prospect's potential. The defensive back's poor play against the sweep, he believed, was the result of poor coaching. Other than that, he only paid attention to three facts: the safety was quick afoot, he was aggressive and eager to tackle, and he held for placekicks, meaning he had good hands, and he was willing to play special teams.

The scout ate lunch in the school cafeteria. He picked at his sausage, decided against finishing it, and rose amid bantering curiosity to bus his tray and leave. He moved around the campus, past wide green lawns and white-columned brick buildings that caused him to think of plantations. He turned one corner, saw the stadium on the horizon, and headed toward it. He walked through a chain-link gate and up to the stands above the 40-yard line. He removed his shirt, laid it along the bench-type seat as a blanket, and stretched out. For the next half hour, the sun baked his face and chest while noontime joggers chugged around the track below.

Later, as the players were filing out for afternoon practice, the scout was walking into the gym. He sought out the trainer. A 15-minute session revealed the defensive back had "average toughness" and that he had missed all of spring practice with a sprained knee, then the flu.

The warmup drills at practice told the scout a bit more. The back showed no signs of a limp in the reaction exercises. He back stepped and sidestepped quickly, if not exceptionally fast. He popped pads in a tackling drill, fronting his man squarely, then driving his helmet into the numbers with an audible grunt. The defensive back's 4.65 speed for the 40 eliminated him from consideration as a professional cornerback, but, at 200 pounds he seemed to have adequate feet, good hands, and big-league hitting skills. "If I had to guess right now, I'd say he was a sixth- or seventh-round prospect with a chance of sticking because of his attitude. He could be a safety. But he looks like a kamikaze who could play special teams, and that always impresses coaches on cutdown days."

When the horn blew, ending practice, the scout hurried to the parking lot. He faced a two-hour drive that night and another school tomorrow. He was beginning to sag from the routine. Another school. Another Holiday Inn. Another 100 pages of *Shogun*.

FRIDAY

The small state college was located on the outskirts of town, at the end of a long boulevard that began in an elegant, shady residential neighborhood, then trailed into a garish zone of body and fender shops, used-car lots, and the inevitable fast-food restaurants and convenience stores. The scout drove to the back end of the campus, where an oversized structure with a crowned tar-paper roof identified itself as the athletic complex.

The building was as big as a Zeppelin hangar and just as high, a domed-over stadium accommodating 16,000 spectators for basketball or football. The sports information director's office was stuck in the corner of the first floor. The man at the desk inside was rummaging through piles of papers when the scout walked in. Thick-jowled and bald, he was biting the stub of an ugly green cigar. He had the look of a man who had been at his job a very long time.

"We got this big offensive tackle, 6-6, 270; I'm pushing him for All-America," said the sports information director after the scout had introduced himself. The scout actually was curious about only one player, a 6-foot 190-pound receiver, not on the combine charts, who had been recommended by a former pro player living in the area. "He's been hurt," the sports information director announced. "Real bad in spring practice. Broke his ankle and hasn't fully recovered."

At the coaching office, the scout stood against a wall under a placard that said, "Just A Dirty Blue Shirt And A Chance To Be A Winner." He was waiting while a Secretary tracked down an assistant coach. She returned moments later, leading a paunchy middle-aged man still puffing from his mid-morning workout.

The scout recognized him as a former assistant with many pro teams. He was one in a category of coaching nomads who began their careers at some high school or junior college, excelled, and were tapped to assist a rising head coach who subsequently never rose. Thereafter, they would hook on late to staffs that were fired after a year on the job. The pattern would repeat itself as the years piled up, and the coaches could recite a litany like, "I've moved twelve times in fifteen years. Damn, that's hard on the family."

This assistant claimed he finally had found a permanent home. His children, now in high school, had formed stable ties with a wholesome community. His wife could plant azaleas one spring and expect to watch them bud the next. The coach belied his contentment a bit by inquiring slavishly after former friends in the pros and telling war stories of incompetent general managers who had fired him. The scout broke in and asked about his seniors.

"To be honest," said the coach, "we don't have a single pro prospect."

"What about your big tackle?"

"If he makes it, I'd be really surprised. He's big enough, but he's slow, and he doesn't have the feet."

"How about your injured receiver?"

"He's coming along real slow. I doubt whether he'll play much this year, and that'll set him back. I really don't think you'd be interested in him. Oh, he's got some talent—he's fast and he can catch, but I don't think so."

The scout had a plane to catch that afternoon, and he was exhausted from a long week on the road. He could write a credible report from the assistant coach's opinion, but something about that opinion nagged at him. For one thing, the coach was proud of his professional background. He would rate a player conservatively, not wanting to align with exuberant college coaches who think all their dray horses are thoroughbreds. For another, he might be feeling let down by the receiver's injury, a common emotion among coaches. They count on a player who turns up hurt, and they grow hostile toward him unconsciously The scout wanted to know more. He asked for some game films, a projector, and directions to the training room.

The trainer lectured him at length on the receiver's injury. "He dislocated and fractured his fibula. It required surgery and the doctor put in a plate and some screws. He has been okayed to resume playing, but the screws won't come out until after the season.

"He's been working out on his own, but he's hit a plateau to where he won't push himself further. The doctors say he can play, but right now, it is up to him whether he will."

The scout passed into the training room and eyed the receiver, a light-skinned black with rippling muscles who was standing on the taping table like the statue of Apollo. The scout stepped forward and greeted him. He asked perfunctory questions and jotted down notes on his steno pad.

"I like him," the scout said while walking to the film room. "There's something about him."

The films vindicated the scout's judgment. In more than three games worth of offensive footage, the receiver shone through the dim lighting on the screen. He moved inside deftly for possession yardage. He caught passes in a crowd without flinching. He streaked deep for several touchdowns. He threw effective blocks on running downs and seemed involved in every play, including his decoy patterns. The scout made a note to carefully check the receiver's progress through the season. "We may have somebody here," he said.

The scout stuck around for afternoon practice, but it revealed little.

At 4 P.M., the scout left the stadium for the parking lot. Under threatening skies, he backtracked to the motel near the center of town, found a sign pointing toward a highway, and another one saying, "Airport 9 Miles." He trailed out of town, past farmhouses and green fields marked by low hills and clumps of trees. At a junction, he turned right and drove another five miles. Light planes were buzzing overhead, and the scout could see the outlines of airstrips along the horizon to his right.

Clouds were bunching gray and ominous when he pulled into the rental car parking zone. Inside the terminal, he checked his baggage and confirmed a seat for the two-hour flight to Atlanta. He walked through a metal detector, down a ramp to the boarding area, where people milled around holding carry-on luggage, raincoats over their arms.

Outside, the clouds gathered darker and lower, as workmen in coveralls and earmuffs gassed and loaded the twin engine YS-11 commuter. Minutes later, the workmen dispersed, and an attendant swung the glass-doored gate open. The scout picked up his briefcase and walked up the steps and into the fuselage of the plane.

The plane warmed its engines to a whining pitch, then skittered down the runway and soared into liftoff, bouncing from one angry cloud to another through its ascent. It was a disquieting voyage, turbulent and slow, making tedious stops at rural Carolina airports before lifting off for the final lap into Atlanta.

The plane leveled off, and the air relaxed for the first time. The scout stared out the oval window at whirring propellers. He thought about his take for the week: two big-school prospects he was sure of, a tackle and a kicker; a small-school safety he felt would make a solid mid- to low-round pick; and an injured small-school receiver who probably would be worth a free agent's contract.

He also thought of a weekend in Atlanta with its edible food and entertaining nights and of two more weeks on the road before he would return home.

JIM KLOBUCHAR

Believe Everything You Hear

Passing a movie theater one day, John McNally saw the name BLOOD AND SAND *on the marquee. "That's it," he told his friend. "I'll be Blood, you be Sand." Thus was born Johnny Blood, an athlete of great ability and a roustabout of unparalleled dimension. Jim Klobuchar, a long-time columnist with the* MINNEAPOLIS STAR-TRIBUNE *and a frequent contributor to NFL publications, caught up with Blood when the Hall of Fame halfback was 70. This story first appeared in* PRO! *magazine in 1973.*

"A PSYCHIATRIST TOLD MY MOTHER I should have been an actor. It never occurred to me, but there might have been a thread of logic to that. My earliest memory is standing on the windowsill of my nursery, pulling up my nightie for the benefit of a small audience across the street. Without knowing it, I might have pioneered a new art form."

—Johnny Blood (McNally)
reflecting on his narrow escape from orthodoxy

The tyranny of time eventually ruins our illusions. About the reindeer and Robin Hood and the called home run.

Time cannot touch Johnny Blood. He is no illusion. If you wish, you may call him Johnny Blood Past. He has the corporeal form of John V. McNally Present, who moves among us performing a kind of droll and graceful penance at the age of 70 by advancing causes and modestly curtailing his poetic eruptions.

It is a grand attempt, but it should not be taken seriously as an act of contrition. The world will pardon much in its folk heroes but it will not allow them to abdicate, and John McNally therefore yields gently to the will of Johnny Blood's public.

So strum no minstrel's mandolin for the departed spirit of Johnny Blood nor consign it to the floating pantheons. Johnny Blood McNally performed such mind-bending deeds and so adroitly sidestepped adversaries like logic, deputies, and linebackers he must rise above mere mythology. You do Johnny Blood no favors by making him a legend. Instead, cherish him. He was authentic, as much as the swashing of the bathtub gin of the era that spawned him, or the moody-whistling trains on which he hoboed.

And if you are a football fan who would like to flash back to the bare-knuckled adolescence of professional football, when the players shouted bets across the line of scrimmage and slugged and cursed and laughed at each other for $100 a game, congratulate yourself that there was no television to glamorize Johnny Blood.

It would have been unbearable to watch the rail-riding vagabond curled in front of a fireplace, reciting "To a Skylark" with a popcorn popper in one hand and a flapper in the other.

How much better to experience Johnny Blood at leisure. Certainly you can sing your ballads, about his transcontinental motorcycle rides with hot-breathed maid—no, make that hot-breathed young women, for the sake of accuracy; about his eighth-floor leap onto Curly Lambeau's window ledge to collect an advance; playing a football game with a punctured kidney; doing a midfield jig to a chorus of Piccolo Pete during a time out; stalling his car broadside to stop the Packers' train, which he had missed owing to the late-rising habits of a blonde.

His football was the football of joy, the expression of an impish Achilles. He was lavishly endowed with ability and nerve and a gift for the improbable play, when nothing else would rescue his team from catastrophe. But the total weight of these qualities never smothered his renegade tilt and usually got no better than a draw. He won football games for the Packers with extraordinary catches and runs, scored 37 pro touchdowns and played on four championship teams. But he contrived to strike a redeeming balance with these achievements by getting fired by the Packers for reporting groggily to practice one day and falling on his rump attempting to punt.

They voted him into the Pro Football Hall of Fame lustily and deservedly. But it was never clear which Johnny fascinated the selectors more persuasively—Blood the champion or Blood the happy heretic.

The dilemma in singing ballads about Johnny Blood's 22 years in pro football is that you have trouble separating the stanzas, the ones in which the truth is merely outlandish from the ones in which the truth is plain horrendous.

"In some ways," Johnny Blood McNally admits, "I was a horrendous character. Maybe the zodiac had it right. I was born under Sagittarius. As I understand it, this made me part philosopher, part stud by decree of the stars. It is a helluva burden for a man to carry and practically impossible to live up to, although I don't deny making the attempt for a couple of years.

"When I look back on it, I can see that some of my unorthodox behavior came out of my upbringing in Wisconsin and had nothing to do with the zodiac. Some of the Blood stories you hear talk of me as though I were some kind of society football player. I did get money from my family later, but they never trusted me with it until I was fifty-five. My mother was a school teacher who got hold of me early and pumped a lot of myths into me, Grecian myths, Irish myths, King Arthur stuff. That part of me was going to be adventure. My father was a small-town businessman and athletic fan, but a left-handed, curly-haired Irishman, which explains a lot.

"My mother was born on a farm in St. Croix County, Wisconsin. Her favorite activity was breaking horses. Maybe she looked on me as another kind of colt. I loved her, but I just didn't cooperate very well and so one day she handed me a poem entitled, 'The Bronco That Wouldn't Be Broken.' Remember that one from your school days? Anyhow, she smiled when she did it. I suppose she was making some kind of statement."

The punctuation for it could have been furnished in ensuing years by professors, railroad dicks, sea captains, Nevada pit bosses, defensive ends, and football coaches, all of whom in some form failed to saddle the obstinate bronco. John McNally was a multi-directional prodigy, a high school graduate at 14, a teenaged economist capable of launching a book on the subject, a dedicated college dropout, and a mirthful revolutionary in general.

The straight arrows of John McNally's youth were the authorities at St. John's in Collegeville, Minnesota, the earnest fathers at Notre Dame, the worried fathers of his girl friends, and that collection of ringing social principles we call Rules.

McNally defied them impartially, including the one against amateur athletes accepting coin for their labors. To spare the feelings of his coach at St. John's, John decided to function incognito for a Minneapolis semipro club. He covered his tracks by selecting the name of Johnny Blood, borrowed from the marquee of a theater where Rudolph Valentino's *Blood and Sand* was playing. The choice was so good it seemed to have providential help, which may not have been a coincidence. "People have told me," John McNally said, "that I'm really a frustrated priest."

The priesthood is one of the more novel other-lives proposed for Johnny Blood McNally by his admirers and biographers, and one of the very few he has not actually attempted. He is the kind of man, with his history and his still-lean and courtly carriage of today, that impels otherwise non-psychic types into rambling notions about reincarnation. Nobody, the theory goes, could possibly pack that much living into one lifetime without some prior experience.

So how will you have it with Johnny Blood? Did he duel against the baron's cutthroats with D'Artagnan? Race the chariots for the hand, or whatever available, of the senator's daughter? Did he sail with Captain Kidd or ride with Zorro?

"Reincarnation," John granted, "is an intriguing concept. Who am

I to say no? I don't believe in it, but I never considered many things impossible. I think I would have been a lousy swordsman, although a good pirate because of certain skills I cultivated at quick escape in my earlier years. I've been a lecturer, miner, dockhand, gambler, seaman, coach, and farm hand. I don't know who else I might have been. If I had any relatives in other lives, it might have been some combination of John L. Sullivan and Errol Flynn. At least that would have been my preference."

Johnny Blood needs no hypnotic regression to make it as a bona fide sage. His life has been filled with a Decameron menagerie of characters, symbolic questings, odd triumphs, and hilarious defeats. It is a kind of pilgrim's progress from the reckless appetites of the warrior-nomad to his sense of duty in a pensive old age.

He has never blushed for the urges of his prime. Yet he does regret 10 years of his middle age in which "I didn't really do a damned thing except to go around obliging people who wanted to dredge up skeletons of another time. I would join them in having one more happy wake for the career of Johnny Blood."

In this he may be making a needlessly hard judgment. Nobody has ever provided aging folk heroes with a manual on how to repudiate the fiction gracefully without spoiling the larger fun generated by the truth. So John has suffered the blarney without protest, fully recognizing that the genuine Blood stories are better. He is also a practical man. It wouldn't do him any good to deny any part of it, including the fairy tales.

Which is another reason John has been welcomed in the newspaper offices across the land with that special kind of hospitality accorded the arrival of an ice cream cart at a kindergarten picnic. Thus his recent public lobbying, first a McNally-inspired campaign to draft Supreme Court Justice Byron R. White for President and later an appeal for pensions to oldtime pros, encountered little resistance breaking into print.

The experience has jarred him somewhat. "I'd want to talk all about why Whizzer White [whom he coached with the Pittsburgh

Steelers] would be so qualified to serve as President in case of a deadlock at the Democratic convention," he said, "and the sports columnist would nod and then ask me if it were true that I once stole a cab in St. Louis in an emergency to protect the reputation of a young lady."

The story, naturally, was true, which sort of consigned Whizzer White to the subterranean sections of the story, to John's mortification.

He is having to battle a similar conflict of interest between John McNally, maverick knight, and John McNally, advocate, in his current mission to extend pro football's pension benefits to the men of the game's formative years. About this he comes as close as he is capable to real anger. "I think," he said, "the lawyers are waiting until the old guys are all dead."

It should not be neglected that among the several lives of John McNally was a promising career as a feed salesman. It ended under provocative circumstances but John concedes himself some gifts of persuasion.

It was such power that enabled him to draw out a book on Basic English from a college library in the thirties while he was touring with the Packers. "It was Ogden and Richards," he remembers. "They invented 'Basic English.' It was all the rage among the young scholars in those years. The incident took place during one of my interludes of intellectual curiosity. I checked out the book from the librarian and then just forgot about it. A couple of months later somebody from the team office called me and said, "Another first, John. According to this letter from Palo Alto you're the first pro football player who ever stole a book from the Stanford Library."

John made immediate restitution, out of his abiding fondness for the academic groves. This affection, if ever doubted, was reinforced in the 1950s when John McNally, a pro football player for two decades and onetime international roustabout, returned to St. John's as a lecturer in economics.

His scholarship was dimmed in the 1920s, however, when he got kicked out of Notre Dame for violating curfew and refusing to identify his accomplices.

Like his contemporary in the fields of arts and letters, Thomas Wolfe, Johnny Blood McNally was bewitched by trains. They were his Arabian carpets of adventure, his deliverance from drudgery and the sites of his random showdowns with the forces of calm and order. He bummed his way around the country on trains, ran across their roofs, challenged the Chicago Bears on a train, and once nearly derailed his own team.

"It was simply an obligation I had to a young woman," he explained of this latter feat. "She was a late riser, which put great demands on chivalry. Anyhow, the Packer train was leaving at ten A.M. for the West Coast, from where we were going to sail to Hawaii for some exhibitions.

"I got a late start for the depot and discovered the train had left without me. There was really no choice. Either I stopped the train, which was then just pulling out of the yard, or I got fined for missing it."

His priorities clear, McNally floorboarded his touring car for three blocks and swung it across the tracks a couple of hundred feet in front of the advancing train.

"I couldn't imagine that the engineer was a callous man and would run the engine through the car," McNally relates, "especially since the lady and I were still in it."

Sensitivity triumphed. The engineer stopped the train, McNally valorously turned over the wheel to the young woman, kissed her auf wiedersehen, and boarded the train.

"Would you believe this?" he asked. "A few months ago, in the spring of 1974, I was visiting in Palm Springs, California. The late Arthur Daley of the New York Times, a really lovable person, had written a column about some of my experiences. One of the girl's relatives saw Daley's column and forwarded it to her, asking whether I was the guy she had talked about years ago. A copy of the letter was sent to Arthur, who sent it to me, and on this day in California I met the girl-on-the-tracks, forty years after the incident. She's a widow living in San Bernardino, and remembers the whole thing very clearly."

One wouldn't wonder. Nor should one be surprised that McNally waited 30 years to avenge another small railroad crisis involving a less hazardous gamble.

It wasn't uncommon for the pro footballers of the 1920s and 1930s to wager against each other on the quirk of the moment before games. Such indiscretion today would invoke immediate thunder and damnation from the league office. But in those days the athletes considered it a legitimate source of walking-around money. No big sums were involved, nor were they available, in view of the relative penury of the shoulder-padded bettors. Ten dollars was standard."We never looked on it as immoral in any way because you always bet on yourself," McNally explained. "Of course, if I were with management I can see how it would have a different complexion. I had a ten dollar bet on this game with Carl Brumbaugh, the Bears' quarterback. We won the game and afterwards I went on the Bears' train to collect the bet.

"All hell broke loose. Somebody got the idea I came on board to challenge the whole Bears' team, which wouldn't have been very bright considering the few escape routes open. I barely got out of there in one piece, and I didn't collect the money from Brumbaugh.

"A couple of years ago they got all of the old Bears and Packers players together for the one-hundredth anniversary Green Bay-Chicago game. I spotted Brumbaugh and said, 'You bastard, you still haven't paid the ten dollars.' He almost keeled over laughing and he paid me the ten dollars. I hate to think what inflation did to the original ten bucks."

It is hard to suppress the notion that it would have made a rare exhibit for the Hall of Fame.

Yet in a substantial way the Blood legendry has inflicted a disservice on the Blood artistry. Players of that era concede there were one or two better runners and one or two better receivers and defensive backs, but none with Johnny Blood's diversity, speed, or gift for climactic play.

"I don't know what my speed was," John acknowledges. "Nobody timed you scientifically. I do know that every now and then we'd get a guy in camp who was supposed to have run the hundred in nine-six. It was nine-six in those days, not nine-one. They must have lost a few decimal points on the train because I could always outrun them when we put the shoes on.

"It's pointless to compare the players of then with the ones today. Sizes are different and the game is different. But yes, I could play in the pros today. I'm sure I'd be a wide receiver. I'd go about one-ninety or so and I know I'd be able to get downfield fast enough. But you see the crucial difference is the sixty-minute business. We played the whole game. Well, if I played the whole game today I wouldn't have to worry about getting mauled by two-hundred-eighty-pound defensive ends because the same guy would have to play offense and you're not going to have flankers weighing two-hundred-eighty pounds running hitch-outs.

"A lot of people today have the impression we played the game in those years with bums and unemployed muleskinners. Listen, there were people in our lineups who became doctors and lawyers or became successful in a dozen other ways. We had a Ph.D. in the lineup once. Duke Slater played, one of the great blacks, who became a judge. And of course Whizzer White, who now sits on the Supreme Court bench and should be president.

"We didn't have the outer space equipment they play with today and sometimes we went without a helmet. All they were in those days were flimsy pieces of leather that were okay for the morale but weren't worth much to the skull.

"The games get a little fuzzy in your memory. Still, I can remember a couple of plays as vividly as though they were on the television screen in front of me right now. I remember lining up on our two-yard line after I went to Pittsburgh as player-coach, and the Bears were going for a touchdown. You know the ball is going to

Nagurski. He's squatting down there with his big wide nostrils, ready to run through the wall. The only thing you know about it is you've got to get in front of him and hit him before he starts rolling. He's already knocked three of our guys out of the game—one with a broken leg, one with a broken arm, and Lord knows what happened to the third. I don't say Nagurski was the strongest runner of all time but I do know he was the best fullback—I mean offense, defense, blocking, and power when he had momentum. So I still have this picture of the two-yard line, of Nagurski hunkering down ready to get the ball, and here he comes!"

John's voice softened as the story progressed, and he halted his recitation to allow the leprechaun's latent smile to frolic beneath his still-clear blue eyes.

"Yes, and then, John," his companion prodded.

"I honestly can't tell you how it ended. I don't know whether I stopped Nagurski or if he scored. The only memory I have is that big son of a bitch coming into the line so incredibly huge he took up all the daylight."

The more philosophic of today's professionals, when away from their accountants, sometimes impute qualities of spiritual fulfillment to the game. They talk solemnly and unapologetically about the fraternal love it creates among players who share the grime and sweat and fears.

"I think we had that bond," John said, "but it was never expressed as love, and I think they beat that word to death nowadays. I'm not going to quibble over words. Football had more spontaneity on the field in our years, which could have meant more fun, I suppose. But I remember the exhilaration they talk about. I remember it from a play where I caught a pass near the goal line. I don't know who we were playing. I think Herber threw it. I just remember going up for it with another guy, and I jumped a little higher. It was an important game, and I knew I had the touchdown when I caught the ball. I was floating, really. It was like the slow motion you see in the television highlights today. I could hear the crowd roaring and it seemed like

I'd never come down. The goal posts were in front of me but this is the God's truth: I actually believed I could have jumped over the crossbar. I just felt elevated, all through me. No matter what the ball player tells you, he just doesn't feel that very often."

And when he felt it no more, Johnny Blood went seeking, for a new respectability in a time and society where rebels were not so quickly indulged. He went back to St. John's in the early 1950s to teach and to coach, with passable success, but even in a place so sequestered he was fundamentally a curiosity. The rakehell becalmed. He looked professional and sometimes he sounded that way, but he was more the pastured bronco then he was the serious intellectual of his fugitive imaginings. He attended graduate school at the University of Minnesota at the age of 50, half-hoping that would launch him into scholastic excitements. But he confessed to himself before he did to others that his spirit was an imposter when confined by blackboard and brick walls. Intellectualism and poetry recitals were fun, easy, and even impressive when the philosopher had a swaying audience of nonpoetic listeners to enchant, and with whom he could sway in unison.

He became a traveling ornament on the pro football circuit, a figure stately and commanding because of his appearance and past, also endearing because of his musty flights into philosophy.

To some of the regulars at Packers or championship games, the middle-aged surrogate of Johnny Blood was tedious and sometimes a simple pain in the rear.

I looked on John McNally then as a lonely man but a very captivating man, honestly searching and struggling but too much the creature Johnny Blood Past to make any permanent break with Johnny Blood of any age.

He married, commuted between St. Paul and New Richmond, Wisconsin, ran a couple of small businesses, and acquired money from the legacy of his mother's publishing family. He divorced after 10 years with expressions of surprise that it endured that long, remarrying several years later. The union is doing well.

And Johnny Blood, 70, is a healthier man spiritually. He gave himself to his Whizzer White cause and the old players' cause because it was ruinous to a man's self-respect to turn his life into a tired puppet show in which new audiences smiled and gaped and appreciated while the well-meaning puppeteer-biographers asked Johnny Blood to reenact it, one more time.

His carriage is straight, the shoulders unbending, and the hair a virile mottled gray. Sometimes he has shortness of breath and he may ask you—no, he will tell you—he does not hear as well. He is not a sad or solemn man, understand. He will talk about the old years if you wish, and he will do so with animation and obvious affection. But he has more peace now.

"You humble me, John," his companion said. "I have known a lot of people who have striven for all the points on the compass that are available to the curious man. Adventurers and seekers. Some of them are good people, but most of them are role players in some fashion. You may have been a character, but you were a helluva character and a very honest character."

John accepted this as a reasonable judgment.

"I've always seen myself as an outrider," he said."You've seen the movies where a guy goes out by himself and hits the bush, a little away from the crowd. Well, I think that was me. I think everybody has regrets of some kind.

"I read. Sometimes I meditate. I wrote some poetry but I don't think it was very good, except for one, which I do remember and can recite, but no more in public. It's too bad about classic poetry, I mean the kind Wordsworth and Keats wrote. It was beautiful and the language was enduring. I regret they don't write poetry like that any more."

There is one truth about youth. It can be overwhelmed by the seasons and taunted by a tremor in the lips, but when it is the youth of Johnny Blood, it is never really destroyed.

They do not write poems any more like John Keats wrote, nor play football like Johnny Blood.

SCOTT OSTLER

Down Home with Terry Bradshaw

Terry Bradshaw was booed early in his career, and his intelligence was questioned later in his career even as he masterfully directed the Pittsburgh Steelers' offense. He seemed even less comfortable with his successes, from his status as the first player selected in the 1970 draft to his four Super Bowl triumphs. Fortunately, Scott Ostler met Bradshaw where the quarterback was most at ease: his 400-acre ranch near Grand Cane, Louisiana, in this 1981 story for PRO! *magazine.*

TERRY BRADSHAW IS STRETCHED OUT on an air mattress, bobbing on the surface of a swimming pool that, if seen from the air, would be a mere blue-green speck in a corner of the expanse known as the Circle-12 Ranch.

If Bradshaw had a worry in the world right now, it would have a difficult time hammering its way into his consciousness.

Pittsburgh and his mountain climb of a football career is a million miles away. So is Nashville and his roller coaster of a singing career, and Hollywood and his obstacle course of an acting career.

Not that Bradshaw doesn't feel relaxed or comfortable on a football field or behind a microphone or in front of a camera. It's just that, be it ever so humble, there's no place like home—especially if home is 400 lush, green acres of meadow and forests near Grand Cane, Louisiana.

Bradshaw floats and bobs and finally says, "Like my agent told me when he came down here for a visit—this place will drive you sane."

That makes it the ideal kind of place for someone like Terry Bradshaw.

You take a country boy and make him into a high school and college football hero, then make him struggle for several years in the pros. Suddenly challenge his equilibrium with four Super Bowl titles, but make him sweat to overcome the label of a bumpkin with a strong arm and a weak mind.

Then let his personality and charm lead him innocently into the entertainment jungle, where polished professionals have been known to turn into lunatics. Let him take his lumps and bumps under the bright lights, and shatter a couple of his made-in-Hollywood marriages, for good measure.

What you wind up with, potentially, is a confused and insecure man. That might have been the Terry Bradshaw of whom *Los Angeles Times* football analyst Bob Oates wrote a few years ago, "Ground under for so many years, Bradshaw has trouble to this day thinking of himself as a champion."

He has no trouble now. Terry Bradshaw gives every appearance today of having come to terms with all the criticism and adulation. He seems remarkably happy and well adjusted for a man whose various careers and relationships have taken so many soap-opera turns.

Last summer, shortly after Bradshaw's would-be television series folded to critical reviews, a sportswriter asked for an interview.

He had been talking about quitting football for acting, and it seemed like a good time to talk about his various glamour careers, especially the one that made him famous. Heading into his twelfth NFL season—if he did decide to head in—what was the state of Terry Bradshaw?

Because his various careers had become increasingly interrelated, it seemed a good time to talk about the singing, the acting, the ranching.

"C'mon down," said Bradshaw.

Bradshaw steers his station wagon, loaded with three eager dogs, off the highway and onto a narrow blacktop farm road lined with tall pine and hickory trees.

"It's a good old hiding place," Bradshaw says, chewing tobacco. "Think you could find it again?" Not likely. It's a winding 30-mile ride from Shreveport, where he grew up, to Bradshaw's ranch, a ride not many autograph seekers or privacy invaders would bother to make, even if they knew the location of the ranch.

But the 400-acre spread wasn't intended as a hiding place. If it was, Bradshaw wouldn't have named it the Circle-12 (his Steelers uniform number) and flanked the driveway entrance with ironwork representations of the Circle-12 brand.

The ranch is intended simply as a place to live and work. Bradshaw purchased these 400 acres about a year ago and later bought another 400 acres nearby (an acre is roughly the size of one football field). He's in the business of raising and breeding cattle and show horses.

The country boy finally has come home to the country. Actually he was raised inside the Shreveport city limits, not on a farm, but the farm roots are there.

"My grandfather had a forty-acre farm," Bradshaw says, "and I loved it. I liked the idea of being out in the country, of waking up to a rooster crowing . . . Mom going out to the barn to get eggs . . . making homemade biscuits . . . raising our own chickens and cattle . . . raising cotton and watermelons.

"We'd take the melons out and sell 'em. We'd drive through the suburbs, or into little towns, and park on the corner and just holler and sell the melons.

"I just liked it, all the fishing holes we'd find, every phase of it. If you were raised on a farm and had to do all the work, maybe you wouldn't like it, but I didn't have to do all the hard stuff.

"Once I got playing [pro football], I thought it would be nice to get enough money that I could buy me some land. My dad found this property and I bought it just about sight unseen. I've cleared the land, improved the house, torn down a bunch of old barns, and now I live out here."

Bradshaw lives alone, unless you count the dogs—his golden Labrador and a couple of other dogs that belong to his uncle.

Bradshaw's first marriage in 1972, to former Miss Teen-Age America, Melissa Babich, lasted about a year. In 1977 he married JoJo Starbuck, a former Olympian and professional figure skater. However, there were career conflicts and they have separated.

If anyone ever does a photo story of the NFL's glamour quarterbacks and their dwellings, Bradshaw's surely would be the least glamorous.

It's a small, square, brick house with two bedrooms and a combination country-style living room and dining room. The house is function and not flash. Even the furniture is down-homey and unpretentious, as are the decorations. Except for a few football trophies and a couple of game balls (most of Bradshaw's trophies and mementos are stashed away in a spare room), you'd never suspect it was the home of football's most successful quarterback.

Bradshaw has made a few changes since he moved in. He added an enclosed sun porch, suitable for Ping-Pong or guitar playing.

Why such a modest home?

"One of my philosophies," Bradshaw says, "is that when all is said and done, what you've built up, you'd better be able to maintain. I didn't want to build a big home and then not be able to pay the electricity. It's a little bitty house, but it's simple and comfortable. When I'm through with football, I won't have to make any major adjustments. I own this one, and it means a lot to me. I'm at the end of my career, and I can't afford to build one of those big rascals."

He did, however, build a big rascal of a swimming pool, an instant escape from the sweltering heat and humidity of summertime Louisiana. It's obviously his favorite spot on the 400 acres. The pool is rectangular, built extra long (44 feet) for swimming laps and extra deep for diving.

You swim at your own risk. Bradshaw has fished out an occasional bullfrog or rattlesnake, and one recent guest was stung by a wasp that was nesting under the slide.

About 50 yards from the pool is a large pond Bradshaw keeps stocked with catfish. "I caught 126 of 'em in three hours," he says.

So much for the R & R portion of the Circle-12. The other 399 acres, while beautiful to look at, are all business.

Bradshaw has several modern steel barns and stable areas, which were built for the show horses that are the real business of the ranch.

The star of Bradshaw's growing animal team is a huge stallion named "Impressive Steeler," which is, Terry says with pride, probably the most popular halter stud horse in America, bringing a stud fee of $15,000.

Bradshaws visits his horses like a proud coach walking through the locker room after a practice.

"I've been foolin' with horses since junior high," he says. "I bought my first mare in 1972 or '73. Slowly I learned more about the breed, about what's popular, what to look for. I'd go out and try to find good mares, just acquire field knowledge, just like you would in football. You just get out and start playing and in time, you learn."

For a while, Bradshaw did most of the hard work on the ranch, until he realized he was overmatched. Now his uncle lives in a home near Terry's, and runs the ranch. But Bradshaw still is very much involved, in everything from mucking out the stalls to clearing the land.

As he drives back to the house, a dog sitting on his leg and a chaw of tobacco in his cheek, he says, "I'm happy here, and I guess that's about all you can ask."

The worst performance Terry Bradshaw ever delivered was in Pittsburgh, but not on a football field. It took place in an arena, when he was one of the feature artists in a country and western music festival. He bombed.

"I'll tell you exactly what happened," Bradshaw says. "I didn't have many songs, anyway, and I didn't know the band I was singing with, and I never rehearsed. A girl went on before me and she sang every song I was going to sing. I stood backstage and thought, 'Oh, my God, there goes my show.' I was so nervous my throat was frozen. I quit after four songs."

It was the kind of performance a lot of people were expecting from Bradshaw when, late in 1975, he announced he would be cutting a country album, and would take his songs on tour.

Yawn. Another famous athlete allowing himself to be exploited for his fame and name, convinced by sycophants that his wondrous athletic talent somehow was transferable to another form of entertainment, thrust into the big time without paying his dues.

That's exactly what Bradshaw expected people to think.

"That's probably one of the reasons I turned down a lot of stuff," he says. "Everyone thinks you're trying to cash in."

Singing didn't come as naturally to Bradshaw. While his name obviously was what got him in the front door of the music business and what brought people to his concerts, singing has been a lifelong passion.

"Music always has been my first love," he says. "I was raised listening to the Statesmen and the Blackwood Family. As a child, I loved to sing. My whole family loved to sing. My older brother Gary is a great singer, my aunt is a great singer. My uncles make guitars and pick and write songs. My aunt's father has written three, four hundred songs. I'm all the time in here pickin' and singing."

However, as Bradshaw quickly discovered, pickin' and singin' on the back porch is not quite the same as entertaining a room full or an arena full of paying customers. "You talk about a diamond in the rough," he says. "I was a piece of coal."

A chance meeting with a record producer led to a contract with Mercury records, which cranked out a quick Terry Bradshaw C&W album and sent him on tour. One song of the album, "I'm So Lonesome I Could Cry," did well, but overall his C&W recording debut could be rated D, for disaster.

"I was kind of phased out of the country music," Bradshaw says casually. "I didn't have much say-so. Mercury released me from my recording contract. It was a tremendous blow. I had gotten close with the producer, and what hurt was that he didn't have the guts to tell me to my face that the contract had been canceled. He sent me a

Mail-o-Gram. I kind of got a taste of how cold people could be in the entertainment business."

Actually, Bradshaw doesn't blame any one person for the failure of his C&W career. It was a team effort, with Terry at quarterback. They tried to create an instant star, cutting all corners, and Bradshaw naively went along.

"The country album was terrible," Bradshaw says. "I'd never been in a studio. I did the recording session live with the band, on one take. They were all great pickers and there I was, standing up to the mike singing those songs. Nervous? It was a disaster."

Through the whole ordeal, records and concerts, "I had nobody helping me, and I wasn't putting one hundred percent into it. I was making speaking engagements and doing endorsements, and then running off to do a concert. It wasn't fair to the public. I had a different band every place I went. I made fifteen thousand dollars in three days singing, and then owed twenty thousand. I just had no idea of what I was doing.

"So I just lost all my confidence, I just kind of backed off."

But not too far off, not completely off stage. He still loved music and believed in his own ability. He was wiser, and still had connections in the music industry.

So, just like Terry Bradshaw the struggling young quarterback, Terry Bradshaw the struggling singer kept plugging. He got himself into a different branch of the country and western music—gospel.

It was a natural. Bradshaw has strong religious beliefs, and there was not as much pressure on him singing gospel, because it's a less intense and competitive field of music.

His work is becoming more polished as his confidence grows, in the studio and in concert. His first gospel album, *Until You*, was well received. His second, *Getting Free*, is due to be released in September. He plans to continue to perform live.

"One thing I always could do is entertain," he says. "I loved making people laugh, just acting crazy. One thing I could always do in concerts, even if I was singing bad, was have fun, make fun of myself . . . although my manager didn't like that."

Bradshaw puts down his guitar, which he has been picking as he talks, and moves to his reel-to-reel tape deck to cue up his latest gospel album.

It's a professional product, good, progressive, country-style music with sophisticated arrangements—strings, horns, background vocals. Bradshaw doesn't have the strong, distinctive style of Merle Haggard or Willie Nelson, but his simple vocals don't send you searching for ear plugs.

It's a nice, mellow country and western album, only instead of singing about bars and girls and broken hearts, Bradshaw sings about Jesus and feeling good.

"I feel like I could have done this album better," he says, "but I always feel that way when I finish something."

Bradshaw brings out a copy of his first gospel album. The back cover has several football photos of him, and on the front cover photo he's wearing a hairpiece to cover his thinning-on-the top hair. He doesn't like the football pictures, and he says he no longer wears the wig. But he's happy with what's inside the covers on both albums.

"People come in here and I play the record and they say, 'Aren't you something, sitting here listening to your own music.' But I like the album. I'm proud of it. Sometimes when I'm listening, I forget I'm singing."

You should understand that it's not just Bradshaw's fame and Super Bowl accomplishments that have gained him entrance into Hollywood and Nashville.

You have to understand that Bradshaw's personality had a lot to do with it. He's like Dolly Parton, one of those rare folks who not only are talented, but instantly likable and natural, on stage and off.

"Historically, successful people try to transcend barriers and get into fields where they have no business," says Jerry Crutchfield, who works with Bradshaw on his record albums. "But the truth is that Terry really is a singer and an entertainer. The incredible thing about Terry—and I have worked with a lot of music personalities—is he seems to have that magnetic attraction. It's unbelievable, he's so recognizable and congenial, such a strong personality."

Bradshaw also has a streak of modesty that makes him seem even more down to earth.

"I'm a little uncomfortable with praise," he says. "I don't like to get stared at for being successful or popular or famous or a star, I don't particularly like the idea that people stare. I forget at times that I am, to those people, something different or special. I can't go Christmas shopping, or go into stores, I can't hardly go into a restaurant. That part [of fame] I don't like, but I don't blame them. It's just that I want to be like *them*."

So with the combination of his sports fame and a big league personality, it seems only natural that Bradshaw would wind up in movies and television, despite the handicap of playing football in Pittsburgh, hardly the entertainment capital of the world.

Until recently, however, his acting jobs mostly were minor, the bit parts and cameo roles, in such movies as *Smokey and the Bandit* and *The Cannonball Run*. Then came the job that threatened to take him away from football. He landed a part in a pilot for a television series, "The Stockers."

He was to co-star with country music star and comedian Mel Tillis in a series about country dirt-track stock car racers.

When he got the role, Bradshaw announced that he would retire from football if the pilot were picked up as a regular series. When the first episode bombed, Steelers fans were relieved. "I wasn't disappointed that it didn't get picked up," Bradshaw says, "but I was disappointed for another reason, namely that the show wasn't that good. After I'd seen it, I was embarrassed."

Ah, another show business lesson for the country quarterback.

"From my understanding," Bradshaw says, "when you do a pilot, you do several episodes and then pick out the best one to show. We did *one*.

"If I'm going to lose in the Super Bowl, I've already played eighteen games, and by golly, if I get beat, it's by a better team or because of breaks, but I've never been embarrassed on the field by not preparing and not knowing what I was doing.

"We jumped into a major effort with inexperienced [production] people, who didn't know what they were doing. There was an awful lot of advertising hype about how great the show was. I certainly wouldn't say anything bad about anyone, but what I saw on screen *should've* been canceled. *I* would have canceled it. It plain and simple wasn't any good."

There probably will be other movies, and other television shows, and more work as analyst on televised football broadcasts. But, for now, Terry Bradshaw has one identity that continues to overshadow the rest. . . .

Terry Bradshaw was over the hill. The Pittsburgh Steelers were over the hill.

Or so the signs seemed to indicate. Last season was a large disappointment for Bradshaw, his team, and their fans. His performances were inconsistent; he showed signs of wear and tear.

He began talking about retirement immediately after winning his fourth Super Bowl in January 1980. Then came the subpar season, the acting career, and more talk of retirement.

The picture was forming: Aging quarterback with no more football worlds to conquer, decreasing motivation, and reluctance to expose his body to mayhem and his game to criticism. Regardless of his acting fortunes, his football career seemed on the wane.

But bouncing around his house last June, a few weeks before he broke a toe playing with his dog, Bradshaw sounded like a kid getting himself psyched up to roar into his first pro football training camp and make an impression.

"I'm probably more excited today than since my rookie year about playing football," Bradshaw says. "That's the good thing that's come out of all this, is that I'm rejuvenated.

"I called Chuck [Noll] the other day and said, 'I'll be at the minicamp. I want you to know that I'm looking forward to it.' He said, 'Fine, that's good news.'

"There's been a lot of negative criticism, a lot of questions. If I would come back, would I give one hundred percent? People will feel, because of the TV show and everything, that football is my second choice, and I don't blame them for thinking that.

"The skeptics will keep me on edge, I won't be lackadaisical. There's nothing greater than a challenge, when you've got something to prove. We've got a couple good kids [Cliff Stoudt and Mark Malone] who want my job, and the fans and the press will be on me.

"Only one of my teammates said anything, that I know of. Jack Lambert said something like, 'By God he'd better have his mind one hundred percent off his outside activities.' I think most of them are glad I'm back, but I'm not going to worry about it too much."

And no more talk of retirement.

"I said it publicly, that I'll stop this foolishness. There won't be any more of this talk. Next time at the end of the season I'll just say 'See ya next year.' I'll play at least four more years, definitely.

"I was just tired after the last Super Bowl [XIV]. I was exhausted. The idea of acting was presented to me, and it was a once-in-a-lifetime opportunity. I felt I could give up football.

"I asked myself why I should want to come back. I think what happened was I got mentally tired from the strain and stress of being champion, and the demands on my time and the stress it puts on the family.

"I started thinking: I'm thirty-two. If I retire, I've done everything I could possibly do. I could get out healthy and pursue other careers. Why not?

"I asked myself, 'Can I handle the pressure [back in football]? *Will* there be other Super Bowls, will I lose my job, or turn into a very average quarterback and then go down in history as being lucky for the things I had accomplished before?'

"I found those things starting to creep into my thinking. I just was tired of the whole scene, getting up every week to face a new team. I just wanted to get away. I was a very tired person.

"But while I was waiting to hear about the pilot, I had all the time here, working from sunup to sundown. The phone wasn't ringing, I wasn't in demand. When I got the news [about the series cancellation], I found myself thinking about football. You can see I've got a few mementos. I found myself day-dreaming, reminiscing. I got a worse and worse longing to compete again. I started thinking about what a fool I'd been. I started to analyze—'Jiminy Christmas, I'm throwing away something I've worked all my life for. Why not play the deck to the end?'

"Everything I have is football, everything I own is because of football—the movies, records. There's nothing wrong with using that [football fame] to help you get into other things that are exciting, challenging, but. . . .

"I just like to throw that little pigskin. I do enjoy the game. To me, it's still a game. I never took it seriously. To me it's still a sport, and I try hard to make it fun . . . if I didn't have to worry about winnin' or losing, God, I'd *never* quit, I'd play forever."

Bradshaw's enjoyment and appreciation for the game now might be owing to the fact that it took him so long to be recognized as a great quarterback—by the critics and by himself. Remember, at one point in his *fifth* season as a Steeler, Bradshaw was the team's third-string quarterback. He didn't make an all-pro team until he was 30.

It didn't really all come together for Bradshaw until 1979—the third Super Bowl championship, the Super Bowl most valuable player award, *Sports Illustrated*'s Sportsman of the Year award, even a spot on the year's "Ten Best Dressed Men" list. ("Wasn't that a hoot?" Bradshaw says. "That just cracked me up. All I ever wear are cowboy boots and shirts, and jeans and hats.")

The early years in the NFL were rocky for Bradshaw. The Steelers weren't making Super Bowl trips, and Terry wasn't getting great reviews. The "good arm, no brains" label stayed with him for a long time. Asked if he ever thinks back to those early years, Bradshaw laughs and says:

"No, I don't drift back too far. If I drift, I drift back to the good times, I don't want to feed my brain all that bad stuff. I'm like an alcoholic—if you get off the damn sauce, you sure don't want another drink. Let that past lie, let it sleep."

So, Bradshaw is eager to play the way he's always played. Before his toe injury, he was running—not jogging—seven miles a day on the roads around his ranch.

"Keep this sucker in shape, and it'll respond," Bradshaw says, referring to his body.

And, at 33, Bradshaw finally is confident of his skills. He's still not his own number one booster and boaster, but he is no longer shy about assessing his game.

Asked to rate himself as a quarterback, Bradshaw squints and says, "I'm a good quarterback . . . and at times I show signs of brilliance. And at other times I give people an upset stomach, or a headache.

"Anybody could have quarterbacked the Steelers and been a winner, and I'm being honest. But I do feel this: I am in awe of great actors, the Academy Award winners, the Dustin Hoffmans and the Richard Dreyfusses and people like that. And as comfortable as they are in their spotlight, I am in mine. I feel very comfortable. I've reached the point where I'm a confident player.

"Other quarterbacks do better things and a lot of them can throw the ball. But they haven't done it in big games."

It's hard to find flaws in Bradshaw's confidence, his maturity, or his attitude. He's come a long way in the last few years.

Obviously, Terry Bradshaw has been down on his farm too long. It's driving him sane.

JIM MURRAY

One Man's Image

Jim Murray has been the superstar columnist of the LOS ANGELES TIMES *sports page for more than 30 years, but his syndicated columns are so popular that his voice long ago overran any regional bounds. Murray's punchy descriptions are the essence of American sportswriting, and his subject for this essay, Bears founder and coach George Halas, was the essence of the NFL's hard-knocking early days. This piece appeared in* MORE THAN A GAME, *an NFL collection published in 1974.*

THEY CAME FROM THE OLD COUNTRY, and they had names like "Anton" and "Stefan" and "Josip" and "Stanislaus" and they had a big edge on people who needed to rest.

Their icon was work. They harnessed up to it like Percherons at birth, and they died in the traces. They were born with a silver shovel in their mouths. Sunup to sundown was their idea of a work day until the electric light came in. Then, they worked till they fell asleep.

They carried their money in their belts where it got as sweat-stained as they were. They didn't trust banks, people, governments, or each other. "Heaven" was a place where you got a lunch hour.

They had short powerful arms, squat immovable legs. God (or environment) built them to shovel, haul, cut, pull, and push. They weren't much on dancing. They were long on reality and short on imagination. An open-hearth furnace is no place for fairy tales. The company store does not sell costume novels.

They came to America, and they disappeared into the steel mills where they hauled the molten ingots or pounded sledges or laid track. They put human as well as processed steel into the backbone of the country.

They farmed the barren fields everyone else quit on. They grew tobacco under gauze. They put tunnels under rivers, beams on buildings. They had rings around their heads from hard hats.

When they went to college, they took courses that meant money. English Literature was safe from them. *The Lives of the Minor Poets* would not get Papa out of the coal mines. Daydreams weren't something you paid good money for. They learned how to build bridges with a pencil or build a machine that could dig ore and let Uncle Louie up from the mine shaft.

Their god was steel and iron and gold. Their god was a man who minded the store. Vacations were for the rich. They all ended up with backaches. So they feared an open window more than an open hearth. Better a hundred-degree heat in the foundry than a few days off at no pay because you couldn't straighten your back.

In football, they were in the line. In war, they were in the infantry. In life, they were in the pits. On a ship, they were down in the hold.

They bit coins and held paper money up to the light. They never took checks. The part of Europe their people came from, they didn't trust their neighbor all that much. He brought flowers one day, a bayonet the next.

George Stanley Halas came from a long line of these people. He came from a craggy land known as "Bohemia" in the old Austro-Hungarian Empire, and it's the heart and lungs of Czechoslovakia now. It's funny that "Bohemian" should come to symbolize a kind of unwashed, frivolous, violin-playing gypsy, because the real Bohemians were the craggy types outlined above, fools for work who sowed the barren sides of the Carpathian Mountains or produced the best mechanics in Europe in the airless factories of the Industrial Revolution. They lived by their backs, not their wits.

George Halas's father was a tailor in America. When he cut you a graduation suit, you could expect to be buried in it. He paid his bills, he was on time with the rent, and you could take his handshake to any bank in Chicago and get a loan on it. He didn't put out the "Closed" sign on the shop until the whole street was empty and the street cars stopped running.

Son George got a chance to go to the University of Illinois and escape a lifetime of needles in the mouth or coal lamp in the hat, and, when he wasn't playing football, baseball, basketball, or soccer, he was washing windows, cutting grass, sweeping floors, or selling sandwiches.

When he left college, his first job was playing right field for the New York Yankees, and he was good enough that it took a hip injury for Babe Ruth to take the job away from him. But he considered two hours of baseball a day to be loafing. So he played football and worked in a stock brokerage on the side.

When he couldn't get his job back from Babe Ruth, George went to work for the Decatur Staleys football team.

The Chicago Bears, you see, started life as an 11-man advertisement for a shirt-starching compound. George worked so hard keeping the team together and successful, that he actually felt guilty taking Sunday afternoons off to block and tackle.

Owner A.N. Staley gave George $5,000 to take the team out of town in 1921. George got a $25 million franchise literally for less than nothing. All Staley wanted was that they keep the name "Staleys" for a year.

When he sank the five grand in pro football, lots of people thought he would be better off throwing it off rooftops or spending it on chorus girls. His mother wondered why he had bothered to learn to build bridges.

Pro football was started by six guys sitting around on Hupmobile running boards in Canton, Ohio, one afternoon in 1920. The only survivor of that group is George Halas. One of the reasons pro football survived is George Halas.

George Halas not only played end, he sold tickets, swept floors, shoveled snow, ushered patrons, coached, counted, flacked, worried, wet-nursed, and evangelized. He spent Staley's get-away money on uniforms, and the first 20 bucks that came through the till, he ran down to the drugstore and bought iodine and tape.

When not a single Chicago newspaperman showed up to cover the game, George hired a press agent. Not even baseball had thought of that. Today, a team would as soon take the field without a quarterback as without a public-relations man. A former one is a National Football League commissioner.

A felicitous nickname, pinned on a trackman-halfback at the University of Illinois, the "Galloping Ghost," turned Red Grange into a million-dollar property and pro football into a billion-dollar one.

George Halas went into partnership with Red Grange. Which is to say, Red got 50 percent of the take from a Bears-Grange tie-up. When Halas saw a line around the block the next morning, queued up to get tickets, he knew pro football was here to stay. Grange had underpriced himself. More than 65,000 people showed up at the Polo Grounds to see him. The rest of the Bears were just $100-a-day spear carriers. In Philly, 40,000 sat in the rain. Coral Gables built a stadium just for him and charged $18 a head.

That the promoters quickly caught on may be seen from George's wry joke that, in St. Louis, a mortician fielded an All-Star team to face Grange, and, after Grange ran wild, the press suggested they should have checked the All-Stars for a pulse.

If all the man hours George Halas put into his Chicago Bears, and, inferentially, into pro football over the past 50 years were to be totaled up, they would probably be found to be running neck-and-neck with those put in by the United Auto Workers over that period.

He is tireless, abusive, contentious, cantankerous; if he were in government, there'd be a stamp out on him by now. Yoked to pro football, he has worked for it on his knees like a charlady, at a desk like a clerk, with a rake like a gardener, at a blackboard like a teacher, with his hat in his hand or a clench in his fists, when he made $56 as he did in 1922 or lost $18,000 as he did in 1932.

Of course, if all there was to George Halas was the 16-hour day and the seven-day week, pro football still would be in its pass-the-hat stage. Halas schemed, raged, plotted, conspired for his foundling sport. He had such uncanny ability to spot motivation in a football player that he got a quarterback (Sid Luckman) out of the Ivy League, ends from obscure campuses (Harlon Hill from Florence State) and fullbacks (Bronko Nagurski) from such frozen north country that they didn't thaw out till the third week of summer practice.

He wrote and rewrote the rules himself, but this didn't stop him from chasing referees up and down the sidelines abusively for enforcing them. He took a kick at a fan once when he was a mere 67 or so. "I knew it was time to retire when I missed," he admitted. He lectured at a clinic once. "People think I invented the game of football," he began, thought a minute, then added: "And I did."

He changed the rules to put the goal posts on the goal line (then got the best placekicker in the business), and was the first to see the wisdom of permitting a forward pass anywhere behind the line of scrimmage. If he spent 16 hours a day working for pro football, he spent the whole 24 *thinking* for it.

He tested ideas by disagreeing with them. He was the first to see that mating with television would be like marrying an heiress. He built the greatest teams the game has ever seen and would have cheerfully poured it on a rival team consisting wholly of his grandparents, maternal aunts, uncles, and infants. What some people thought was his biggest blunder of all time, defeating Washington 73-0 in the 1940 title game, actually was a showman's stroke. That dramatic score demonstrated two things: pro football's proficiency and honesty.

The Halas act is hardboiled, but old friends know the right ventricle is full of fudge. The crust is hard but it's meringue. He cries at sad movies, is as sentimental as a Carrie Jacobs Bond lyric.

What Ford was to autos, Rockefeller to oil, Vanderbilt to railroads, or Morgan to money, Halas was to football. It must give a man great satisfaction to see an enterprise he was given $5,000 to take off somebody's hands grow into an industry with a waiting list of millionaires and cities waving blank checks and bidding to be let in.

On the other hand, satisfaction is time consuming. And for the old Bohemian workhorse, he finds he can squeeze it in about 1976. You see, that's a Leap Year, and he can give it five minutes on February 29. While he's shaving.

PAUL ZIMMERMAN

It Was Pro Football and It Was New York

Paul Zimmerman, better known as Dr. Z to the hundreds of thousands who read SPORTS ILLUSTRATED, *has been challenging, delighting, and infuriating well-read football fans for years. Zimmerman is noted for his analysis of strategy and personnel, but he also can approach the sport from its lighter side. Writing for* PRO! *magazine in 1972, he examined the New York Titans, one of the original AFL teams and an organization not exactly known for traveling in luxury.*

A FEW MONTHS AGO they had a football game in New York's Randalls Island, an old stadium in the shadow of the Triborough Bridge.

About 2,000 fans showed up to watch the New York Fillies lose to the Midwest Cowgirls. Girls football. A flaky night, but it brought back memories.

"It reminded me," said a fan with a past, "of watching the old Titans play."

The old Titans. Just mention the name and you're bound to get a laugh. Larry Grantham and Don Maynard, who were Titans from the beginning, can laugh, too, but it's a laughter born of sadness.

"Well, it was pretty rough in those days, particularly the financial aspect of it," Grantham said. "You know, you're twenty-two years old . . . first time in the big city . . . trying to raise a family . . . and you're not sure your paycheck's going to clear.

"Sometimes Don and I hear these kids moaning about one thing or another, and we just look at each other and smile."

Grantham was a 210-pound linebacker of ordinary build but finely tuned football instincts. He played 13 seasons, and in his twelfth, 1971, he was voted the Jets' most valuable player.

Maynard was a Giants' reject, by way of Canada. They didn't like his sideburns or cowboy boots, a decade ahead of their time in 1958. He lasted 13 memorable seasons, too.

"I'll never forget the first time I ever laid eyes on Don," Grantham said. "It was at our first training camp in 1960—Durham, New Hampshire. I got to camp late, as usual, and the first guy I saw was Don, sitting on one of those old New England-style stone fences.

"He was sitting there with a big hat on, and cowboy boots. He looked like he was waiting for the rodeo to start. He had blue jeans on, and a belt with a big brass buckle that had number thirteen on both sides. And written across the face of it was 'Shine.' That was his nickname in college.

"I'll never forget that 'Shine' belt as long as I live."

For three seasons, 1960 through 1962, the Titans bore the image of one man, Harry Wismer. Harry's sportscasting had become legendary. "He announces a football game," Jimmy Cannon once wrote, "like a holdup victim hollering for a cop."

Harry once announced a runner going from the 45 . . . to the 50 . . . to the 55-yard line. For a couple of seasons he did the commentary for the day-old taped replays of Notre Dame games. His trick was to announce, "Neil Worden is now in the Notre Dame backfield," and sure enough, Worden would carry the ball on the next play. Of course he'd been in the backfield all along, and Wismer had already reviewed the tape. But it made Harry seem like a prognosticating genius.

The AFL was bankrolled by millionaires in that first season of 1960—oilmen Lamar Hunt in Dallas and Bud Adams in Houston, insurance tycoon Ralph Wilson in Buffalo, hotel man Barron Hilton in Los Angeles—but Harry had hustled his way in by the side door.

He married Henry Ford's niece. Harry knew how to present an idea, but he always operated on the brink of bankruptcy. So he cut corners and saved money. Lord, how Harry saved money!

"An underfinanced club with a very poor image," was Lamar Hunt's capsule of the old Titans. It was a mild evaluation.

The Los Angeles Chargers once wrote to the Titans for team pictures. The return mail contained 100 head shots of Harry Wismer. The Chargers' public relations man, Bob Burdick, once visited the Titans' office to pick up some tickets. The office was Wismer's apartment at 277 Park Avenue. The actual entrance, though, was on Forty-Eighth Street, and a lot of people never found it.

"When I rang the doorbell, a Swedish cook stopped me and said, 'What you want?'" Burdick recalled. "The ticket office was the bedroom. The coaches' office was the kitchen, and the press agent's office was a butler's pantry on the way to the bathroom. Two people couldn't squeeze by it at the same time.

"When I went into the bedroom, there were thousands of dollars worth of tickets lying all over the bed. No one was there. The two ticket men had been arguing about who'd be the first one to go out for lunch, so they both left. While I was there, a guy came in looking to buy two tickets. He left a ten-dollar bill on the bed, picked up a pair, and left."

The Titans' press agent was Ted Emery, who came from Dartmouth. His operating budget was zero. When he asked for stationery for his releases, Wismer told him to visit the stationery stores and request free samples.

A few years later Grantham mentioned that Weeb Ewbank was the first coach to give them a playbook ("a sensible kind of thing for a pro football team to have"). Sammy Baugh, the original Titans' coach, countered with, "before you can have a playbook you've got to have paper."

But Harry made sure the Titans stayed in the newspapers. He would greet all reporters with, "Congratulations." He would phone them at midnight . . . 2 A.M. . . . 4 A.M. . . . with bogus rumors of trades, serious illnesses, even deaths. He would step into a crowded elevator and announce, "Well, they just shot Castro." Sometimes Khrushchev. Just to keep in practice.

Subway posters advertised "Harry Wismer's Titans of New York." When the team took the field the band would play "I'm Just Wild About Harry." After a while nobody was, but what the hell, it was pro football and it was New York.

The money men in the early AFL were signing a few top draft choices away from the NFL, but the Titans got nothing in those drafts. "Drafting means nothing," Harry told his general manager, Steve Sebo. "Watch the other teams' cut lists. You'll do all right."

"There's no way you can win games," Baugh said, "by using people who aren't good enough to make the teams you're trying to beat."

But somehow Sammy Baugh's Titans of 1960 and 1961 managed to go 7-7 each season, which was a minor triumph. It was not until 1967 that the Titans—by then the Jets—were able to win as many as seven again. Baugh had some legitimate stars in those days—the long-range pass-catch threat of Al Dorow to Maynard or Art Powell, plus quality runners in Bill Mathis and Dick Christy. It was a team that could have been developed by adding a few good draft choices.

One thing it did leave, though, was the memory of some indelible characters. There was Hubert Bobo, the crazy linebacker with the two bad knees.

"We were playing cards one night on the plane trip home from a game," Curley Johnson, the punter, once recalled. "Bobo was angry about something, so he was punching every guy who dealt too slowly."

"Didn't you do anything about it?" someone asked Curley.

"Do anything? I was the most nervous guy there. It was my deal next."

The trip they still talk about is the one from Abilene, Texas, to Mobile, Alabama, on a preseason swing in 1960. Wismer decided that the 900-mile trip would be cheaper by overnight train than by plane, since he would also save a dinner bill (Harry used to book 8 P.M. flights for West Coast trips to avoid paying meal money). Harry assured the Titans they'd be in an air-conditioned train all the way.

Of course there was no air conditioning, and the trip through the late-summer Texas oven was a nightmare. There wasn't even any hot water for shaving. By the time they reached Mobile, the team was just about out of clean clothes. In Mobile they learned a parade had been scheduled in their honor.

"Everybody in ties," Sebo ordered. So of course Maynard dutifully knotted a tie over his T-shirt.

Billy Mathis, a 220-pound, crew-cut halfback from Clemson, had just been obtained in a trade, and he met the Titans at the station.

"He looked like the greatest thing we'd ever seen, a real All-America," Grantham said years later. "He was clean.

"I signed with the Titans for what I thought was a fifteen-hundred-dollar bonus," Grantham says. "I found out later that it was really an advance against my salary.

"All of us eventually got the back pay coming to us when the league stepped in and took over the team during the 1962 season. But I think Sammy Baugh took a pretty good beating financially. I know for a fact that if a kid was having problems Sammy would slip him something out of his own pocket.

"In 1960 six of us got together and rented an apartment. Me and my wife, Nick Mumley and his wife, Dick Jamieson and his wife. We found a place in New Rochelle, but the lady wanted two hundred dollars security. We pooled our money and came up short. I went to Sammy and asked him for four hundred dollars. Three other couples needed two hundred dollars for another apartment, and I was borrowing for all of us.

"Our apartment had a bedroom and a living room. We had the lady put in extra beds. Thank God we were all good friends. I remember we had a system worked out about raincoats. If anyone had to get up in the middle of the night, he or she grabbed a raincoat and put it on.

"Anyway, when I went back to Sam to pay him his four hundred dollars, he looked at me and said, 'I never loaned you but two hundred dollars.' I told him, 'No, Sam, it was four hundred dollars—honest.' That's the way he was. He never kept any records, just gave people money when they needed it."

The lessons of those early days aren't forgotten. A few days before Super Bowl III, some writers asked Weeb Ewbank about Maynard.

"I think Don's got every penny he ever made," the coach said. "They say that he checks into a hotel with two empty suit cases, but they're full when he leaves. Soap, toilet paper, towels . . .you name it."

"Isn't that terrible, what they said about Don stuffing his suitcase with toilet paper?" someone said to his wife, Marilyn, the next day.

"It's worse for me," she said. "I've got to unpack those suitcases. It isn't easy, smoothing out all those crumpled toilet tissues."

In 1963, though, Sonny Werblin took over. He brought backers—and money.

"I remember one practice we had at our Peekskill camp," said Paul Rochester, a defensive tackle.

"Sonny was up there that day, with his big car with the bar set up in back. I knew practice was going to be something special—to impress the boss. Sure enough, it started raining—then hailing. Hailstones as big as golf balls.

"We kept practicing, though. There we were, taking our stances with hailstones bouncing off our rear ends, and Sonny watching the whole thing from his car."

The old Titans were officially dead.

Whatever Happened to Old Whatshisname?

Where have you gone Sidney Youngelman? And Pasquale Lamberti? And Lowe Wren? (Or was it Wren Lowe?) And Thomas Tharp? And Wayne Fontes? And Frank D'Agostino? And Frederick Julian? (Or was it Julian Frederick?) And Dewey Bohling? And Americo Sapienza? And Blanche Martin? And Thurlow Cooper? And Hall Whitley? (Or was it Whitley Hall?) And Gerhard Schwedes? And Moses Gray? And John Klotz? And Hubert Bobo? (Or was it Bobo Hubert?)

Ah, names . . . but then maybe the name of the game is all wrong. Maybe it is not "where have they gone?" and "where are they now?" but "who were they then?"

Surely Blanche Martin is a character in Tennessee Williams' new play . . .

Surely Gerhard Schwedes is a member of Willy Brandt's cabinet . . .

Surely Frank D'Agostino is singing in a lounge in Las Vegas . . .

Surely Sidney Youngelman can tell you why seersucker wears better than gabardine . . .

Surely Americo Sapienza discovered football . . .

Surely none of those things are right.

All of them—Blanche Martin, Hall Whitley, Hubert Bobo, Sidney Youngelman, Americo Sapienza . . . and ad infinitum—were members of the New York Titans (circa 1960–62).

A total of 91 men wore the uniform of the Titans . . . and some of them (though not a lot of them) will admit it today.

One ex-Titan with a long memory is Bill Atkins, now the defensive backfield coach of the Buffalo Bills. Bill checked into New York in 1962, when the Titans' ship was sinking.

"Bulldog Turner, our head coach [Turner replaced Sammy Baugh as coach before the '62 season], really made a sincere effort to improve the team," said Atkins, "so he was constantly shuffling players, bringing in new ones, getting rid of those who weren't helping the team. But he had competition from Harry Wismer [the Titans' owner], who kept players he liked rather than those who might help the club.

"So when Bulldog cut a guy, the fellow would have to go to Harry and see if it was true or not."

Sometimes it wasn't. One player, Ed Kovac, was cut and rehired five times.

Turner was something of a character himself. Alex Kroll, one of the few draft choices the Titans signed, is now a vice president with Young and Rubicam, Inc., an advertising agency. Kroll recalls the final game of the 1962 season. Wismer had been unable to meet his payroll, the AFL had taken over operation of the club, and Bulldog was readying his team to play the Houston Oilers.

"He gathered us together," says Kroll, "and reminded us that this was the last game of the season. 'There probably won't even be any New York Titans next year,' he told us. 'So most of you are playing in your last pro game. Most of you aren't good enough to play anywhere else.'"

The statement was only a half-truth. Larry Grantham and Don Maynard are proof of that.

Grantham came to the Titans as a receiver, but he was moved to linebacker not long after he arrived. He has been a linebacker for the Jets (née Titans) ever since—although the longevity did not seem apparent at the time. In the 1961 edition of *All-Pro Football*, Murray Olderman wrote: "Grantham is a scrapper but the Mississippian only weighs one ninety-five, which is hardly keeper size."

Maynard, who teamed with Art Powell to give the Titans an awesome one-two receiving punch (in three years they combined to catch 375 passes), holds the all-time NFL record for most yards gained receiving (11,834).

Success also has followed other ex-Titans. Bob Mischak, one of the co-captains, is plebe football coach at Army. Lee Grosscup, who quarterbacked the '62 club, is a sportscaster with ABC. Safety Dainard Paulson is a high school coach in his home state of Oregon. Running back Bill Mathis, who went on to several productive years and climaxed them by playing in Super Bowl III, is an investment broker in Manhattan. Al Dorow, the quarterback who threw 26 touchdown passes in 1960, coached in Canada the last couple of seasons. And Sammy Baugh, the kind man who shepherded the Titans through their first two seasons, lives a life of leisure on his ranch near Rotan, Texas.

Three years. The New York Titans lasted three years before the end came. Before it ended (of course) with a whimper not a bang.

In a first-person story written for *Sports Illustrated* three years ago, Kroll wrote:

"The final day of Titans football ended with the score 44-10 in favor of the Oilers and 50 to 75 onlookers present, not including the two teams. Still, there seemed to be a small personal consolation for coming to the park that day. The game had been billed as the last ever in the Polo Grounds. Shea Stadium was supposed to be ready for the Mets' opening day in April. So I had seen the end of a historic ball park. The Polo Grounds, where John McGraw and Bill Terry, Tuffy Leemans, and Charlie Conerly had built legends, had seen its last legend. Us. As for myself, I would be the last man ever carried out of the Polo Grounds on a stretcher. It was a record of sorts.

"But the completion of Shea Stadium was delayed a whole year. Early the next spring the Mets' Rod Kanehl ran into the outfield wall and had to be carried out. So even this consolation for playing with the Titans was not to be granted. It came later. To Grantham, Maynard, and Mathis in the Super Bowl. To the rest of us in the secure knowledge that we had been the last major-league team to play almost entirely for laughs."

Most of the Titans are gone . . . but they are hardly forgotten. Still, some questions remain unanswered.

Like . . . where have you gone Sidney Youngelman?

PHIL MUSICK

A Football Man

Phil Musick was in Pittsburgh throughout the Steelers' glorious ride of the 1970s. He covered the team for the PITTSBURGH POST GAZETTE, *then later wrote a column for the paper. After that he became host of one of Pittsburgh's most popular radio talk shows. In 1976, Musick profiled Bert Bell for* PRO! *magazine. Bell, a seminal sports figure in Pennsylvania, was NFL Commissioner for 13 years, until he had a heart attack while attending an Eagles-Steelers game at Philadelphia's Franklin Field.*

FOR BERT BELL, life was a ball in the beginning. Later, when he was NFL commissioner, it was a football.

A poet's moon hung in the evening sky, scattering its beams down upon an easy sea. Lonely gulls wheeled and soared through the soft silence. A couple strolled the sand to the whisperings of an ebbtide. The girl, a bride, was lovelier than roses. The huge, yellow ball in the sky seemed made for a honeymoon. The man glanced up at it.

"Frances," said Bert Bell, "I just wish I had a punter who could kick that high."

He was born on Philadelphia's Main Line amid such turn of the century wealth and power that it took John O'Hara more than a dozen books to completely describe it. They hung the name deBenneville on him. As soon as he could, he began calling himself Bert, and through most of the important days of his life he loafed in suburban Philly drugstores and a place called The Tavern with guys named Ox Smith and Clyde the Soda Jerk.

His grandfather was a congressman, his father the attorney general of Pennsylvania, his brother the state's governor. Bert Bell was a Football Man.

His best friends were an Irishman from Pittsburgh, who before he was anything else was a horseplayer, and a man who was the son of an immigrant Bohemian tailor from Chicago. And the only time Bert Bell had any serious money as an adult, he died six days before he could spend it to buy a professional football team.

He had a nanny when he was two, a pony when he was six, a tux when he was 12, and a Marmon roadster when he was 17. Through most of his life, he wore tan gabardine from Memorial Day to Labor Day, blue serge the rest of the year, and yet the only thing that ever really impressed him had laces across the top of it. When Ox Smith and Clyde the Soda Jerk and Jiggs Torchiana and some other guys from The Tavern bought him a new hat one year, they took his old one and jumped up and down on it. Nobody could see any difference.

His mother's first name was Fleurette; his father's middle name was Cromwell. He was Bert to millions, had a nose a hawk would've been proud of, and spent much of his time in saloons where when someone would spit on the floor, nobody got uptight.

He had a rich kid's fling that lasted a decade; went to war; ran a couple of hotels; put down his glass and never touched another drop because a stunner from the Ziegfeld Follies asked him to; talked like a stevedore; loved maybe more than anything else a good fight, and made a respectable title of the word "czar."

In the truest sense, he was a Football Man. He quarterbacked, he coached, he bought a pro team. He swept the grandstand, shoveled snow, hustled tickets, flacked, cajoled, worried, fought, and fussed. And when the stock market got his last $50,000, he borrowed $2,500 and bought a football team.

"For me," he liked to say, "there was nothing else. Football was my life."

After 13 years as commissioner of the National Football League, he died one 1959 afternoon at an NFL game. It was like Caruso dying during the third act of Pagliacci.

Time has pulled Bert Bell out of perspective, warped even the cynical Westbrook Pegler's thought that "Bert Bell is the man who most typifies America." His contemporaries, save for the Irishman, Pittsburgh Steelers' owner Art Rooney, and the crusty legend from Chicago, George Halas, are mostly dead. His goodly virtues—honor, respect, fairness, trust . . . lord, even honesty—have been eaten up by Watergates and pursuit of the two-car garage and dueling the government across a 1040 form.

Bert Bell's accomplishments stand, however. And maybe that is the way to get a handle on the stocky Football Man. What he did: the draft . . . whipping the rival All-America Football Conference with the ultimate weapon, time . . . dealing openly and quickly with the game's first scandal . . . leashing the monster, television . . . bending the Halases and George Preston Marshalls to his will for that trite objective: the good of the game . . . protecting professional football from gambling . . . and running the NFL so skillfully that in time he came to czardom because he held the most powerful of all clubs—the threat to quit.

The body of Sir Christopher Wren, the architect of St. Paul's in London, is buried on the grounds. Inscribed on his tombstone are the words: "If you would see his monument, look around."

Bell's monument is the National Football League, and the words of those who helped him build it, the Halases and Rooneys and Maras.

Bell was not afraid to wield his power, either, even though owners occasionally balked. San Francisco's Tony Morabito once said publicly, "I'm going to try to get Bell's job." But Bell survived. "Unless you permit me to save the game by running it my way, I will give it back to you," he said.

"He'd have delegates staked out in advance; he always knew how many votes he needed to pass something, and where to get them," says Giants' owner Wellington Mara. "He could persuade you. Politics is the art of the possible and Bert knew what could be attempted. He passed important pieces of league legislation in four-day meetings by holding them until the last two hours, because he knew we all wanted to go home. There wouldn't be big-league football today without him."

Bert Bell seemed destined to become NFL commissioner, to guide it through growing pains into maturity. It was as though he'd subconsciously prepared for the demands of the job by spending the first 30 years or so of his life having one long, raucous, ball.

"Before he got married, Bert touched all the bases," chuckles Rooney. And so Bert did. There was football, and there was fun, and there was damn little else. He bounced out of three prep schools, football the only thing tying him to the educational process. He was a quarterback. He was skinny, and cocky to a degree that fights would occasionally break out in the stands at Penn between Bell supporters and detractors. He couldn't do much but punt and win. And hang so tough that he once played a game at Penn with a broken shoulder, and accepted his father's offer of $50 if he would have a busted nose re-broken and re-set. The game got into his blood at Penn. The war interrupted the process and he spent two years working in a field hospital under almost continuous shelling by the Germans. He survived, came back in 1919 to play his senior season, and quit days after it had ended.

Football had gotten him off the Main Line—"if I can survive deBenneville, I can survive anything," he used to say—and football would keep him off it. For eight years, he was a part-time assistant coach at Penn and Temple, and a full-time hell-raiser.

"He was a very spoiled young man," says Bell's daughter, Janie. "For a long time, he lived the life of Riley. He had all the money he wanted, and he was athletically inclined. His mother died when he was seventeen and he was very much the apple of his father's eye. No matter how much he had drank the night before, he'd always get up and have breakfast with his father."

Janie Bell, and her brothers, Bert Jr. and Upton, inherited the Bell virtues, which formed the rules he implemented in all of his dealings as commissioner of the NFL. "Once, before I started school, for some reason I stole a couple of pieces of penny-gum at the drugstore in Narberth where my father loafed," she says. "When we got home, he asked where I got the gum. I finally told him. He got the car out and took me clear back to the drugstore to pay the man and tell him what had happened."

In the turned-down-hose, turned-up-nose naughtiness of the 1920s, though, Bell had not yet discovered the drugstore in suburban Narberth. He still spent most of his time chasing the good life. Years later, when a coach drowning his sorrows in scotch challenged the ability of a teetotaler like Bell to understand the need for whiskey, he was told, "If I never have another one, my daily average will still be pretty good."

He gambled, always reserving the month of August for the races at Saratoga and, at night, the plush gambling spots. And of course he played the market. But it was football that formed the values that would take hold later.

Bell's diet didn't get bland until the stock market crashed, and Frances Upton appeared. John C. Bell bailed his son out of a financial bind—although Bert Bell never again had anything resembling a fortune—and Frances Upton put him squarely upon the football road.

The pride of Florenz Ziegfeld, she was one of the great beauties of the early 1930s. And, just as it happens on the soap operas, she brought out the best in Bell. One night in 1932 in a Margate, New Jersey, restaurant, she told Bert Bell, "It's me or drinking." Bell tilted the glass in his hand, drained it, and put it down on the table. "I'll never take another drink," he told Frances Upton. He never did, either. Four months later, Bert and Frances were secretly married. "My grandmother told my mother, 'She's crazy for marrying him,'" Janie Bell says. "But my mother always said, 'I knew he had willpower and character.'"

Unfortunately, Bell didn't have any money. But Frances Upton Bell, who'd costarred in a Broadway musical with Eddie Cantor, did. Her husband borrowed $2,500 in 1933, went into partnership with three former Penn teammates, and bought the Frankford Yellowjackets. A year later, the Yellowjackets became the Philadelphia Eagles. Bell bought out his partners, and proceeded to establish new standards for losing money and football games for 12 seasons.

"That's what made him such a good commissioner, he understood the problems of owning a club then," Rooney recalls. Rooney is the Steelers' patriarch now. At 74, he is a grand old man in pro football. But through the World War II years, with the NFL still clinging to existence, Rooney and Bell were partners in the Pittsburgh franchise. In 1940, a wealthy Pittsburgh bon vivant, C. Alexis Thompson, purchased the Steelers. A complex three-way agreement was reached, which concluded with Thompson running the Eagles and Rooney and Bell the Steelers.

Ask what exactly transpired, Rooney grins and throws up his hands. "Things were different then," he says. "Money was tough to come by."

It certainly was in Philadelphia. "Bert ran the club out of Lew Tendler's saloon," Rooney says. "He'd give the bartender at Tendler's the tickets to sell, hoping a live one would come in, and he'd run off to the newspapers and radio stations trying to get some publicity for the team. He'd sell tickets on the street corners. Anything. Everything."

The everything included coaching and fighting the early season competition, baseball's Athletics and Phillies.

"One time, the Eagles were playing the same day the Athletics were," Rooney says with a laugh. "It was cloudy, but everybody was going to the baseball game, so Bert gave a guy five dollars and a megaphone, and sent him over to the ballpark to yell, 'No game today, rain.'"

Bell wasn't much of a coach, but he lasted until the Steelers were badly beaten in successive preseason games in 1941. "He called me up and said, 'We've got to do something drastic,'" Rooney remembers. "I said, 'I know. You got to quit.'"

Bell's resignation speech was brief and candid. "I believe it to be in the best interests of the Pittsburgh fans that I resign," he said.

When Johnny came marching home again from World War II, the National Football League was at a crossroads. The owners were not comfortable with commissioner Elmer Layden. He had been competent enough, but the problems of the day needed more than competency. Beyond that, Layden was a college football man, one of the Four Horsemen. By mutual agreement, it was decided Layden would not return for the 1946 season.

Who would replace him? At a meeting in January, 1946, the owners looked to one of their own—Bert Bell. "He understood our problems, what it was like trying to run a club then," says Rooney.

At the league meetings, he could tell stories for hours. He knew the disappointment of working 18 hours a day and then seeing a thousand fans in the stands. Trying to talk pro football to newspapermen who thought the game was a bit uncivilized and who wrote instead of Gehrig and DiMaggio and Williams. Trying to struggle through until next season.

Bell hadn't stuck his old fedora on the rack in the commissioner's office before all the challenges to the league, which had simmered during the war, began to bubble. Congress was taking its first serious look into the game. Television was about to drastically alter the American lifestyle. The gamblers still lurked, better organized, allied now with a population recently versed in the virtues of living hard and quickly. There was a need for balanced competition. And there was competition.

Bell's first days on the job were spent dealing with the rival All-America Football Conference. Men with money had founded it in 1946. Shortly, the confrontation began to get costly. Player salaries skyrocketed. In four cities, the leagues fought on common ground for the fans' loyalty, and the AAFC made inroads. It also made overtures to the established league for a common draft, inter-league play, and a championship game.

Bell held his ground. He never mentioned the AAFC by name. The other league, he called it. "We're not interested in the other league."

Some NFL owners were. The war was expensive, and their pockets had begun to spring leaks. Fans and writers poured abuse on Bell for his rigid stance. He stood like a rock, waiting for time to fell the AAFC. In 1949, there was an unconditional surrender, and the NFL absorbed AAFC franchises in Cleveland, Baltimore, and San Francisco.

Bell's authority was enhanced. He'd fought down panic in the ranks.

Most importantly, he'd been right when some owners had been wrong . . . for a second time. Three years before, on the eve of the 1946 championship game, New York gamblers had attempted to fix a point spread. Bell's hand fell on the offenders like a stone. He suspended New York Giants' fullback Merle Hapes before the game and Giants' passer Frank Filchock after it.

"Bert was death on gambling," says Halas. "He watched the odds like a bookie. He'd go into gambling joints right in Philly to check out rumors."

Gambling threatened the game Bell loved. He would not permit such threats, from any quarter. He hired a retired FBI official to police the NFL and each year he made the same speech to the players: "Gamblers bet millions on our games. You boys go around knocking the officials and people will get dirty ideas. Watch out for the wise-guys . . . the winkers.

"They're not gamblers or bookies or even fans. They are winkers. They come up to you in a restaurant and say, 'You're Jimmy Smith, let me buy you a dinner.' Then they go back to the bar and say, 'Bet such-and-such real big. You just saw me talking to Smith, didn't you?' Watch out for winkers."

Being commissioner was not easy. But for Bell, the choice was always clear. There was right, come hell or lousy gate receipts.

Right was not televising a game in a town in which fans had spent good money to buy tickets. In Detroit the week before the Lions played Cleveland for the 1957 championship, there was an outcry to have the sold-out game televised. Bell would not hear of it. The governor and two Michigan senators implored him, then attacked.

"I don't believe there is any honesty in selling a person a ticket and then, after you've taken his dollars, decide to put the game on television, where he could've seen it for nothing," said Bell. "As long as I have anything to do with this league, home games won't be televised, period."

He also fought hard for balanced competition, the foundation upon which a prosperous league now rests. It took Bert Bell's powers of negotiation to stop a handful of teams from dominating the league as they had over the first 25 years. "Bert showed them that grabbing off players was a two-way street, and suddenly they all got religion," says a veteran NFL official.

The draft was the religion. Recalcitrant owners had it stuffed down their throats, but it worked. The Pittsburgh Steelers, for example, won nothing for 40 years, then rebuilt from the draft, and won successive Super Bowls.

And he fought hard to stop the strong from feeding off the weak. Powerful teams had always played weaker teams early in the year, the drawing of the schedule always bringing strife. "Early in the year, weak clubs should play weak clubs, strong ones should play strong ones," Bell commanded. "It's the only way to balance competition."

"The schedules would always take several days and Bert always found time to politic," Mara says. "All the clubs were very jealous of the schedules and no one trusted anyone. After a while, people started walking out of the league meetings and saying, 'Let Bert do it.'"

Bell did it. As he did everything pertaining to his affair of the heart with the NFL. "His mission in life was football," says Halas. "He had a sure instinct for conducting the business of the game."

Bell's interest in the game never waned. A week before he died, he'd made a tentative deal to purchase the Eagles following the 1959 season. "He died before he could sign the papers," says Upton Bell. Had the deal gone through, Bell would have resigned as commissioner.

Sadly, Bell missed a fight he would've enjoyed when the American Football League was formed in late 1959. Lamar Hunt, the AFL's founder, had kept Bell fully informed of the new league's plans and progress.

"I always felt Bert would've given us a fair shake," says Hunt.

Bert Bell would not have known any other way to do it.

SHELBY STROTHER

The Coach Is a Soft Touch

Shelby Strother was an award-winning columnist who worked for four newspapers, lastly the DETROIT NEWS. *The witty, earthy Strother was struck down by liver cancer in 1991, at 44. His rich legacy includes several features for* GAMEDAY *magazine and a book,* NFL TOP 40, *chronicling the greatest games in league history. This story, about the poignant relationship between then-Cardinals coach Gene Stallings and his son, who has Down's Syndrome, reached* GAMEDAY *readers in 1987.*

THE DAY BEFORE, when the rain came hard, then harder, and the wind began to howl, and a huge tree fell across the dirt road leading to Gene Stallings's Hike Away Ranch, there wasn't much else to do but go look for his steel chain saw.

No time for toughness or courage or compassion or sensitivity. Just do what you have to do.

"It rains like that sometimes out here," Stallings says. "I guess it comes with the territory. There have been times when a storm was coming up and I've had to wake my children in the middle of the night to help bale hay, to get it in before it gets wet. You just have to take it as it comes."

Stallings, the head coach of the St. Louis Cardinals, smiles. Inside his home in the woods outside of Paris, Texas, his wife Ruth Ann and their four daughters are busy making a Texas-sized lunch. His son is keeping his granddaughter occupied. And Stallings is building an unexpected pile of firewood.

Out here, the stereotypes fall like uprooted timber, get sawed up by the reality of the moment. They talk all around the National Football League about how tough Gene Stallings is. They speak of him in terms such as rugged . . . disciplinarian . . . stern taskmaster . . . one tough customer. They say Gene Stallings is tough as a boot.

Tough as a boot. When you hear he's from Texas and owns and works his own cattle ranch and that he used to play football for Paul (Bear) Bryant, was head coach at Texas A&M, and used to help Tom Landry coach the Dallas Cowboys, you jump to this conclusion. With all that exposure to fire and ice and things western, the guy must be . . . tough as a boot.

And you stop right there. Don't go beyond the callused hands and the leathery face with the squint lines that a lifetime of working in the sun will give. You see the lean, sinewy frame and the broad shoulders and the strong jaw and you've already made up your mind. The outer fabric is all you see—because it's so tough.

But is that all there is? How deep is that boot anyway?

Boots are tough. They get water-logged, and mud cakes the square toes and they're tough enough, rough enough, to do their job. And the skin is so thick that even a rattlesnake's best bite or life's cruelest fate can't break through. The boot can take it, whatever it is.

But what if you could turn the boot inside out? And see the insides? What of the boot that is soft and gentle and tender and comfortable on the inside? What of the guy who once jumped into a dangerous sucking-bottom pond to help save a calf from drowning? What of the fellow who secretly visits children's hospitals with religious regularity and is one of the softest touches in the NFL when it comes to charity and any event or organization involving children? What of the man who never missed a piano recital or drillteam exhibition by one of his daughters and who wouldn't think of playing golf without his favorite cart driver, his son? When one of his cows is having trouble during the delivery of a calf, is "tough" the way to describe the man with the frantic, concerned eyes as he struggles to help bring new life into the world? And what can you say about a father who takes his special son and creates a special world, the same world he's laid out for all his family?

No, you don't have to wait too long for the other boot to drop with Gene Stallings.

Tough as a boot? How about soft as a boot?

"Oh yes—that's Bebes, all right," Ruth Ann Stallings says, smiling. "I call him Bebes. Everyone does who grew up with him. His older brother couldn't say Baby Gene. It came out Bebes. But, yes—you just described Gene Stallings perfectly. There is so much sensitivity, so much caring and love inside that man. And so many people never get to see the real Gene Stallings."

At the moment, the real Gene Stallings is on a homemade dock that knifes into one of the two lakes on his 600-acre ranch. His son Johnny is sitting beside him. They both are holding fishing rods, staring at the still, fresh water. Waiting for a big one to bite.

Catching a bass out of your own lake can be one of the genuine pleasures in a man's lifetime. But today the fish are safe. The Stallings fish only for the companionship. A man and his son, together on a hot summer day in the Texas countryside. So close together they cast a single shadow.

Gene and Johnny Stallings enjoy the stillness of the day. Out there on the dock, there is no need for the toughness. Gene Stallings can let out some of his compassion, along with his strength, and turn inside out. And let those stereotypes just kind of splinter and crumble in a nice, neat pile.

Ruth Ann Stallings watches her menfolk. She smiles once more and says, "He's been such a good father to all our children. But for Johnny, who's special, you know, the main thing is that he's always been one of the family. We learned a lot about unselfish love when Johnny came into our life. And Bebes has always made sure that whatever we do, Johnny's included."

The father and his son walk toward the house. He walks slowly but his son still takes three steps to his one. They hold hands and smile at each other.

"Daddy, can we ride horses?"

"Yeah, we'll ride horses, Johnny."

"Daddy, you ride Blue. I'll ride Jody."

"Okay, Johnny. That's what we'll do."

And the smiles crackle back and forth once more. For the moment, the clouds are parted from Johnny Stallings, who is afflicted with one of life's low blows, Down's syndrome.

On a hot summer day in Texas, new conclusions are made. It has to do with flinching at something in front of you, then finding out what it is instead of turning around. It has to do with playing the cards you are dealt. There are things to do on the ranch. Work. Calves to wean, fences and corrals to build, meadows to clear. There is a pro football team in St. Louis to reassemble, make stronger, tougher, better. Different fences need mending and building. But today, there is time for a man and his son to wet a line. To saddle up Blue and Jody. To take care of important things.

Inside the modest, tidy home, Laurie, Jackie, Anna Lee, and Martha Kate Stallings are telling stories about their father to a visitor.

"He was always there," Laurie says. "He'd be at our choir performances or he'd be in the stands during halftime when our drill team was marching, or be there whatever it was. He'd never stand up and cheer—that's just not the way he is—but he was always there."

Three of the daughters—all but 17-year-old Martha Kate, who still is in high school—attended Abilene Christian College. All three tell loving stories of the horrible blue station wagon their father "allowed" them to use when they were away at school. Martha Kate says she dreads the day her father tells her he's got just the car for her to use in college. They giggle as they tell stories of former boyfriends who were required to go through the rites of passage that involved coming to the Stallings house and meeting the family, including Daddy, the one with all the stereotypes. Such as the one boy who sat at the supper table and decided to take the dare about eating the huge jalapeño pepper Stallings had just laid out on his plate. They reminisce of days in the yard when he taught them how to throw a ball. Then suddenly, squeals of laughter.

"Until Daddy built all these fences and corrals for the cattle," Anna Lee says, "we used to have this thing called the human chain. He'd come in and say 'All right everybody, we gotta form the human chain.' And we'd all join hands and go to work."

Then Jackie says, "And of course, with Johnny he's so patient and caring. When Johnny came into our life, our family became so much fuller and closer. And Daddy had a lot to do with that, along with Johnny."

The story is of love. A man and his wife. Their four daughters. And their son. . . .

In the summer of 1962, life was about as full and rich as it could be for Stallings. He was a hot-shot assistant coach on Bear Bryant's staff. The season before, Alabama had gone undefeated, and had won the national collegiate championship. Now, recruiting was going well. And any day now, 27-year-old Gene Stallings would become a father for the third time. He already had two beautiful daughters. Maybe this time he would get a son.

A son . . . someone to hunt and fish with, someone to toss a football back and forth with. It was June in Tuscaloosa, Alabama. And life seemed to get better by the day.

On June 11, 1962, Ruth Ann went into labor. Everyone was all smiles as they went to the hospital. If it was a boy, they already had a name picked out. John Mark Stallings.

Ruth Ann remembers when her third child squirmed into existence.

"I was awake during the delivery," she says. "I wanted it that way. I was so hoping I could give Bebes a son. So, you can imagine how thrilled I was when the nurse told me it was a boy.

"But almost immediately she got this strange look on her face. Then the doctor came over and he was all concerned, too. I didn't know what had happened."

The next day, a doctor came into the hospital room where Ruth Ann was recovering. The new father was at her bedside. The doctor held nothing back. He said there was a problem with their son. He was retarded. A mongoloid.

The young coach heard the words and they sounded horrible. And his first emotion was anger. Then a gasp of helplessness. Then Gene Stallings fainted.

"Passed out flat," he says. "There's so many emotions that come over you. You feel so many things."

"You share so many dreams for your children," Ruth Ann says. "You never expect things to go wrong, not right from the beginning."

The explanation was simple if not gentle. It was a cruel phenomenon called Down's syndrome. Simply put, during the assembly line where life is built, the twenty-first chromosome triples instead of doubles. A mistake. One of God's fumbles.

The prognosis was bleak. There were all sorts of complications associated with the syndrome. The baby's mental development would be forever stunted. His heart was bad. John Mark Stallings probably would not live long. Given the complications, it was just as well.

Gene Stallings stares at the floor as the memory strafes close, too close. Then with those piercing eyes that often render words useless, the glare softens. And he clasps the strong, rough, callused hands together.

"They said he'd never live to be four," he says. "Then they said he wouldn't make it past eleven."

Soft becomes softer. The voice of the rancher, the coach, the father is low. Then quiet. Then the eyes rage with pride. The hands become fists. The voice booms.

"The other day, June eleventh in fact, Johnny had his twenty-fifth birthday."

Across the room, Johnny sits on a couch, straight back, his cowboy boots barely touching the floor. Watching his daddy watching him. The smiles collide in the middle of the room.

"A little TLC goes a long way," Stallings says.

"When are we going to ride horses, Daddy?"

"In a bit, Johnny. We'll ride. I promise."

When Ruth Ann and Gene Stallings were allowed to take their new son home from the hospital in 1962, they still had not completely adjusted to the fact their baby never was going to be normal.

"He looked like any other baby. The symptoms of Down's syndrome hadn't come out yet," Ruth Ann remembers.

"I used to hold him and say to Ruth Ann, 'Why, this baby is fine,'" Stallings says. "'Come look, there's nothing wrong with this boy.' I kept up like that for weeks, months. I was praying the doctor was wrong, wishing and hoping somebody had made a mistake. But they hadn't."

Then came the decision. There were all kinds of options how the baby could be handled. For the Stallings, there was only one.

"We decided we would keep him in an environment of home and family," Gene says. "Part of the family. If we went to the country club, Johnny was going with us. If the girls had some boy come visit, Johnny would be the first member of the family we'd introduce. We decided a long time ago to keep our little boy happy and healthy and safe. We'd just surround him with love."

If you call Coach Stallings, bear with him if he can't come to the phone right away. He may be playing dominoes. It may be because he's watching the video of *Mary Poppins* or *The Sound of Music*, or *Old Yeller* for the hundredth time. Together with Johnny, and anyone else who wants to be there. Or, he may be out riding horses.

Johnny Stallings has this charm about him. Ask any of the Cardinals football players who their biggest, most constant fan is. Who is always hanging out with them after practice? Playing cards, smiling, waving, hugging each of them before they leave to go home?

"I'm telling you," Stallings says, "Johnny has something you and I don't have. And that's a guaranteed one-way ticket to Heaven. I really think that. That boy doesn't have a mean thought or breath in him. We've always had a touching, feeling family. A good family. Johnny, though, has given us such an extra dimension. We're blessed. We really are."

The ranch is called Hike Away. It is 600 acres of fertile land located a few miles out of Paris. It is a land almost packed away in cotton. A time warp. In Paris, at the Two Kiss Drive-In, a Dr. Pepper is 29 cents, a cheeseburger 75 cents. They wash your windshield at the self-serve station. At Gene Stallings's place, the creature comforts are even more basic. There is no TV. The only phone used to be in the barn. The radio gets turned on only if someone wants to know the weather report. And, if you want to read the paper, you have to go into town and buy one.

But the 60-tree fruit orchard soon will bear peaches and apples and plums and apricots. Pregnant cows dot the rolling hills as far as the eye can see. The two lakes are stocked with fish. The lush scenery, the soft and shrill sounds of nature in concert, the vibrant, energetic, alive feelings of a small chunk of the world thriving, is at once both a sensual and a humbling feeling.

"One of the things our family has always done is get what we call a pokin' stick," Stallings says. "That's just any stick or branch that you can use to go discovering, looking for nature and varmints. Just following animal tracks is fun. Like I said, there are excellent bass out there in the lake. Turtles, too. And over at Pine Creek, there are all kinds of things. I saw a quail just an hour ago. I always wanted to own land because of all the stuff that came along with it."

Including the work. Seventeen years ago, when he bought the property, it was a wilderness. Today, he says the place is barely carved out enough to resemble a dream.

"I'll never get it all done," he says. "I just hope I can get it in good enough shape to pass on. For me, it's a place where I can lick my wounds, let off some steam, wean a few calves, and just enjoy my family and life in general."

Stallings jumps in his truck and heads out to take inventory. He wheels down a pasture, stops and points to a hill. "Now this meadow over here is where I'm keeping some heifers."

The sight of the virgin cows, some of them lying, some standing contentedly, causes him to nod approval.

In a minute Stallings is pointing out a fence he built. He says he has come to appreciate a well-built fence, a good tight brace, a catch pen that works.

"Know what I really want to do? I want to grow good things. Grow good grass, raise good cows."

There is work to be done. And, because of the rain, a day less to do it. Training camp is rushing closer. Soon he will have to leave Hike Away and head for "my real business." The ranch is also a farm—"Ruth Ann planted the orchard"—and the garden offered all sorts of fresh vegetables last year, including a bumper crop of jalapeños.

"I'm also getting to where I know what I'm doing with a cutting torch. Things are looking good. I enjoy this. I enjoy the change of pace. A man needs to work hard, I mean, really hard. It's good. Good all around. Digging post holes is hard work, but it's good for a man."

Hard work was never a problem for Stallings. In high school, he helped his father with the family roofing business—"just about the hottest work you can do"—and for six summers in a row, he was a roughneck on the oil rigs.

Ruth Ann remembers the man she fell in love with as "someone you knew was good for his word. This was in high school in the early fifties and Bebes wore this flattop haircut and was really a nice-looking man. And he was so good in sports, a real Big Man on Campus."

And she was prom queen two years in a row, although when one of her daughters mentions that, she blushes.

"It sounds like a perfect love story, doesn't it?" she says while rolling dough for fresh blackberry cobbler. "Well, that's just what it was."

When they graduated, she went to East Texas State and he, upon her urging, accepted a scholarship from Texas A&M.

"I wanted him to go there instead of one of the other schools," Ruth Ann says, smiling. "It was a military school and an all-boy school."

The four daughters laugh in chorus.

"Kind of selfish of me, wasn't it?" Ruth Ann adds, bending down to put dessert in the oven.

They had planned to marry after Stallings's junior season, "but Coach Bryant wouldn't let us. Bebes was a captain and he wanted the team captains to live in the dorm."

On the weekend after the Aggies' upset of Texas on Thanksgiving Day, Gene Stallings took a bride.

"He was an excellent catch," Ruth Ann says.

Gene and Ruth Ann had two daughters, then a son, then two more daughters. After all the problems with Johnny at birth, Stallings admitted the decision to have more children was "the tough one."

"But the doctors had just come out with this test to study the chromosomes," he says, "and it showed that we weren't liable to have any more difficulties. That the problem with Johnny was just a quirk. So we decided to go ahead. In this family—the more, the better."

"Our family has just evolved closer and closer," Ruth Ann says. "It's not been anything conscious. There's just always been a lot of love. But Johnny taught us about unselfish love. Most people love and expect something in return. Not Johnny. And now it's spreading to our girls' husbands. One of them is a surgical resident. Another just got his doctorate. And the other is a tax accountant who is thinking about law school."

"I like family. The family unit is important," Stallings says. "I like to be around family. I'm proud of mine."

It is time to eat.

The Stallings stand and walk to the middle of the room, asking their visitors to join them. Everyone joins hands, forming a lovely circle. Indeed a human chain. And Gene Stallings asks Johnny to give the blessing.

First a smile, then a pause to remember the words, then an enthusiastic, "Dear God, thank you for. . . ."

Heads bowed, hands squeezing, the next several moments vibrate with meaning. Then comes the avalanche of baked chicken, cabbage, zucchini casserole, fresh tomatoes. There was plenty to eat at Gene Stallings's house that hot summer day. With blackberry cobbler to finish.

Afterwards, Stallings, who sits even taller in the saddle when he looks out over his personal herd, asks, "Would it be all right if the girls sang a song or two?"

Constant ear infections when he was a baby left Stallings deaf in his right ear a long time ago. No sweat though. Take 'em as they come. Deal with the ordinary moments; turn them around in your favor. A slight and subtle tilt of the head so his good ear is in perfect position. The five women in his life sing softly, sweetly. His only son smiles proudly, tapping his hands on the table in accompaniment. Gene Stallings closes his eyes and taps his boot ever so gently on the floor.

Outside, two saddled horses are waiting.

IRA BERKOW

Wordsmith

Red Smith was the guiding light for a generation of sportswriters, and nobody knew his work better than Ira Berkow, NEW YORK TIMES *sports columnist for 20 years. When Smith died in 1982, Berkow explained his co-worker's prodigious contributions to* PRO! *readers. Berkow has authored numerous books, including one on his Chicago origins called* HANOVER STREET.

RED SMITH'S HEALTH was failing, and his son Terry, after several tries, finally convinced him in early January to cut back on his columns for the the *New York Times* from four a week to three. Smith was 76 years old—a newspaperman for 55 years. The red hair that inspired his nickname now was a soft white, but he remained commandingly literate, and still the most acclaimed sports columnist in the nation.

Buoyed by his success, Terry then suggested that his father not attend Super Bowl XVI in Detroit, but write his column after watching the game on television.

Red adjusted his dark-rimmed glasses and stared at his son with watery, pale-blue eyes. "Nothing doing," he said, his voice getting stronger. "I'm going to the Super Bowl, and then next month I'm going to the Holmes-Cooney fight in Las Vegas, and the month after that I'm going to spring training."

It wasn't to be. Red Smith died January 15.

The first of his three-a-week columns was his last. It appeared on Monday, January 10. Smith's column not only was his livelihood, but his life. Three columns a week? He used to do seven. He wrote in his final column: "[And] between those jousts with the mother tongue, there was always a fight or football match or ball game or horse race that had to be covered after the column was done. I loved it."

And people loved Red, as a writer and as a man.

The day after Smith died, Dave Kindred wrote in his *Washington Post* column: "If we could all be so courtly, be so economical and light on the typewriter, make the damn machine sing the way Red did, helping a few people smile of a morning and explaining in one-syllable words what Bowie Kuhn and Marvin Miller are up to—and if we could be Red Smith, we would be, and that is his legacy to his craft."

His fans were legion. They ranged from Hemingway (who praised Smith through a character in his novel *Across the River and into the Trees*) to Beau Jack, the lightweight boxing champion who was unable to read or write.

"Don't let his size fool you," pitcher Tom Seaver once told a younger player about 5-foot 7-inch Smith. "He's got a Nolan Ryan fastball, a Sandy Koufax curveball, and the league he plays in is the best there is."

When Smith won the Pulitzer Prize in 1976—only the second sportswriter to be so honored—the Pulitzer Committee cited him for not simply sports writing but "distinguished commentary."

Smith's graceful prose could touch the range of emotions, could make one laugh out loud, could prick the pompous. It would give insight and inform—and, invariably, delight.

Smith would write of his problems as a fisherman and once described the black bass as a "derby-wearing, cigar-smoking fish to whom a hook in the mouth is no worse than a bad cold."

On visiting the great race horse Secretariat, retired on a Kentucky farm: "He acknowledged the attention with quiet assurance. He knew perfectly well that he was the attraction, he agreed it was only fair, and he stayed there posing as long as an admirer remained. If he were a singer, it would be said that he was generous with encores."

He also could be moved to anger, though he never failed to do it in graceful language. When, for example, the panjandrums of the Olympic Committee chose to resume the 1972 Olympic Games following the massacre of Israeli athletes, Smith wrote: "Walled off in their dream world, appallingly unaware of the realities of life and death, the aging playground directors who conduct this quadrennial muscle dance ruled that a little bloodshed must not be permitted to interrupt play."

Smith had strong convictions about the role of sports in society. He did not take the position that the two are completely separate entities. "Sports is not really a play world," he said. "I think it's the real world. Not in who wins or loses as it is reflected on the scoreboard, but in the people in sports who are suffering and living and dying and loving and trying to make their way through life just as bricklayers and politicians are."

He added: "The man who reports on these games contributes his small bit to the record of his time."

Walter Wellesley (Red) Smith, born in Green Bay, Wisconsin, in 1905, certainly made his contributions not only to the record of his time, but to joy in his time.

He was graduated from Notre Dame in 1927 and immediately set out on a journalistic career, first with the *Milwaukee Sentinel*, then with the *St. Louis Star*, the *Philadelphia Record*, the *New York Herald Tribune*—where he became the most widely syndicated sportswriter in the country—and, in 1971, the *New York Times*.

On Wednesday, January 20, at the memorial Mass of Red Smith, some 500 people filed into St. Patrick's Cathedral on Fifth Avenue in Manhattan. Those attending included the men and women who respected him as a professional, the young writers to whom he was gracious when asked for advice, and his family—his wife Phyllis; his two children Catherine Halloran and Terry Smith (now a *New York Times* reporter in Washington), and Smith's five step-children, six grandchildren, and two great-grandchildren.

Celebrating the Mass, the Reverend John Quinn noted that Smith once said, “Dying is no big deal. The least of us will manage that. Living is the trick.”

“It is the trick,” said Father Quinn, “that Red Smith mastered.”

JOHN WIEBUSCH

Bronko Nagurski

The stories surrounding Bronko Nagurski, the greatest fullback of the 1930s and one of the most admired NFL players of all time, are boundless. Did he really knock down all 11 members of the Northwestern defense on a 12-yard touchdown run for the University of Minnesota? Did he truly lift a truck off a dying man all by himself? John Wiebusch, editor-in-chief at NFL Properties, explored the facts and fictions of a football legend for PRO! *magazine in 1983.*

LEGEND (LEJ'END), n. 1. An unverified popular story handed down from earlier times. 2. A body or collection of such stories. 3. A romanticized or popularized myth of modern times. 4. A person who achieves legendary fame.

—*American Heritage Dictionary*

In the Gordian knot of real and unreal, of what happened and what might have happened, Bronko Nagurski is all the above, a man bigger than life when he played, a name bigger than life today.

His name. To say it is to say strength and power and hair-on-the-chest maleness. Bronk-o Nag-ur-ski. The sounds are almost chauvinistic. Bronko Nagurski. Treetop tall, able to leap football fields in a single bound, earth mover. Paul Bunyan in the midst of us.

One year when it rained from St. Patrick's Day till the Fourth of July, Paul Bunyan got disgusted because his celebration of the Fourth was spoiled. He dived into Lake Superior and swam to where a solid pillar of water was coming down. He dived under this pillar, swam up into it, and climbed with powerful swimming strokes. He'd gone about an hour, came splashing down, and as the rain stopped, he explained, "I turned the damn thing off." This is told in the Big North Woods and on the Great Lakes with many particulars.

—Carl Sandburg

Bronko Nagurski lives in International Falls, Minnesota, on the Canadian border. The Rainy River flows through International Falls five months of the year. The other seven months it is frozen rock-solid. International Falls is called the Icebox of the Nation. Men in plaid wool shirts with ruddy faces smile through their beers there and say, "You got to be hardy to live here."

Bronko Nagurski has been there all his life, for 66 winters and 66 summers. He has been there pumping gas in the station that bore his name until a couple years ago. He has been there answering questions about where the smallmouth bass were hitting. He has been there in the Big North Woods, leading a quiet life while legends grow around him.

Red Grange can't swear the story is true. But he says the man who told it to him swears it was and that's good enough for him.

"A few years ago," says Grange, who played with Bronko Nagurski on the Chicago Bears, "Doc Spears, Bronko's coach at the University of Minnesota, was in Florida visiting me. I asked him how he'd ever come across a guy like Bronko in a place like International Falls. Spears said that he had gone up there from Minneapolis to see another kid. He thought the kid's name was Smith. Spears told me that just outside of International Falls he saw this young kid pushing a plow. There was no horse or anything else—just this kid pushing a plow! Spears stopped the car and asked the kid just where he might find this Smith fellow. Well, Doc swears the kid with the plow just picked it up and pointed in the direction. Doc knew that Smith or no Smith, he had to have this kid, too. The kid was Bronko Nagurski."

One bright spring morning Paul Bunyan discovered that the billions of feet of logs that he and his men had cut and dragged down to the banking grounds during the winter were land-locked in a lake in Northern Minnesota. Without blinking an eyelash, Paul ordered Ole, his great Swede blacksmith, to make an enormous shovel. Paul took this shovel one morning before breakfast, and started to dig a canal through to the Gulf of Mexico. He took his direction from the path the wildfowl had cleft in the air during their last migration. He shoveled so fast that soon the sun was darkened as if by a total eclipse. The dirt that flew over his right shoulder formed the Rocky Mountains, and what he hurled in the opposite direction (there wasn't any room in the sky, you understand, to throw the dirt one way) became the Appalachians. Paul reached the Gulf at the end of the first day just as the sun was about to set. He flicked a hundred gallons of sweat from his brow with his forefinger, flung his shovel down with a grunt and a smile, and galloped back to camp before the last light was put out for the night.

—James Cloyd Bowman

In three years with the University of Minnesota varsity, the teams Bronko Nagurski played with lost only four games, three of them by one point and one by two points.

But it is not the winning or the losing they remember. It is Bronko Nagurski. In three years he played every position except center and quarterback and in his senior year, in 1929, Grantland Rice named only 10 men to the All-America football team. Bronko Nagurski was named at both tackle and fullback.

In a game against Northwestern that year they say Bronko Nagurski scored a touchdown from 12 yards and that during that run every member of the Northwestern defense took a shot at him. When Bronko came down in the end zone it was only because he hit a stack of lumber.

A similar thing had happened the year before, when Minnesota played Wisconsin. Bronko had suffered an injury to his spine but he insisted on playing with a steel brace. It was a game for the Big Ten championship and Wisconsin needed only a tie to win. Late in the game, with both teams scoreless, Minnesota moved close to the Wisconsin goal line. They gave the ball to Bronko Nagurski four consecutive times and on the last effort he took it into the end zone. There were six Wisconsin players on his back when he scored.

Paul Bunyan was very big for his age, of course, but he was never clumsy as many big boys are. Once—the first time he ever went hunting—he sneaked his father's old shotgun out of the house and set forth to see what he could find. He kept his sharp eyes wide open and at last he saw a deer stick its head around a tree four or five miles away. He blazed away at the animal with the old gun, and then was so anxious to see if he had killed it that he started for the spot, lippity-cut. He ran so fast that he outran the load he had fired from the gun, with the result that he got the full charge of the buckshot in the seat of his breeches.

—Wallace Wadsworth

He joined the Chicago Bears of the National Football League in 1930, but he was preceded by his reputation. Already he was a folk hero. There was the story about how he ran six miles to and from high school every day in International Falls (even in the winter) . . . about how he had single-handedly lifted a truck off a dying man . . . about how he had rescued another man who'd been buried under a pile of logs at a sawmill.

The pros were disbelievers and it is not difficult to see why. They sought softness in the legend early.

In 1930, the Green Bay Packers were the lords of professional football. They had Johnny Blood (McNally) to run the ball and a man-mountain tackle, Cal Hubbard, to clear a path. Hubbard weighed 250 pounds; he was a big man by the standards of any age but four decades ago he was Herculean.

The story is told by Red Grange:

"The Bronk and I were on one side protecting the punter on

fourth-down plays. Well, the game was getting along and the Packers were beating us and Hubbard passed me after one play and said, 'Next time you guys punt, let me by. I won't block the kick. I just want to get a shot at that Nagurski and see if he's as tough as they say he is.' So the next time we went into punt formation I let Hubbard get past me and I turned around to watch. I'm telling you, Hubbard socked the Bronk a good one, but the guy who went down was Hubbard himself. Hubbard caught up with me as we left the field. He said, 'The kid is as hard as they said he was.'"

I will endeavor to give you an idea of the size of the real Paul Bunyan, something no other man has been able to give the public without resorting to untruths.

From the soles of his feet to the roots of his hair he split the atmosphere exactly 16 feet 11 inches. His weight, he told me, was 888 pounds.

But what interested me most was his face. He had the most unusual eyes I ever have seen. The distance between his eyes was 17 inches. They were the size of ordinary saucers. His nose resembled a fresh leg of mutton. When he opened his mouth in one of his prodigious yawns, one could have inserted a ten-quart pail.

—Earl Clifton Beck

In 1963, Bronko Nagurski was a charter member of the Pro Football Hall of Fame. He did not receive his Hall of Fame ring until the following year, however. The reason for the delay was that the L.G. Balfour company had made a size 19 1/2 ring. Balfour officials still believe the ring is the largest ever made in the United States.

George Halas shakes his head at the memory. "I assure you that you will not see a more remarkable physical specimen anywhere," says the man who coached Bronko as a professional. "He was six feet, two inches and he weighed two hundred thirty-four pounds and it was all—literally all—muscle, skin, and bone. He didn't have an ounce of fat on him. A lot of men have passed in front of me but none with a build like that man."

Beattie Feathers played with Bronko Nagurski. "He had the most incredible natural strength I've ever seen," says Feathers. "One time we were up in Green Bay working out on the Saturday afternoon before the game. We were all just running around and tossing the ball about when Halas called us into the huddle. The starting team gathered around Halas and he told us to line up in formation to run a few plays. I didn't see Bronko and I said to Halas, 'Coach, we don't have a fullback.' I didn't realize it, but Bronko was standing right behind me. Well, Bronko gave me what he thought was a friendly bop on the helmet, and it knocked me down. He was so big and powerful I don t believe even he knew how strong he really was."

Gene Ronzani was the Bears' quarterback for most of the Nagurski years. "Here I was coming out of Marquette," said Ronzani, "and I tell you, just the thought of playing with Bronko Nagurski scared the hell out of me. And when I saw him I became more of a believer. Not only was he as big and strong as advertised and not only was he a humble fellow and an all-around good guy, but he was the second-fastest man on the Bears. And his toughness! He had a bad knee and sometimes he would come limping back to the huddle. I'd ask him if he wanted a time out and he'd say, 'Time out? Hell no, let's play football.' Then he would slap his knee on either side with that big hand of his—slapping the cartilage back in place. We'd shake our heads and away we'd go and Bronko would carry the ball."

The epic battles of the day were between Clarke Hinkle, fullback and linebacker for the Packers, and Bronko Nagurski, fullback and linebacker for the Bears. It was survival of the fittest then; it is mutual admiration today.

"I felt I could play football with anyone," says Hinkle, "and I was particularly anxious to go after Bronko because he was the best. The first time I came up against him I made the mistake of letting him come to me before I made the tackle—or tried to make it. I needed seven stitches to close up the cut on my chin. It was murder, but you had to go after him to be effective. If you didn't you were through.

"Once I went over right tackle and cut toward the sidelines and I saw that Bronko had me cornered. I knew that in blocking or tackling he rarely left his feet. Nor did he wrap his arms around a runner in making a tackle. He merely used to block or tackle with his shoulder or hip or forearm—and that got the job done. This one time I pivoted straight toward Bronko before he hit me. I lowered my shoulder and smashed into and over him. He suffered a broken nose and a fractured rib on that play but it didn't keep him out of the rest of the game."

In 1936, two members of the Pittsburgh team attempted to stop Bronko Nagurski from reaching the end zone. One man suffered a broken shoulder; the other was knocked out.

And so as the train carried the Pittsburgh team home from Chicago they played cards and talked about the Bears' fullback. Suddenly the train gave an unusually violent lurch and the bodies of football players were strewn in the aisles.

"Run for your lives, men," shouted halfback Warren Heller. "It's Nagurski!"

One day Paul Bunyan climbed a tree during a violent windstorm. After he got to the top it started to blow eighteen hurricanes. After a few minutes Paul and the tree went sailing off into space.

After traveling for days in the air, Paul began to drop. When he hit he made a hole over nine hundred miles long and a good many miles wide. Paul was so tired that he fell asleep before investigating his new surroundings. He had a terrible nightmare that caused him to sweat so much that the hole was filled with water. Years later Henry Hudson found this hole and named it Hudson Bay after himself.

—Earl Clifton Beck

Maybe truth isn't stranger than fiction (as Lord Byron wrote), but sometimes it's almost a dead heat . . .

Once in a game against Portsmouth in 1933, Bronko Nagurski went 45 yards for the winning touchdown, sending two linebackers flying in different directions, running over the defensive halfback, and straight-arming the safety aside before colliding with the goal post and caroming into the brick wall at Wrigley Field in Chicago. "The last guy hit me awful hard," Bronko said after he was revived.

Once in a game against Green Bay in 1934, Bronko powered through three tacklers into the end zone, crashing head-on into the steel netting protecting the box seats.

Steve Owen was the coach of the New York Giants. He once said of Nagurski, "He's the only man I've ever seen who runs his own interference."

Lest you smile at fond remembrance, consider this from Beattie Feathers: "When we got near the goal line we didn't put any blockers ahead of Bronko. He was fast but he was not a quick starter and we didn't want to take a chance of him getting tripped up by his own blockers. So he'd just blast through the line without any interference."

Gene Ronzani: "He had that strong forearm and those enormous shoulders and he'd just stick his arm out and batter people out of the way."

Mel Hein, center-linebacker for the Giants: "Coaches always told you to tackle a big running back low, so I tried to tackle Bronko low the first time I faced him and he stampeded me. But if you tried to tackle him high, he kept right on going. Actually, we found that the only sure way to bring him down was to have at least two tacklers. And often that didn't work."

Chris Crosshaul was a careless cuss. He took a big drive down the Mississippi for Paul Bunyan and when the logs were delivered in New Orleans it was found that he had driven the wrong ones. It was up to Paul to drive them back upstream.

No one but Paul Bunyan would ever tackle a job like that. To drive logs upstream is impossible, but if you think a little thing like an impossibility could stop him, you don't know Paul Bunyan. He simply fed Babe (the blue ox) a good big salt ration and drove him to the upper Mississippi to drink. Babe drank the river dry and sucked all the water upstream. The logs came up river faster than they went down.

—W. B. Laughead

Bronko Nagurski was more than just another routine Superman.

"He could do it all," said Doc Spears, his college coach. "He could have been an All-America at any position."

Charles Johnson and Dick Cullum are two of the most respected sports journalists of the last century. Both men saw Bronko Nagurski play for the University of Minnesota and for the Bears. Both men wrote about what they saw for Minneapolis newspapers. And their opinions virtually parallel that of Doc Spears.

"Bronk really could have been the best at anything he tried," says Johnson.

"In many ways, Bronko was the Babe Ruth of football. They both could do it all. The difference was the Bronk did it less flamboyantly because that was his nature. He's a very basic, very simple man who's uncomfortable when he gets a lot of attention."

"The truth is," says Cullum, "that Bronko Nagurski may not even have been the University of Minnesota's finest fullback. That distinction may belong to Herb Joesting (a senior fullback in Bronko's sophomore year). But I don't disparage Bronko's talents as a fullback . . . hardly. He was an All-America and I think he was the best fullback ever to play in the NFL.

"But the man's versatility was so remarkable. I remember one game at Iowa when Minnesota was severely crippled and had to lose. But Nagurski played tremendously at five positions—end, tackle, guard, halfback, and fullback. When Bronk went to the Chicago Bears he fit immediately into the fullback position and was not tried anywhere else.

"Yet his friends could not help but wish he had tried some other positions, too. They knew he was a better end and a better tackle than he was a fullback, yet he was enough fullback to be called the best in NFL history. That's a measure of greatness."

In the 1930s, Grantland Rice wrote: "Bronko Nagurski was a star end, a great tackle, and a great back—an All-America in any one of these positions."

Paul Bunyan was of tremendous size and strength, the strongest man that ever swung an axe. He had curly black hair which his loving wife used to comb for him every morning with a great crosscut saw, after first parting it nicely with a broadax, and a big, black beard that was as long as it was wide and as wide as it was long. He was rather proud of this beard and took good care of it. Several times every day he would pull up a young pine tree by the roots and use its stiff branches in combing and brushing it smooth.

—Wallace Wadsworth

The statistics of the early days of professional football were something less than official and the yardage totals attributed to Bronko Nagurski can only be approximate. It is certain that he carried the ball over 800 times and gained over 4,000 yards.

But is that the measure of the man? Hardly.

How do you measure his blocking? In the first 27 years of the NFL, only one man, Beattie Feathers, rushed for 1,000 yards in one season. Feathers gained 1,004 yards in 1934 for the Bears and the men who were there claim Nagurski ran interference on almost every play.

How do you measure the 60-minute player? "If I'd played one way," Bronko Nagurski once said, "I could have played another fifteen years."

And isn't it significant that the plays one of the great runners of all time is remembered best for are passing plays?

In 1932, ties didn't count and the Bears (6-1-6) and the Portsmouth Spartans (6-1-4) tied for the NFL title. They played it off in an indoor game in Chicago Stadium and in the fourth quarter of the scoreless tie the Bears threatened. Nagurski carried the ball three consecutive times inside the Portsmouth 10 but on fourth down the Bears were still one yard short. Nagurski got the ball again. He faked a plunge, then drilled a jump pass to Red Grange in the end zone.

"I had slipped in the end zone," says Grange, "and I was flat on my back. Bronko saw me and hit me and that was the game's only touchdown. He wasn't a great passer technically, but he was always on target."

In 1933, the NFL divided into two divisions for the first time. The Bears opposed the New York Giants in the championship game and their knockout punch was the passing arm of Bronko Nagurski. The big fullback passed to Bill Karr for one touchdown, then brought the Bears a 23-21 victory when he passed to Bill Hewitt, who lateraled to Karr to complete a 25-yard touchdown play.

"Bronko would buck up to the line," says Mel Hein of the Giants, "and you'd have to come in to meet him as a linebacker. Then he'd stand straight up and lob a little pass. We all knew it was coming but we couldn't afford to concentrate on it because we couldn't afford to give Bronko any running room."

A favorite lumberjack sport is rolling a log. A man stands on a big log afloat in the water and starts turning it with his feet, keeping his feet going so that he is always on top and standing safely upright, no matter how fast he gets the log to whirling under him. Paul Bunyan could roll a log so fast that it made foam on the water solid enough for him to walk ashore on, and he is known to have crossed wide rivers in this way. Not all of this foam which he thus caused has disappeared to this day, and occasionally small bits of it may still be seen floating down many streams after a heavy rain.

—Wallace Wadsworth

He was the player of his time—perhaps of all time—but his time was not a time of great reward because it was the time of the Great Depression.

In 1965, Bronko Nagurski told Milton Richman of *United Press International*: "The first contract I signed with him (owner George Halas) was for five thousand dollars. Even though I had a good year, my salary was cut to forty-five hundred my second year. The depression was on, the club was losing money and we had to take cuts.

"I got thirty-seven hundred my third year with the Bears and that's where my salary stayed for a number of years. They upped my pay to five thousand in 1937 when I talked about retiring and when I asked for six thousand in 1938 they turned me down. I went home figuring they'd call me, but they never did. Not until five years later."

In 1943, World War II had decimated the Bears' talent. Three tackles and two guards were gone from the 1942 team and Ralph Brizzolara, the Bears' interim general manager (Halas also was in the service) called Nagurski, then nearly 35, and asked if he was interested in coming back to play tackle. He was.

"And once he started to play," says Ronzani, "he was the same old Bronk."

In his first game, against the Packers, he was hit by Ted Fritsch, a young fullback. Fritsch was knocked unconscious. The legend was back.

Nagurski remained at tackle for most of the season, until injuries sidelined both of the Bears' fullbacks for the final game of the regular season against the Cardinals. Bronko Nagurski carried the ball 17 times for 84 yards that day, scoring one touchdown and setting up two others. The derring-do helped the Bears turn a 24-14 deficit into a 35-24 victory.

The Bears trounced the Washington Redskins for the NFL championship in the following month, and Nagurski saw action again at fullback. In his farewell to football, he scored a touchdown.

Even when he was an old man, or what would be old for most men, Paul Bunyan was so quick on his feet that he could blow out the light in the bunkhouse at night; and be in bed and asleep before the room got dark.

—W. B. Laughead

Bronko Nagurski remains a man of basics, a man who does not demand much of life except a square deal. And he doesn't feel he's always gotten that. He feels his career was shorted . . . he feels that his days as a professional wrestler (he was an enormous attraction in the 1930s and 1940s) were degrading . . . he feels that he and other early players should be included in the Players Association pension plan (they are not).

In recent years he has had to undergo major surgery on his knees and he has been dogged by arthritis. He no longer grants interviews (and he seldom did, even a decade ago), choosing instead to guard his privacy.

He lives in International Falls with his wife of more than 30 years, Eileen, and one of their six children, Kevin, a high school senior and an outstanding hockey player (there also are five older children, three sons and two daughters, and four grandchildren).

"I have no regrets," he says. "Nothing I could change, anyway. I watch a lot of modern football and I wonder if I could be happy playing it because I could only play half the time. And I wonder what I'd be playing. I like to carry the ball, but I expect that they'd end up using me the same way the Bears do Dick Butkus now. I'd like that, too. I was very much like Butkus—big and mobile. Besides, I guess I liked defense a little better."

Fifty pounds over his playing weight, he is asked to confirm a story about how he used to enter a room holding his wife out at arm's length.

"That's right," he said, "and I can still do it, only Eileen won't let me."

Who made Paul Bunyan, who gave him birth as a myth, who joked him into life as the Master Lumberjack, who fashioned him forth as an apparition easing the hours of men amid axes and trees, saws and lumber? The people, the bookless people, they made Paul and had him alive long before he got into the books for those who read. And some of Paul is as old as the hills, young as the alphabet.

—Carl Sandburg

PHIL BARBER

LXII

Lasers down the sidelines? A female coach named Dawn Shula-Rodriguez? Holographic images of Super Bowl LXII beamed back to the home fans in Los Angeles and Hong Kong? It was all part of Phil Barber's vision of the NFL future, written for the Super Bowl XXVI game program in Minneapolis. A seven-year veteran of NFL Properties' editorial staff, Barber edited that program for two years, GAMEDAY *and* TEAM NFL *magazines for three.*

RIO DE JANEIRO, February 21, 2028—Could any conclusion to any event have fit better? After two wacky, tumultuous weeks in a city that had gone certifiably *louco* over a football game, could any concluding image have been more appropriate than a loose ball bouncing freely, if erratically, toward an unmanned end zone? For evidence of the game's dramatic nature, take a look at the Super Bowl LXII highlight compilation, which NFL Films had put onto magnetic reso-disc and packaged before most of the fans had boarded the monorail.

From the moment one stepped into the Rio heat and realized that, yes, February is a summer month in South America, it was obvious this would be a Super Bowl like no other. From the tiny NFL shields that Brazil had sewn onto all national flags to promote the game to the giant football scenes projected onto the surrounding mountains at night, the developing giant spared few flourishes.

Perhaps the most amazing sideshow at Super Bowl LXII was the "NFL in Yo' Face" attraction at Disneyworld Rio, where the league held its gigantic party Friday night. Of course, everyone had seen the advertisements for this billion-dollar creation, but few could have been prepared for it. Just to suit up in the authentic NFL uniform of one's choice satisfied a nearly universal deep-seated desire, but the full production was unreal. A mixture of film images, real-life game sounds (and smells), and actors portraying savage defensive linemen, it was the closest most of us ever will get to taking a snap against an NFL defense. It was so realistic, in fact, that I was charged with intentional grounding on a crucial third-down play.

But it wasn't the fanfare, diverting as it may have been, that made this particular Super Bowl week so memorable; it was the two teams involved, the conference champions. This was the ultimate clash of worlds: the high-tech Hong Kong Dragons, the first team to train completely underwater, versus the blood-and-guts Los Angeles Raiders, who still wear silver and black as other teams move to fuchsia and mauve. The far-flung Eastern (Hemisphere) Conference against the Western Conference, made up primarily of long-time NFL teams. New versus Old. The Offense of the '30s vs. the Defense of the '20s.

The week-long interview process, conducted wholly through two-way closed-circuit television, was almost as colorful as the face-to-face press conferences of old. In only a limited number of cases was the plug pulled because of a displeasing query. The star of Super Bowl week was Hong Kong's Takehiko Tsuchiya, the latest NFL head coach to be described as a "genius." Admittedly, the label isn't far from the mark this time. Born in Japan, educated at Tokyo University, Oxford, and MIT, Tsuchiya claims he "never watched a complete football game" until he worked on a certain doctoral thesis, an analysis of motion and force that concentrated on wide receivers being pummeled while running crossing patterns.

Since the completion of that project, Tsuchiya has thought about little other than football. Using his own copyrighted software programs to break down every NFL game of the last 25 years play by play, Coach T. claims to have determined the ideal formation and play for every conceivable situation, against any opponent.

"After running through five hundred thousand simulations of the game," he declared to an astonished press corps on Tuesday, "I have concluded that we will win 27-21 . . . or possibly 30-21, depending on whether my kicker converts a third-quarter field-goal attempt. In addition, we will outrush the Raiders by 120-130 yards, and will hold an approximate two-to-one lead in time of possession."

"Why even play the game?" one reporter teased.

"The international television and sponsorship rights were negotiated long ago," Tsuchiya replied without smiling.

The coach's conclusions would have sounded like wild rantings, of course, had his team not soundly thrashed the NFL competition throughout the 2027 season. The Dragons, after finishing the regular season 18-2 and setting a league record with 249 rushing yards per game, were being compared to the greatest teams in NFL history, storied casts such as the '78 Steelers, the '89 49ers, the '03 Patriots, and, yes, even the '17 Conquistadors.

The Raiders, in contrast, stumbled and staggered a few times along the way to a 14-6 regular-season record. But after their 24-14 victory over "North America's Team," the rejuvenated Dallas Cowboys and their Doomsday V Defense, it was clear Los Angeles was a team to fear. The Raiders' catalyst, of course, is young Wingin' Willie Wadholm-Jermain, who became the first NFL quarterback ever to surpass 7,500 passing yards (7,584) in a single season in 2027. It was only four years ago that Wadholm-Jermain led the Canadian football team to a gold medal in the 2024 Winter Olympics, and his legend has mushroomed ever since.

Though most of Wadholm-Jermain's teammates are too young to remember Al Davis, Ken Stabler, Howie Long, and the other Raiders of bygone eras, they seem to be cut from the same idiosyncratic mold. They curse, spit, and laugh just like Raiders always have, and apparently always will. Another indication of how much things stay the same: Who but the Raiders would appoint the NFL's first female head coach? The decision to promote Dawn Shula-Rodriguez from offensive coordinator two years ago was met with reaction ranging from hearty applause to snickering. Men's rights groups even protested. But there can be little debate now as to whether Ms. Shula-Rodriguez inherited any of her grandfather's coaching genes. (Don Shula retired in 1999 as the winningest coach in NFL history.)

Shula-Rodriguez also has managed to retain her sense of humor under tremendous pressure. When asked Thursday if she had devised a new game plan to combat Tsuchiya's Fusion Age attack, she replied, "Yeah, we've installed the Run-and-Shoot," a tongue-in-cheek reference to the long-outmoded offense popularized in the 1990s.

The venue itself was a topic of much conversation as the game approached. The Brazil Dome—*O Domo Brasileiro*—is a model for all future super-stadiums. To put 118,000 spectators in comfortable pivoting seats, all of which provide good views of the on-field action, is impressive enough. But to think that the electricity for the arena—from the lighting to the heightened-resolution scoreboards to the card scanners at the merchandise stands—is completely solar-generated is to try the imagination.

The outside world first was treated to a glimpse of O Domo during the 2026 World Cup soccer finals (won by the upstart U.S. team, as if you needed a reminder), but the accommodations have gotten even better in the short time since. Each seat now is equipped with a personal video monitor that allows the fan to view the game action from his or her choice of camera angles, along with slow-motion replays of every down. Finally, the comforts of the living room, minus a robotic food server, in the midst of a cheering throng.

Of course, the Brazil Dome wasn't the only stadium filled to capacity on Super Sunday. As were the last few Super Bowls, this year's game was played "live" in the home arenas of the two participating teams. Well, almost live—as the real Super Bowl LXII battle was waged here, holographic images of the game action simultaneously were beamed onto the fields of the Los Angeles Coliseum and Hong Kong's Giant Olive.

Kickoff, if you remember, originally had been scheduled for

4:00 P.M., Rio de Janeiro time, but was moved to 5:30 when a long-range forecast indicated ultraviolet radiation would be "heavy to unhealthful" about noon, when many fans would have been enjoying the exhibits outside the stadium.

The schedule change made it easy for all fans to be in their seats for the pregame festivities, which were highlighted by a musical extravaganza called "Jump Back! The Godfather Turns 100." It was a rollicking tribute to James Brown, born in 1928. An address by NFL Commissioner Derrick Thomas—who joked about his former team, the Kansas City Chiefs, failing to repeat as Western Hemisphere champions in 2027—was followed by the National Anthems of the United States and Brazil, both performed by Old Kids on the Block. Many an eye misted as 55-year-old Donny thanked the audience for being a part of the Old Kids' worldwide reunion tour.

Then came the coin toss. When Roger Staubach, 86 years old and still looking fit as a midshipman, strode across the field to greet the 10 or 12 team captains and decide possession of the opening kickoff, the whole event took on a different perspective, at least for me.

Could it really have been 50 years ago that Staubach led the Cowboys to a 27-10 victory over the Denver Broncos in Super Bowl XII? I was only 13 years old at the time, but I remember the game well. Thinking about it set my mind wandering through the many changes the game of football has experienced over the last five decades.

For instance, Super Bowl XII was the first one played indoors, at the original Louisiana Superdome. Yesterday's game also took place under a roof, but back in January of 1978 that meant an artificial surface. It was long before we learned how to grow natural grass indoors, before AstroTurf was outlawed. I remember joining those voices that harped about artificial turf; now I almost would say that I miss it, if only for the sake of nostalgia.

Of course, the equipment has changed dramatically. Gone are the hard-plastic helmets, bulky pads, cage face masks, and relatively loose-fitting uniforms of the seventies. The NFL player of 2028 would sooner play with radioactive waste than take the field without his lightweight titanium helmet, skin-tight latex uniform equipped with durable airbags, and form-fitting cleats with built-in ankle wraps. And in-helmet radios for sideline-to-field communication? They would have seemed like science fiction back in '78.

The players have changed, too. Despite what most old fogies such as myself will tell you, today's players are bigger, stronger, and faster than those of my childhood. Sure, with 55 players on each active roster, they can afford to be more specialized as well (Dragons linebacker Tex Hager enters the lineup only on third-down plays with between 8 and 12 yards to go for a first down), but consider this comparison: The Cowboys' heaviest offensive lineman in Super Bowl XII was center John Fitzgerald, who weighed 260 pounds; the Raiders' starting offensive line for Super Bowl LXII *averaged* 335 pounds.

In 1977, footballs still were made of leather; assistant coaches numbered eight or nine per team, as opposed to the 21 on the Dragons' sideline yesterday; the goal posts were much wider (they were narrowed from 18 feet 6 inches to 12 feet 6 inches in 2018, when field-goal percentages routinely crept above 90); and, gasp!, *there was no such thing* as instant replay in officiating. Who among us NFL fans would be brave enough to live without subjection to review now?—although, with sensors on the ball and laser beams across each sideline, goal line, and end line, plus another at the first-down marker, the replay official doesn't get involved as much as he once did.

We interrupt this sentimental flashback to bring you . . . halftime! A lot of people thought last year's production at Wembley Stadium—a lifelike re-creation of the bombing of London during World War II—was the ultimate halftime show, but LXII's might have been its equal. This year's included a salute to the joint U.S.-Japanese space program, complete with 200 anti-gravity gymnasts and a working model of the manned capsule scheduled to blast off for Mars in 2030. More appropriate to the South American setting was a traditional ceremony by native Guarani dancers.

For highlights of the game itself, please turn to one of the 40 or so other Super Bowl stories in this News Mail. Anyway, you probably were watching as closely as I was at the end of the fourth quarter when, despite a large advantage to the Dragons in yardage, first downs, and time of possession. the score was tied at 17-17. You probably witnessed the scene as Dragons quarterback James Kaplan-Lopes-Baban dropped back to pass with the clock winding down and was hit by two Raiders defensive ends at once, the ball squirting free and bouncing, drifting into the Hong Kong end zone, where Los Angeles linebacker Nik Pontino fell on it for the winning score.

Moments later, the game was over, and the ecstatic Raiders dumped a tub of kelp-and-pollen liquid protein supplement over the head of Shula-Rodriguez. Still damp in the locker room afterward, she said, "The only hard drives that win football games are in the heart, not in a computer."

What a coach! What a woman! Maybe we'll see her at Carnival next weekend.

Notes: The ratings for the Global Broadcasting Company's telecast were tabulated immediately after the game, and the worldwide audience was estimated at 1.45 billion. The American television audience was placed at 204,312,000, making Super Bowl LXII the third-most-watched program in United States history, behind games L and LVII. Nine of the all-time top 10 broadcasts have been Super Bowls, the sole exception being the farewell episode of "The Simpsons" in 2011 . . . The capacity in-stadium crowd consumed approximately 33,000 soy dogs, 40,000 bags of peanuts, 24,000 *churraquinhos*, 7,500 iguana burgers, 13,000 gallons of water, 8,000 gallons of soft drinks, and 13,000 gallons of Chug beer substitute . . . One of the nearly 1,000 photographers outlining the Domo Brasileiro field was John Biever, who at the age of 80 is the last surviving member of the "Super Bowl Club," meaning he has photographed every Super Bowl. Biever shot LXII with a 1990s-era antique

Canon . . . Late in the second quarter, the Raiders' defense was flagged for illegal zone coverage. It was the first time the new rule, designed to help open up the passing game, had been applied in the Super Bowl . . . Each member of the Raiders received a silverplated ear- or nose-ring, cast as a miniature Vince Lombardi Trophy . . . About 20 minutes before the game, the Sony blimp and the General Electric blimp—two of the many circling O Domo—inadvertently bumped. Angry words were exchanged, but no injuries were reported . . . The featured attraction at Super Bowl Card Show XXXIX, housed in an enormous tent outside the stadium, was NFL Pro Set's current 2,750-card set, which includes full movement-and-sound images of every NFL player active in 2027.

WELLS TWOMBLY

Airedales and Indians

Where do you start with a football team that was named after a strain of Airedale, played in the hometown of acting President Warren Harding, and featured players named Wrinkle Meat and Long Time Sleep? The Oorang Indians of 1922-23 are but a blip on the screen of NFL history, but because of their unique existence—captured with a smile by Wells Twombly—they are not forgotten. Twombly was a SAN FRANCISCO EXAMINER *columnist who died in 1979. His story on Jim Thorpe's team premiered in* PRO! *in 1976.*

IN 1921, A MAN NAMED Walter Lingo founded an all Indian team in Marion, Ohio, that publicized his dog kennels.

It seems incomprehensible now, in an age of imperial presidents and multimillion dollar stadiums, but there was a time when Marion, Ohio, had in its municipal bosom a chief executive who conducted a campaign from his front porch and a National Football League franchise that represented a dog kennel.

Was any small midwestern city ever more blessed than Marion in the early twenties? There was Warren Harding, the only journalist ever to hold the highest office in the land, the only man nominated and elected primarily for the reason that he looked as if nature had especially designed him to be president with that handsome, carved-in-granite profile and those strong, trustworthy eyes. If reporters wanted to interview him . . . well, trains stopped in Marion and the candidate was right there rocking away on his front porch.

Then there were the Oorang Indians, surely the most accurately named team in the long, gaudy history of professional sports in America. No prince of the Roman Catholic Church ever returned punts for the St. Louis team. The only oilman ever involved with the Houston club was the guy who owned it. Hardly anyone ever left the mills of United States Steel in order to block for the Pittsburgh team. But the Oorang Indians were all Indians . . . Original Americans.

They included Cherokees, Mohawks, Chippewas, Blackfoot, Winnebagos, Missions, Cadoos, Sac and Fox, Senecas, and Penobscots. They ranged from full-blooded Indians such as the immortal Wrinklemeat, who was all Cherokee, to Jim Thorpe, who was three-eighths Irish, to Xavier Downwind, who had more French blood than Chippewa, to Nick Lassa, who was only slightly Cherokee and was called Long Time Sleep because his more ethnically pure teammates had a helluva time waking him in the morning.

The Oorangs, who are listed in the *NFL Record Manua*l as "Marion," were the invention of an incredible promoter named Walter Lingo, who admitted to three major passions in his life—a breed of large and aggressive Airedale that he personally considered to be a wonder dog, American Indian lore, and hunting. Remarkably he managed to combine all three of them for two giddy years through the medium of football. A sport of which he really wasn't fond.

What a man Walter Lingo was! He was full of boys' book bravado, a person who could easily have taken Frank Merriwell out chasing bears in the Ohio uplands. He was the owner of King Oorang, whom he modestly billed as "the world's greatest all-around dog." Lingo wrote endless miles of press releases about his beloved breed. Even though the nation was zany over Rin Tin Tin, and German shepherds were selling like no other variety of dog, Lingo was convinced that he could change the market by sheer dint of his ability as a publicity expert, a charge he did not deny.

"About sixty years ago," he wrote in his own monthly magazine, "the common man of Great Britain found it necessary to create a dog different from any other in existence. The bird dog became lost in the bush when at stand, the hound was too noisy, and the retrievers lacked stamina. Therefore these folks secretly experimented by a series of crossbreeding old types, including the otter hound, the old English sheep dog, the black and tan terrier, and the bulldog. From this melting pot resulted the Airedale, so named because he was first produced by the people along the dale of the Aire river between England and Scotland. The new dog combined the good qualities of his ancestors without their faults. It was a super dog."

Through an incredible series of breedings, bringing in great Airedales from all over the world, Lingo came up with King Oorang, whom *Field and Stream* called the "greatest utility dog in the history of the world." In his kennels at LaRue, 14 miles outside of Marion, he conducted one of the country's first great puppy factories. It was a mail-order business, providing over 15,000 Oorang Airedales for purchasers from all over the United States, Canada, Central, and South America. At least 1,000 females were out on contract to farmers in Ohio who, in return for one Oorang, were willing to sell all the puppies back to Lingo at cost.

"There are a large number of clerks employed in the Oorang office at LaRue," said Freeman Lloyd, a prominent dog-show writer of the period. "They do nothing but keep records on the temperament, instincts, and pluck of the various Airedales being bred and born here. There are kennel men, night watchmen, crate makers, hunters, and trainers. The writer has covered thousands of kennels all over the world and nothing has been seen or imagined such as Walter Lingo's mail-order dog business."

There never would have been any Oorang Indians playing out of Marion during the brief term of Warren Harding if Lingo had not been fascinated by Indians. They were mythic creatures, he thought. They were strong, fierce, instinctive hunters. And one early winter day in the year 1921, with the former publisher of the *Marion Star* seated somewhat hesitantly in the White House, this incredible myth-maker brought two of the greatest players ever to graduate from the Carlisle Indian School to his LaRue plantation to hunt some possum.

By this time both Pete Calac and Jim Thorpe were getting a bit long in the tooth. In fact, Thorpe had just washed out of major league baseball a couple of years earlier, hitting .327 for the Boston Braves despite the fact that John J. McGraw of the New York Giants insisted that he could not hit a curveball. ("I must have hit a few of them, especially that last year," he said.) Despite his original genius, Thorpe was not a child anymore. When he met Lingo he insisted that he was 37, but there are people who say he was a year or two older.

Over a toddy or two, it was agreed that Lingo would purchase a franchise in the National Football League, an item that cost a thumping $100 in those days. By way of comparison, a superior Oorang Airedale male was priced at $150. Then again, Lingo was selling 100 pounds of Oorang dog biscuits in genuine burlap sacks with the kennel's name on the sides for $10. In other words if you had lived in Green Bay and wanted to buy the Packers you could have done so for the price of ten sacks of dog biscuits.

This is not to say that Lingo's hounds weren't popular. They were the subject of a series of boys' books written by Horace Lytle. The main character was Oorang Sandy and he was featured in such thrillers as *The Monarch of Moose Lake* and *The Heart of a Pal* and *The Mightiest Eagle*. They cost $1.75 each and James Wallen of the *Chicago Tribune* said they were "a big performance in writing."

One edition of *Oorang Comments*, which Lingo wrote and edited, showed two dogs underneath the carcass of a spotted leopard with the caption: "This big cat put up a hard fight with tooth and claw, but the two brave Oorangs were too much for him and he was killed after a mighty battle. The two dogs look a bit worse for wear but the next day they added another cat of similar size to their string of trophies."

It was questionable whether the Indians were there to play football or to give Airedale exhibitions at halftime. Lingo himself wasn't quite sure. In a book that was a marvelously bumptious piece of self-puffery called *Me and My Dogs*, he wrote that several famous Indians were part of his organization. He posed them in what he supposed were native costumes and gave them enough guns to wipe out the entire Seventh Cavalry.

"Speaking of using Indians," he wrote, "let me tell you about my big publicity stunt. You know Jim Thorpe, don't you, the Sac and Fox Indian, the world's greatest athlete who won the all-around championship at the Olympic Games in Sweden in 1912? Well, I found him a bit down and out and I invited him to come hunt with me in Ohio, those Indians being almost as good as my Airedales when it comes to tracking game. Assisted by two other famous Indian stars, Joe Guyon and Pete Calac, he headed a company of fifty Indian athletes and toured the country with a trained pack of Oorang Airedales. They played football against the leading big city teams.

"They gave exhibitions with my Airedales at work trailing and treeing a live bear, and fancy rifle shooting by Indian crack shots, with the Oorang Airedales retrieving the targets. The program also included Indian dancing, fancy tomahawk work, knife and lariat throwing by Indian performers. The climax was an exhibition of what the United States's loyal Indian scouts did during the war against Germany, with Oorang Airedale Red Cross dogs giving first aid in an armed encounter between scouts and Huns in no man's land. Many of the Indians and dogs were veterans of the war—the Oorangs up front."

Lingo became friendly with Thorpe when a neighboring farmer accused the Oorang Kennels of raising a nation of sheep killers. With no reluctance at all, Thorpe, the greatest athlete of his time, testified that he once knew an Oorang Airedale that had saved a six-year old girl named Mabel from being trampled by an enraged bull that had somehow violated her father's farm. The bull was stomping straight toward the child, having been attracted by her bright red dress. Escape was impossible, Thorpe said. But a loyal and indomitable Oorang Airedale had leaped at the beast's nozzle at the correct time.

She was saved, an event that would have made Rin Tin Tin proud.

There was never a time when Lingo was stuck for a dog story, a fact that absolutely amazed Thorpe. All one had to do was mention an incident and Lingo was off and running. In time, the club's head coach would invent situations and the owner would tell you what he insisted was a true story. At a dinner on the evening before the Oorang Indians played the Chicago Bears, Lingo went on at length and in stark detail about an Airedale that had personally defeated two enraged sows. The dog was just a puppy, but he grabbed two of the fiercest beasts in the world and killed them both.

"That man Lingo even told stories that made us look bad," said Thorpe. "He had a couple of us breaking in on this pioneer woman while she slept and having her rescued by a pair of Oorang Airedales. They never had Oorang Airedales on the Kansas frontier, but he said they were there anyway. It made good news for his kennels and that's all he thought about. I did what I was paid to do. I sure couldn't play football for him because I was getting up toward forty and I couldn't breathe so good."

The football players testified constantly about what good and faithful buddies their Airedales were. They insisted that their dogs could kill bear, wolf, and deer in a single gulp. They said that no other dog could catch a dead duck floating on the water like an Oorang Airedale.

"What I love most about my Indians is that they know more than my dogs," said Lingo. "That is something most white people can't understand. I love Indians for that reason."

Professional football was the stepchild of the sports pages in the early twenties, but there was sufficient interest to warrant the expenditure of $100, which is exactly what it cost Walter Lingo to advertise his dog business on the playing fields of the nation. In an era that saw the creation of such athletic oddments as the Pottsville Maroons, the Racine Legions, the Milwaukee Badgers, the Dayton Triangles, and the Hammond Pros, there is no question that the Oorang Indians managed to stand out. It was agreed that aging and ailing Thorpe would be head coach and that he would play whenever it was possible.

"It was a wonderful promotion," said Mrs. John Knaur, a niece of Lingo's who still lives in LaRue. "His Airedales were larger than most and they were used for hunting and for guard work. Right up until the time that Castro drove him out of Cuba, [President Fulgencio] Batista bought about a dozen of them a year. The Indians were hired mostly as dog trainers, because my uncle had this idea that there was almost a supernatural bond between Indians and animals, something that white people didn't fully understand. They lived in a big house he rented for them. My uncle wanted them to play in LaRue, but there wasn't a playing field here. However, Marion had one."

Marion was booming along with Harding. One of Harding's closest friends, Ralph Lewis, had sold his pickle business and was raising money for a 150-room hotel; the President himself had contributed $2,000. There were now more than 30,000 people in the city and it was rapidly turning from an agricultural city to an industrialized center. In honor of the president, Al Jolson had consented to play in Marion's only theater, the Chautauqua Auditorium in Garfield Park.

As a descendent of the famed war chief Blackhawk, Thorpe had been given an Indian name, Bright Path, because his mother was convinced that he was the reincarnation of his ancestor. Lingo, who was not much of a football fan, insisted that Jim Thorpe drop his magic name and bill himself as Chief Bright Path.

The Oorang Indians got the very best of care, Lingo boasted in his magazine. The same dietician and the same trainer who fed his Airedales and cared for their physical well-being also tended to his Indians. How much more concern could a man show for his red brothers?

An ancient poster advertising the team shows an Indian with a feather in his hair, but bare-chested with buckskin pants and regulation puttees, striding across a World War I battlefield, an Airedale at his side. Naturally, the dog is wearing a Red Cross blanket. Both creatures have noble expressions. "During the Recent World War Oorang Airedales and Oorang Indian Scouts More Than 'Did Their Bit.' Come see both of them This Sunday at The Marion County Fairgrounds."

There were also pictures of Thorpe—or Chief Bright Path—

standing in silhouette with the feathered regalia of a plains chieftain. It was explained that even though he was 38 years old he was still an ardent sportsman. "One of the secrets of his great lasting powers is the fact that he never quits training," said one of Lingo's more picturesque press releases. "Playing baseball in the summer, football in the fall, and hunting with Oorang Airedales in the winter keeps his body in the pink of physical condition at all times."

It further said that Thorpe was an expert at track and field, lacrosse, basketball, soccer, hockey, handball, tennis, golf, billiards, and bowling as well. He was a genius with a gun, rifle, or pistol. He was also a great roper and rider. Thorpe undoubtedly was a master at some sports that had not yet been invented. Even though the former Carlisle Indian School phenomenon could hardly get his muscles together for more than a few plunges into the line a game, Lingo was paying him $500 and he was going to get his money's worth in free advertising.

When the Oorang Indians opened the 1921 season against the Indianapolis Belmonts, they lined up this way: Long Time Sleep and Stilwell Sanooke were at ends, Xavier Downwind and Baptist Thunder at tackles, Elmer Busch and Ted Lone Wolf at guards, and Ted St. Germaine at center. The backfield had Joe Guyon at quarterback, Reginald Attache and Pete Calac at halfback, and David Running Deer at fullback. Among the reserves were Peter Black Bear, Joe Little Twig, Dick Deerslayer, Bemus Pierce, Newasha, Laughing Gas, Red Fang, and Arrowhead.

In their very first game, they not only hammered Indianapolis, which was not an NFL team, 33-0, but they took away $2,000 in profit and a Cherokee tackle named Chief Johnson, whom Thorpe stole from the Belmonts at halftime. The Indianapolis players protested that the Oorangs had used too many All Americas—Busch and Thorpe from Carlisle, Calac from West Virginia Wesleyan, St. Germaine from Yale, and Guyon from Carlisle and Georgia Tech.

"I doubt if any of our players ever walked across a college campus," said Robert Eddy, the Indianapolis general manager. "They said that they would leave their All-Americas out of the lineup and they didn't. The whole thing was played in a snowstorm. Thorpe gave the darndest exhibition of kicking at halftime that anybody had ever seen. Our club never stood a chance against them."

Despite their name and their excellent opening, the Oorangs were somewhat less successful than Sitting Bull was against George Armstrong Custer. They simply were not a good football team. They did not take Walter Lingo all that seriously. They did about what they pleased and won only three games in two years, losing 16 and finishing twelfth one season and eighteenth the next, beating out only the Rochester Jeffersons and the Louisville Brecks.

"The passing years have given them a powerful image," wrote John Short in the *Marion Star*, Harding's old paper. "The records tell you differently. They came and they gave the game incredible color at a time when it needed color badly. But you can look up the facts. The Chicago Bears beat them badly, even though Thorpe did his damndest. There are only a few people left alive who saw them play. But every one of the players is gone. There is a legend that Harding went to some of their games, but that simply isn't true. It never happened. Fancy makes it seem possible."

Ed Healey, a Dartmouth guard who played for the Chicago Bears against the Oorangs, blamed their lack of success on Thorpe, who was not a good coach. Healey claimed the Oorang team had no discipline. Whatever they felt was proper, the Oorangs did. "They were tough sons-a-guns on the field, giving you an elbow here and a knee there. But off the field they were marvelous, a whole lot of fun. They just had a good time and didn't care that much about football. The man who owned the Oorangs had them doing shows with his dogs at halftime. That was what the team was all about . . . it was there to advertise those Airedales. The Indians knew that football wasn't important to Lingo, so they just partied all the time."

The late Leon Boutwell said that on one occasion a bartender in Chicago at a place called the Everyman's Saloon decided that because the laws of Illinois demanded that a place call it quits at 2 A.M. that he stop serving drinks. He told the Oorang Indians that they would have to abide by those rules. They rejected this notion as being absurd. They took the bartender, put him in the telephone booth, and turned it upside down. They poured until 7 A.M., then went out and got slaughtered by the Bears.

The Indians played only a handful of games in Marion, spending long weeks on the road moving from Rochester to Toledo to Chicago to Minneapolis to St. Louis. In addition to the exhibitions with the dogs at halftime, Long Time Sleep wrestled a bear on the field. Whenever a carnival came to Marion, the Oorangs would send Long Time Sleep up against the guy every carnival had, the one who'd take on all comers. All you had to do was stay two rounds with the show's champion. The Oorangs would clean up and then party until dawn's early light.

"White people had this misconception about Indians," said the late Leon Boutwell, a Chippewa who played quarterback with the team for a short time. "They thought we were all wild men, even though almost all of us had been to college and were generally more civilized than they were. Well, it was a dandy excuse to raise hell and get away with it when the mood struck us. Since we were Indians we could get away with things the whites couldn't. Don't think we didn't take advantage of it."

One afternoon in St. Louis, a bunch of the Oorangs were whooping it up in a saloon when they decided that they had gone a bit too far with their merriment. They thought it best to get back to their hotel. The trolley was, unfortunately, headed in the wrong direction. The muscular men did the obvious. They picked up the trolley, turned it around on the tracks, and told the conductor where they wanted to go. He turned the trolley into an express.

"My uncle had grown weary of football by 1924," said Mrs. Knaur. "It was cutting into his profits from the kennel, so he turned the franchise back to the league. The Oorang Indians had served their purpose, which was to publicize the Airedales. If the team had won more games, perhaps he could have kept up the sponsorship. But it wasn't worth it. Some players moved on to other teams. Some, like Long Time Sleep, went back to the reservation. A few settled around LaRue and Marion and their children and grandchildren still live here."

It was time to go. The boom was over in Marion. The man who got to be president because he looked like one, Warren Gamaliel Harding, had been disgraced in the Teapot Dome oil scandal. A few months later he would be dead. The Oorang Indians were scattered. Never once since has Marion come up in expansion discussions. A pity! All it has left are its memories and the finest Airedales in the world.

MICKEY HERSKOWITZ

Goodbye, Johnny U.

Johnny Unitas, that most All-American of NFL heroes, was a throwback to a more innocent time. When he retired after the 1973 season, the fond farewells were many and varied. This version, written by Mickey Herskowitz for PRO! *magazine in 1974, captured the Hall-of-Fame quarterback at his most candid. Herskowitz, a columnist for the* HOUSTON POST *and author of numerous popular books, is one of the finest sports commentators of his era.*

JOHNNY UNITAS left football pretty much as he came into it—without ceremony. One day he was on the field, straining to recapture the rich talents of a spent career, and the next day he was sitting in front of a press conference, explaining dryly, "Your mind is willing but your body just wears out."

The scene was a little disjointed for some of us. Pickets milled outside the front gate. And the field—the one Unitas had walked away from—was wrong. It was catching a breeze off the blue Pacific, not Chesapeake Bay. For most of his fans, the time to get sentimental had been a year and a few months before, when the Baltimore management decided the services of Johnny U. were no longer needed. The treatment was cold and a little mean, but no worse, when you get down to it, than England selling the London Bridge.

So Unitas, voted the greatest quarterback of pro football's first 50 years, ran out the string in San Diego, where the owner, Eugene Klein, called him "a living work of art." The dramatic gesture has always been alien to Unitas's character, and to his work. Everything about him—his style, dress, speech—suggests understatement, and this is the way he went.

He was on the practice field when the moment of truth arrived. "The legs just wouldn't respond." he said. "They were sore and swollen and I couldn't maneuver. I stepped in a hole and sprained the left knee and the ankle slightly. I was getting a message."

As he limped off the field, John Unitas said to himself, "I think it's time to get out." It was a Sunday morning, and he went directly to Tommy Prothro, who had not exactly inherited a jelly roll when he hired on to coach the Chargers.

"Tommy," said Unitas in his best dropback-and-fire manner. "I think I'm gonna retire. I just can't do the things I'd like to do out there."

Prothro looked at him for a moment and nodded. "That might be best, John," he said, gently. "It must be embarrassing to someone like yourself, who has been able to do the things you've done, to find that it has become an effort."

"No," Unitas corrected. "It's not embarrassing. It's just the fact that I can't do them."

And so it was done. No theatrics. No evasion. No cute lines. Just Johnny Unitas, speaking with a directness that erased all doubt, the way a wet thumb wipes chalk from a blackboard. It was one of the qualities we came to know and enjoy. Even when he sparred with the press—which he did well. He didn't exactly trust the press, see, but he wasn't paranoid about it.

A moment that flashes to mind occurred during Super Bowl V week in January, 1971, the Colts against the Dallas Cowboys. During a group interview, he was asked about the system then favored by Tom Landry, in which Craig Morton received all the plays from the bench.

John allowed that he could never tolerate such an arrangement. "If the coach sent in all the plays," he said, "you might as well have a dummy back there." Suddenly, he sat up straight in his chair and his eyes narrowed. "Now, don't you guys go writing that I called Morton a dummy. I know you guys."

It took awhile, but the guys got to know him, too. They learned that he would not let you dig much below the surface. But his answers, far from being bland, had bite. And in all that he said or did, his enormous pride showed through.

I wondered, in that moment of melancholy that most men would feel, if Unitas thought about what his life would have been like if he had not made that contact with the Colts.

"They called me," he said.

I rephrased the question. "The connection," I said. "That's what I meant. I know they called you. But what if you hadn't connected with them? With any team. What would you have done?"

"I don't know," he said. "I don't think about things like that. What might have happened did happen."

There aren't many cornball stories like it anymore. Getting cut by the Steelers. A season of semipro ball for the Bloomfield Rams at six bucks a game and getting paid, in cash, in the basement of a dairy. The call from the Colts and, shazam, two championships before the 1950s had run out. He could do what the great ones always did: race the clock, and bring his team from behind.

But he was much more than that. He may have been pro football's Last Hero. We have plenty of superstars, of course. Television and big money make them easy to find. But there are not many heroes left, of the kind little kids can admire and copy, and whose stories are the kind you can read with your breakfast cereal. And that is what is poignant about the leavetaking of Johnny U.

You do not put it quite that way to Unitas, of course, unless you are prepared to watch a grown man throw up. But I got the idea across, and Johnny thought about it.

"That's what disturbs me about so much of what is written today," he said.

"The derogatory things. I know, the newspaper people say, 'We've got to print it like it is.' But I'd hate for my kids to idolize someone who is into drugs, who treats others with contempt, who thinks his talent is a license to behave any way he wishes. I've busted my ass all my life to watch where I go, what I do, with whom I'm seen. I've spent nineteen years in it and a few guys make headlines for smoking pot and now the public thinks all pro football players are potheads.

"Some of the fun has gone out of the game. The thing that was so irritating was that the players coming into the league today wouldn't take the time, or put forth the effort, of those of ten and twelve years back. They were more concerned then with the game and the team. Little else mattered. You don't have that now. They don't want to spend the time.

"That's one reason I wouldn't want to coach. I couldn't put up with a lot of the horse manure the coaches do now from some of the players. I wouldn't have any patience with the phoniness of some of 'em, and the lack of dedication. I'd probably end up with a squad of twenty-five. There are too many factions on the teams now. You got everything from temperance guys to women's lib.

"It's like one fellow said; he had been with a team a year and he got traded before he could learn all the handshakes."

It was very much in character that Unitas would be the first veteran to cross the picket line of the NFL Players Association, when the Chargers opened camp last summer. "Football has given me every opportunity I've ever had," he said, simply. "No one else I know, from a poor section of Pittsburgh, from a poor family, has been able to sit down for lunch with three or four presidents of the United States."

In the end, Unitas had played out one less than his uniform number—18 years. He was a winner. He was great. He brought us to the stadium and he made us cheer. He attempted more passes and completed more for more yards and touchdowns than anyone else who ever played the game.

Of course, it was a job, and he was paid well for it, and maybe there is no need to romanticize what he did. But there is a suspicion that we will not see another like him, and the urge is not to let him get away unapplauded, as John would have it. "I came into the league without any fuss," he said. "I'd just as soon leave it that way. There's no difference that I can see in retiring from pro football, or quitting a job at the Pennsy Railroad. I did something I wanted to do, and went as far as I could go."

To appreciate how far, you have to know the conditions under which he came to the Baltimore Colts. Weeb Ewbank was looking for a backup quarterback (to George Shaw) when he invited Unitas to a tryout camp. "He came in," recalls Weeb, "and we took pictures of him in practice. Not movies. Still pictures. In those days, we didn't have any film equipment. The only good stills did was, when you had a bunch of kids at a tryout, you could keep the pictures in front of you and it helped to remember which ones they were.

"We took pictures of John under center, and again when he set up and right at the last, when he followed through. That was the thing we noticed right away, the way he followed through. It was exceptional. The pictures showed it clearly. His arm went through so far that he turned his hand over like a pitcher. I often wondered how he kept from injuring his arm, because it was like throwing a screwball, and all those guys end up with crooked arms. When he followed through his fingers turned over and you could see the back of his hand. And when he used to throw a lot of times, with this tremendous follow-through, he'd snag his fingernails on the back of a guy's shirt or he'd jam his fingers on somebody's helmet. He had to be careful of that. I worried that he might get what they call a tennis elbow but, boy, I saw the way he could throw and I never bothered him about it. You knew right away. He was in camp in no time at all and we knew that as soon as he learned the offense he would be our quarterback."

Years later Ewbank would be across the field, coaching the New York Jets, on what may have been the saddest Sunday of John Unitas's career—the day the Jets upset the Colts in Super Bowl III. Unitas spent most of the game as a spectator, coming off the bench late in the third quarter, trying to wake up the echoes one more time, rallying the Colts as he had done so often. And on the Jets' bench a strange thing happened. Seeing the quarterback he had developed at

Baltimore, Ewbank forgot himself. Weeb actually clapped his hands and shouted out to the field, "No interceptions now, John."

Later, when it was over, a writer asked Unitas, "How good is Joe Namath?"

"Sixteen to seven," Unitas replied, saying it all.

Carroll Rosenbloom, who owned the Colts then (and now the Rams), and whose relationship with Unitas was almost paternal, got his first tip about the crewcut Louisville University product from Art Rooney, whose Steelers had rejected him. "He had been in camp a few days," recalled Rosenbloom, "and Rooney called me about something or other. He said, 'Carroll, you got that boy Uni-TASS. I want to tell you something. My sons tell me that guy was the best-looking quarterback we had in camp and my coach [Walt Kiesling] never let him THROW the ball.' After that, I watched John in practice. He was so relaxed, so loose, and a very likable kid. This whole time we were wondering if we needed to trade for another quarterback, or if Unitas could do the job backing up George Shaw. We went into Chicago and were leading that game by ten points and, in the middle of the second quarter, they ruined Shaw's career. The Bears hit him high and low and across the mouth, broke his nose and knocked out most of his teeth, and he was a sight. They had to carry Shaw off, and Unitas had to come into the game. I must say he looked horrible and we lost it [58-27]; in fact, the first pass Unitas threw was intercepted for a touchdown.

"I went down to the locker room. John was never one to show his emotions, but he was sitting in front of his locker, still hadn't taken off his uniform and had his head hanging between his legs so that all you could see was the top of that crewcut. I walked over and got him under the chin and lifted his head up. I said, 'Now look, John, that was not your fault. You haven't had an opportunity to play and no one is blaming you. You're not only going to be a good one in this league, you're going to be a great one.'

"Well, I was just trying to build him up, get him out of the dumps. I wasn't sure right then he'd even make the club. But many times over the years John would ask me about that, how I could be so sure he'd make it. I'd tell him, 'What the hell, John, I'm an old jock. I know talent.'"

Johnny Unitas knew he had arrived—knew he had it made—when he returned to New York two weeks after quarterbacking the Colts to that colossal victory over the Giants in the title game of 1958. The Colts had won in sudden death, in what was to become The Greatest Game Ever Played.

He and his wife wandered into what was then one of the city's most exclusive night spots, the Harwyn Club, and the headwaiter recognized him, the hot new celebrity in town. "Right this way, Mr. Unitas," he sang out. They were led to a corner table, the most prominent in the joint. It was at that very table, the headwaiter confided proudly, that Eddie Fisher and Liz Taylor had their rendezvous the night before Eddie flew home to Hollywood to tell Debbie Reynolds he wanted a divorce.

It was not your ordinary table. It wasn't your ordinary decade, either. But Johnny Unitas was right for the times and perfect for pro football, which had begun to take off. The 1958 sudden-death encounter, more than any other single event, gave the game new visibility, and Johnny U. was its hero.

With a touch of irony, Unitas says, "I've always felt that it wasn't a real good football game until the last two minutes, and then the overtime. We played pretty well but we should have blown New York out of the stadium and we didn't, then we had to come from behind in order to tie and then go on to win it. Just the fact that it was the first overtime in championship play, that was enough to make people feel they had seen something fantastic.

"They always forget that the month before, in the game that clinched the division championship and put us into the playoff, San Francisco had us down twenty-seven to seven at the half and we came back to beat 'em thirty-five to twenty-seven. That was a much better game. Our defense shut out Y.A. Tittle in the second half, and that was quite an accomplishment."

You ask Unitas how it feels and what it has meant to him.

"I'm not philosophical," he reminds you, "one way or another. With me it has always been point blank—yes or no, can you or can't you. I just couldn't play anymore. It was time to quit and get out. I was taking up someone else's time.

"The people you meet, the friendships, the characters you have the enjoyment of playing with—there have been so many, Alex Hawkins, Big Daddy Lipscomb, Jim Parker, Bert Rechichar, I could name a dozen—that's what you take out of it. For me the thrill wasn't only in winning. It was working with people who were as dedicated as you are, working at times like a big machine.

"Mentally, I haven't changed. I feel the same. I care the same. If I could have gotten a leg transplant I'd play for another thirty years. But I couldn't move anymore. The way it was, it was like standing in the middle of a road and saying, 'Okay, Buick, run me down.'"

Maybe one only imagines it, but a little emotion, a glimpse of regret, seemed to flicker lightly between the words. You have to look for it, of course. For 19 years Unitas has been about as emotional as a large rock.

But he was hardly humorless. It was a wry kind of humor, the kind that worked for a slow grin, not a belly laugh. Once he said that he never believed in looking back, and he added a familiar line, "Something might be gaining on you."

He was told that he had selected a quote from a legendary source, and he seemed honestly unaware. "Who said it," he asked, "Paul Brown? Benjamin Franklin?"

"One of your contemporaries," came the answer. "Satchel Paige."

"Oh," said Unitas, "is he old?"

Another time he described what it was like in the huddle: "When the score's loose, and you're way ahead, even the guards are offering you plays. When it gets nice and tight, you ask somebody for help and you don't hear a damned thing."

Now for the first time in 20 years, Johnny Unitas at 41 has found himself around the house in September, watching the leaves turn, enjoying the colors of autumn in his own yard, performing the chores familiar to us ordinary mortals.

The house is a five-bedroom, rambling white stucco, with two front pillars lending a colonial touch. It sits on seven acres of prime Maryland woodlands, the real home field now for the Unitas team, which includes three dogs and now a sixth child, Francis Joseph. He was four months old when Unitas retired, and probably the only guy around less concerned than his old man.

He spent his first weeks as a civilian "mowing the grass, cutting down trees, splitting wood, and changing diapers." He has the restaurant in Baltimore, "The Golden Arm," and land interests in Florida, and no one expects Johnny U. to spend much time dwelling in the past.

But the times and the game have changed. Remember the fifties? Ike was just what the country needed, a president who didn't meddle in the affairs of government. We escaped our problems by plunging into sports, and some guys would have played football for an ice cream cone. Unitas, the son of Lithuanian immigrants who became the most admired quarterback of his time, was part of that era. There may not be another folk hero like him; it just doesn't happen that way anymore.

It was a touch of pride that no one can begrudge him, that prompted Unitas to emphasize the fact that the legs, not the golden arm, finally undid him. You suspect that if the NFL ever adopted a designated passer rule, ol' Johnny Unitas might come back.

JERRY IZENBERG

"Time to Tee it Up"
from *No Medals for Trying*

Syndicated sports columnist Jerry Izenberg has covered NFL football for more than 30 years, most recently for the NEWARK STAR-LEDGER. *In 1989, he spent a week with coach Bill Parcells and the New York Giants as they prepared for a crucial game with their division rivals, the Philadelphia Eagles. What materialized from that week was* NO MEDALS FOR TRYING, *an intimate look at the inner workings of a football organization from top to bottom. In this selection, the fourth quarter is about to begin and the score is tied. We soon learn if all the preparation paid off.*

FOURTH QUARTER

So this is what everyone thought it would be. The Eagles and the Giants never do it simply. They never do it gracefully. This series has become shot-and-a-beer football played by two teams and two coaching staffs that would spit in your eye if you told them they bore any resemblance to each other.

And it may be that at times they do not. But put them on the same field and the result is always the same. Somebody will make a terrible mistake and spend the rest of the game trying to mitigate it—and they generally do.

Then, invariably, it will come down to the fourth quarter and what wins it will be as unexpected as it is dramatic. Both sides had that thought with which to conjure when the clock started running in the fourth and the Philadelphia Eagles took possession of the wind.

It began with the Eagles' defense suddenly falling upon the

Giants' offensive line as if they had turned the pages of this particular book back to the game's opening minutes.

The message is delivered to the Giants immediately. On second and 3, Anderson hammers his way for four yards but Jumbo is caught tripping and they are set back 5 yards. The Eagles are coming with all they have and if Simms didn't know better, you couldn't blame him for thinking that it wasn't weather-induced vapor streaming from their mouths—it was pure fire.

Simms rolls to his right, sets up to throw and then sees the Eye of the Dragon. Untouched by human hands, Mike Pitts is barreling through an alley of flesh and headed straight for him. There is no time to throw and nowhere to go. Pitts levels him and the Giants lose another 9 yards.

On third down, Simms must throw after moving forward to avoid a forest of white jerseys and he has no chance to complete his pass to Turner. Now Sean Landeta must come off the bench and kick into the maw of the wind from the Giants' 49.

Once the ball gains altitude it seems to freeze and fall straight down. It rolls dead on the Eagles' 26.

Cunningham goes straight into the wind for Byars, but this time the wind is friend to no quarterback. The ball sails beyond everyone's reach. On second down, he sends Sherman bulling straight ahead for 2, but Ron Solt, the right guard, is detected putting a stranglehold on Howard's waist and it costs the Eagles 10.

After what follows next you cannot find a frostbite case in the stands or a man on the Giants' bench who does not think they are about to win this game.

On second and 20 Cunningham tosses short to Byars, coming out of the backfield. But Adrian White has read the play perfectly. He slants from left to right and slams Byars to the ground 3 yards behind the line of scrimmage. It is now third down and 23 to go at the Eagles' 12.

This is where number 12 kills you—and the Giants know it. This is where he slides and glides and scrambles and ambles and suddenly you have to go all the way down to the other end of the field for the next snap.

But not this time. Cunningham drops back . . . and back . . . and back. But the lanes are plugged and Erik Howard fights through a wall of blockers, pushing them toward the quarterback. Marshall comes in from the side. Howard strips away David Alexander in the final instant and nails Cunningham to the artificial turf.

Much of the quarterback's body falls across the goal line. Marshall is leaping in the air with his closed palms pressed flat against each other and held over his head, signaling a safety.

But the refs spot the ball at the Philadelphia 2.

As the defense leaves the field, they are met by the Giants' entire team. The crowd is standing and screaming. The wind is rattling toward the Giants' goal line. With such a set, "The Twilight Zone" could tape thirty episodes.

Now the Giants' punt return team is on the field, remembering all the film and all the planning centering around Runager's lack of distance. Unnoticed in the confusion, Cunningham has walked to the sidelines and he is talking to Buddy Ryan.

They know something that nobody on the other side of the field does. Back on Thursday, with the wind howling down in South Philly, Randall Cunningham sought out Gizmo Williams and told him: "Don't make any plans after practice today. You and me got a date."

Alone in Veterans Stadium, there was Randall Cunningham with a bag of balls and Gizmo was down the field. Cunningham was working on his punting.

"I can kick," Cunningham would later say. "I kicked in college. I know all about that wind up in the Meadowlands. I thought there just might come a time when I could fool everybody." At the University of Nevada at Las Vegas, number 12 had been the team's regular punter and had led the nation one season. Just a year earlier he had set the Giants back on their heels with a surprise 55-yard quick kick in Philadelphia. But that was gimmick stuff.

He kicked and kicked on Thursday until his leg began to hurt.

"Now," Randall Cunningham said. "Buddy, I'd like to do it now."

"Well, go ahead, if you think you can get it done."

So, suddenly, Randall Cunningham was running back onto the field, waving Runager off to the sidelines.

Years from now, the Giants who played in this football game and the men who sat up night after night with nothing but number 12 on their minds will be able to tell you that they had stopped Randall Cunningham from beating them with his right arm—he would complete just nine passes for 130 yards.

And they had stopped Randall Cunningham from beating them with both his legs—he would run for just 10 yards, 7 of them on one play.

What they could not do was stop him from beating them with his right foot.

Parcells is watching Meggett standing all alone in the face of the wind, thinking "He'll catch it. They're doing the right thing. Cunningham can outkick Runager. But this is our park. We win these games. Meggett will catch it and will stick it in the end zone."

Cunningham is standing straight up at the point where the blue-and-white artwork meets in the end zone. At six-foot-four, he is a solitary figure outlined against the glare of the stadium lights.

And the wind is breathing on the back of his helmet like a living thing.

Just down the road in the state's largest inner cities, places like Newark and Jersey City and Paterson, they call this kind of wind the Hawk. They know all about the Hawk. It rattles down empty streets and slams into deserted doorways and only a fool would stand in its path. When the Hawk visits the Meadowlands, it grows teeth. All week long the Giants had prayed for it. The Hawk won a lot of games for them in this park. In the Year of the Super Bowl, it even won a conference championship for them, blowing the Washington Redskins into submission.

In thirty seconds the Giants would learn something they had never even once considered. The Hawk belongs to no man.

With the Giants' kick return linemen breathing fire in front of him and the Hawk blowing pure ice at his back, Randall Cunningham took the snap and put his foot into the ball.

Back at the Giants' 38-yard line, David Meggett watched the ball, which seemed to take forever to drop. It was angled off to his left and he was sliding over trying to get a fix on it. At the last possible instant he decided to field it on the bounce.

The ball had traveled 60 yards in the air. When it hit, the Hawk pursed his lips and started to blow. The ball skipped. It slithered. It rolled. By the time Meggett picked it up, he was on his own 7-yard line. Desperately, he tried to turn it upfield. He managed just nine yards before Sammy Lilly and Dave Rimington sandwiched him and sprawled him on the ground.

And for an instant there was a hint of the stone-cold, cemetery silence of which Parcells had spoken when he was recalling the opener down in Washington. The only noise you could hear was coming from underneath green capes on the Eagles' sideline.

As Meggett came to the sidelines, Parcells walked over to him. "Come on," he said, "you've got to play with your head." And then, as the enormity of the moment seemed to set in and as though it had suddenly reaffirmed what every coach knows—that all the hours of talking and planning mean nothing if your people can't translate them into the deed on Sunday—he said in a much louder voice: "This is the championship. Don't you understand what we're doing here? This is the championship game!"

Randall Cunningham had punted the ball 91 yards—a third of which had accrued when the ball was permitted to drop untouched.

The Giants were 84 yards from the Eagles' goal and they had to move the ball into the bite of the Hawk.

And then there were the teeth of the Eagle defense.

On the first play, Simms fails to connect with Mowatt on a bad pass and it costs even more when the Giants are penalized for an illegal formation.

Second and 15, the ball on the 11.

Simms is not in the shotgun. At the snap of the ball, Reggie White breaks free of Riesenberg and is headed toward Simms. At the other side of the line, Mike Golic is hooked with William Roberts. But now Golic forces him back, spins off his block, and is running free. Simms sees White and takes two steps forward to avoid him. In that instant, Golic has circled in from behind the quarterback and wraps him up. The ball squirts free and Pitts recovers it on the 7.

In the stands, they are chanting for one more miracle: "defense . . . defense . . . defense." As for the Eagles, they have dumped old slant 31 in the garbage can for this one. Now they will go with the red zone plays that got them here.

On first down, Cunningham lofts the fade to the corner Belichick had worried over during the week. Pepper Johnson is out there just as they practiced it, but the receiver, Robert Drummond, has a step on him. Both men go up. Drummond juggles the ball and it squirts away, falling for an incompletion.

Again the chant: "defense . . . defense . . . defense." And again, Cunningham goes to an old formula. He lays the ball in Byars's stomach and the big back hits the right side of the line. The Eagles' line gets off the ball quickly. Byars's legs are churning. Banks hurls himself into the hole just as Reasons angles in from the side. The ball is spotted at the 2.

Over on the sidelines, Cunningham is talking with two coaches, shaking his head, and gesturing. He knows what he wants to call now and apparently they are going to let him. As he trots back out, the Giants are shouting at each other and shaking their fists. They have been here before in this very game. Now they are telling each other it can be done again.

Cunningham is over center, calling the cadence. Behind him, Byars is the lone set back. At the snap, Keith Jackson, lined up on the right side, throws his body into John Washington and drives him back. Byars reads off a block by his right guard, Ron Solt, who moves Pepper Johnson in the other direction and he powers through the hole and into the end zone.

There are ten minutes left in this game, but as far as the Giants are concerned it might as well be ten seconds.

The Giants will never again get closer than the Eagles' 30-yard line.

POSTGAME LOCKER ROOM

Phil Simms is slumped in an upright position on one of the training tables. Ronnie Barnes is trying to clean up Simms's left hand, which is covered with blood and has been bleeding ever since it was hit full force by someone's helmet. As Barnes works, Simms is motionless, his chin on his chest. The trainer crouches to cut the tape off his ankles. Both Tim and Wellington Mara have paused to pass some kind of encouragement to him but he stares straight ahead. Now George Young is talking to him. He draws no response.

Out in the big locker room there is more silence. Odessa Turner sits motionless on the stool before his locker. The sprained knee, with which he had continued to play, throbs bitterly. But he is as angry with himself and with the offense's failure as the rest of them. He does not limp off to Barnes for treatment.

David Meggett is away from his locker. In a moment, they will open the doors and let the press inside. When they arrive, Meggett will not be there.

Down the hall, in the big classroom, Bill Parcells faces the worst moment of the afternoon. Meeting the press in New York is like nowhere else. The television people and the still cameras, the largest number of beat writers and columnists and sidebar writers in the league make movement almost impossible. Today their ranks are swelled by a large Philadelphia contingent and a variety of writers from around the country who are here because of the game's overall significance.

He is totally surrounded by them. Because professional football is a business, he does not have the luxury to mourn or curse or smack the wall in private. The league rules say the locker room must be open twenty minutes after each game and the coach must meet the press.

"You couldn't say that this was one of Phil Simms's better days," he starts. "I told them [the Giants] before you came in that you cannot make mistakes like that and win. I think you'll try to win but that's up to you. It looks like Philadelphia will win the division. There isn't much we can do about that now. Yes, I think Meggett should have caught the ball and, yes, he's fumbling too much."

Within the hour, he would leave the building. Judy Parcells had already said good-bye to her children and was headed home to wait. There would be no steak dinner at Manny's tonight.

Back in the dressing room, Phil Simms had returned to his locker. He knew what was coming but he had to do the right thing.

"It's hard to go out there and screw it up but I did it," he said. "I can't blame the protection. I had enough time to dig myself out of the hole I put us in. My ankle wasn't the reason. I could move well enough to buy the time I needed. And it wasn't the gloves. I've played long enough not to make those mistakes."

And then he limped away.

Johnie Cooks is exhausted. "We might see them again in the playoffs," he says. "Who knows? But what we're gonna find out these next few weeks is who wants to win around here and who wants to pay the price."

In the row of lockers across from Cooks, Erik Howard is shaking his head. His hand is swollen again. There is blood on his pants. "We [the defense] hold 'em to 3 points until the last quarter and they win—ridiculous. We gave it away. We [the defense] don't get out there until we're down 14-0, we fight our way back in. We even stop 'em on the goal. Shit, Merry Christmas, Philadelphia. We should have gift-wrapped the damned thing, mailed it to them, and not even bothered to show up."

7:30 P.M., UPPER SADDLE RIVER, NEW JERSEY

He is sitting in the brown chair in the family room, the halfeaten sandwich by his side. On the television screen, the Chicago Bears and the Minnesota Vikings have become a blur. Now he sighs, rises from the chair, and walks slowly up the stairs to bed.

At 4:00 A.M., his private demons will hammer him awake. He does not go back to sleep.

At 6:00 A.M., he is on his way back to the office.

CHARLES MAHER

Even His Best Friends Will Tell Him

Think your job is thankless? Talk to Norm Schachter, long-time NFL official. The peacekeeping zebras of the gridiron can't take an airplane or go home to their families without hearing about the call they blew a few hours earlier. Charler Maher profiled Schachter for PRO! *magazine in 1973. Maher worked for the* ASSOCIATED PRESS, *then the* LOS ANGELES TIMES, *before moving to Idaho in the early 1980s, where he now lives in semi-retirement.*

YEARS AGO, WHILE OFFICIATING a Rams 49ers game in Los Angeles, Norm Schachter made a call against the home team. The fans, willing as always to examine one side of every question, let him have it.

Schachter's oldest son, Tom, then about nine, was in the stands. His father had a talk with him afterward.

"Tom, you've got to take it as an impersonal thing when the crowd gets on your dad like that. You have to realize these are home-team fans and they get excited. Legitimately so. I know you probably hear a lot of talk in the stands, and I hope you didn't take it personally."

"I took it personally," said Tom. "You blew the call."

Schachter, the NFL's senior official, is used to the zings and arrows. He's second-guessed on not one job but two. Once a high school principal, he's now an assistant superintendent in the Los Angeles school system, in charge of 52 San Fernando Valley schools with a combined enrollment of 60,000. A school administrator, like a football official, gets a lot of help from the sidelines.

Norm illustrated his predicament not long ago in an interview at his home. He said he'd be flying east to do a game and the guy in the next seat would be a football fan. He'd swear he'd seen Schachter somewhere before. A conversation would start, and before long the guy would be asking for tickets, or for inside information on a game, or for an explanation of a disputed call the Sunday before.

"So I started saying I was a high school principal," Norm said. "But then all the militancy started in the schools and people would get on me about that. An educator can always get advice. So I took to saying I was an undertaker. It worked. Nobody would talk to me."

They talk to him plenty on the field. But they may not always be as angry as they look. Sometimes, they may just be playing to the crowd, as the mischievous George Halas was one afternoon in Chicago.

"I was working the Bears-Giants championship game in 1963," Norm said, "and Halas came out on the field at halftime. He ran up to me with his program and started waving it in my face. It looked as if he were really chewing me out but all he said was, 'Which way do we go in the second half, Norm?' I said, 'The other way, coach.' He got about ten yards away, then whirled and came storming back at me, waving that program in my face. When he got up to me he said, 'Thanks.' By now, the fans were really turned on. You should have heard them. I figured I'd be lucky to get out of there alive."

Then there was a game in New York. The Cowboys against the Giants. As Norm remembers, a division title was riding on it.

"Pete Gogolak came in to kick a field goal from the twelve. One of the Cowboys—I think it was Bob Lilly—broke through and blocked the ball. Gogolak, without breaking stride, caught the ball with his left foot as it came off the ground and kicked it again. Greatest bit of reaction I ever saw. Darned if the ball didn't sail between the goal posts."

Was it good?

"Well, sixty-two thousand people thought it was good," Norm said. "I guess everybody watching all over the country did. But I threw my flag. The Giants all charged me. 'What's the flag for?' they said.

"'I don't know,' I said. 'But something's wrong.'

"And it was wrong. I'd reacted instinctively, as you do with experience. You can't kick a loose ball. If Gogolak had caught the ball with his hands, and had control of it, he could have kicked it again. But this was a loose ball. I called it a touchback and gave the Cowboys the ball on their twenty.

"Don Meredith (the Dallas quarterback) came running in and said, 'Nice call, Norm.' Of course, he had absolutely no idea what I'd called."

Another time Schachter was working a game in Cleveland. Frank Ryan, the Cleveland quarterback, had just gotten a doctorate in mathematics.

On second-and-nine, the Browns made seven yards. But the other team was offside.

Schachter: "Frank, you've got an option. You made seven, so it will be third-and-two. Or you can take the offside and it's second-and-four."

Ryan: "Second-and-four? Wait a minute, Norm. How do you get four?"

Schachter: "Well, Frank, you work it this way: You start with nine and take away five. That leaves four. Back home, we call that basic math."

Ryan called Schachter something else. But he was smiling when he did it.

Schachter had another ready comeback when challenged by Bob Skoronski on an unforgettable, unbearable afternoon in Green Bay. It was the 1967 NFL title game between the Cowboys and Packers. Game-time temperature: 13 degrees below zero.

"I blew my whistle to start the game, and that was the last whistle anybody really heard all day," Norm said. "All the whistles froze. I guess nobody knows that. We called the whole game verbally and with arm signals.

"Joe Connell, my umpire, tried to blow his whistle, but he just got a little tweet. When he took the whistle out of his mouth, part of his lip came with it. I'd put a rubber nipple on mine so it wouldn't freeze to my lips.

"Television needed a time out in the fourth quarter so I called one. Well, it was really freezing now. Skoronski, the offensive captain for Green Bay, came running up."

Skoronski: "Norm, who the hell called that time out?"

Schachter: "I did."

Skoronski: "What for?"

Schachter: "For the players' pension fund."

Skoronski: "Great call. Great call."

Schachter remembered another title game, one that got people down on him for a call he didn't even make. "It was the sudden-death game between Green Bay and Baltimore in 1965," he said. "Don Chandler won it for Green Bay with a field goal. The call was disputed, but I'm sure it was good.

"On a play like this, I don't make the call. I just relay the signal. I've got other things to watch. For instance, whether somebody runs into the kicker. But they thought I called it. I'm told that Chuck Thompson of Baltimore, who announced the game, ended his sports show for three months after that by saying, 'Good night, Norm Schachter, wherever you are.'"

Referees run into second-guessers everywhere. Before Super Bowl V in Miami, Schachter had breakfast at his hotel coffee shop.

Waitress: "May I have your order?"

Schachter: "I don't know whether to have ham and eggs or sausage and eggs."

Waitress: "That'll probably be the toughest call you have all day."

Schachter: "Well, let me have the ham and eggs."

Waitress: "You blew that one, too."

Years earlier, on the morning of a 49ers-Colts game in Baltimore, Norm was having breakfast in a hotel dining room. It was being remodeled, and there was a partition right behind him. A waitress accidentally bumped it, and it started to fall on him. Leo Nomellini of the 49ers, seated nearby, jumped up and grabbed the partition.

"Saved me from getting a hell of a bang on the head," Schachter said. "I said, 'Thanks, Leo. I appreciated that.'

"Leo was a good player. Worked hard. Seldom fouled. But that afternoon I caught him and called a penalty."

Schachter: "Leo, you're using your hands."

Nomellini: "I knew I should have let the damn thing fall on you."

Sometimes, the language is not that polite. A Minnesota player once blew his noodle and cursed at Schachter. Schachter called a 15-yard penalty. Norm Van Brocklin, then coaching the Vikings, asked Schachter at halftime what the penalty was for.

Schachter: "Number fifty-eight called me a son of a bitch, coach, and nobody calls me a son of a bitch except you."

Van Brocklin (smiling): "You son of a bitch."

That wasn't the worst thing that ever happened to Schachter in a Minnesota game. In 1969, the Vikings played the Colts on the second weekend of the season. For Schachter, it turned out to be the end of the season.

"I saw the right tackle for Minnesota miss his block, and I knew the defensive end was going to get to the quarterback, Joe Kapp. I moved back, waiting for Kapp to get hit, and he got it, from the blind side. He fumbled. I went behind him to cover the play. The tackle who had missed the block was coming back to try to help out. I stumbled and he ran up my back. I heard a pop, like a gun."

The tendon on Schachter's right leg had snapped. "It was pulled right off the bone and severed," he said. "A Baltimore player picked up the fumble and went about seventy-nine yards, but Don Shinnick was holding so they brought the ball back. I'd been wiped out on a play that didn't even count.

"I did four and a half hours of therapy a day for the next year. I'd exercise in the morning ten or fifteen minutes, then ride the stationary bicycle five miles. On my lunch break at school, I'd swim about twenty minutes, and in the afternoon I'd drag myself around the track about a mile. Then I'd use the whirlpool for a half hour and walk two miles at night. It was a four-shower day for me."

Schachter got into officiating in 1941, while coaching high school ball in Redlands, California. "I think it was a college scrimmage," he said. "They needed somebody to fill in. I liked it right away."

Norm went into the Marines in 1941, but he returned to officiating in 1942. He worked hundreds of football, basketball, and baseball games in the Los Angeles area. Then, in 1953, he got a call from Bert Bell, the NFL commissioner. Norm has not had many fall weekends off since.

"I fly about 120,000 miles a season," he said. "I guess I must have flown two million miles altogether. The league office tells us about ten days in advance where we're going, and we leave home Saturday morning. The home team will leave a projector in the referee's name at our hotel, and the league sends out a film of the game we worked the week before. We meet after dinner to look over the film, review our mechanics, and see if there's anything we might do better.

"Most of our officials don't really need the jobs. Most have been very successful in other fields. We have druggists, lawyers, deans of colleges, business people. Officiating is just something they enjoy doing.

"For me, it's more than a part-time job. I make up the tests they give officials and work on the rule book. It runs about eighty-seven pages now and we're redoing the whole thing. I spend about a half hour a day on the rules. You can turn to any page in the book and ask me about a paragraph, and I can probably quote the rule. If you miss on a judgment call, that's one thing. Everybody's going to do that once in a while. But I'd hate to be wrong on a rule, to have forgotten something I should have known."

Schachter gave up coaching years ago but admits he still does a little of it—in his head. Before the offensive team lines up, he'll often call the play to himself, trying to anticipate what the quarterback will do.

"About nine times out of ten you can tell what they're going to do," he said. "I may change my position when I know something is coming up, but I'll change only slightly so the players won't pick up on it and key on me. I try not to go near huddles. When you've done enough games, you just about know what hole they're going to look for.

"In our job, you can't really watch the game. One of my prime responsibilities as referee is to watch the quarterback. The referee has overall command of the game and stands behind the offense. The umpire is behind the defense, close to the line. The field judge is downfield. The head linesman runs the chains, keeps track of the downs. Across the field from him is the line judge. The back judge is on the same side, only downfield. None of us can really see the game. I mean the whole game. If you get caught up in it, you'll miss something in your own area of responsibility. I went over to the sideline one time and there was a young official standing there, really wrapped up in the game. 'Wow!' he said. 'Great play!' I knew he wasn't going to be around very long. He wasn't."

To keep his job, an NFL official must consistently be in position to make the correct call. To be in position, he must be in condition. Schachter works out every day, riding his stationary bicycle five miles.

But everything considered, he probably gets his best workout on Sunday.

"I think we cover a good four or five miles during the afternoon," he said. "And that's not even counting after the game, when they chase us."

RAY DIDINGER

The Best Team of the Best Years

Ray Didinger has been writing insightful stories for Philadelphia newspapers (first the defunct BULLETIN, *then the* DAILY NEWS*) for more than 25 years, which isn't long enough to give him detailed recollection of the Eagles of the late 1940s. So he looked up several of the principals of those championship teams—they played for the NFL title three consecutive years, winning in 1948 and '49— including quarterback Tommy Thompson, tackle Al Wistert, and Pro Football Hall-of-Fame halfback Steve Van Buren. Didinger's flavorful story first ran in* PRO! *magazine in 1983.*

THE GREAT WAR WAS OVER. At last.

Sixteen million American men and women were back from the conflict, picking up the textbooks and lunch pails they had put down four years earlier, finally reunited with their dreams.

It was a festive time, a time of peace and prosperity, pride, and hope. America was alive, vital in a way it had never been before. It was a nation of star-spangled idealists, determined to build a new and better world.

Sam Goldwyn summed up the mood of the country with the title of his Oscar-winning film, *The Best Years of Our Lives*. The late forties really were The Best Years.

They were the years when 53 million Americans had jobs, when unemployment was less than two percent. The national income tripled, and the economy swelled with $150 billion in postwar money.

They were the years of convenience and leisure, the years of the first drive-in banks, frozen food, television, and the Kinsey Report. They were the years of jukebox swing, Henry Aldrich, and Give-'em-hell, Harry.

In many ways, the Philadelphia Eagles were a metaphor for that time. They were a diverse and cocky bunch, unpolished and a bit ragged around the edges, cast together not so much by planning as by fate.

They came from college campuses, B-24s, and fox holes, from shipyards and steel mills, from the sandlots and the trade schools, from the tenements and the Bayou.

One-by-one, they straggled into Philadelphia and they became the champions of professional football, the duffel-bag dynasty. They were The Best Team of The Best Years.

We weren't typical college kids. There were a lot of guys like me, just back from the war. I was in the 35th Infantry. Went in as a private, came out a second lieutenant. Yeah, we saw some heavy fighting. We were in the Battle of the Bulge. I don't like to talk about the war, even now. I just know when I got out, I was happy to be alive.

—Pete Pihos, end, 1947–1955

Al Wistert was an All-America tackle at Michigan. He was captain of the College All-Star team that upset the NFL-champion Washington Redskins.

Al Wistert was a winner, a man accustomed to success and pampering. For him, joining the Eagles as the top draft pick in 1943 was like being sold into bondage.

"The Eagles were a lousy team back then," Wistert recalls. "They had been around ten years, and they hadn't had a winning season yet. Their players were the ones nobody else wanted.

"My first year was the year the Eagles and the [Pittsburgh] Steelers merged. They called the team the Steagles. All that meant was we had twice as many lousy players because the Steelers were just as bad as the Eagles.

"I'll never forget when I showed up for the first practice. We trained at St. Joseph's College on City Line Avenue. We dressed in this dingy, little room under the stands. Two 60-watt bulbs hanging from the ceiling. We couldn't even see to lace our shoes.

"We didn't practice on the main field. We practiced on this other field, behind a gas station on 54th Street. It was like a prairie. Weeds three feet high. Broken bottles, trash thrown all over the place.

"The coaches weren't even there. They didn't get the wake-up call at their hotel. The players were standing around, not doing anything. I remember Bill Hewitt, a veteran, smoking a cigarette. I couldn't believe my eyes.

"At Michigan, the facilities were first class, the practices were run like clockwork. Everything reflected pride and a winning attitude. Here I was in the pros and it was a farce. Nobody seemed to know, or care, what went on.

"My first impression of Greasy Neale [head coach] was he was the most uncouth man I ever met," Wistert says. "He cussed and swore. Foul language bothered me back then. I wasn't used to it.

"I was raised by my mother and three sisters. I never heard that kind of language around the house. I never heard it playing ball in high school or college, either. My coaches didn't believe in it.

"At Michigan, I was coached by Fritz Crisler, who played his college ball under Amos Alonzo Stagg. Stagg, of course, once studied to be a preacher. He never swore, neither did Fritz.

"So I joined the Eagles, and here was Greasy calling us every name in the book. It actually hurt my play. One day, Greasy took me aside and asked what was wrong. I said, 'I can't play for you. You don't know how to handle men.' We didn't speak the rest of the year.

"But I came back the following season and my feelings for Greasy changed. I began to see through all that shouting. I realized Greasy didn't mean anything by it. He was just a stickler for perfection. He was driven to win."

Earle Neale came up the hard way. As a young man, he was a center fielder for the Cincinnati Reds. Later, he took a job as an assistant football coach at Yale University.

Greasy wasn't exactly the Ivy League type, but he had a knack for beating Harvard, so the Eli family made allowances. He might have stayed at Yale forever except Lex Thompson, the dashing steel tycoon who owned the Eagles, lured him to Philadelphia for $8,000 a year.

Thompson, in a complicated deal, swapped his Pittsburgh franchise with Bert Bell and Art Rooney for the Eagles. Bell tried to run the whole operation himself, with little success. He coached the Eagles for five years and won 10 games. Finally, in 1941, Bell bailed out.

Neale had to rebuild the franchise from the ground up. It wasn't easy with a war going on; good players were hard to find. He won four games his first two years and five in 1943, the year the Eagles merged with the Steelers.

But Neale was pouring a foundation. Each year, he added a few quality athletes. Two-way linemen Wistert, Frank (Bucko) Kilroy, and Vic Sears. Running backs Bosh Pritchard and Jack Hinkle. Quarterback Tommy Thompson, blinded in one eye by a childhood accident.

All the while, Neale was putting his X's and O's in order. On offense, he had the Eagles running a T-formation patterned after the Chicago Bears. On defense, he created his own alignment, a 5-2-4 that became known as "the Eagle defense" and was imitated by NFL teams well into the next decade.

"Greasy was the smartest football man I ever met," Tommy Thompson says. "His memory was fantastic. I remember sitting with him at a Brooklyn-Giants game one year. Pug Manders took the ball and ran up the middle. It looked like any other play to me. But Greasy said, 'Hey, I remember that play. Brown used it against Yale in '33. Third play of the second quarter.'

"He'd do the same thing preparing for our games. He'd say, 'Remember what this team did against us last time?' Then he'd rattle off our last game, play-by-play. We didn't need films. Greasy had it all in his head."

The Eagles had the coach, they had the quarterback, they had a defense that no one could quite figure out. But what turned them into championship caliber was the 6-foot, 200-pound halfback they selected in the first round of the 1944 draft.

Steve Van Buren was born in Spanish Honduras, grew up on a banana farm, and almost didn't play high school football because he was too small.

He worked in a steel mill for a year, added 35 pounds, then went to Louisiana State University, where he spent two seasons blocking for a Single-Wing tailback named Alvin Dark, later an all-star shortstop with the New York and San Francisco Giants.

Van Buren didn't carry the ball until his senior year, but he wound up breaking the Southeast Conference rushing record. Coach Bernie Moore later apologized to Van Buren, saying he had done him a "terrible injustice."

Van Buren told Moore not to worry. "Everything turned out all right," he said. That was Van Buren's nature—quiet, unassuming, just one of the boys.

His talent, however, set him apart. He was a 1980s runner turned loose in the 1940s, a big, punishing back with a sprinter's speed. He could run the 100-yard dash in 9.8. No one in the league could catch him at 50 yards.

Neale called Van Buren the greatest runner he ever saw, better than Jim Thorpe and Red Grange. "Grange had the same ability to sidestep," Neale said, "but he didn't have Van Buren's power to go with it."

"When Steve carried the ball, he struck fear in the heart of the defense," says Russ Craft, the Eagles' all-pro defensive back (1946–1953).

"He leaned forward so much and ran so hard, you could actually see the dirt flying off his cleats. When he hit the line, he looked like a bulldozer going through a picket fence.

"I saw him knock off more headgears than you could count. I saw him bust up a lot of faces, too. This was the era before the mandatory face masks. Thank God he seldom got mad on the field. He might have killed somebody."

Van Buren signed for $4,000 that first year. He teamed with Thompson and Hinkle, averaged 5.5 yards per carry, and the Eagles finished 7-1-2. That quickly, a franchise was delivered from the ashes.

After the season, Neale went to Van Buren's apartment to sign him for 1945. Typically, Greasy came straight to the point.

"Greasy told me, 'Steve, whatever you ask for, we've got to pay you. But we'd like to pay you $7,500,'" Van Buren recalls. "I said, 'That's fine.' I signed, and that was the end of it.

"I wouldn't have argued if he had said five thousand. I wasn't much for haggling. I liked playing football, and I liked Philadelphia. I didn't worry that much about money. Nobody did back then.

"The players today might say we were stupid, but at least we were happy."

We weren't offered endorsements. Steve was the only one, and he wasn't interested. I remember this guy from a cereal company offered Steve a lot of money to plug his product. Steve tasted it and threw the box on the floor. He said, 'I wouldn't feed that to my dog.' The guy got mad and walked out. Steve just laughed. That's the way he was.

—Jack Hinkle, halfback, 1941–47

By all accounts, the post-war Eagles were a team of extraordinary spirit.

Off the field, they gave the appearance of being loose, almost cavalier. On the field, they played with a fierce, unrelenting will.

"You hear about teams giving 110 percent?" says Wistert, the team captain. "We gave 150 percent every time out. We had talent, sure, but we played over our heads in those championship years.

"Man-for-man, I don't know if we stacked up with the Cardinals and the Rams. They were truly great teams. The [Chicago] Cardinals had the Dream Backfield. The Rams had Bob Waterfield, Tom Fears, Elroy Hirsch, Tom Harmon, Glenn Davis. But we beat them. Down deep, I think we wanted it more."

The Eagles stuck together. Once a Los Angeles player took a swing at Greasy Neale on the sidelines. He quickly was pummeled by a half-dozen Eagles.

"We were like a family," Wistert says. "Most of the guys lived in the Walnut Park Apartments. Forty bucks a week. Players, wives, kids, all in there together.

"We had team picnics in Fairmont Park. Everybody showed up. Lex [Thompson] would come down from New York. Greasy would be there. We'd play touch football. Guys would be diving, rolling around, laughing.

"Greasy was a big part of that feeling. Once we had the [great] team, he backed off. He didn't rant and rave like he did in the early years. He'd stop practices after an hour and say, 'Let's go play golf.' He knew when we were ready.

"We traveled by train in those days, and Greasy would organize card games. Pinochle, that was his passion. Penny-a-point. He'd be in there with the rest of us, dealing the cards, telling jokes. I never saw a team so totally together."

Bosh Pritchard contributed to that atmosphere. Pritchard was a 5-10, 165-pound halfback from VMI, a jackrabbit who could take a routine play, cut here, cut there, and zip for six points.

Pritchard's quickness was the perfect complement to Van Buren's power. Against Washington in 1949, Tommy Thompson faked to Van Buren, then handed off to Pritchard, who went 77 yards without being touched.

But football was only one facet of Pritchard's personality. The truth is, the man really wanted to be in show business. Singing, acting, Bosh could do it all. At least in his own mind.

During the war, Pritchard was in the Army, stationed on the West Coast. On weekends, he played football for the semipro San Francisco Bombers. At halftime, he sang with the band. "The Crooning Halfback," that was his billing.

Following his discharge, Pritchard signed with the Eagles for $6,000. Greasy wouldn't let him sing at halftime, so he did his performing after the games. Bosh didn't care where. Any place that had a microphone and an audience would do. If they didn't have a microphone, well, that was okay, too.

"We'd go into a club," Russ Craft says, "and we'd take bets on how long it would be before Bosh was up on the bandstand. Actually, he was a pretty good singer, but we needled him something awful."

"I was the team funny man," Pritchard says. "Today, I guess they'd call me a flake. But Greasy encouraged it, particularly before games. He said I kept the boys loose.

"I'd get on the team bus and I'd say, 'All right, all together now. . . .' And I'd start singing the VMI fight song. They'd laugh and boo. That's how we'd get ready to play."

Pritchard wasn't the only Eagle with a flair for the arts. Guard Walter (Piggy) Barnes worked on a television show, "Action in the Afternoon," which was produced live on the lawn behind the WCAU studios on City Line.

The show was a Western serial best-remembered for its scenes of cowboys and Indians shooting it out while Philadelphia transit buses rumbled past.

Today, Walter Barnes is a full-time actor who appears regularly in Clint Eastwood films.

We all had offseason jobs. Why? Hell, we needed the money. I sold beer, so did [Mike] Jarmoluk and [Ben] Kish. Wistert taught school, Pritchard was on the radio. A few guys worked construction. We weren't stars in those days. We were just guys scratching out a living.

—Jack Ferrante, end, 1941, 1944–1950

Even now, looking back four decades, the accomplishments of the Greasy Neale Eagles boggle the mind.

They won three straight Eastern Division titles (1947–49). They won 31 games, lost seven, and tied one. The last two years, they outscored their opponents 761-290.

They won back-to-back NFL championships in 1948 and 1949,

shutting out the Chicago Cardinals (7-0) and Los Angeles Rams (14-0). No NFL team before or since ever posted consecutive shutouts in championship play.

Van Buren led the league in rushing four times. He became the first man in NFL history to gain 1,000 yards twice. Thompson led the league in completion percentage one year, touchdown passes another.

Pihos, the 6-1, 215-pound end, was the league's top pass receiver three straight years. Joe Muha played fullback and linebacker and also was the game's best punter.

Neale's innovative Eagle defense was the state of the art. Kilroy, the middle guard, anchored the line. Alex Wojciechowicz played linebacker and scared off any receiver who had ideas about coming across the middle.

"Wojie was the toughest guy on the team," Hinkle says. "He looked like a big, shaggy dog. A sad-eyed St. Bernard. But he'd rip your head off."

Johnny Green was a 6-1, 200-pound end with a similar disposition. Neale offered a $10 reward for every quarterback sack and every forced fumble. Green would pick up $100 almost every week.

"We had a great defense," Russ Craft says. "We felt like nobody could score on us. Our linemen bottled things up tackle-to-tackle. Kilroy, Wistert, and Sears were the best. Wojie, Muha, and later [Chuck] Bednarik were excellent linebackers. Smart, fast.

"The guys who were under the most pressure were the cornerbacks, me and Pat McHugh. Teams knew they couldn't beat us up the middle, so they tried the flanks. We held up our end most of the time."

In 1947, the Eagles played in their first championship game and lost to the Cardinals 28-21. The game was played on a frozen Comiskey Park field, and the Eagles were forced to wear sneakers. (Their cleats had been filed down to sharp points, and the officials ruled them dangerous.)

"Worst footing ever," Van Buren says. "I slipped and fell twice just coming out of the huddle."

The next year, the Eagles and Cardinals met again for the title. This time, the game was played in Philadelphia's Shibe Park in a blizzard. The Eagles won 7-0, the only touchdown coming on a 5-yard run by Van Buren.

Ironically, Van Buren almost missed the game. He awoke in his suburban home that morning, looked out at the heavy snow, and went back to bed, assuming the game would be postponed.

An hour passed, and Van Buren decided he ought to go, just in case. So he made the familiar trek, riding the trolley to 69th Street, taking the Market Street subway to City Hall, then transferring to the Broad Street Line.

He rode the subway to Lehigh Avenue, then trudged eight blocks through the snow to the stadium. He helped win the NFL championship, then repeated his ride on the subway and trolley home.

"I remember that day very well," Van Buren says. "The snow was so heavy we [the players] had to help the ground crew roll the tarpaulin off the field. Can you imagine the two teams doing that today before a Super Bowl?

"The footing wasn't too bad. It was sloppy, but not slippery. I could run okay, I just couldn't see. I'm not kidding. It was snowing so hard, I couldn't even see the Cardinals' safety, Marshall Goldberg.

"When we won . . . well, that was the ultimate. We had worked so hard, finally the reward was there. The feeling in that [locker] room was just tremendous. Ol' Greasy . . . even he was choked up."

In 1949, the Eagles had their best season, winning 11 of 12 games. Chuck Bednarik joined the team that year, giving the Eagles five future Pro Football Hall of Famers (Neale, Van Buren, Pihos, and Wojciechowicz were the others).

They defeated the Rams for the title in a driving southern California rain. Thompson passed to Pihos for the first score. A rookie, Leo Skladany, blocked Bob Waterfield's punt in the end zone for the other.

Van Buren carried the ball 31 times for 196 yards, an NFL Championship Game record.

"Steve was hell on a leash that day," Pihos says. "The mud was up past our ankles in the second half, but he just kept pounding away. Steve never complained. He never got tired. His stamina was unbelievable."

"The only disappointment was the money," Pritchard says. "We figured with the game being played in the Coliseum (90,000 capacity), we'd have the biggest live gate in NFL history. That would mean more money for us.

"But, with the rain, only 27,980 people showed up.

"Our shares turned out to be $1,094 each. Guys were saying, 'But I was gonna buy a car with my share. . . .' Our wives were even madder than we were."

The Eagles didn't realize it at the time, but their golden era was coming to an end.

The fifties brought in a new power, the Cleveland Browns, from the All-America Football Conference. Knee injuries struck down Van Buren and Pritchard. Age caught up with the noble warriors in the trenches.

Neale had several run-ins with the meddlesome new owner, James P. Clark, including a wrestling match in the Yankee Stadium locker room following a bitter 7-3 loss to the Giants.

To no one's surprise, Neale was replaced prior to the 1951 season. That signaled a decline in Eagles fortunes which lasted until 1960, when the team won another NFL championship.

But the memory of those Eagles lives on in Philadelphia's rabid football community. It also lives on in the hearts and minds of the men who made it happen.

The championship teams had a reunion at the Eagles' training camp last summer. The old gang gathered on a muggy August afternoon and sat around a lounge at West Chester State University, reminiscing.

"It was great seeing the guys again," Pete Pihos says. "Finding out where they were living, what they were doing, how many grandchildren they had.

"It's funny the way time changes some things and not others. I mean, here we were, a bunch of old-timers, gray hair, bones creaking, but we still had that winning attitude.

"We were the champions of professional football. That's something no one can take away. Not now. Not ever."

WILL McDONOUGH

Gate-Crashers and Frog's Legs

"My favorite Super Bowl memories are drawn from those people who added flavor and human qualities," Will McDonough wrote in the Super Bowl XXVIII game program in Atlanta. As a veteran of all 27 Super Bowls to that time—he covered the AFL's Chiefs in Super Bowl I—McDonough had plenty of characters to write about. He is a much-read columnist for the BOSTON GLOBE *and a fixture each Sunday on NBC's "NFL Live."*

THE ASSIGNMENT WAS to cover the Kansas City Chiefs as they prepared to play the Green Bay Packers in Super Bowl I. Get out there a few days early, my boss at the *Boston Globe* told me, and stay at the same hotel as the Chiefs. Unheard of today, a reporter rooming at the same place as a Super Bowl team. But that's how it was in 1967.

I drove from the Los Angeles airport to Long Beach. It was dark, it was raining, and fog engulfed the hotel. The scene was like something out of the movies. It was a fitting introduction to this event, because the whole idea of the game was shrouded in mystery. One opinion seemed universal, however—the contest figured to be a mismatch.

Now, while sometimes things are what they appear (Super Bowl I was a mismatch, with Green Bay dominating), there are times when even the most vivid imagination cannot see what lies ahead.

Hard feelings ran deep in those days. NFL players and even the writers who covered them seemed indignant at the mere thought of having to play an AFL team. Len Dawson, the great Kansas City quarterback, was sitting at a coffee shop one morning when a writer from Cleveland approached. "Lenny," said the NFL writer, "I'd like to talk to you for a few minutes." Dawson, who had played with the Browns, shook his head. "Why? You never talked to me the years I was in Cleveland."

Access to players never was a problem then. That's a far cry from today, when you almost need an act of Congress to get an interview, then have to battle MTV reporters to ask a question.

A few days before the first Super Bowl, I drove up to Santa Barbara, where the Packers were staying. I asked to see quarterback Bart Starr. Next thing I knew, Starr appeared in the hotel lobby and told me to come to his room.

Interview a player in his hotel room before the Super Bowl? Not a chance of doing that today.

I felt bad for the Chiefs that Sunday! My heart was with them, as were the hearts of most of the AFL writers. It was a personal thing with us. The late Tex Maule of *Sports Illustrated* basked in the spotlight. He was an NFL guy, and he told anyone who would listen that Green Bay would dominate.

He was right. The AFL writers had to bite their tongues.

The bashing continued in the locker room. Legendary Vince Lombardi was asked about the Chiefs. "Well," said the Packers head coach, "they can't play with the good teams in our league. They couldn't play with the Lions or Bears [Green Bay's chief rivals in the NFL Western Conference]."

After filing my story, I went back to the hotel and sat around a small press room with Kansas City head coach Hank Stram and a few NFL writers. Stram, told of Lombardi's comments, was devastated. He talked about the game, but every couple of minutes he'd say, "Did Vince really say we weren't that good? That we couldn't play at that level? Vince is a friend. Did he really say that?"

That summer, returning to the *Boston Globe* after a Red Sox game, I passed the wire machine and saw that Kansas City had defeated

Chicago 66-24 in a preseason game. I said to myself: "I'm sure that was for you, Vince."

But even Lombardi came around. The day before Super Bowl III in January, 1969, I was with Jimmy Cannon, the late and very great New York columnist and a friend of Lombardi's. "Kid," Cannon told me, "I think they [the Jets] have a shot."

I laughed. Hell, the Jets were 19-point underdogs. It was just a hopeful New Yorker talking, I thought. "No, I was talking to Vince," Cannon said, "and he thinks this kid [Joe Namath] can beat them [the Baltimore Colts]. They're better than they used to be."

In more than 30 years of sportswriting, that game remains my biggest thrill. Namath was masterful, but I'll always remember hearing of coach Weeb Ewbank's pregame speech. "When we win," he told his players, "don't carry me off the field. I have a bad hip. I don't want to get hurt."

His players thought it was a ploy to show how confident he was.

But Ewbank was serious. In the AFL Championship Game two weeks earlier, he was carried off the field and a fan had pulled so hard on his leg that he required hip surgery later that year.

If Super Bowl III was vindication for the AFL, it also was sweet justice for the writers from the junior league. Maule got an earful from us. The tables had turned.

Respect grew the next year when Stram, Dawson, and the Chiefs beat the NFL's mighty Vikings at Tulane Stadium. It was the most bizarre Super Bowl week ever. It was abnormally cold in New Orleans, the Mississippi River was frozen, rumors circulated that Dawson was involved in gambling, and nobody seemed convinced that the Jets' victory the year before was real. I truly believed the Chiefs would win, but they were huge underdogs.

This was the game in which a hot-air balloon crashed into the stands during halftime. Fortunately, many of the fans were huddling under the stands to escape the cold, so no one was badly hurt.

Which is more than I could say for myself. Sick with the flu, I decided to eat something solid for the first time in days. I opened my box lunch, had a few bites, turned to a Cleveland writer, Chuck Heaton, and told him the chicken was pretty good.

"That's not chicken," he said, "it's frog's legs." I think I could have outrun Otis Taylor in my sprint to the men's room.

Super Bowl history books tell us all about the great plays and the players who pulled them off. My favorite Super Bowl memories are drawn not from people who performed between the goal posts, but from those who added flavor and human qualities.

People such as Skipper McNally. Skipper was a character, a guy from the Boston area who'd had bit parts in some good movies such as *Charly* and *On the Waterfront*. Skipper was a gate-crasher: he loved the spotlight, and what brighter spotlight than America's premier sporting event? In New Orleans for Super Bowl IV, he devised a scheme. When the team bus approached Tulane Stadium, Skipper put on his Vikings windbreaker and yelled out: "Team's here. Clear the way. Team's here." He ran beside the bus as it went through the gates and past security.

When it became apparent the Chiefs would win, Skipper changed gears. He put on a Kansas City windbreaker and moved to the other sideline. His goal was to help carry off the winning coach, to get his picture in *Sports Illustrated*. So as time ran out, there was 5-foot-9 Skipper McNally next to 6-foot-9 Ernie Ladd, the former Chief who was cheering on his ex-mates.

"Grab the coach," said Ladd. Skipper obliged. He made his SI photo and also the NFL highlight reels because NFL Films had wired Stram. On the film, you can hear Stram calling out: "Where's Grant [Vikings head coach Bud Grant], where's Grant?"

Skipper was tired and sore, in no mood to carry Stram any longer. "Coach," you can hear him say on the tape, "bleep Grant. Let's get out of here."

In 1977, a great guy who had suffered terrible disappointments on the football field, Raiders head coach John Madden, got to taste Super Bowl success. That day in Los Angeles didn't start well for Madden. A bundle of nerves, he was in such a rush to head to the

Rose Bowl that he left four players at the hotel.

He fined himself for making them late. Later, after a 32-14 rout of the Vikings, Madden celebrated by shaking hands with folks in the parking lot, then retiring to a trailer with his boyhood friend, USC coach John Robinson. Madden still is the same unpretentious man today.

At Super Bowl XVI, San Francisco head coach Bill Walsh got to Detroit earlier than his team. He had gone somewhere to pick up an award, so he decided to meet the players when they arrived at the hotel in Detroit. Dressed in a bellhop's uniform, Walsh greeted the 49ers and kidded with them, telling them they were going to get their butts kicked. Several players absorbed the abuse before Walsh was recognized.

When Super Bowl XXI came to Los Angeles, I was doing some television work for CBS, and it was a new experience. It's a major production, but much of it is done on the fly. My pregame interview from the field was going to be with Denver owner Pat Bowlen, but at the last second my producer nixed the idea. "Do something else," he said.

So we opted for a quick piece on stadium security. I positioned myself near the Giants bench and immediately got smacked a few times by a woman with a baton. I was standing where the band needed to line up, she yelled.

Stay there, said my producer, even if it meant getting hit. Which it did.

The security piece included something about gate-crashers (I would have loved to tell the story of Skipper) and a skydiver who had warned that he was going to parachute in during the National Anthem. He never did. Who knows? Maybe he decided to wait for a heavyweight championship fight seven years later.

Later, we headed to the losers' locker room for interviews. An NFL official was furious because we got there before the Broncos, so he made us hide in the showers. That's where we were when coach Dan Reeves talked to his players.

Moving toward the locker room just before halftime that day, I went past a group of people who were getting ready to entertain. A man dressed as a clown tapped me on the shoulder. "Hey, pal, I haven't been out there yet, who's winning the game?" I told him it was close, but the Giants were starting to play well. "Whew, good," he said. "I have a bet on the Giants." It was Mickey Rooney.

I've known Buffalo Bills owner Ralph Wilson since the old AFL days. His team lost to the Giants in Super Bowl XXV, remembered forever as the game in which Scott Norwood's 47-yard field goal attempt in the final seconds was wide right.

Two years later, Wilson invited me to the Kentucky Derby. He had a financial interest in the favorite, Arazi. I glanced at the racing form as we drove to Churchill Downs. "Ralph," I asked, "what number did Scott Norwood wear?" He thought for a moment and said, "Eleven." I showed him the racing form and pointed to horse number 11, Arazi.

The program said Arazi liked to run wide right. We laughed at the irony.

I don't know much about racing, so I tried to follow Arazi. I knew his jockey wore a red cap. Toward the stretch the horses bunched and I focused on the finish line. I thought I saw a jockey with a red cap finish first. I thought Arazi had won.

Wilson pulled back from his binoculars. He didn't say a word. He simply made a sweeping motion with his hands: wide right. I told Wilson I thought Arazi had won. (He hadn't.)

"Will, the day of the Super Bowl," Wilson said, "when Norwood kicked that ball, when the ball was in the air, I was up in the box. I jumped off the ground and said, 'We won!' But then it went wide right. So I won the Super Bowl for three seconds."

Three glorious seconds . . . 27 memorable games. It's all a matter of perspective.

SCOTT OSTLER

Confessions of a Super Pirate

Scott Ostler has been taking a skewed look at the world of sports for years, as a columnist and feature writer with the Los Angeles Times, The National, *and now the* San Francisco Chronicle. *He has been named California sportswriter of the year five times. Ostler's hands-on experience with pro football began with an adolescent foray onto his father's roof, as he explained in this piece written for the Super Bowl XXVIII program in Atlanta.*

I AM A DISTRACTION.

That is my function during Super Bowl Week. As a big-time sportswriter and member of the media, my job is to annoy the players and coaches, to distract their attention from the business of game preparation in an effort to provide reports on the mood of your favorite team.

We bring you reports like, "Today, the mood of the Buffalo Bills can be characterized as annoyed and distracted."

We are not the only distractions, of course. Among the nuisances that have been known to interfere with the players' mental focus are meals, brushing after meals, low-flying aircraft, Nintendo Game Boy, hotel maid services, and world wars.

Yet, despite the distractions, somehow the game takes place every year. Apparently, I am only a minor pain in the neck.

There was a Super Bowl, however, when I was a big pain, when I brought the pro football and TV establishment to its knees. Me and 100,000 other brave pirates.

We staged a grass-roots, roof-top insurrection that sent shock waves through the corridors of the NFL, AFL, NBC, CBS, FCC, and—who knows—maybe the CIA.

We stole the Super Bowl.

It was January 1967, and I was annoyed. Because I was a teenager then, saying that I was annoyed is redundant, but I was extra annoyed because of the Super Bowl.

Brief background: The NFL finally decided to acknowledge the existence of the upstart AFL by agreeing to a showdown championship game.

Cool! The AFL was a fun, wide-open league, exemplified by the champion Kansas City Chiefs. It would be great to see what the zany Chiefs could do against the mighty, NFL-champion Green Bay Packers. Who knows? Maybe the Super Bowl would become an annual event.

The game would be played in the Los Angeles Memorial Coliseum, and would be televised nationally by both NBC and CBS. Tickets, however, were not selling briskly. Can you imagine a problem selling Super Bowl tickets? Hello, Coliseum switchboard? What time does the Super Bowl start?

What time can you get here?

Yes, that's an old joke, but it was new in 1967.

The situation wasn't quite that bad, but the Coliseum seating capacity was 90,000-plus, and not quite 62,000 tickets would be sold. Even if a lot of the fans were overweight, the stadium would look to be a box-office bomb on TV.

To goose ticket sales, NFL Commissioner Pete Rozelle pulled the TV plug. About six weeks before the game he announced that the telecast would be blacked out in the greater Los Angeles area.

This, remember, was before satellite dishes or pay-per-view. It was buy a ticket or forget it. As a starving college student in L.A., I couldn't afford a ticket, and the nearest city that would receive the telecast was San Diego.

Then local radio station KRLA promoted a do-it-yourself TV

antenna that would allow you pick up the game at home. A Super Bowl blackout buster!

You could get your instructions by mailing an envelope to the station. It still was two weeks before the game, but being a college student, I procrastinated for 13 days, and had to drive to the KRLA studio in Pasadena.

Years later I learned that KRLA came up with the idea six weeks before Super Sunday. "But we figured if we announced it too soon, Rozelle would black out San Diego," then-station manager John Barrett said later.

The idea was no more than a whim to the folks at KRLA, a throwaway bit of fun. They didn't understand the power of pro football. Mail poured into the station, and the phone lines were jammed with requests for antenna instructions. Everyone at the station—accountants, news directors, secretaries, janitors—was pressed into mail and phone duty for two weeks.

The demand snowballed, and the Saturday before the game KRLA deejays, including Kasey Kasem and Bob Eubanks, announced that the instruction sheet could be picked up at the station. A massive traffic jam ensued.

The station distributed about 20,000 copies of the instructions, friends passed them along to friends, and an estimated 100,000 Super Bowl antennae were lashed together and mounted on buildings across the L.A. basin.

I hurried home and set to work. The antenna consisted of five or six varied lengths of coat-hanger wire attached to a broomstick, which then was wired to your regular rooftop TV aerial.

It was so simple that a fool could put together the antenna in 20 minutes. Mine took two hours because I lacked certain tools, such as electronic aptitude. But I worked happily, humming the theme song from "Mission Impossible." The cost was about 50 cents, not counting the broom I destroyed or the $100 worth of damage to my parents' landscaping and roof, suffered during installation.

I hooked it up Super Sunday morning, turned on my TV, and got pure, dazzling . . . snow. A quick check of the skies. No, it was not snowing over Los Angeles. The instructions said to twist and rotate the antenna until the picture came in.

Like a pilot flying through a snowstorm, desperately trying to make radar contact, I kept twisting and adjusting the antenna, while my buddy inside the house monitored the screen, until . . . A PICTURE! YESSS!

I felt like the villain in a James Bond movie. Try to keep me from watching your Super Bowl game NOW, Missster Rozelle. A-HA-HAHAHAHAHA!

My buddy and I kicked back with snacks and soda pop. The TV reception was not fabulous, but we definitely could tell it was a football game, even if it was hard to make out minute objects, such as the football . Had it been a color TV, we would have been able to tell which players were Chiefs and which were Packers.

No matter. What was important was that we were watching the game, and that the people of Los Angeles had delivered a message. Never again would the NFL try to black out a Super Bowl game. (Of course, never again would the Super Bowl not be sold out.)

From a personal standpoint, the rest is history. Inspired by my first crude foray into electronics, I went on to invent the VCR and the microwave oven.

Just kidding. Years later I did learn to use a VCR and a microwave oven, though I often confuse the two. I also became a sportswriter, which means I get paid to watch Super Bowls, often from great seats, with free snacks.

Snacks? I get invited to the NFL Commissioner's Party, pal. Astronauts say that the only man-made objects visible from the moon are the Great Wall of China and the seafood buffet table at the Commissioner's Party.

But you know what? For me, the Super Bowl never will be cooler than it was in '67.

Beginning from that first fuzzy image, I became a knowledgeable, professional Super Bowl watcher. Allow me to pass along some valuable insights into viewing the game, on TV and in person.

Don't complain. Got lousy seats? They could be worse. You could be seated on one of the team benches.

It is a fascinating place from which to experience the flavor of the game—the sounds, the intensity, the Gatorade. But you have no idea what's going on. Watching a game from the sidelines is like standing way too close to a LeRoy Neiman painting.

This explains why coaches often seem confused after the game. "I was generally pleased with my team's performance, but I'll know more when I study the tapes and find out whether we won or lost."

Watch the talkers. For some reason, the players who do the most talking the week before the game almost always excel on Super Sunday. I exaggerated at the start of this piece when I said the media are a nuisance. Most players actually enjoy their daily chats with the press, and the most convivial players almost always wind up starring in the game.

Prime example: Joe Theismann in Super Bowl XVII, where he quarterbacked the Redskins to a win over Miami. That week Joe would talk your pen dry.

I sometimes wonder what kind of work Theismann went into after football.

Focus. Don't get hung up on extraneous things. Watching one Super Bowl for example, I absentmindedly began pondering the metaphysics of the Miami Dolphins' helmets, causing me to miss five or six crucial commercials.

The Miami helmet features a dolphin wearing a tiny helmet with a 'D' on the side. Shouldn't that dolphin be wearing a Dolphins helmet, which would have a picture of a dolphin wearing a Dolphins helmet? If the Dolphins are in the Super Bowl, make it a point not to think about this.

Update your gridspeak. Don't mark yourself as a football dinosaur by referring to passes as either "long" or "short." That confusing terminology has been greatly simplified by coaches and TV announcers. Passes now are thrown "underneath the coverage" or "up top." "Nickel package" is another handy term that can be dropped into almost any football conversation, even if you have no idea what it means.

Other useful words and phrases include: Smashmouth football, situation substitution, hang time, red zone, rotating zone, no-parking zone, speed-up offense, speed rush, foot speed, and foot fault.

Digress. If the game becomes a one-sided rout, spice up the conversation with philosophical topics. For instance, aren't you glad the NFL never has resorted to trendy singular nicknames?

The league will lose big style points in my book if it ever starts naming teams the Pittsburgh Steel, the Miami Prickly Heat (helmet: a dolphin with a rash?), the Buffalo Buffalo, or the New England Style Clam Chowder.

Ignore the QB. Novice fans focus exclusively on the quarterback and wind up missing some of the most interesting action on the field.

Try watching the guy who stands behind the head coach and keeps his headphone wire neatly coiled. This is a vital task. One slip-up and the coach could become hopelessly tangled in his own cord, unable to get out of the way of that oncoming railroad train.

Watch for a play from President Clinton. It is rumored he will resume the tradition of the U.S. president designing a play for his favorite team. Richard M. Nixon started and ended this tradition by suggesting a play to Dolphins coach Don Shula for Super Bowl VI. The play failed, and Nixon soon was demoted to private citizen.

Reminisce. People around you at the stadium—or in the bar or living room—love to hear stories about the old days.

Why, I remember when there were no end-zone nets to catch extra-point and field-goal attempts. Balls booted into the stands would touch off spirited free-for-alls.

True story: I dove into one such scrum, grabbed the ball, and tugged—only to find that I had an armlock on a bald man's head.

That couldn't happen today, of course, because of the advent of spray-on hair.

Jim Klobuchar

Memory Layne

If you say, "They don't make players like Bobby Layne anymore," you are mouthing more than a cliché. Layne, the much-loved quarterback of the Detroit Lions when they ruled the NFL in the 1950s, could carouse, drink, curse—and win football games—as well as any player of his day. Jim Klobuchar, a fixture on the pages of the Minneapolis Star-Tribune *for some 35 years, was the perfect person to catch up with Layne in 1975 for* PRO! *magazine.*

He would thrust his maskless jowls into the faces of his quailing accomplices in the huddle. Do you remember?

Bobby Layne delivering an ultimatum to the penitents. He would stand with his hands on his hips, promising tears and demanding sweat and quite possibly a kick in the tail. MacArthur played the scene more majestically, but the general never had the handicap of a bad Saturday night in Philadelphia.

Layne in closeup, his helmet barely able to contain the puffy cheeks of this old gnome in umbrage, was one of the imperishable portraits of his time. You could freeze an entire epoch with one still picture that absorbed the era's rhythm and scent, evoked its saints and demons. It was a time when the television cameras were converting pro football from the club fight cultism of the postwar years to the Sunday communion it became to millions of people for whom God mercifully ordained doubleheaders and split screens.

Here was Vince Lombardi, in his first years, standing beside the Packers' bench. He wore a camel's hair coat and projected a grimace so kinetic and willful it stirred bafflement among the viewers in the way Leonardo da Vinci did with Mona Lisa. You could read it any way you wanted. From certain angles it was a snarl of exhortation. But Lombardi zealots saw it as one of those Biblical smiles of certitude, first employed by St. Michael.

And there was John Unitas, standing without flinching in his protective pocket, pumping his fake, anchored in his hightop shoes, winging the ball 50 yards to Lenny Moore on third and one.

And Bobby Layne. They gave a banquet in Dallas for all the Texas Hall of Famers last year. There were so many great Texas athletes and sure-enough immortals in that number somebody asked where the Oklahoma recruiters were. There were Ben Hogan, Sammy Baugh, Doak Walker, Byron Nelson, Jimmy Demaret, and a few hundred others. They came out of the Panhandle, the country clubs, and the cactus. Lamar Hunt was the impresario and Bob Hope was the toastmaster.

He got Bobby Layne and he fractured the house. "I want to introduce the only man who ran an X-rated huddle in the NFL," he said.

Nobody talked about charisma when Bobby Layne played football. The operative word then was aura. The exact composition of Bobby's aura always fascinated chemists, since it was widely believed to consist of equal parts sulphur, gunsmoke, Texas natural gas, and bourbon.

There is still some residual sulphur when the man enters a room today, diluted by the years, of course, but unmistakable. He was one of the real ones, Bobby Layne, an undefeatable buccaneer, a crony and contemptuous autocrat, a hell-raising man and football virtuoso.

He sat at a restaurant table in Minneapolis, affable, brown, and stunningly trim. For four months Bobby Layne had been eating grapefruit, rice, and dry toast. That is the gospel. He had sheared off 25 pounds and seemed fearful of being swept away when the restaurant door opened. "The doctor done it," he said with a minimum of exuberance.

"Jog every day," he said. "Me and my dog. In a park near

Lubbock." The brown-haired waitress was tarrying. "Dietin', hon," Bobby clucked. "Gimme just one of those lil' ole hamburger patties, and what they call cottage cheese, and one nice icy gin and tonic, hon."

His luncheon companion, a newspaperman, did not expect to be dining that afternoon with Bobby Layne because it was, after all, Minneapolis, and Layne normally lunches in Lubbock with his domino partners. A couple of days before, he had blown their appointment in Lubbock because of a busted battery on a private plane flying him from Mexico, leaving the reporter to count motels and heat waves for excitement in Lubbock. Two days later Layne called from the airport in Minneapolis. "I owe you one, podner," he said.

He reminded the interrogator of Van Brocklin, chummy and uproarious as a social person, sardonic in his judgments of non-achievers and therefore the non-equals. But kinder than Dutch. They both belonged to a time when the game was clubbier. Its friendships and admirations and hatreds were more intimate than today, when the big money and celebrity of the game have removed some of its musketeer camaraderie.

But Bobby himself was always a money man, once the game's highest-paid practitioner at $25,000 and proud of it.

"But all that partying, Bobby," the interrogator jogged him. "You don't mean to tell America a lot of that is fiction."

"I'd say the parts between Thursday and Sunday, yeah. Before that you sort of had to relax. Buddy Parker, now, there was a man of wisdom. Our coach at Detroit and Pittsburgh. One of the greatest ever. Buddy used to tell us, 'There's three things guys like to do in this business: drink, carouse, and play cards for money. I know very few guys who can do two of them well, and not many guys who can do one of them well. But if you ever try to do all three around here, you're busted.'"

The ultimate pity of the Bobby and Buddy alliance is that pro football was just a few years short of its engulfing popularity when they flourished, so the millions didn't really know. Buddy was a kind of choleric genius, a man whose setbacks seemed so soaringly tragic —and sometimes comically tragic—because of his magnificent rages.

"How that man suffered," Bobby acknowledged, not quite tragically. "I remember visiting his house after a game one night and we all had a few drinks, and the drinks got to Buddy because we heard this voice from Buddy's bedroom and there he was on his knees, and he's praying, and he says, 'Why does Paul Brown have all those backs who run and run and run, Lord, and I don't have any?'"

But surely the Lord listened some of the time?

"Well, we had some great running backs at Detroit, sure, but there was this one year everything went wrong and we lost the first six games of the season and we're flying back from the West Coast. When we got to Denver Buddy couldn't take it and he called Bert Bell, the commissioner. 'Every s.o.b. on this team is on waivers,' he said."

The waitress brought another plate of dry toast and teased her raspy client with a smile. Bobby is an instant social smash in almost any environment—bar, duck blind, airliner, or rodeo bleachers. He is breezy, confident, and generous. Partly because of this but more because of his naturalness, service people—the barmaids and porters—love him. Bobby joshed the waitress and allowed that since it was Tuesday, it would be all right to add a moderate amount to his glass.

There are football players who become an immediate part of the brotherhood, having passed the sifting process that is never defined but is activated in the dormitories and training rooms the moment the player walks into camp. The process can sometimes miscalculate the player's competitive value, but it rarely errs in evaluating his character, his fitness to belong. Layne was accepted within weeks after he joined the Chicago Bears. This was despite the boxcar numbers on his salary ($77,000 for three years including bonuses, a plutocratic figure for those days) and a general attitude among the pro players of the day that gave rookies the same kind of popularity accorded food poisoning and flat tires.

He failed with Chicago when Sid Luckman decided quarterbacking needed an elder statesman. This left Johnny Lujack and Bobby as the backup quarterbacks, and for Bobby, Chicago was a foreign country. He muddled through a bad rookie season, struggling with adjustment problems and an ailing baby. Accordingly, George Halas—after explaining the situation in a way that earned Bobby's respect—dealt him to the New York Bulldogs. It was not Halas's most charitable move.

"But you couldn't spend a year with that Bears' outfit without learning something," Bobby affirmed. "One of my punishments for being a rookie was to cater to Bulldog Turner's hunger. They had him on the fat man's table. At night, Bulldog sounded like he was actually starving to death. He just came in from the mess hall watching all of his buddies whomp down those steaks and goodies and all, and he was dying. He would order me to go to the commissary to get him some food. I'd tell him the commissary was closed and he'd say, 'Break in! What the hell kind of league do you think you're playing in?' So I'd go break into the commissary and I did it fast, because the way Turner sounded, if I didn't come back with the goods, he was gonna eat me."

The New York Bulldogs were one of the great busts of pro football history, a welfare line masquerading as a football team. Layne led the Bulldogs in forward passes, yards gained rushing, and concussions. The team was owned by the late Ted Collins, a man of strong but strange loyalties who, in midseason of a 1-10-1 year, told Charlie Ewart that he could stay on as coach but not to show up for practice.

All that spared Layne certain dismemberment the following season was a trade to Detroit. And in two years, he was a championship quarterback.

His Monday parties at the Stadium Club were widely credited with saving Detroit from the first Eisenhower recession. Bobby often paid the full damages. This flowed partly out of love for the sporting times but it also represented Bobby's gratitude for having been raised a quarterback. "You had to be a politician," he admitted. "I loved a lot of those guys but you had to spread your money around a little, too. It was awfully tough, the line between playing the big shot and being a good guy with fellas who made less. You couldn't spread it too thick. But let me tell you. When I was with guys like Harley Sewell, and Charley Ane, and Dick Stanfel, I was sincere about picking up some of those checks. They were something fierce.

"They ever tell you about Stanfel? You could go through a complete game film and never see Stanfel miss a block, or not knock some guy down. I didn't respect many people more than Stanfel. Once we were playing the 49ers, trying to get in for a score just before the half. I didn't want to use another time out there. We ran a sweep to the sidelines and Stanfel comes back to the huddle, wheezing and hacking and out of breath. He's real hoarse and he mumbles to me, 'Bobby, gimme a time out.' I was really a hardbutt about those things, you know, so I just said flat out to Dick Stanfel, 'The hell with your time out.' So I called another play.

"Stanfel made his block, and then he had to go off the field. The doctor looked at him later and diagnosed it. A broken back. Dick Stanfel made this block with a broken vertebra and you know what I felt like, don't you, because the next day Dick was wearing this cast up to his neck.

"We had the guys. Hunchy Hoernschmeyer, Doak Walker, Cloyce Box, Jack Christiansen, Jim David, Dorne Dibble, Joe Schmidt, Gene Gedman, oh hell, I could name them all. Leon Hart, Lou Creekmur, Yale Lary, guys like that. Later John Henry Johnson. Man, he would unjoint you, John Henry would. But he was a little quirky. He was afraid of crawling things. One day I got there a little early before the afternoon practice. You'd work out in the morning, then lay around after lunch just dreading the second one. Everybody sort of slouched to the training room anyway. I found one of these small grass snakes. John Henry was one of those who would sit around with his football pants halfway up, waiting to go out. I had taped this snake to the inside of his pants, so just the head moved. And John Henry, he finally went to lift his pants up and here's this snake with its head twitchin' and flickin'. And John Henry saw that, and he damned near leveled the building. He tore through the locker room yelling.

"Joe Schmidt was all I saw after John Henry ran out the room. Schmidt was lying on the floor helpless from laughing.

"But you never got in John Henry's way unless you were ready. I'll never forget Larry Wilson of the Cardinals, and this says as much about Larry as it does about John Henry. Larry was the guy who perfected the safety blitz. You had to have some kind of death wish to invent the safety blitz. But Larry Wilson may have been the toughest guy pound for pound who ever played this game. He'd stand there across the line and his mouth would be open. He didn't have any teeth, which made him look like Popeye.

"He worried the hell out of coaches with the safety blitz, and quarterbacks weren't exactly immune either. We were playing the Cardinals and Buddy says he's got the solution. Parker was always maneuvering and jostling. You had to set your alarm at midnight to get up before Parker.

"'What we gonna do,' Buddy told us before the game, 'is take care of Larry Wilson real early with that safety blitz. John Henry, we want you to uncoil on him. We're gonna hide you someplace in the backfield and when he comes, pop him.'

"Sure enough, Larry Wilson comes with the safety blitz. He waited real long, like the third play. We got John Henry hunkered down low in the backfield and all I can say is, 'Here he comes!'

"Larry Wilson busts through and John Henry unloads. Legal, but he's real brutal, you know. Wilson went down like he was hit by a train. He's just laying there stiff. I actually thought he was dead. They finally brought him back to consciousness and hauled him off the field. I sort of regretted it, and I told one of the guys, 'You got to admire Larry Wilson for what he tried to do. I hope he's not gonna miss too many weeks.'

"He didn't. As a matter of fact, what he missed was one play. He was back in for the one after that. And two plays later you know what they came with? That's right. Larry Wilson and the safety blitz. I just told John Henry, I said, 'I'll be goddamned.' And John Henry said I took the words out of his mouth.

"Now see that's the difference. You can take that from a good ball player. Not only was he a good ball player but he played straight football. That day Ed Meadows laid me out in our game with the Bears. I never said Ed Meadows deliberately tried to take me out of the ball game. Never said that. I do remember my pals from Lubbock being up for the game and they were at a party where there were a lot of Bears' players. And they said some of the Bears were willing to bet I wouldn't get past the first quarter. Great kidders, those Bears.

"I'll say this about the play. I just handed off to Gene Gedman and I was watching him run when Meadows hit me. The lights just went out. I'd be the last guy to say he meant to do it. I'll put it this way: he could have avoided it."

An old conversational prune that always turns up in the barroom arguments surfaced here. What about dirty football, especially back in that pro football era of dogfights and no-man's-lands?

"All I can judge by is what happened to me," Bobby Layne said. "A lot of the guys went out of their way to avoid hurting a guy. Well, when I say 'guy,' I mean me. Hardy Brown of the Forty-Niners collapsed a lot of people with the shoulder shot he gave, but he was kind to me, I'll say that. Old Hardy would say, 'Gotcha, don't move.' And I'd say, 'Don't worry, buddy, don't worry.'"

A little haze was beginning to film the eyes of the warrior. It might have been the nostalgia or the vintage of the libation. The San Francisco hotel desk clerk who walked into a postgame suite years ago and found $800 worth of mirror smashed by an enraged Bobby Layne (the Lions never did understand the 49ers in the years he played) might be reluctant to call him a sentimentalist.

But mention Ernie Stautner. Watch the transformation. Superimpose the battle mask of Bobby Layne and his snarling tomato face in the Steelers' huddle. Let it fade now, and meld with

Bobby Layne at age 48, a sun-soaked Texas businessman with most of his furies banked. His irreverences are still largely intact, but most of his remembrances are warm and generous—the confections of the old pro.

"Ernie and I rented a house not long after I joined Pittsburgh," he said. "I remember telling Art Rooney I didn't need any more money in salary and that I was even willing to take a cut, in exchange for Art paying my living expenses, which sort of scared Mr. Rooney. Ernie was one of the greatest.

"I was a little shook when I first joined Pittsburgh. At Detroit, everything was first wagon. In Pittsburgh, hell, they couldn't even boo big-league style. The fans got on me one game and Ernie really let them have it in the newspapers. So now the whole town is on Ernie. Next week, we're playing at home, and Ernie is the captain. We line up to run out from the ramp at crappy old Forbes Field. Ernie goes first. You know, shoulders back, knees up, the works. The fans booed. Ernie figured he could cope with that because the rest of the team was coming out behind him. He kept running and looked back to see how far the rest of us were behind.

"There wasn't another ball player out of the ramp. We just decided we're gonna have a little fun with Ernie and let him go out there solo. The fans were just blasting the hell out of him and we're standing there in the shade laughing and giggling and Ernie almost died. He just stood there like he's been thrown overboard by his mother. Now I call that some kind of ingratitude on our part but that dumpy old stadium did that to you.

"Wednesday night at midnight was when Ernie and me would stop partying. We were always ready for the game. I don't care what the gossips tell you. Some games we were readier than others, probably. I'll never forget Ernie the day the doctor got in late and was supposed to give him Novocain for his shoulder and he grabbed the wrong bottle and gave him enough Demerol to kill a horse. Ernie almost died. They took him to a hospital and he was in a coma for a while. I went to see him. Ernie talked like he was going to die. Finally he said he needed a priest. The good man arrived and Ernie kinda croaked to him, 'Father forgive me for I have sinned. This is my confession. Father, there ain't much time so I'm just sort of gonna hit the high spots . . .'"

The waitress arrived with the check, which Layne speared instantly with a move that radiated experience. "I'll tell you why I'm glad to pay this check, hon," he told the waitress. "A fifty-dollar bill is the unluckiest bill there is. Did you know that? Never had any luck with it, gambling, anything else. I got one more fifty-dollar bill in my wallet here, and I'm lookin' for a way to get rid of it, too."

The waitress said she just never looked at it that way before.

Bobby rose. Back to Lubbock, and his oil investments and real estate and cronyism, the hunting, fishing, domino and card playing at the club, football on television in season—"too damn much of it for the ladies of the house, just too damn much, and too damn much for Bobby, too.

"Dutch [Van Brocklin] coached here, yeah. Too bad about him and Atlanta. Greatest quarterbacking job ever was what Dutch did in Philadelphia. Dog team, last to first."

"And what about Layne in Detroit?"

"He didn't do badly, either. I ever tell you about Creekmur? Now, there was a guy who . . ."

The waitress couldn't believe the tip.

STEVE CASSADY

The Selection Process

No element of NFL football is more shrouded in secrecy and deception than the maneuverings that surround the drafting of college players. Steve Cassady, who wrote many memorable articles for PRO! *magazine in the late 1970s and early 1980s, gained access to one team's "War Room" on draft day, 1983, painting a picture that more resembles a high-level cabinet meeting than what we associate with the normal functioning of a sports league.*

Editor's Note—*The following story chronicles the actual events in one team's NFL draft room, an area usually off-limits to members of the media. However, certain facts have been changed to masquerade the identity of the team.*

ONE BY ONE, the football people filed past the only other men on the streets—workers in forest green coveralls lugging refuse cans from the side of the building to disposal trucks at the curb. They disappeared through double glass doors into the club's administrative offices. All of them carried briefcases. Some held steaming Styrofoam cups.

The general manager was the first in, at 6:10, followed in the next 20 minutes by the director of player personnel, five scouts, and the head coach. Inside the room where they gathered, they hung up coats and moved about, some directly to swivel chairs around one of two boat-shaped conference tables, others to a counter in front, where they poured coffee into insulated mugs or grabbed doughnuts from a stack of pastry boxes.

They were settled 10 minutes after they had arrived. The front table, where the coach and general manager sat as advisers, overseers, consultants, still was tidy. Blank pads stacked in a neat pile. Pencils sharp and lined in a row. Bound materials in order between bookends.

The other table, where the director of player personnel sat with the scouts, already was chaos. Books of computer printouts, binders of player biographies, scouting reports, full-form player photos, medical reports—all were strewn at random angles. Interspersed between the books were ashtrays the diameter of frisbees, open tins of snuff, and yellow pads on which the scouts furiously scratched notes.

Off to their right, on the west wall, was the big board, a graphic display of football information. The board was 20 feet wide and went from floor to ceiling, a blank wall transformed into a draft-day mural. Strung across the top were rating numbers—from the lowest draftable score, 4.0 at the right, to the highest that year, 9.1, at the left. Up and down the borders on both sides were the positions, from center at the top, to safety at the bottom. Under the horizontal headings, rectangular cards were attached magnetically, each with a player's name written in bold block letters. Underneath the name on the card, in smaller letters, were height, weight, time in the 40-yard dash, and general-rating score. As the draft progressed, the cards of the chosen would be taken down and placed on boards elsewhere in the room, under the headings of the teams that drafted them. The idea was to know who was available by reading the board two ways. You look at the 8.7's column. You read down and see how many players are left in that category. You scan to a position, reading it across to see how highly rated the remaining players are. You can do that for any number, for any position, any time.

On the east wall, opposite the big board, was a similar mural, with more than 700 names charted in a more concentrated order. It had horizontal column heads designated by position. Under those headings were vertical lists of prospects in descending order of their ratings, from 3.9 to 1.0 to Reject. Free agents would be signed from this list. Between it and the names on the big board, no college senior with football ability or experience had been missed. The scouts hadn't overlooked a name.

By 6:45, the room was filled with support people—the team physician, the orthopedic surgeon, the two trainers, a computer programmer and operator, office administrators, and several secretaries. The conversation at the scouting table was picking up in pace, equal parts serious inquiry and idle banter. The director of player personnel asked out loud about a linebacker from the head coach's alma mater.

"Got to consider what's come out of that school," said one scout reading a chart through half-glasses. He smiled without looking up. The coach was talking to the general manager about something else and wasn't paying attention.

"Yeah," added a scout who wore a turquoise and silver ring with matching belt buckle. "Gotta hope they plucked the rotten apple out of that barrel twenty-five years ago, before it spoiled the whole damn bunch." The coach talked on, oblivious to the exchange.

The director dipped some tobacco inside his lower lip and asked about a 4.0 receiver who set pass catching records at a West Coast school. "Tell me again why we rate him so low."

The scout with the West Coast territory, the only one at the table not wearing cowboy boots, answered. "Couldn't run a 4.8 forty if we started him downhill. Tell you what, though. He's got the best hands of anybody up there."

The coach swung his chair and looked at the free-agent board. He noticed a reject linebacker from a big football school. "Damn shame," he said, repeating the linebacker's name solemnly. "Kid started as a freshman. Had everything, size, speed, heart. All those injuries—now look at him."

"Knees already starting to atrophy," added the West Coast scout.

At 7 A.M., one trainer stationed himself near the big board, the other at the phone on the desk in front. The general manager looked at the clock on the wall and said, "Why don't we see what's going on." The head coach, who was telling of a former player from another team who now was doing time in jail, stopped in mid-sentence. He took a deep drag on his cigarette and said, "Here we go."

The trainer punched a series of phone buttons and waited while the singsong of computer tones connected him to draft headquarters in a ballroom at the New York Sheraton Hotel.

"Anything yet?" he asked into the receiver.

The coach and general manager stared his way.

The scouts and director of player personnel all leaned back in their chairs, eyes on the trainer.

Pause.

"Baltimore used only nine seconds," the trainer yelled out. "They took Elway."

The other trainer took down John Elway's card, the only 9.0+ on the big board. The reaction was silence for a split second.

"I'll be a son of a gun," drawled the director of player personnel, breaking the spell. He swiveled forward, spit in a cup, and resumed his paperwork. Draft day in an NFL war room had begun.

From the moment they all had arrived, the mood in the room was calm but expectant. Calm, because all the battles had been waged in pre-draft meetings. Scouts' biases, coaches' preferences, and executives' judgments had been sifted through reel after reel of game films, through a virtual library of scouting reports, through computer printouts and player profiles. Decisions had been made, priorities set, a consensus reached. The team knew going in what it needed and whom it wanted.

Expectant, because no matter how thorough the planning, how shrewd the forecasts, nobody could say for certain how the draft would unfurl. They would be prepared for their task, but draft-day action is a deck that won't be stacked. Invariably, they end up playing the hands they are dealt.

With Elway taken, and the remaining 350 or so prospects clustered between scores of 8.9 and 4.0, they whiled away the time with paperwork and conversation. Every few minutes or so, the trainer phoned for an update, ringing off each time with a variation of the same promise: "Check with you in ten." "Check in five." "Call back in seven." "Talk to you in four."

The going was slow in the first round, every team taking most of its allotted 15 minutes, nervous about the magnitude of the first pick. Elway to the Colts . . . Eric Dickerson to the Rams . . . Curt Warner to the Seahawks . . . Chris Hinton to the Broncos. At a slack point between picks, the head coach resumed his story about the player in jail:

"Whatever they got him for—holding, dealing, it wasn't as heavy as it could have been. See, they got this compound next to the main prison, minimum security or something, where they keep the light offenders. This guy had a five-year sentence. They told him if he was good—which if they knew him like I did, they wouldn't have wasted their breath—he'd stay in minimum security and be out in twenty months. This guy's so smart—the next thing I hear he's serving his full term in D-block inside the main prison."

"He was never known for his mental gymnastics," laughed one of the scouts who had known the player in college.

"Who drafted him?" asked another. "Some way we could put him in our division, on another team, when he gets out?"

"Ten away," said the trainer, riveting all attention back to the board.

At the signal, one of the scouts, a big man, a former pro lineman wearing a white shirt, navy tie, light blue slacks, and silver lizard-skin cowboy boots, rose from his chair and lumbered to a portable blackboard at the back of the room. Holding the top of the board with his left hand, he wrote out a list of names in large cursive letters with his right—the names of the 10 highest-rated players left on the big board, from a nose tackle rated 8.9, down through a group of linebackers, receivers, offensive linemen, and defensive backs around 8.7, 8.6, 8.5, down to a wide receiver who was an 8.2.

In theory, any of the 10 would do in this year's draft, the first 30 choices were projected as stars. That was the theory anyway. In practice, theories are muddied by need . . . the way it was at that moment. Both the head coach and the director of player personnel had one name in mind, a fast wide receiver with game-breaking ability their offense currently lacked.

The picks went on. The nose tackle at the head of the list remained. So did the gilt-edged receiver, now in second spot, with three erasures in between. Below him, after an interval of one erasure and several other names, was another receiver with legitimate first-round talent, but not the spectacular skills of the other.

"Bait-cutting time," muttered the director of player personnel. "First round critical. Got to have a star, a dominator, a Pro Bowler . . . somebody who can push us into the playoffs. Just need one. Want that guy."

But if the prime receiver gets chosen, then what? Then reread the hand: "Don't need a nose tackle. Good though. Can we pass up a guy that talented? Easy to find a place for him. Maybe work a trade with one of the guys we got now. . . . Not much of a gap between the nose tackle and the receiver we want. No criticism if we pass up the nose. Big gap between nose tackle and next best receiver. Open ourselves up, we pass on talent and go for need, if the best guy around at that position is an 8.2 . . . too big a risk."

The trainer announced the most recent choice at draft headquarters, a running back. "They got free agents with bad knees playing the tackles," screamed the coach rhetorically. "What the hell they doing taking a running back? They got no blockers for him."

"Probably let a backfield assistant make that pick," said the scout with the half-glasses, looking over them toward the coach. "They usually got a grip on the big picture."

The coach smiled.

Banter now filled the gaps between phone calls. The owner, a man with a firm executive bearing that gave way occasionally to jokes—mostly his own—had come in and was instigating. He looked at the big scout who had drawn the names on the board, then over at the coffee urns.

"Which is the pot you made?" he asked. "I want the other."

"Neither," yelled the man with the turquoise ring. "He didn't get here early enough."

"How would you know?" said the general manager, laughing. "You didn't either."

The owner asked for the extension number of the coaches' offices. He mentioned the offensive line assistant. "I'm gonna tell him Dave Rimington [two-time Outland Trophy winner from Nebraska, an 8.9 center] is still up."

"We're not looking to take a center," said the scout with the ring.

"I know," said the owner. "I just want to get his hopes up."

"That's cruel," chuckled the general manager.

The ringing phone jangled everyone alert. Eyes looked to the board. It was the Giants' turn.

"Kinard," said the trainer, referring to the safety from Clemson.

A single spot was between the team and its choice. It was held by a club with three well-known needs—offensive line, cornerback, and wide receiver. On the board were the nose tackle, an offensive tackle, the wide receiver, and a cornerback named Smith.

The owner had since replaced the trainer at the phones. His style was different. Instead of announcing facts as they arrived, he nodded as he heard the details, writing them down and uttering single syllables that revealed nothing to the rest of the room. The picks were a secret until the owner placed his information on a transparent form, slipped the form into an overhead projector, and flashed the results on the wall.

The scouts weren't thrilled by the owner's system. They sat there fidgeting, their choice imminent, the fear pervasive that someone would take the receiver they coveted.

The owner looked at his watch, then punched telephone buttons.

"Anything yet?" He nodded. The scouts strained to read his gestures for insight. None was forthcoming.

"Uh-huh," he nodded and wrote. Still no sign.

"Uh-huh." Same thing.

"They did?" The scouts sat back, resigned to wait.

"Okay."

"Last name. Uh-huh. How do you spell that?"

At that, one of the scouts, the one with the lizard-skin boots, bent forward and remarked in what was intended to be a whisper, "At least we know it ain't Smith." But he missed by several decibel levels. It came out as a kind of croak, loud enough to reach the front. The football people tried stifling their laughter, but it didn't work. The owner shook his head. He slid the transparency into the projector and flicked the switch.

It was the offensive tackle.

"They turn in his name yet?" asked the general manager, still uneasy, afraid to celebrate prematurely. "It's official? They announced it at the front?"

"They announced it. It's official," said the owner.

The general manager sank in his chair and smiled.

"Beautiful," said the director of player personnel, dropping his pencil on the tabletop and rising.

"All right!" exclaimed the scout with the lizard-skin boots.

"We got him!" shouted the head coach. "He's ours!"

It was seven minutes more before the director instructed the owner to submit the wide receiver's name. It took that long because teams contact draftees before announcing choices, partly to show proper interest to a new employee, partly to protect themselves with last-minute assurance against a horrible mistake. As the scout with the shoes put it, "To see if he's still alive. We'd look awful damn silly drafting a guy that got hit by a car on his way home from school yesterday."

The day figured to run long. In normal years, the draft was conducted over two days. Six rounds the first, six the second, 15 minutes between choices the first two rounds, five minutes in rounds three through twelve. This year, the interval between choices was the same, but the whole thing would go start-to-finish without a break, supposedly to stymie the USFL.

The reasoning, which caused eyeballs to roll every time it came up, was tied to the plan of the draft. In theory, first- and second-round picks figure to start right away. Third and fourth to make the team and eventually start. Five and six to make the team and maybe some day be starters.

Anyone taken after round six, therefore, is considered a second-day player, at best a long shot to make the club. Knowing that, the reasoning went the USFL could attract seniors unchosen the first day with a variation of the following pitch: "Look what the NFL thinks of you. Late round, low money. Don't even expect you to make the team. Come with us, play right away, sign for the same money as high-round choices." The NFL wouldn't tempt that possibility, even for 24 hours—a worry viewed cynically by some.

"I can feel it already," said the head coach in mid-morning, rubbing his hands together. "We're gonna kick the crap out of the USFL today." He laughed sardonically.

It was approaching afternoon. The team had taken a linebacker in the second round, and now was huddled in debate over the third pick, two spots before the choice came due. Ten minutes earlier, New England had called to deal a pair of reserves for the third-round pick—a quarterback and a running back. The general manager had turned them down without consulting the others. It would have been unanimously refused anyway. He knew the consensus was to firm up the secondary.

The choices primarily were between a fast cornerback who maybe didn't like to hit, favored by the scout with the lizard-skin boots ("He's got balance . . . runs a 4.45, 4.5, faster if he has to"), and a safety by the one with the silver and turquoise ring. ("We need help in the middle, we've seen him at safety, we know he can play the position.")

"Yeah," said the first scout. "Good safety. Good corner. Take the corner every time. No contest."

"He's not big enough, your guy," countered the second. "What is he, 172?"

"'Bout that . . . damn, you gotta take speed whenever you can. Inside, outside. We can always get inside guys later. Slow guys will still be there next round."

The director heard the debate while asking about other prospects. He turned to the doctors for medical information on a linebacker and a defensive tackle.

"Got blood work on both," the doctor answered. "First guy's fine on all other counts. Saw him in Tampa [at the camp conducted by the scouting bureau the team belonged to]. Other guy, a no-show for the physical. No EKG, no chest. History's okay."

The director asked about another linebacker.

"Weak shoulders," said the orthopedic surgeon, a young, broad-shouldered man with a frizzy perm, a mustache, and a growing paunch. "Wouldn't take him unless you got nobody you like better."

The general manager, who had been on the phone in his office, returned, excited. "Got a deal," he yelled.

"We're on deck," announced the owner from his seat by the phone. "About five minutes away."

"Shoot," said the director.

"Green Bay. Our pick in this round for theirs and an extra fourth."

"Where'd that put us?" asked the director.

"Four lower than we are right now," answered the general manager. "I'd do it." He looked around.

The director surveyed his people. No dissent from the scouts. He looked at the general manager. "Go for it." Then to the owner: "Hang on to the line. Tell 'em we got one cooking."

The director continued his questioning, this time about a big defensive lineman. "He quick enough to be a stunting tackle? He sure looks strong enough."

"We're up," said the owner. "Three minutes."

"Don't know that much about him," said the scout with the half-glasses.

"Got the body and quickness to play anywhere he wants . . . if he wants," said the West Coast scout.

The general manager returned. "Deal's off . . . they backed out. Go with who we got. How much time?"

"Two minutes," said the owner.

The director looked at the scout who favored the fast cornerback. "What do you think?"

"Good height, over six foot. Damn good speed. Damn good cover guy. You got a 4.4 guy who can cover. I say go with him."

He looked at the other. "You?"

"It's easier to find inside guys, but I don't believe this one'll hit enough. We damn sure need help inside, for our Five-Pack. I like the other guy. Not spectacular but solid. At least we're pretty sure he'll deliver a blow."

The director paused. He pointed his chin at the coach. "You've seen the corner on film. You think he'd help?"

"I've only seen him on one film," said the coach, "so I can't say for sure. But you're asking me what I think. Off that one reel, I'd say no."

"One minute," yelled the owner. The director bunched his forehead into furrows and rubbed across it with his hand.

"Gentlemen, I'm about to make a very unpopular decision." He mentioned the name of the defensive tackle with the questionable attitude. "Put him through," the director said to the owner.

"I see something there," was all he added, an explanation that set fingers drumming and pencils tapping all along the scouting table. The scout who wanted the fast corner said, "Don't check my blood pressure after this one."

The one with the ring reached for his coffee. "This could drive me back to whiskey," he moaned.

The hours piled up, the picks went on, the postures sagged. Ties were loosened at the collar or hung on chair backs. The general manager sat silently, blowing into hands laced together in the form of a steeple. The scout who was not wearing cowboy boots had his feet on the table, shoes unlaced.

"Take these peanuts away from me," said the one with the half glasses. "I been grazing on 'em all morning." He reclined, boots on the table, hands behind his head.

The director asked no one in particular about a defensive tackle with a 6.8 rating: "Look him up, see how long his arms are."

The scout with the half-glasses, leaning back with his hands behind his head, said, "How you gonna face the line coach if you pick another defensive player?"

"Let 'em talk to their wives if they want sympathy," said the director, laughing.

By round seven, the garbage bags inside the room were overflowing with doughnut remains, pizza crusts, leftovers from fatty cold cuts, coleslaw and chips, empty cans and coffee cups with teeth marks on their rims.

The left side of the big board was swept clean to the 5.0s, except for several USFL players and random other names currently drawing questions by the general manager. He was walking along the board, jabbing at cards like a professor pacing in front of his class soliciting student discussion.

"How 'bout this guy?" he asked, his index finger on the card of a 6.5 safety from a small northeastern school.

"Good hitter, plays good. History of injuries, though," said the director. He nodded toward the orthopedic surgeon.

"Dislocated his patella in high school," said the doctor. "Thing we don't know, is it an old injury that's healed? Or an old injury that's gonna start acting up and giving him trouble?"

He pointed to a tight end, another 6.5, noticing his size and his 4.6 speed. "Don't see any reason not to consider a tight end right about now, especially a big son of a gun like this who can run. Something wrong with him?"

"Strong rumors," said the director, causing the general manager to grimace knowingly.

He pointed to a running back from a powerhouse football school, also a 6.5. "We could do worse than taking a fullback 'bout now."

"Attitude," said the director. "Sucker hates everybody including himself. Nothing racial . . . that's what we thought at first. But that's not it. Blacks, whites—he can't get along with anyone. Bad practice player. Tells the trainer, 'It's my body, I'll let you know when it's ready to go.'"

"Hope the Colts get him," broke in the coach. "Like to hear his first conversation with Kush."

It went that way for several rounds, sifting out rejects with the higher ratings, mining talent among the others. The director and the scouts worked up a strong case in the ninth round for a 6-foot 4-inch, 305-pound center with a fairly high rating that every other team seemed to be ignoring because his small southeastern school had won only four games in four years and the center's football skills still were terribly unrefined.

"They say he can pump 230 pounds thirty reps," said the scout with the lizard-skin boots.

"He's got weight lifter's pecs," added the coach, admiring the center's photo in the picture binder.

"We take him, we're going to have to pay extra airfare on the charters," quipped the scout with the turquoise ring as he looked over the coach's shoulder.

"I saw him," said the one with the unlaced shoes. "Worked him out. Got a twenty-nine-inch vertical jump . . . 305 pounds. Gets off the ground like Doctor J."

"Five ahead of you," announced the team treasurer, who now was manning the phones.

"Big stud like that, that can run 4.9 and jump three feet," said the director. "He's still around when we come up, we're going to take him."

Just before the team's pick in round 11, the general manager walked to the board and pointed to a flanker whose name he had been squinting at from his table. The player was good-sized with a 4.8 rating from a midwestern school. "What's his story?"

"Looked good as a sophomore," said the director. "But he's gotten progressively worse. Right now, he drops everything thrown his way. Check the name next to him—4.5 speed, 4.6 score. Interests me. He hasn't been consistent. Didn't start his whole career. But he interests me. . . ."

"Made some plays in a game against Cal," added the scout with the half-glasses.

"Coach says he's a bad practice guy," said the one with the unlaced shoes. "But he may be the best athlete on the team."

"'Bout this time," said the one with the lizard-skin boots, nodding toward the free-agent board, "I'd as soon pick somebody over there who at least has a cut-dog's chance of making it."

"Here's where we start taking the basketball players," said the scout with the ring.

"We got a pick coming up fast," pleaded the director.

"Got to take somebody." He mentioned a linebacker from a West Coast school that one of the scouts had voted for earlier. He looked at the scout. "I think we're better off taking a run at the receiver now, and hope your backer is still there next round."

Nobody argued. The director told the treasurer to submit the receiver's name 15 minutes later when the treasurer announced, "We're up." The director flopped into his chair and looked at his watch. It was 11:45 P.M.—more than 17 hours after his work day had begun. "One round to go. We got any beer over here?"

"It's all on the other side," said a secretary, referring to the conference rooms at the opposite end of the stadium complex. "I'll send a runner."

"Best idea I've heard since they decided to do the whole draft in a single day," offered the tired voice of the scout with the lizard-skin boots.

"By the way," he asked, seeming to address the ceiling. "How ya think we're doing against the USFL?"

"Kicking ass," said the coach, perking up, clenching his fist and holding it in the air, laughing.

The final round's debate was a tribute to the long day's effect on group humor, which was turning as dark as the sky outside. It began with discussion of an offensive tackle with a medical problem, whose card had slipped from sight behind the corner of the curtain on the right-hand side of the board. They had been talking about the linebacker whom they had passed over in the round before, thinking of reasons for and against. ("We'll have trouble with him," joked one scout. "I hear he's planning to graduate on time with a degree in economics.")

Somebody remembered the tackle from a long-ago scouting mission. "Where the hell'd his card go?" he asked, scanning the 4.0s. The trainer walked to the edge of the board and retrieved the card, which was obscured from view. He held it up like a diving judge. The card revealed a 4.0 rating with a "D" notation, meaning discuss, meaning he was rated that low for medical reasons.

"Who's got the file on him?" asked the director.

"I do," said the orthopedic surgeon. "Interesting case."

"You gonna tell us what it is?" asked the coach, baiting him and smiling before he could continue, "or are you planning to conduct a seminar?"

The doctor was flustered for a moment. "Heart," he said cryptically.

The room was silent.

"What's the story?" asked the director.

"Prognosis good. It's a bad problem . . . some kind of a murmur . . . but there's a good chance. . . ."

"Let me get this straight," said the coach. "It's a bad case . . . but it's good?"

"No," said the scout with the unlaced shoes. "It's a good case that's bad. Good for the doctor's pocketbook . . . bad for the patient's health."

"What case ain't?" said the one with the half-glasses. "Good for the doctor's pocketbook, I mean. Every time somebody has a shin splint treated, some doctor shows up in the Marina owning a new sailboat."

The surgeon, his face red, tried recovering by looking at the director and getting back to the subject.

"Thinking of him to make your team?"

"Not with your recommendation," answered the director, smirking. More laughter followed.

"No," said the doctor. "I mean, you bringing him just for camp, or is he in your long-range plans?"

"Camp, why?"

"'Cause," said the doctor, finally giving up and joining the gallows exchange. "I guess what I'm saying is he'll last at least till training camp ends, so he'd be okay to pick."

"Sick," said the general manager, laughing anyway.

The coach was doubled over, snorting through his laughter. "You're a regular Albert Schweitzer, you are," he said. "A real humanitarian." The name "Albert" stuck through the time of the final choice, when the director—to no argument—sent through neither the tackle nor the linebacker.

He picked another linebacker, a quick-footed if undersized athlete from the free-agent board he suddenly decided just might have the "cut-dog's" chance the scout with the lizard-skin boots had mentioned earlier. It seemed a good time to proceed on instinct.

"Let's wrap it up," said the director. He stuffed printed materials into his beaten-up leather briefcase.

"Now let's get a beer," said the coach, an idea everyone liked even better. "C'mon, Albert," he said, putting a bearish arm around the doctor's shoulder. "I'll buy you one."

Around the table a few minutes later, drink in hand, the scout with the lizard-skin boots asked, "You ever hear about the guy who goes into a bar. . . ." Everybody groaned, but the scout was undeterred.

"He's dressed in high cowboy fashion. Shirt, jeans, hat. Except for his feet. On his feet, he's wearing tennis shoes. The bartender serves him and looks funny at his getup. The guy says, 'I see you're wondering about my outfit. Well, let me tell you, everything I wear has a purpose. This hat, for instance. It protects my head against the cold in winter. It keeps the sun from beating down on me in summer. These jeans—they're tough, long-wearing, and comfortable. This shirt is cotton, with snaps that pull open if I ever get caught in the brush. And these sneakers—'" the scout paused for maximum dramatic effect, "'—these arc so nobody will mistake me for a goddamn football scout.'"

He laughed convulsively. The doctor laughed. They all laughed. The 18-hour work day was over.

Acknowledgments

Grateful acknowledgment is made for permission to reprint the following works:

"The Eighty Yard Run" by Irwin Shaw. Copyright © Irwin Shaw. Reprinted with permission. All rights reserved.

"All Flesh Is One" by Ray Bradbury. Copyright © 1970 by Ray Bradbury. Reprinted by permission.

"Oh, What a Lovely Game" by Andy Rooney. *Super Bowl XXVI Game Program.* Copyright © 1992 by NFL Properties, Inc. Reprinted by permission.

Selection from *End Zone* (retitled "The Language of Football") by Don DeLillo. Copyright © 1972 by Don DeLillo. Used by permission of Viking Penguin, a division of Penguin Books USA, Inc.

"Breaking the Field" by James Dickey. *Super Bowl XXVIII Game Program.* Copyright © 1994 by NFL Properties, Inc. Reprinted by permission.

"Tom Landry: God, Family, and Football" by Gary Cartwright. *Sport.* Copyright © 1969 by Gary Cartwright. Reprinted by permission.

Selection from *A Fan's Notes* (retitled "One for Steve") by Frederick Exley. Copyright © 1968 by Frederick Exley. Reprinted by permission of Random House, Inc.

"Farewell the Gods of Instant Legend" by Haywood Hale Broun. Copyright © 1969 by NFL Properties, Inc.

"The Lesson I Learned from Vince Lombardi" by Lee Iacocca, as told to Murray Olderman. *Sport.* Copyright © 1972 by Lee Iacocca. Reprinted by permission.

"Hero Worship on Sunday Afternoon" by August Wilson. *Super Bowl XXVI Game Program.* Copyright © 1992 by NFL Properties, Inc. Reprinted by permission.

"A Game of Passion" by Ray Bradbury. From *A Game of Passion.* Copyright © 1975 by NFL Properties, Inc.

"Alias Little Mo" by Gay Talese. Copyright © 1957 by The New York Times Company. Reprinted by permission.

"In the Pocket" by James Dickey. From *More Than a Game.* Copyright © 1974 by NFL Properties, Inc. Reprinted by permission.

"Cruncher" by Sandy Grady. Reprinted by permission of the author.

"Those Raider 'Renegades'" from *Hey, Wait a Minute (I Wrote a Book!)* by John Madden with Dave Anderson. Copyright © 1984 by John Madden, Inc. Reprinted by permission of Random House, Inc.

Selection from *I Can't Wait Until Tomorrow 'Cause I Get Better Looking Every Day* (retitled "Who Did They Think They Were Messing With—The Rams?") by Joe Namath and Dick Schaap. Copyright © 1969 by Random House, Inc. Reprinted by permission of Random House, Inc.

Selection from *I Am Third* (retitled "Pick") by Gale Sayers with Al Silverman. Copyright © 1970 by Gale Sayers and Al Silverman. Reprinted by permission of the William Morris Agency, Inc. on behalf of the author.

"The Dream Is Alive" by Tim Green. *GAMEDAY.* Copyright © 1993 by NFL Properties, Inc. Reprinted by permission.

Selection from *Off My Chest* (retitled "Big Daddy") by Jim Brown with Myron Cope. Copyright © 1964 by Jim Brown with Myron Cope. Reprinted by permission.

Selection from *Run to Daylight* (retitled "The Morning After") by Vince Lombardi with W.C. Heinz. Copyright © 1963, 1991. Used by permission of Prentice Hall/A Division of Simon & Schuster.

"Barnstorming" by John Wiebusch. *PRO!* Copyright © 1977 by NFL Properties, Inc. Reprinted by permission.

"Once Upon a Time In Dallas" by Mickey Herskowitz. *PRO!* Copyright © 1972 by NFL Properties, Inc. Reprinted by permission.

"A Remembrance of Paul Brown" by Ray Didinger. *PRO!* Copyright © 1990 by NFL Properties, Inc. Reprinted by permission.

"The Search" by Steve Cassady. *PRO!* Copyright © 1991 by NFL Properties, Inc. Reprinted by permission.

"Believe Everything You Hear" by Jim Klobuchar. *PRO!* Copyright © 1973 by NFL Properties, Inc. Reprinted by permisison.

"Down Home with Terry Bradshaw" by Scott Ostler. *PRO!* Copyright © 1981 by NFL Properties, Inc. Reprinted by permission.

"One Man's Image" by Jim Murray. From *More than A Game.* Copyright © 1974 by NFL Properties, Inc. Reprinted by permission.

"It Was Pro Football and It Was New York" by Paul Zimmerman. *PRO!* Copyright © 1972 by NFL Properties, Inc. Reprinted by permission.

"A Football Man" by Phil Musick. *PRO!* Copyright © 1976 by NFL Properties, Inc. Reprinted by permission.

"The Coach Is a Soft Touch" by Shelby Strother. *GAME DAY.* Copyright © 1987 by NFL Properties, Inc. Reprinted by permission.

"Wordsmith" by Ira Berkow. *PRO!* Copyright © 1982 by NFL Properties, Inc. Reprinted by permission.

"Bronko Nagurski" by John Wiebusch. *PRO!* Copyright © 1983 by NFL Properties, Inc. Reprinted by permission.

"LXII" by Phil Barber. *Super Bowl XXVI Game Program.* Copyright © 1992 by NFL Properties, Inc. Reprinted by permission.

"Airedales and Indians" by Wells Twombly. *PRO!* Copyright © 1976 by NFL Properties, Inc. Reprinted by permission.

"Goodbye, Johnny U." by Mickey Herskowitz. *PRO!* Copyright © 1974 by NFL Properties, Inc. Reprinted by permission.

Selection from *No Medals for Trying* (retitled "Time to Tee it Up") by Jerry Izenberg. Copyright © 1990 by Jerry Izenberg. Reprinted by permission of Macmillan Publishing Company.

"Even His Best Friends Will Tell Him" by Charles Maher. *PRO!* Copyright © 1973 by NFL Properties, Inc. Reprinted by permission.

"The Best Team of the Best Years" by Ray Didinger. *PRO!* Copyright © 1983 by NFL Properties, Inc. Reprinted by permission.

"Gate-Crashers and Frog's Legs" by Will McDonough. *Super Bowl XXVIII Game Program.* Copyright © 1994 by NFL Properties, Inc. Reprinted by permisison.

"Confessions of a Super Pirate" by Scott Ostler. *Super Bowl XXVIII Game Program.* Copyright © 1994 by NFL Properties, Inc. Reprinted by permission.

"Memory Layne" by Jim Klobuchar. *PRO!* Copyright © 1975 by NFL Properties, Inc. Reprinted by permission.

"The Selection Process" by Steve Cassady. *PRO!* Copyright © 1983 by NFL Properties, Inc.